The Living Will and the Durable Power of Attorney for Health Care Book*

***With Forms**

Phillip G. Williams

Contemporary Public Health Issues
Volume 1

Updated, revised, and expanded edition of *The Living Will Source Book* (1986)

The P. Gaines Co.
PO Box 2253, Oak Park, Illinois 60303

Since laws are subject to differing interpretations, neither the publisher nor the author offers any guarantees concerning the information contained in this publication or the use to which it is put. Although this publication is designed to provide accurate and authoritative information concerning Living Wills and Durable Powers of Attorney for Health Care, it is sold with the understanding that neither the author nor the publisher is engaged in rendering legal or other professional advice. If legal or other expert assistance is required, the services of a competent professional should be sought. *Adapted from a Declaration of Principles jointly adopted by a Committee of the American Bar Association and a Committee of Publishers.*

Library of Congress Cataloging in Publication Data

Williams, Phil, 1946-
The living will and the durable power of attorney for health care book, with forms / Phillip G. Williams.
p. cm. -- (Contemporary public health issues : v. 1)
Updated, rev., and expanded ed. of: The living will source book, 1986.
Includes bibliographical references.
Includes index.
ISBN 0-936284-23-4 (pbk. : alk. paper) : $19.95
1. Right to die--Law and legislation--United States--States. 2. Power of attorney--United States--States. 3. Right to die--Law and legislation--United States--States--Forms. 4. Power of attorney--United States--States--Forms. I. Williams, Phil, 1946- Living will source book. II. Title. III. Series.
[DNLM : 1. Ethics, Medical--United States--legislation. 2. Life Support Care--United States--legislation. 3. Right To Die--forms. 4. Right To Die--United Sates--legislation. 5. Terminal Care--United States--legislation. W32.5 AA1 W7L]
KF3827.E87Z9587 1991
344.73'04197--dc20
[347.3044197]
DNLM/DLC
for Library of Congress 90-15715
CIP

Manufactured in the United States of America.

Table of Contents

DEDICATION

We dedicate this volume to Attorney Luis Kutner, originator of the Living Will, whose foresight directs all our efforts to achieve what has become a central goal of modern life, the right to a natural death.

ACKNOWLEDGMENTS

We gratefully acknowledge the assistance of the staff of Cook County Law Library in the preparation of this book, especially the unflagging efforts of Jack Foreman, who doggedly persisted in finding the answer to every question raised.

Introduction

The Importance of the Living Will and Durable Power of Attorney for Health Care in Today's World

The Living Will, a signed, dated, and witnessed document which permits an individual to authorize in advance the withholding or withdrawal of artificial life-support measures in the event of terminal illness or injury, has taken on new meaning and urgency in light of the recent United States Supreme Court ruling in the Nancy Cruzan case.

Because Nancy Cruzan did not fill out a Living Will, the state of Missouri ruled that she could not be removed from life-support devices, in spite of the fact that she had been in a persistent vegetative state for the past seven years. Her friends and relatives testified to her saying before her accident that she would not want to be kept alive under such conditions. This was not, however, considered sufficient evidence of her wishes by the state court. The inescapable implication is that the state of Missouri regards the only convincing proof of one's desires in such an instance to be that expressed in written form, in, for example, a Living Will.

There are several cruel ironies at work here. It was in 1983 that Nancy Cruzan had the automobile accident that left her comatose. Missouri did not pass a Living Will law until 1985, however. It seems highly unlikely that Nancy would have executed a Living Will prior to the state's legislative recognition of this legal right via statute. For the Missouri courts to require a written documentation of her desires prior to the state's own passage of the law that authorizes such a document in its jurisdiction seems unreasonable. The Missouri Living Will law explicitly forbids the withholding or withdrawal of nutrition and hydration. Therefore, even if Nancy had executed a Living Will in Missouri, it would not have allowed her to be removed from the life-support systems that are sustaining her existence without a court battle.

In its landmark ruling, the United States Supreme Court upheld the right of the state of Missouri (and other states as well) to require that individuals spell out their wishes regarding a natural death clearly (with the implication that only a written expression, that is, a Living Will, could satisfy the stringent application of the law in the case of Missouri). In this respect, the ruling is a narrow one, yet it also indirectly raises broader constitutional questions as well. In its ruling, the Supreme Court issued valuable guidelines concerning its own position on the question of the right to die. Surprisingly, the Court expressed the view that a competent individual has the right to refuse life-saving treatment, including food and water. Writing the majority opinion, Chief Justice William Rehnquist stated, "We assume that the United States Constitution would grant a competent person a constitutionally protected right to refuse lifesaving hydration and nutrition. " This statement presupposes, of course, that the "competent person" has filled out an advance directive expressing his or her wishes about such matters beforehand, in writing, if the state so requires.

Associate Justice Sandra Day O'Connor in a concurring opinion lent support to the use of a Durable Power of Attorney for Health Care document as well. Such a document allows one to appoint someone else to make health care decisions for oneself in the event one becomes incompetent or unconscious. Regarding the Durable

Power of Attorney for Health Care, Justice O'Connor noted that "these procedures . . ., which appear to be rapidly gaining acceptance, may be a valuable additional safeguard of the patient's interest in directing his medical care." She concluded with the observation that states may well be constitutionally required to honor the decisions of such "surrogate decisionmakers."

In spite of the refusal of the United States Supreme Court to release Nancy Cruzan from the limbo of her tragic, vegetative existence, the Court *has* clarified the urgent need for every American to do what Nancy did not do: to fill out two forms—a Living Will and a Durable Power of Attorney for Health Care—which can authorize the removal of one's body from life-sustaining devices when one is terminally ill or in a persistent coma. By the same token, those who wish to have their lives prolonged as long as possible by medical technology, even if they are permanently comatose or terminally ill, can use the same two documents to record their desires in writing as well. (In December 1990, with new testimony from friends about her orally expressed wishes admitted as legal evidence in the Missouri courts, Ms. Cruzan was at last permitted to die, almost eight years from the day she originally became comatose.)

Chapter 1 of this book provides background information on the historical, legal and ethical issues related to the Living Will and the Durable Power of Attorney documents and the right-to-die movement. Chapter 2 contains the text of the Uniform Right to Die Act, the model for all laws in this country on this issue. Chapter 3 consists of a state-by-state compendium of the specific texts of the Living Will laws of each state with legislation specifically addressing this issue (at present, 42 states and the District of Columbia have such laws). The state of New York's Orders Not to Resuscitate law has a more narrow focus than the Living Will laws of other states but is included in this chapter. In Appendix A, you will find, alphabetically listed, the Living Will forms specified by law for each state. You may photocopy the appropriate form for your state and use it to draft your own personal Living Will. The form should be filled out after reading your state's Living Will law in Chapter 3, if you reside in a state with such legislation. If you do not find your state represented in Chapter 3, read the Uniform Right to Die Act in Chapter 2 instead and use the generic Living Will form found in Appendix B. In Appendix C, you will find the Durable Power of Attorney for Health Care forms for use in those states which specifically have drafted laws and forms for use in this area. If you do not find your state listed in Appendix C, use the generic Durable Power of Attorney for Health Care form and instructions found in Appendix D.

The right-to-die movement can measure real progress since the passage of the first Living Will legislation in 1976 in the state of California. Paradoxically, the fact that most states have now passed Living Will laws poses a grave danger to individuals who do not wish their dying prolonged by medical technology. There may exist a greater likelihood at present than ever before that a physician will refuse to end artificial life-support measures, regardless of the utter hopelessness of the patient's situation, unless the patient has signed a Living Will and/or a Durable Power of Attorney for Health Care.

From the legal standpoint, some states have taken a more permissive approach to the right to die than Missouri has. The Florida Supreme Court, for example, has recently ruled that relatives or guardians can order removal of feeding tubes from brain-damaged individuals who expressed orally a preference for dying rather than being kept alive by such means, even though such individuals have not signed a Living Will. In spite of the Florida ruling, the United States Supreme Court's upholding of Missouri's hard-line approach may signal a trend. The Supreme Court decision supports greater formality of expression of one's wishes about dying in writing and adherence to the letter of the law. The Supreme Court's implied view seems to be this: if state law provides a vehicle for making one's wishes about one's dying known and legally effective, strict attention to the steps specified by the state legislature may reasonably be required. Consequently, those who neglect to fill out a Living Will and a Durable Power of Attorney for Health Care may run a greater risk of being kept alive indefinitely against their wishes today than at any other period in the past, in spite of the proliferation of legislation addressing this issue.

Chapter 1

Historical, Legal, and Ethical Issues Surrounding the Living Will and the Durable Power of Attorney for Health Care

"The ultimate civil liberty is the right to choose when and how to die at life's end."

—Derek Humphrey

Definition, origin, and brief history of the Living Will

The Living Will is a signed, dated, and witnessed document which permits you to authorize in advance the withholding or withdrawal of artificial life-support measures (also referred to as "death-delaying measures" by some state laws), in the event of your terminal illness or injury. The term "living will", first coined by Chicago attorney Luis Kutner in the 1950s, is obviously not new, although it is only in the last decade that a majority of states have passed so-called "natural death" or "death with dignity" statutes. These laws give an explicit legal basis for the right of individuals to make Living Wills. It is the view of legal scholars that individuals residing in states without such legislation still have a common law right to execute a Living Will. While the recent Supreme Court ruling in the Nancy Cruzan case did affirm the constitutional right to avoid unwanted medical treatment, it left to individual states the right to decide what proof it will require of a patient's clear desire to discontinue medical interventions. In the case of Ms. Cruzan—whose accident occurred two years before Missouri passed its own Living Will law—the implicit assumption by the court that *written* evidence of her wish to end life-support in the event of a terminal condition will alone constitute clear and convincing proof of her wishes seems unreasonably burdensome. While Ms. Cruzan could have exercised her common law right to execute a Living Will in Missouri in 1983, her chances of doing so were very slim.

Bishop Fulton Sheen was the first person officially to execute Kutner's "testament permitting death" without heroic medical treatments; actor Errol Flynn was the second.

In 1968, Concern for Dying, a New York educational council, became the first organization to produce and distribute Living Wills. Since that time, millions of copies have been placed in the hands of those wishing to make advance directives about their own dying.

In 1976, the tragic case of Karen Ann Quinlan gripped the attention of the American public. Irrevocably brain damaged, Ms. Quinlan had subsisted in a coma for eight years on a respirator when her parents obtained permission from the New Jersey court to remove their daughter from the ventilator. She did not die until much later, however; her life was sustained for yet another ten years by a feeding tube. Her case dramatized for many Americans the need for advance medical directives such as the Living Will to prevent such life-in-death dilemmas. She gave a name and a face to the modern-day horror of a body subsisting in a persistent vegetative state, kept biologically functioning indefinitely by artificial means.

In the same year, California passed the first Living Will law in the nation, allowing individuals to express in writing their wishes not to be kept alive by mechanical means if there were no possibility of improvement. Within ten years, about half the states in this country had comparable laws. Today, 42 states and the District of Columbia have Living Will legislation. All but one of the remaining eight states[1] have legislation pending on this issue.

In 1990, the United States Supreme Court refused to authorize the parents of Nancy Cruzan, another comatose victim, to halt the administration of artificial feeding and hydration to their daughter and permit her to die. The Court's decision in the Cruzan case, in light of the absence of the existence of a Living Will, again highlights the necessity of such a document for every American who agrees with its premises.

The origin of the Durable Power of Attorney for Health Care

In spite of the widespread acceptance of the Living Will as a means of communicating the individual's wishes about dying, certain legal problems remain in many states' laws. A relatively new document, the Durable Power of Attorney for Health Care (DPA/HC), has been created to address these difficulties, which range from the unresolved situation in which the patient and the doctor fundamentally disagree, in principle, on the withholding of life-sustaining technologies to the absence of proxy provisions and the inability to enforce legally a Living Will in many circumstances. The Power of Attorney is not new, of course, only the explicit application of it to health care decisions. The concept of "durable" is central. Whereas a Power of Attorney

1 These eight states without death with dignity statutes at present include Massachusetts, Michigan, New Jersey, Nebraska, Ohio, Pennsylvania, Rhode Island, and South Dakota.

normally *ceases* to operate if the principal becomes incapable, a *durable* Power of Attorney comes into play at exactly the moment when the principal can no longer act because of mental or physical incapacity. The DPA/HC designates a proxy to make health care decisions for you if and when you become incapable of doing so for yourself.

Currently, some 25 states and the District of Columbia have laws in place explicitly permitting the creation of a Durable Power of Attorney for Health Care.Only 13 of these states and the District of Columbia provide DPA/HC model forms for use in their jurisdictions (these state-mandated forms are found in Appendix C).[2] New York's recently passed Health Care Proxy Act establishes the right of New York residents to create a Health Care Proxy, which legally functions in the same way as a DPA/HC although, technically speaking, it is not authorized under the New York Durable Power of Attorney statute.[3] Likewise, Kentucky now allows for the appointment of a health care surrogate to make medical decisions in one's stead.[4] Utah's Living Will law includes within it a Power of Attorney to designate another to make treatment decisions for someone who is incapacitated,[5] while Minnesota's law is a hybrid form which combines a Living Will and a DPA/HC into one document, making provision for the appointment of a proxy.[6] The following states, furthermore, also have *as a part of their Living Will acts* a proxy designation option, permitting a surrogate to make medical decisions on behalf of a terminally ill individual (in some cases, a terminally ill minor): Arkansas, Delaware, Florida, Idaho, Indiana, Louisiana, Minnesota, Texas, Utah, Virginia, and Wyoming.

In those states without any form of legislation providing for the creation of a health care proxy, it is generally assumed by legal experts that health care decisions do fall under the authority of general Power of Attorney statutes. This assumption has been established as legal fact by court decisions in a number of states, including Arizona, Colorado, Hawaii, Iowa, Maryland, and New Jersey.To function as a health care document, such Powers of Attorney clearly must be made durable by including such language in them as, "This Power of Attorney shall not be affected by the subsequent disability or incompetence of the principal," or "This Power of Attorney becomes effective upon the disability of the principal," or similar words showing the intent of the principal that the authority conferred shall be exercisable notwithstanding his or her subsequent disability or incompetence. What is not clear, in states with no Durable Power of Attorney for Health Care law and no definitive legal precedent of applying a general Power of Attorney to medical decisions, is

---

2 The 14 providing model forms are California, Georgia, Idaho, Illinois, Kansas, Nevada, Ohio, Oregon, Rhode Island, Tennessee, Texas, Vermont, West Virginia, and the District of Columbia.

3 The New York form is found in Appendix C as well.

4 The Kentucky form has also been included in Appendix C.

5 Since the Utah Power of Attorney form is a separate, detachable document distinct from the state Living Will declaration, it has been included in Appendix C.

6 The Minnesota proxy designation is found in Appendix A, since it is a part of the state Living Will declaration, not a separate form.

whether these general Powers of Attorney convey the authority to *refuse* health care. It is for this reason that Powers of Attorney specifically covering health care decisions, including the decision to refuse treatment, are being adopted by many state legislatures. If you do not reside in a state which has authorized a specific DPA/HC model form (see Appendix C for the 14 existing statutory DPA/HC forms to date), it is recommended that you use the generic form in Appendix D.

The DPA/HC goes into effect only when one is no longer able to make health care decisions for oneself. Then the proxy you have designated in the DPA/HC will make health care decisions for you, in light of your wishes conveyed orally or in the form itself. There are legal safeguards if your agent makes decisions not in keeping with your known wishes. If you regain your competency, furthermore, your power to make health care decisions reverts to you.

If you have both a Living Will and a DPA/HC, the DPA/HC takes precedence over the Living Will. Under normal circumstances, it will be advantageous to have another individual acting in your behalf if you are incapacitated to make decisions about whatever health care matters arise, especially in the case of situations that might not have been anticipated in your Living Will (a new life-support technology developed *after* your execution of the document, for example). One of the chief advantages of the DPA/HC, then, is its greater flexibility, since it allows your agent to respond to concrete situations that your Living Will may not adequately cover or even take into account. The DPA/HC is also legally enforceable, whereas your Living Will may or may not be, depending on a variety of factors, such as your specific requests in the document in light of your current state laws, the presence or absence of legal sanctions against physicians and other health care workers who refuse to honor a Living Will in your state, and so on. You must remember, too, there may be certain situations in which the Living Will would govern, although you have both documents legally executed. If, for example, the agent you designate in the DPA/HC is not available to act in your behalf, then your wishes expressed in the Living Will would rule.

The DPA/HC can also function in place of legal guardianship or conservatorship, in the realm of health care. It may not prevent your having to go to court to obtain guardianship of someone who has become incapable if you must assume not only health but financial responsibilities for the incapacitated individual as well. But it will tide you over in the case of an emergency, if medical decisions must be made before there is time for guardianship to be legally established.

Ethical grounds of the Living Will and the Durable Power of Attorney for Health Care in the modern medical context

The Judaeo-Christian concept of 'the person' underlies the rationale of advance medical directives such as the Living Will. The right to be self-determining, to function as an agent instead of a patient even in sickness and death, is grounded in a fundamental religious premise about the nature of the person as an end in oneself, possessing innate value and dignity.

The view of life and death implied by a world in which the making of advance medical directives is not only a right but a necessity is a terrifying one in which technology, as in some nightmarish science fiction novel, has taken on a life of its own. These "advances" in medical science which allow the dying to be kept biologically functioning indefinitely by artificial means can no longer be viewed without a deep sense of irony and fear. Noting the absurdity of always doing what is possible by means of state-of-the-art technology, many ethical thinkers have expressed grave reservations about the attempt to preserve physical life without regard to the broader human context. To keep bodily functions going when there is no reasonable chance of an individual's recovery of a sense of self or wholeness; to resuscitate a terminally ill patient against his or her express wishes; all such acts of medical derring-do remain morally repugnant for those who see the person as more than a slab of writhing flesh. The fragmentation of the person into impersonal medical functions represents the last step in a peculiarly modern process of dehumanization, culminating in the disregard of the spiritual dimension of human life in the name of some mechanistic, inhuman ideal of Life. The rational application of medical technology to sustain 'life' at any cost not only violates the individual's legal right to consent to or refuse medical treatment (unless opposed by a compelling state interest), but also one's ethical right to choose death when the body is hopelessly ill.

In the modern hospital context, many persons in advanced stages of terminal illness are unconscious or otherwise seriously impaired when life-prolonging procedures are applied. A Living Will document provides one universally recognized means of advance expression of one's wishes concerning medical treatment while one is still capable of deciding for oneself. As already noted, a growing number of states also specifically recognize by law one's right to have a guardian make treatment decisions when one is no longer competent to do so oneself (the Durable Power of Attorney for Health Care and comparable instruments of appointment of a health care agent). Some states, furthermore, as noted above on page 11, while not having passed a statute authorizing the creation of a DPA/HC, make provision in their Living Will legislation for another type of health care proxy.

Personalized instructions

In addition to a general declaration forbidding the artificial prolongation of the life of a terminally ill or comatose person, most states with natural death laws now permit personalized instructions. Space is sometimes provided on the Living Will form itself for you to specify that your dying is not to be prolonged by certain medical procedures which you will then have the opportunity specifically to list, such as the application of artificial respirators, cardiopulmonary resuscitation, intravenous or nasogastric or gastronomy tube feeding, blood transfusions, surgery, including amputation, organ transplantation, radiation treatment, dialysis, and so on. If no space is provided on the form itself for personalized instructions, attach your personalized instructions to the standard form, along with a statement that additional instructions are based on your constitutional or common law rights. In the case of the Durable Power of Attorney for Health Care forms of specific states, the same allowance for personal instructions is usually made. Some state forms distinguish two types of personalized instructions on the DPA/HC, one specifically concerning life-sustaining (or death-delaying) procedures that you do or do not want used and the other cataloging other desires, special instructions, and any limitations you might want to place on the authority of the agent you have designated to make health care decisions for you.

Another frequently included personal direction in a Living Will document is the making of a gift of one's body or body parts for transplantation or other purposes under the Uniform Anatomical Gift Act.[7] Most existing state DPA/HC statutes also authorize your appointed health care agent to make an anatomical gift from

7 See Phillip Williams, *Life from Death: The Organ and Tissue Donation and Transplantation Source Book, With Forms*. Contemporary Public Health Issues, Vol. 2. (Oak Park, Ill.: The P. Gaines Co., 1989).

your body as well as to request an autopsy and dispose of your remains, unless you specifically deny these rights to your proxy in the document.

If any additions to a Living Will are of a personalized nature and in conflict with state law (as in the case of the request for withholding of food and water in some states), they may be disregarded by the attending physician, however, unless an appeal to the court of jurisdiction proves successful.

The food and water controversy

Turning off a respirator when a patient is in an irreversible coma and following a patient's prior approval of a "do not resuscitate" order are recognized as standard medical practice in many sectors. Today, the main ethical and legal battles are being fought over the controversial issue of withholding food and water. Nineteen states with right-to-die laws explicitly forbid the withholding or withdrawal of nutrition and hydration from terminally ill patients. Four states disallow health-care workers to withhold nutrition and fluids necessary to alleviate pain or to maintain patient comfort. Two more states specify that nutrition and water cannot be stopped if death by starvation or malnutrition would result. While over half the states with Living Will legislation specifically prohibit the withholding of food and water from terminally ill patients in some or all circumstances, regardless of whether the patients themselves have requested it, only four states make specific provision for the patient to *request,* in the Living Will declaration, the withholding or withdrawal of artificially administered nutrition and hydration by nastrogastic or gastrostomy tubes or intraveneous feeding. Colorado for one recently rewrote its law to allow for the withdrawal of food and water at the patient's request. Thirteen other states do not explicitly ban the withholding of nutritional supplements. The newly emerging Durable Power of Attorney for Health Care statutes show a similar division between states that permit and those that deny the right to forgo nutritional support. Ohio, for instance, does not allow withdrawal of nutrition and hydration unless two physicians agree that such feedings would not provide comfort and, furthermore, would do no good or would even shorten one's life, while Vermont gives the option to the signer of the Durable Power of Attorney to forgo all treatment, including artificial nutrition and hydration.

In 1986, the Ethical and Judicial Council of the American Medical Association approved a policy statement which affirms the ethical right of physicians to withhold *all* means of life-prolonging treatment, including "artificially or technologically supplied nutrition or hydration," from patients who are permanently unconscious even if death is not imminent. This "withholding" only applies to persons in a persistent vegetative state, of course, and only covers artificially administered feeding. In the past, one obstacle to the implementation of Living Wills requesting such removal of life-support measures, especially the stopping of artificial nutrition and hydration, often was a medical paternalism which simply refused to take patients' wishes regarding medical treatment—or the cessation of it—into account. Growing public awareness of and education about patient rights, evidenced by the ground swell of new natural death legislation in dozens of states, have been paralleled by the medical community's increasingly affirmative recognition of patient rights. The AMA's policy statement about nutrition and hydration has found legal support in a number of state court decisions permitting the withdrawal of nutrition from comatose patients even in cases when death was not imminent. In other states such as Missouri, Ohio, and New York, of course, a patient's right to die in such cases has *not* been affirmed by the courts. The legal issue remains a vexing one, because it is often decided on narrow technical grounds, as in the Nancy Cruzan case.

In the noted case of Karen Quinlan, although the respirator was eventually turned off with court approval, Karen continued to breath on her own; because she was fed artificially, she lived on, comatose, for some ten years more. It is precisely this form of "living death" that the Living Will and the Durable Power of Attorney for Health Care concepts are designed to prevent. With some 10,000 comatose individuals in this country today who are being sustained by artificial feeding (often against the express wishes of their families), the issue of "forced" feeding remains one replete with tragic consequences for those trapped between life and death by an impersonal legal system.

No clear-cut consensus regarding the definition of "medical treatment" has emerged from the courts, with some permitting the withdrawal of artificial nutrition and others prohibiting it. The AMA statement, while not legally binding, bolsters the argument of those who favor withholding artificially administered sustenance as well as other forms of life-prolonging medical treatment for the terminally ill.

A California appeals court in a case involving Elizabeth Bouvia, a quadriplegic victim of cerebral palsy, ruled that a patient's legal right to refuse medical treatment extends to the rejection of a feeding tube. Thus, the California appeals court affirmed a patient's basic and fundamental right to refuse medical treatment, even though it leads to death.

The recent United States Supreme Court ruling in the Nancy Cruzan case also upheld this right, in spite of the fact that it did not reverse the Supreme Court of Missouri's refusal to withhold artificial nutrition from Nancy Cruzan and allow her to die. Because Nancy did not have a Living Will, her desire to have artificial feeding stopped could not be clearly established, according to the strict standard of evidence required by the state of Missouri in cases where a patient is incompetent. Her parents' wishes were not taken into consideration. In the United States Supreme Court ruling, the Justices' commentary on the case affirmed the constitutional right to refuse medical treatment, including life-support treatment. This right appears to override the law in those states which explicitly prohibit the withholding of nutrition, furthermore, *provided that,* in the case of an incompetent patient, one's wishes for the withholding or withdrawal of artificially administered nourishment have previously been spelled out clearly when one was of sound mind (in Missouri, this entails a statement so directing in writing, in a properly executed Living Will). The United Sates Supreme Court, however, only indirectly alluded to this right, confining itself for the most part to the more limited question of whether the state of Missouri has the right to demand unequivocal evidence of an incompetent patient's wishes for a "natural death" (obviously, a written statement of one's desires comprises the clearest form of such evidence). In answering this question in the affirmative, the United States Supreme Court cleared the way for every state to demand adherence to its own right-to-die litmus test. The downside of this recognition of state sovereignty in such matters is a situation in which one terminally ill person residing in one state may be allowed to die according to his or her wishes while someone else in similar circumstances living in another state may be kept alive against one's will. Instead of depending on the state courts to reconstruct one's views—based on the testimony of friends and relatives—of whether one would wish to be kept alive when suffering a terminal condition, the person truly concerned that his wishes regarding dying be respected will put them in writing, based on the Missouri example.

In the final twist of a lengthy court case involving Sidney Greenspan, who remained for six years in a vegetative coma, a Cook County Circuit Court judge in Illinois ruled in October 1990 that a feeding tube keeping Mr. Greenspan alive could be removed. His case parallels that of Nancy Cruzan, since he, comatose, had no Living Will or Durable Power of Attorney for Health Care. In this instance, the testimony of his wife was finally admitted as clear and convincing evidence that Mr. Greenspan would not have wanted to be kept alive under such circumstances. (Nancy Cruzan was similarly permitted to die after almost eight years, owing to friends' testimony regarding her wishes). The existence of a Living Will and/or DPA/HC would, in all likelihood, have shortened the period of six years of "living hell," in the words of Sidney Greenspan's wife.

Patient and physician safeguards

Advance directives such as the Living Will and the Durable Power of Attorney for Health Care have medical, legal, and ethical dimensions. Such documents involve patient directives concerning special medical treatments. They are also legal documents. In certain states, for example, Living Will legislation carries fines and imprisonment or other sanctions if its terms are not adhered to by the attending physician. The Durable Power of Attorney for Health Care has behind it the force of law as well. Finally, the existence of such documents depends upon certain ethical principles regarding human rights, including the right to a quality of life which goes beyond merely physical duration and, in the absence of such quality, the right to die. The Living Will and the DPA/HC concepts provide medical, legal, and ethical safeguards for both patient and doctor, allowing a patient with a terminal condition the right to die without artificially protracted suffering and prolonged dying, as well as protecting the physician and other medical personnel carrying out the patient's wishes from civil or criminal liability or charges of unprofessional conduct.

Legal basis in the Constitution and common law

To date, 42 states and the District of Columbia have passed legislation giving individuals the express right to execute Living Will documents (the New York statute, as noted, applies narrowly to only the issue of do not resuscitate orders). A number of states, furthermore, as discussed on page 11, have passed either a Durable Power of Attorney for Health Care statute or some other form of health care proxy law, allowing persons to appoint a surrogate to make health care decisions for them when they are no longer able to do so themselves. It is the opinion of civil libertarians that the rights granted by Living Will and Durable Power of Attorney for Health Care laws are guaranteed by the Constitution and by common law, in the absence of specific Living Will and DPA/HC legislation. In other words, the fundamental rights which these laws address are operable even in those states which have not passed legislation dealing with this particular issue. These include the constitutional guarantee of individual privacy and the common law right to personal self-determination. Persons living in states without specific Living Will legislation can still fill out a Living Will, as explained below. The same applies to the Durable Power of Attorney for Health Care. A general DPA/HC form for use in those states without specific legislation on this issue is included in Appendix D.

Specific state laws governing the execution of a Living Will

Since the laws of states with Living Will legislation vary considerably on specific issues and some are more limited in scope and application than others, this book includes point by point the legal statutes for each state, as well as an appendix (Appendix A) with the required or recommended Declaration or Directive form which each state legislature has approved. The text of each state's law will explain whether that state's appended form must be followed verbatim or whether a generic form may be used. Since forms are provided in both cases of those that must be adhered to exactly and those that are given as a general model only, we suggest that you simply use the specific state form for your state, whether required or suggested, to avoid confusion. A few states, namely Delaware, New York, and New Mexico, have Living Will legislation but do not provide a required or recommended form. In such a case, the general Living Will form in Appendix B should be used. Likewise, for individuals residing in states without specific legislation in this area, the general Living Will form with instructions in Appendix B should be followed.

Definition of key terms

Each state with Living Will legislation generally provides a definition of key terms used in its natural death laws. The terms frequently defined in this fashion include "Attending Physician", "Adult" (most often, someone at least 18 years of age), "Declaration" or "Directive" or "Terminal Care Document" (the Living Will document executed in accordance with the natural death laws of that state), "Hospital", "Terminal Condition", "Qualified Patient" (someone who has executed a Declaration and who has been diagnosed to be in a terminal condition). One term, that used to designate the medical treatments that prolong dying, is of particular significance. In Mississippi, it is called "life-prolonging mechanisms"; in Missouri, "death-prolonging procedures"; in Maryland, "life-sustaining procedure". Regardless of the terminology employed, it is important to note what this key term includes as well as excludes in each state's natural death legislation, which has a direct bearing on other specific, personalized directives you may wish to make. In general, life-sustaining procedures or mechanisms include any medical treatment, procedure, or intervention which uses mechanical or other artificial means to sustain, restore, or supplant a spontaneous vital function (a mechanical respirator, for example). Most states specifically exclude pain medication and other forms of "comfort care" (in other words, these types of treatment are to be continued after a Living Will document takes effect and other forms of treatment are withdrawn).

Although the texts of each state's Durable Power of Attorney for Health Care statutes are not included in this book, these laws parallel closely those authorizing the Living Will. A series of definitions similarly defines the context in which a DPA/HC becomes operable, by establishing the legal definition of a "terminal condition", for example, as well as other key terms. Most states' DPA/HC forms likewise provide space for personalized instructions. While some states' forms explicitly inform the person filling out the form that the designated agent has the power to authorize the withholding of nourishment and fluids if such action is in keeping with the desires of the principal, other states do not spell out the limits of the agent's authority. One state, Ohio, qualifies the right of the agent to decide to withhold food and water in so many ways that the decision can be made only under the direst of near-death circumstances. Some states, such as Texas, note on the form what actions *cannot*, by law, be performed by the agent in that particular state's jurisdiction: consent to voluntary inpatient mental health services, convulsive treatment, psychosurgery, or abortion, in the case of this particular state. Many states include a blanket statement that the agent cannot choose any procedure or action which would be contrary to state law.

Witnesses

All states require some form of witnessing of both the Living Will and the Durable Power of Attorney for Health Care forms. Typically, two nonrelative witnesses are required to sign the documents. Many states offer the option of acknowledgment before a Notary Public instead of witnesses. A few states require both witnesses to sign and a Notary Public. Without the witnessing and/or acknowledgment before a Notary Public, the documents are *not* valid. Each state's laws in Chapter 3 explain what form of witnessing is required for a properly executed Living Will document in that state. The Living Will forms themselves, found in Appendix A, will also state the necessary procedure to follow. The generic form included in Appendix B, for those residing in states without specific Living Will legislation, gives the option of witnessing by two individuals or acknowledgment before a Notary Public. Many individuals, even those living in states with right-to-die laws which give a choice between witnesses and a Notary Public, choose both. Having two witnesses sign *and* getting the form acknowledged by a Notary Public (while not legally required) help to underline the power of conviction of the signer.

Witnessing of a DPA/HC follows the same pattern. Most states give the signer an option of having two witnesses' signatures or that of a Notary Pubic appear on the document. The procedure to follow is again explained on the forms themselves, which are found in Appendix C. Those residing in states without forms appearing in Appendix C can use the generic form in Appendix D to execute a DPA/HC, choosing between two witnesses and a Notary Public, or using both if they so wish.

Personalized directions in advance directives in conflict with state law

The chief "gray area" in Living Will law, as already pointed out, concerns the issue of the withholding or withdrawal of nutrition and fluids. While some states specifically exclude food and water from the definition of life-sustaining procedures that may be withheld or withdrawn, other states' laws include them. What happens if you are an individual who wants artificial feeding and hydration stopped if you are in a vegetative coma, for example, but you live in a state whose right-to-die laws explicitly forbid such action? Regardless of what your state law says at the moment, it is crucial that you spell out your own personal wishes about this and other matters as well. The Supreme Court ruling in the Nancy Cruzan case lends strong support to the rights of an individual to have artificially supplied nutrients withheld or withdrawn *even if state law currently denies that right.* Because legal precedents in this area are still far from clear, your wishes may or may not be honored. By making your desires known in writing, however, you greatly increase the chances of their being followed.

Since a Living Will document filled out at present may not become operable until some distant point in the future, your state laws may at that time allow for the implementation of your directive to withhold food and fluids. Even if the present laws continue in effect, your directive may be considered advisory by your physician and may prove to be legally implementable under certain circumstances.

From reading the text of your state's right-to-die legislation in chapter 3, you can determine if your state's laws explicitly exclude nutrition and hydration from the category of life-sustaining procedures. If so, your state law, as it now stands, does not allow for their withholding or withdrawal under *any* circumstances. In spite of this injunction, you *must* specify food and water, artificially administered, as other forms of treatment to be stopped during the dying process, if, in fact, it is your desire to do so, either by adding personalized instructions to the state Declaration form, if allowable, or attaching a separate written statement, also signed and dated, to this effect. Those living in states which do explicitly allow the withholding or withdrawal of nutrition and hydration must also include specific instructions in the form about their wishes in this regard.

Some states, such as Alaska and Colorado, now authorize the individual specifically to request that nourishment *not* be administered intravenously or by gastric tube in the event of a terminal condition.

Ideally, all states will eventually follow the example of Tennessee, which legislatively distinguishes between artificial feeding (which may be discontinued in the event of a terminal condition) and normal feeding (which may not, under any circumstances, be stopped).

Overview of Living Will state laws

A brief overview of some of the many variables in Living Will legislation from state to state provides an excellent introduction to the issues at stake. All the states with Living Will legislation specify that minors *cannot* execute a document nor can adults who have never been competent. Most states define an adult as someone eighteen years old, but there is some variation in this regard—in Oklahoma, for instance, one must have attained twenty-one years of age to qualify. Some states, furthermore, make an exception for so-called "emancipated minors," who are entitled to execute a Living Will in the same manner as an adult. An emancipated minor must generally have attained at least fourteen years of age and be married and/or economically independent.

A little more than half the states with natural death laws at present specify that a Living Will document is invalid during pregnancy. (In these states, the fetus, if viable, must be carried to term and delivered before the Living Will can be implemented.) In a few states, only one attending physician is required to diagnose a patient's condition as terminal, but almost all states require two physicians' concurring diagnoses. In Maryland, for example, two physicians must so certify, and in Mississippi the diagnosis of a terminal condition by the attending physician must be verified by two other physicians (three physicians in total must concur, in other words).

Maryland, Indiana, and North Dakota make specific provision in their statutes not only for a Declaration authorizing the withholding or withdrawal of life-sustaining mechanisms during a terminal condition but also for a Declaration directing the *initiation* or *continuation* of life-sustaining procedures under all circumstances. Indiana's term for the document, the provisions of which can be requested in writing in any state, is a Life-Prolonging Procedures Will.

North Dakota law specifically excludes persons in a coma whose death is not imminent from being defined as in a "terminal condition" and does not allow Living Wills to be activated under such circumstances. In contrast, the New Mexico Living Will statutes permit the withdrawal of life-support mechanisms if an individual is suffering from a terminal illness *or* is in an irreversible coma. A difference of viewpoints about whether a coma *in itself* may be grounds for disconnection of life-support systems emerges from these two states' approaches to the same problem. All such definitions prove crucial in the attempt to decide who is entitled to a "natural death". Most state laws do not even broach this issue at present, leaving it to the medical authorities and the courts to decide.

Missouri's law enjoins that "communication regarding treatment decisions among patients, the families and physicians is encouraged." If this advice were universally followed, the various medical, legal, and ethical dilemmas that arise in the course of implementing Living Wills would perhaps be resolvable more often.

In a few states, such as Louisiana, the law outlines a nonjudicial procedure whereby another person may make a Declaration on behalf of comatose or incompetent patients who have no Declaration. Under Louisiana law, other individuals, including a judicially appointed curator, spouse, adult child of the patient, the patient's parents, the patient's sibling, or another relative may make a Declaration on his or her behalf, provided he is comatose, incompetent, or physically or mentally incapable of communication and has been certified by two physicians as having a terminal and irreversible condition. Of course, there are judicial procedures, such as guardianship, available in all states which permit similar action on behalf of comatose or incompetent terminal patients without a Declaration. As the case of Nancy Cruzan illustrates, however, under a guardianship arrangement if the patient has no Living Will and no Durable Power of Attorney for Health Care, the guardian will not necessarily be allowed to make decisions that the patient would have made had she or he been competent to do so.

Approximately one third of the states make legal provision for fines and imprisonment or other sanctions in the case of physicians who fail to adhere to the patient's rights set forth in the state Living Will legislation.

The Mississippi and Hawaii right-to-die statutes explicitly raise the issue of transplants. According to these states' laws, a physician participating in a decision to withhold or withdraw life-sustaining mechanisms from a patient at his or her wishes may not participate in transplanting the vital organs of the patient to another person.

All states require witnesses to the Declaration, as already noted. Most states exclude as witnesses persons related to the patient by blood or marriage, those entitled to a portion of the patient's estate as heirs or claimants, those responsible for the patient's health care costs, and employees or patients of the medical facility in which the patient is being treated. A few states, such as Hawaii, require the Declaration to be notarized in addition to being witnessed by two individuals, although, as pointed out, it is advisable that all Living Will documents be notarized to show the seriousness of one's intentions.

Under Missouri law, a potential inheritor who acts contrary to the patient's wishes expressed in the patient's Living Will may lose the rights of inheritance to the extent such loss is provided for by the patient's last will and testament.

In California, the Living Will Declaration expires after five years and must be reexecuted to remain in effect. A few other states previously had such limited life Declarations (Georgia and Idaho), but their laws have recently been revised to eliminate this provision.

Almost all states provide for formal or informal means of revoking the Declaration. In Georgia, the revocation, to be effective, must show the individual's recognition that he intends to revoke the Living Will, not the other kind of will which disposes of his estate.

In several states, such as California, the wording of the state-mandated Living Will Declaration form must be followed exactly. By contrast, most states offer their own version of the Declaration form in their statutes but describe it as a "suggested" or "recommended" model only. Most states do allow for personalized instructions. In California and Oklahoma, the Declaration must be executed (or reexecuted) *after* the diagnosis of a terminal illness in order to be legally binding.

More and more states have revised their laws to recognize Living Will documents executed out of state. This provision is important because it allows for the implementation of your Living Will in the event you are in a state other than your home state and become terminally ill or injured.

Right-to-die laws and suicide, euthanasia, mercy-killing, and aid-in-dying

The "natural death" which results when a person who is terminally ill is removed from life-support equipment is often confused with other, more controversial means of dying. The form of death which occurs when a Living Will is implemented is permitted by law in all fifty states and the District of Columbia. The difference between this type of death and that produced by suicide, euthanasia, mercy killing, and aid-in-dying lies in the relation between the individual and the act of dying. The first waits for death to take place, for nature to take its course. It does nothing actively to hasten death, although it does not shun pain medication, which may indirectly hurry death's arrival. By stopping all mechanical aids which have supplanted vital functions and which, if kept in place, would in many cases sustain bodily functions indefinitely, the physician implementing a Living Will throws the body back on its own resources, allowing it the death toward which it presses.

By contrast, aid-in-dying, which is currently illegal in the United States but legal in The Netherlands, involves direct physician intervention by medical means to end a patient's life in as humane and painless a manner as possible. Where aid-in-dying is legal, it is only performed in the case of terminally ill patients who have repeatedly requested in writing that their lives be ended to spare them further suffering. A physician is not legally bound to follow a patient's wishes in such cases; he has the option of doing so if he can, in good conscience, end another's life under such circumstances. An initiative (the "Death with Dignity Act") was introduced in California in 1989, seeking to allow individuals with a terminal illness to request aid-in-dying from a licensed physician. The California initiative failed but is scheduled to be reintroduced in 1992. Versions of the same act are slated for introduction in Oregon and Washington as well. To date, no state has legalized such practices.

Suicide, the active taking of one's own life, while no longer a criminal act, is not to be confused with the form of involuntary death which the Living Will and the Durable Power of Attorney for Health Care advocate. In the United States and Great Britain, the Hemlock Society promotes a form of drug-induced suicide for the terminally ill which it refers to as "self-determined death" or "self-deliverance". In numerous books and workshops, it presents the most painless and effective ways to end one's life. The Hemlock Society carefully distinguishes its goals from the suicide of an irrational, emotionally depressed person. Its advocacy of "auto-euthanasia", to use another of its own terms, is always grounded in the reality of a terminal condition without hope of recovery, when physical suffering becomes intolerable.

The term "euthanasia" from the Greek literally means a "good death". In light of the connection of this word with the Nazis, it cannot appear other than as an exceedingly ambiguous concept today. "Good from whose perspective?" it seems to demand our inquiry. It originally meant a voluntarily chosen, painless form of death administered to those suffering from an incurable and painful terminal illness; it covered both the "self-deliverance" type of death advocated by the Hemlock Society as well as the aid-in-dying concept. These meanings of the term have all but been lost today. Euthanasia remains tied to its most recent and bloody advocates. In the 1930s, German Nazis killed about 100,000 mentally or physically deformed German citizens and called it "euthanasia". The individuals eliminated in this manner were not necessarily sick or old and dying, however. In their quest for racial and genetic purity, the Germans simply decided to eliminate any individuals they regarded as possessing defective genetic elements. The Nazis thus saddled the word "euthanasia" with the significance of a thinly disguised form of murder justified in the name of eugenics ("good genes"). The Hemlock Society, as noted, has attempted to recycle this term and give it a new twist to refer to its own program of "auto-euthanasia" for the terminally ill.

Mercy-killing is the act of someone that we might refer to as a "loving killer". This form of murder of a loved one by a family member or friend in order to end suffering is a felony. Both aid-in-dying, a physician-assisted termination of life, and mercy-killing are sometimes termed "assisted suicides", since both occur in a situation in which an individual, assisted by another, opts for death rather than a continuation of suffering.

The role of hospitals

Hospitals throughout the country are having to come to grips with the new level of public awareness surrounding Living Wills and Durable Powers of Attorney for Health Care. In the past, most hospitals had no policy at all on such matters, or, at best, only an informal one. Today, more and more hospitals are including Living Wills and Durable Power of Attorney for Health Care forms with all admissions.

MacNeal Hospital in Berwyn, Illinois, has been a forerunner in developing a complete hospital program in this area. Since 1987, it has required all patients admitted to the hospital to specify the level and types of medical intervention they wish to receive if they become unconscious and at risk of dying. Through the use of tailor-made forms, patients, in consultation with their physician, specify the degree of life-support they would want as well as what treatments they do not wish to have. The forms can be revised at any point during the individual's hospital stay.

Clearly, not every hospital will opt to require patients to fill out forms reflecting their wishes in such matters. Since the Supreme Court decision in the Nancy Cruzan case, many more hospitals are making advance medical directives forms available to their patients and are asking them on a voluntary basis to put their treatment preferences in writing.

Some hospitals have had a long-standing practice of asking new admissions if they have a Living Will, and, if so, requesting a copy of it for the medical record. Most of the nation's hospitals are responding to the current situation by developing a policy of soliciting information, in one form or another, from their patients about their health care decisions in the event of terminal illness or injury.

A new federal law taking effect in November 1991 (originally termed the Patient Self-Determination Act) legislates hospital involvement in these issues. The law will require all hospitals and nursing homes receiving Medicare and Medicaid funding to inform all patients of their right-to-die alternatives under state law.

"Significant others" and your Living Will and Durable Power of Attorney for Health Care

Once you have filled out a Living Will Declaration and a Durable Power of Attorney for Health Care, you should discuss these documents with your physician, attorney, clergy, spouse, relatives, close friends, or others who may be involved in decisions related to your dying. When you fill out a DPA/HC, you must appoint a proxy to make health care decisions for you. It is especially important that you discuss your wishes with the person you have designated as your health care "attorney-in-fact" (who, of course does not need to be an attorney but may be anyone, from a friend to a relative who is willing to serve in this capacity as your representative). Several states require the proxy to sign the DPA/HC form itself, as an indication that the person has been notified about his or her appointment and agrees to play this role.

You will want to provide your doctor a copy of both documents for inclusion in your medical records. The person whom you have appointed to serve as your health care agent on your DPA/HC form should also receive copies of your Living Will and DPA/HC. You may want to give copies to other of the above-named individuals as well. If you doctor indicates that he or she is unwilling to comply with the tenets of your Living Will, you may want to find another doctor more sympathetic to your concerns in this important area.

To avoid confusion, it is advisable to keep one original copy of each document for yourself and provide photocopies to the other individuals mentioned above. This will facilitate making changes in the Living Will declaration and DPA/HC at a future date. If you wish to alter either document, you should execute an entirely new one and destroy the outdated original. You can then provide updated photocopies to others as well, with instructions to destroy the earlier version.

Living Will registry

Concern for Dying maintains a Living Will registry. In the event of an accident or sudden illness, a wallet card mini-will provided by this organization will alert medical staff to contact the registry for a copy of your complete Living Will. The registry service is especially recommended for those without family members or close friends, although in certain circumstances it may benefit anyone who completes a Living Will Declaration.

The staff of Concern for Dying will ensure that your document is filled out correctly, assign you a registry number, and keep a copy of your Living Will on file. If you or your representative acting on your behalf needs counseling or legal guidance in implementing your Living Will, one of their staff members will advise you. For these and other services pertaining to the Living Will, ranging from emotional support to legal counseling, contact:

Concern for Dying
250 West 57 Street
New York, New York 10107
Telephone (212) 246-6962

Chapter 2

Uniform Rights of the Terminally Ill Act (1989)

The purpose of uniform acts is to provide state legislatures with a model to follow in drawing up legislation on a given topic. In the case of the Uniform Rights of the Terminally Ill Act, the first version was not passed until 1985, some nine years after the first state (California) had passed a Living Will law. In 1989, the National Conference of Commissioners on Uniform State Laws revised this act, as explained in the Prefatory Note below. It is the text of the 1989 Act that is included in this chapter.

While the Uniform Act does not parallel exactly any particular state's legislation, it provides a compendium and overview of the major issues that every state's Living Will laws must deal with. The Uniform Act not only serves as a summary of existing legislation; it also incorporates future trends that, in the view of the National Conference of Commissioners, need to be recognized. The Uniform Act covers two areas that only a few states, to date, have addressed: (1) that of delegating a health care proxy and (2) the authorization of near relatives to approve withdrawal or withholding of life-sustaining mechanisms in the event of a terminal illness of an incompetent patient who has not executed a declaration. In the case of (1), while some states do provide space in their Living Will declaration for the nomination of a proxy (see page 11), a number of states have also recently passed laws authorizing the use of the Durable Power of Attorney for Health Care, and more are expected to follow suit. This accomplishes the same end, through a different legislative route. Concerning (2), Arkansas, Louisiana, and Texas, for example, have made provisions for this procedure in their statutes so the next-of-kin can authorize withholding of life-support mechanisms in the case of individuals in a terminal condition who have not executed a Living Will. Many of the situations in which individuals are being kept alive in a vegetative state are due to the failure of most states to permit near relatives to make the treatment decision in the case of patients whose wishes were not documented in writing but, according to the testimony of friends and relatives, did not wish to be kept alive indefinitely by artificial measures.

Those living in states without a Living Will law should read the text of the Uniform Act as a prelude to filling out the generic Living Will form in Appendix B. Those seeking information on the legislative process and an overview of right-to-die issues will also find the Uniform Act of interest. Those only wanting to fill out a legal Living Will that fulfills the requirements of their state can skip this chapter and turn to the text of their specific state's law in Chapter 3.

PREFATORY NOTE

The Rights of the Terminally Ill Act is designed to provide various means by which an individual's preferences can be carried out with regard to administration of life-sustaining treatment. The Act permits an individual to execute a declaration that instructs a physician to withhold or withdraw life-sustaining treatment in the event the individual is in a terminal condition and unable to participate in medical treatment decisions. In the alternative, the Act permits the individual to execute a declaration designating another individual to make decisions regarding the withholding or withdrawal of life-sustaining treatment. Finally, the Act authorizes an attending physician to withhold or withdraw life-sustaining treatment in the absence of a declaration upon the consent of a close relative if the action would not conflict with the known intentions of the individual.

The scope of the Act is narrow. Its impact is limited to treatment that is merely life-prolonging, and to patients whose terminal condition is incurable and irreversible, whose death will soon occur, and who are unable to participate in treatment decisions. Beyond its narrow scope, the Act is not intended to affect any existing rights and responsibilities of persons to make medical treatment decisions. The Act merely provides alternative ways in which a terminally-ill patient's desires regarding the use of life-sustaining procedures can be legally implemented.

The purposes of the Act are (1) to establish a procedure which is simple, effective, and acceptable to persons who desire to execute a declaration, (2) to provide a statutory framework that is acceptable to physicians and health-care facilities whose conduct will be affected, (3) to provide for the effectiveness of a declaration in states other than the state in which it is executed through uniformity in scope and procedure, and (4) to avoid the inconsistency in approach that has characterized early state statutes in the area.

The Act's basic structure and substance have been drawn from existing legislation in order to avoid further complexity and to permit its effective operation in light of prior enactments. Departure from existing statutes has been made, however, in order to simplify procedures, improve drafting, and clarify language. Selected provisions have been reworked to express more adequately a specific concept (i.e., life-sustaining treatment, terminal condition) or to reflect changes in established procedure (i.e., the qualifications of witnesses). The Act's stylistic and substantive departures from existing legislation were pursued for the purposes of clarity and simplicity.

The 1989 Act reflects changes and additions to the original Rights of the Terminally Ill Act, approved by the Conference in 1985. The principal changes are noted in the Comments, but they can also be briefly listed. First, Section 2 has been expanded to permit individuals to designate other persons to make decisions regarding the withholding or withdrawal of life-sustaining treatment. Second, under new Section 7 consent to withholding or withdrawal of treatment may be obtained in the absence of a declaration. With few exceptions, changes in the original Act have been limited to Section 2 and (new) Section 7, so that states that have enacted the earlier version can easily incorporate the new provisions.

UNIFORM RIGHTS OF THE TERMINALLY ILL ACT (1989)

§ 1. Definitions.

As used in this [Act],[1] unless the context otherwise requires:

(1) "Attending physician" means the physician who has primary responsibility for the treatment and care of the patient.

(2) "Declaration" means a writing executed in accordance with the requirements of Section 2(a).

(3) "Health-care provider" means a person who is licensed, certified, or otherwise authorized by the law of this State to administer health care in the ordinary course of business or practice of a profession.

(4) "Life-sustaining treatment" means any medical procedure or intervention that, when administered to a qualified patient, will serve only to prolong the process of dying.

(5) "Person" means an individual, corporation, business trust, estate, trust, partnership, association, joint venture, government, governmental subdivision or agency, or any other legal or commercial entity.

(6) "Physician" means an individual [licensed to practice medicine in this State.]

(7) "Qualified patient" means a patient [18][2] or more years of age who has executed a declaration and who has been determined by the attending physician to be in a terminal condition.

(8) "State" means a State of the United States, the District of Columbia, the Commonwealth of Puerto Rico, or a territory or insular possession subject to the jurisdiction of the United States.

(9) "Terminal condition" means an incurable and irreversible condition that, without the administration of life-sustaining treatment will, in the opinion of the attending physician, result in death within a relatively short time.

§ 2. Declaration Relating to Use of Life-Sustaining Treatment.

(a) An individual of sound mind and [18] or more years of age may execute at any time a declaration governing the withholding or withdrawal of life-sustaining treatment. The declarant may designate another individual of sound mind and [18] or more years of age to make decisions governing the withholding or withdrawal of life-sustaining treatment. The declaration must be signed by the declarant, or another at the declarant's direction, and witnessed by two individuals.

(b) A declaration directing a physician to withhold or withdraw life-sustaining treatment may, but need not, be in the following form:

---

1 The word "Act" is bracketed so that state legislatures may fill in the term that they prefer to use, whether Act or Statute or Chapter or Title.

2 Likewise, the age of 18 is bracketed in the definition of a "qualified patient" so that states with a different age for qualifying this status may insert whatever age is appropriate. Throughout the text of the Uniform Act, words or phrases are bracketed to signify that individual states are to supply their own terms.

DECLARATION

If I should have an incurable and irreversible condition that, without the administration of life-sustaining treatment will, in the opinion of my attending physician, cause my death within a relatively short time, and I am no longer able to make decisions regarding my medical treatment, I direct my attending physician, pursuant to the Uniform Rights of the Terminally Ill Act of this State, to withhold or withdraw treatment that only prolongs the process of dying and is not necessary for my comfort or to alleviate pain.
Signed this .... day of ...., ...
Signature.......................................
Address...
The declarant voluntarily signed this writing in my presence.
Witness...
Address...

Witness...
Address...

(c) A declaration that designates another individual to make decisions governing the withholding or withdrawal of life-sustaining treatment may, but need not, be in the following form:

DECLARATION

If I should have an incurable and irreversible condition that, without the administration of life-sustaining treatment, will, in the opinion of my attending physician, cause my death within a relatively short time, and I am no longer able to make decisions regarding my medical treatment, I appoint .... or, if he or she is not reasonably available or unwilling to serve, ..., to make decisions on my behalf regarding withholding or withdrawal of treatment that only prolongs the process of dying and is not necessary for my comfort or to alleviate pain, pursuant to the Uniform Rights of the Terminally Ill Act of this State.
[If the individual(s) I have so appointed is not reasonably available or is unwilling to serve, I direct my attending physician, pursuant to the Uniform Rights of the Terminally Ill Act of this State, to withhold or withdraw treatment that only prolongs the process of dying and is not necessary for my comfort or to alleviate pain.]
Strike out bracketed language if you do not desire it.
Signed this .... day of ...., ...
Signature...
Address...

The declarant voluntarily signed this writing in my presence.
Witness...
Address...

Witness...
Address...

Name and address of designees.
Name..
Address...

(d) The designation of an attorney-in-fact [pursuant to the Uniform Durable Power of Attorney Act or the Model Health-Care Consent Act], or the judicial appointment of an individual [guardian], who is authorized to make decisions regarding the withholding or withdrawal of life-sustaining treatment, constitutes for purposes of this [Act] a declaration designating another individual to act for the declarant pursuant to subsection (a).
(e) A physician or other health-care provider who is furnished a copy of the declaration shall make it a part of the declarant's medical record and, if unwilling to comply with the declaration, promptly so advise the declarant and any individual designated to act for the declarant.

§ 3. When Declaration Operative.
A declaration becomes operative when (i) it is communicated to the attending physician and (ii) the declarant is determined by the attending physician to be in a terminal condition and no longer able to make decisions regarding administration of life-sustaining treatment. When the declaration becomes operative, the attending physician and other health-care providers shall act in accordance with its provisions and with the instructions of a designee under Section 2(a) or comply with the transfer requirements of Section 8.

§ 4. Revocation of Declaration.
(a) A declarant may revoke a declaration at any time and in any manner, without regard to the declarant's mental or physical condition. A revocation is effective upon its communication to the attending physician or other health-care provider by the declarant or a witness to the revocation.
(b) The attending physician or other health-care provider shall make the revocation a part of the declarant's medical record.

§ 5. Recording Determination of Terminal Condition and Declaration.
Upon determining that a declarant is in a terminal condition, the attending physician who knows of a declaration shall record the determination and the terms of the declaration in the declarant's medical record.

§ 6. Treatment of Qualified Patients.
(a) A qualified patient may make decisions regarding life-sustaining treatment so long as the patient is able to do so.
(b) This [Act] does not affect the responsibility of the attending physician or other health-care provider to provide treatment, including nutrition and hydration, for a patient's comfort care or alleviation of pain.
(c) Life-sustaining treatment must not be withheld or withdrawn pursuant to a declaration from an individual known to the attending physician to be pregnant so long as it is probable that the fetus will develop to the point of live birth with continued application of life-sustaining treatment.

§ 7. Consent By Others to Withdrawal or Withholding of Treatment.
(a) If written consent to the withholding or withdrawal of the treatment, witnessed by two individuals, is given to the attending physician, the attending physician may withhold or withdraw life-sustaining treatment from an individual who:

(1) has been determined by the attending physician to be in a terminal condition and no longer able to make decisions regarding administration of life-sustaining treatment; and

(2) has no effective declaration.

(b) The authority to consent or to withhold consent under subsection (a) may be exercised by the following individuals, in order of priority:

(1) the spouse of the individual;

(2) an adult child of the individual or, if there is more than one adult child, a majority of the adult children who are reasonably available for consultation;

(3) the parents of the individual;

(4) an adult sibling of the individual or, if there is more than one adult sibling, a majority of the adult siblings who are reasonably available for consultation; or

(5) the nearest other adult relative of the individual by blood or adoption who is reasonably available for consultation.

(c) If a class entitled to decide whether to consent is not reasonably available for consultation and competent to decide, or declines to decide, the next class is authorized to decide, but an equal division in a class does not authorize the next class to decide.

(d) A decision to grant or withhold consent must be made in good faith. A consent is not valid if it conflicts with the expressed intention of the individual.

(e) A decision of the attending physician acting in good faith that a consent is valid or invalid is conclusive.

(f) Life-sustaining treatment must not be withheld or withdrawn pursuant to this section from an individual known to the attending physician to be pregnant so long as it is probable that the fetus will develop to the point of live birth with continued application of life-sustaining treatment.

§ 8. Transfer of Patients.

An attending physician or other health-care provider who is unwilling to comply with this [Act] shall take all reasonable steps as promptly as practicable to transfer care of the declarant to another physician or health-care provider who is willing to do so.

§ 9. Immunities.

(a) A physician or other health-care provider is not subject to civil or criminal liability, or discipline for unprofessional conduct, for giving effect to a declaration or the direction of an individual designated pursuant to Section 2(a) in the absence of knowledge of the revocation of a declaration, or for giving effect to a written consent under Section 7.

(b) A physician or other health-care provider, whose action under this [Act] is in accord with reasonable medical standards, is not subject to criminal or civil liability, or discipline for unprofessional conduct, with respect to that action.

(c) A physician or other health-care provider, whose decision about the validity of consent under Section 7 is made in good faith, is not subject to criminal or civil liability, or discipline for unprofessional conduct, with respect to that decision.

(d) An individual designated pursuant to Section 2(a) or an individual authorized to consent pursuant to Section 7, whose decision is made or consent given in good faith pursuant to this [Act], is not subject to criminal or civil liability, or discipline for unprofessional conduct, with respect to that decision.

§ 10. Penalties.

(a) A physician or other health-care provider who willfully fails to transfer the care of a patient in accordance with Section 8 is guilty of [a class ____ misdemeanor].

(b) A physician who willfully fails to record a determination of terminal condition or the terms of a declaration in accordance with Section 5 is guilty of [a class ____ misdemeanor].

(c) An individual who willfully conceals, cancels, defaces, or obliterates the declaration of another individual without the declarant's consent or who falsifies or forges a revocation of the declaration of another individual is guilty of [a class ____ misdemeanor].

(d) An individual who falsifies or forges the declaration of another individual, or willfully conceals or withholds personal knowledge of a revocation under Section 4, is guilty of [a class ____ misdemeanor].

(e) A person who requires or prohibits the execution of a declaration as a condition for being insured for, or receiving, health-care services is guilty of [a class ____ misdemeanor].

(f) A person who coerces or fraudulently induces an individual to execute a declaration is guilty of [a class ____ misdemeanor].

(g) The penalties provided in this section do not displace any sanction applicable under other law.

§ 11. Miscellaneous Provisions.
(a) Death resulting from the withholding or withdrawal of life-sustaining treatment in accordance with this [Act] does not constitute, for any purpose, a suicide or homicide.
(b) The making of a declaration pursuant to Section 2 does not affect the sale, procurement, or issuance of a policy of life insurance or annuity, nor does it affect, impair, or modify the terms of an existing policy of life insurance or annuity. A policy of life insurance or annuity is not legally impaired or invalidated by the withholding or withdrawal of life-sustaining treatment from an insured, notwithstanding any term to the contrary.
(c) A person may not prohibit or require the execution of a declaration as a condition for being insured for, or receiving, health-care services.
(d) This [Act] creates no presumption concerning the intention of an individual who has revoked or has not executed a declaration with respect to the use, withholding, or withdrawal of life-sustaining treatment in the event of a terminal condition.
(e) This [Act] does not affect the right of a patient to make decisions regarding use of life-sustaining treatment, so long as the patient is able to do so, or impair or supersede a right or responsibility that a person has to effect the withholding or withdrawal of medical care.
(f) This [Act] does not require a physician or other health-care provider to take action contrary to reasonable medical standards.
(g) This [Act] does not condone, authorize, or approve mercy-killing or euthanasia.

§ 12. When Health-Care Provider May Presume Validity of Declaration.
In the absence of knowledge to the contrary, a physician or other health-care provider may assume that a declaration complies with this [Act] and is valid.

§ 13. Recognition of Declaration Executed in Another State.
A declaration executed in another state in compliance with the law of that state or of this State is valid for purposes of this [Act].

§ 14. Effect of Previous Declaration.
An instrument executed anywhere before the effective date of this [Act] which substantially complies with Section 2(a) is effective under this [Act].

§ 15. Uniformity of Application and Construction.
This [Act] shall be applied and construed to effectuate its general purpose to make uniform the law with respect to the subject of this [Act] among states enacting it.

§ 16. Short Title.
This [Act] may be cited as the Uniform Rights of the Terminally Ill Act (1989).

§ 17. Severability Clause.
If any provision of this [Act] or its application to any person or circumstance is held invalid, the invalidity does not affect other provisions or applications of this [Act] which can be given effect without the invalid provision or application, and to this end the provisions of this [Act] are severable.

§ 18. Effective Date.
This [Act] takes effect on _________.

§ 19. Repeal.
The following acts and parts of acts are repealed:
(1)
(2)

Chapter 3

Texts of Specific State Laws Governing the Execution of a Living Will

This chapter consists of a section-by-section presentation of each state's natural death laws. Eight states, to date, have passed no legislation in this area. The laws of the other 42 states as well as the District of Columbia are included below, in alphabetical order.

Alabama: Natural Death Act

§ **22-8A-1. Short title.** This chapter shall be known and may be cited as the "Natural Death Act."

§ **22-8A-2. Legislative intent.** The legislature finds that adult persons have the fundamental right to control the decisions relating to the rendering of their own medical care, including the decision to have life-sustaining procedures withheld or withdrawn in instances of a terminal condition.

In order that the rights of patients may be respected even after they are no longer able to participate actively in decisions about themselves, the legislature hereby declares that the laws of this state shall recognize the right of an adult person to make a written declaration instructing his or her physician to withhold or withdraw life-sustaining procedures in the event of a terminal condition.

§ **22-8A-3. Definitions.** As used in this chapter, the following terms shall have the following meanings, respectively, unless the context clearly indicates otherwise:

(1) Attending physician. The physician selected by, or assigned to, the patient who has primary responsibility for the treatment and care of the patient.

(2) Declaration. A witnessed document in writing, voluntarily executed by the declarant in accordance with the requirements of section 22-8A-4.

(3) Life-sustaining procedure. Any medical procedure or intervention which, when applied to a qualified patient, would serve only to prolong the dying process and where, in the judgment of the attending physician, death will occur whether or not such procedure or intervention is utilized. Life-sustaining procedure shall not include the administration of medication or the performance of any medical procedure deemed necessary to provide comfort care or to alleviate pain.

(4) Physician. A person licensed to practice medicine and osteopathy in the state of Alabama.

(5) Qualified patient. A patient, who has executed a declaration in accordance with this chapter and who has been diagnosed and certified in writing to be afflicted with a terminal condition by two physicians who have personally examined the patient, one of whom shall be the attending physician.
(6) Terminally ill or injured patient. A patient whose death is imminent or whose condition is hopeless unless he or she is artificially supported through the use of life-sustaining procedures.
§ 22-8A-4. Written declaration; requirements; form. (a) Any adult person may execute a declaration directing the withholding or withdrawal of life-sustaining procedures in a terminal condition. The declaration made pursuant to this chapter shall be:
(1) In writing;
(2) signed by the person making the declaration, or by another person in the declarant's presence and by the declarant's expressed direction;
(3) dated; and
(4) signed in the presence of two or more witnesses at least 19 years of age neither of whom shall be the person who signed the declaration on behalf of and at the direction of the person making the declaration, related to the declarant by blood or marriage, entitled to any portion of the estate of the declarant according to the laws of intestate succession of this state or under any will of the declarant or codicil thereto, or directly financially responsible for declarant's medical care. The declaration of a qualified patient diagnosed as pregnant by the attending physician shall have no effect during the course of the qualified patient's pregnancy.
(b) It shall be the responsibility of declarant to provide for notification to his or her attending physician of the existence of the declaration. An attending physician who is so notified shall make the declaration, or a copy of the declaration, a part of the declarant's medical records.
(c) The declaration shall be substantially in the following form, but in addition may include other specific directions. Should any of the other specific directions be held to be invalid, such invalidity shall not affect other directions of the declaration which can be given effect without the invalid direction, and to this end the directions in the declaration are severable. [*See Appendix A for a copy of the recommended form.*]
§ 22-8A-5. Revocation of written declaration. (a) A declaration may be revoked at any time by the declarant by any of the following methods:
(1) By being obliterated, burnt, torn, or otherwise destroyed or defaced in a manner indicating intention to cancel;
(2) By a written revocation of the declaration signed and dated by the declarant or person acting at the direction of the declarant; or
(3) By a verbal expression of the intent to revoke the declaration, in the presence of a witness 19 years of age or older who signs and dates a writing confirming that such expression of intent was made. Any verbal revocation shall become effective upon receipt by the attending physician of the above mentioned writing. The attending physician shall record in the patient's medical record the time, date and place of when he or she received notification of the revocation.
(b) There shall be no criminal or civil liability on the part of any person for failure to act upon a revocation made pursuant to this section unless that person has actual knowledge of the revocation.
§ 22-8A-6. Certification and confirmation of terminal condition. An attending physician who has been notified of the existence of a declaration executed under this chapter, without delay after the diagnosis of a terminal condition of the declarant, shall take the necessary steps to provide for written certification and confirmation of the declarant's terminal condition, so that declarant may be deemed to be a qualified patient under this chapter.
§ 22-8A-7. Competency of declarant; liability of participating physician, facility, etc. The desires of a qualified patient shall at all times supersede the effect of the declaration.
If the qualified patient is incompetent at the time of the decision to withhold or withdraw life-sustaining procedures, a declaration executed in accordance with section 22-8A-4 is presumed to be valid. For the purpose of this chapter, a physician or medical care facility may presume in the absence of actual notice to the contrary that an individual who executed a declaration was of sound mind when it was executed. The fact of an

individual's having executed a declaration shall not be considered as an indication of a declarant's mental incompetency. Age of itself shall not be a bar to a determination of competency.

No physician, licensed health care professional, medical care facility or employee thereof who in good faith and pursuant to reasonable medical standards causes or participates in the withholding or withdrawing of life-sustaining procedures from a qualified patient pursuant to a declaration made in accordance with this chapter shall, as a result thereof, be subject to criminal or civil liability, or be found to have committed an act of unprofessional conduct.

§ 22-8A-8. Refusal of attending physician to comply with declaration; penalties for willful concealment, etc., of declaration or revocation. (a) An attending physician who refuses to comply with the declaration of a qualified patient pursuant to this chapter shall not be liable for his refusal, but shall permit the qualified patient to be transferred to another physician.

(b) Any person who willfully conceals, cancels, defaces, obliterates or damages the declaration of another without such declarant's consent or who falsifies or forges a revocation of the declaration of another shall be guilty of a Class A misdemeanor.

(c) Any person who falsifies or forges the declaration of another, or willfully conceals or withholds personal knowledge of the revocation of a declaration, with the intent to cause a withholding or withdrawal of life-sustaining procedures contrary to the wishes of the declarant, and thereby, because of such act, directly causes life-sustaining procedures to be withheld or withdrawn and death to be hastened, shall be guilty of a Class C felony.

§ 22-8A-9. Withholding or withdrawal of procedures not suicide; execution of declaration not to affect sale, etc., of life insurance nor be condition for receipt of health care services; provisions of chapter cumulative. (a) The withholding or withdrawal of life-sustaining procedures from a qualified patient in accordance with the provisions of this chapter shall not, for any purpose, constitute a suicide and shall not constitute assisting suicide.

(b) The making of a declaration pursuant to section 22-8A-4 shall not affect in any manner the sale, procurement, or issuance of any policy of life insurance, nor shall it be deemed to modify the terms of an existing policy of life insurance. No policy of life insurance shall be legally impaired or invalidated in any manner by the withholding or withdrawal of life-sustaining procedures from an insured qualified patient, notwithstanding any term of the policy to the contrary.

(c) No physician, medical care facility, or other health care provider, and no health care service plan, health maintenance organization, insurer issuing disability insurance, self-insured employee welfare benefit plan, nonprofit medical service corporation or mutual nonprofit hospital or hospital service corporation shall require any person to execute a declaration as a condition for being insured for, or receiving, health care services.

(d) Nothing in this chapter shall impair or supersede any legal right or legal responsibility which any person may have to effect the withholding or withdrawal of life-sustaining procedures in any lawful manner. In such respect the provisions of this chapter are cumulative.

(e) This chapter shall create no presumption concerning the intention of an individual who has not executed a declaration to consent to the use or withholding of life-sustaining procedures in the event of a terminal condition.

§ 22-8A-10. Provisions of chapter not an approval of mercy killing, etc. Nothing in this chapter shall be construed to condone, authorize or approve mercy killing or to permit any affirmative or deliberate act or omission to end life other than to permit the natural process of dying as provided in this chapter.

Alaska: Rights of Terminally Ill Act

§ 18.12.010. Declaration relating to use of life-sustaining procedures. (a) A competent person who is at least 18 years old may execute a declaration at any time directing that life-sustaining procedures be withheld or withdrawn from that person; but the declaration is given operative effect only if the declarant's condition is determined to be terminal and the declarant is not able to make treatment decisions. The declaration shall be signed by the declarant, or another at the declarant's direction, and in either case shall be witnessed by two persons or a person qualified to take acknowledgments under Alaska Statutes 09.63.010. The witnesses must be at least 18 years old and may not be related to the declarant by blood or marriage. A person may not charge a fee for preparing a declaration.

(b) It is the responsibility of the declarant to provide a copy of the declaration to the declarant's physician. A physician or other health care provider who is provided a copy of the declaration shall make it a part of the declarant's medical records.

(c) A declaration may, but need not be, in the following form. [*See Appendix A for a copy of the form*].

§ 18.12.020. Revocation of declaration. (a) A declaration may be revoked at any time and in any manner by which the declarant is able to communicate an intent to revoke, without regard to mental or physical condition. A revocation is only effective as to the attending physician or any health care provider acting under the guidance of that physician upon communication to the physician or health care provider by the declarant or by another to whom the revocation was communicated.

(b) The attending physician or health care provider shall make the revocation a part of the declarant's medical record.

§ 18.12.030. Recording determination of terminal condition and contents of declaration. When an attending physician who has been provided a copy of a declaration determines that the declarant is in a terminal condition, the physician shall record that determination and the contents of the declaration in the declarant's medical record.

§ 18.12.040. Treatment of qualified patients. (a) A qualified patient has the right to make decisions regarding use of life-sustaining procedures as long as the patient is able to do so. If a qualified patient is not able to make these decisions, the declaration governs decisions regarding use of life-sustaining procedures.

(b) This chapter does not prohibit the application of any medical procedure or intervention, including the provision of nutrition and hydration, considered necessary to provide comfort care or alleviation of pain. The declaration may provide that the declarant does not want nutrition or hydration administered intravenously or by gastric tube.

(c) The declaration of a qualified patient known to the attending physician to be pregnant is given no effect as long as it is probable that the fetus could develop to the point of live birth with continued application of life-sustaining procedures.

§ 18.12.050. Transfer of patients. (a) An attending physician who is unwilling to comply with the requirements of Alaska Statutes 18.12.030 or who is unwilling to comply with the declaration of a qualified patient under Alaska Statutes 18.12.040 shall withdraw as attending physician but the withdrawal is effective only when the services of another attending physician have been obtained.

(b) If the policies of a health care facility preclude compliance with the declaration of a qualified patient under this chapter, that facility shall take all reasonable steps to notify the patient or, if the patient is not able to make treatment decisions, the patient's guardian, of the facility's policy and shall take all reasonable steps to effect the transfer of the patient to the patient's home or to a facility where the provisions of this chapter can be carried out.

§ 18.12.060. Immunities. (a) In the absence of actual notice of the revocation of a declaration, the following, while acting in accordance with the requirements of this chapter, are not subject to civil or criminal liability or guilty of unprofessional conduct:

(1) a physician who causes the withholding or withdrawal of life-sustaining procedures from a qualified patient;

(2) a person who participates in the withholding or withdrawal of life-sustaining procedures under the direction or with the authorization of a physician;

(3) the health care facility in which the withholding or withdrawal occurs.

(b) A physician, a health care professional or a health care facility is not subject to civil or criminal liability for actions under this chapter that are in accord with reasonable medical standards.

§ 18.12.070. Penalties. (a) An attending physician who fails to comply with the declaration of a qualified patient or to make the necessary arrangements to effect a transfer under Alaska Statutes 18.12.050 has no right to compensation for medical services provided to a qualified patient after withdrawal should have been effective or after transfer should have occurred and may be liable to the qualified patient and to the heirs of the qualified patient for a civil penalty not to exceed $1000.00 plus the actual costs associated with the failure to comply with the declaration, and this shall be the exclusive remedy at law for damages.

(b) A person who wilfully conceals, cancels, defaces, obliterates, or damages the declaration of another without the declarant's consent or who falsifies or forges a revocation of the declaration of another may be civilly liable to the qualified patient and to the heirs of the qualified patient.

§ 18.12.080. General provisions. (a) Death resulting from the withholding or withdrawal of life-sustaining procedures under a declaration and in accordance with this chapter does not, for any purpose, constitute a suicide or homicide.

(b) The making of a declaration under Alaska Statutes 18.12.010 does not affect in any manner the sale, procurement, or issuance of a policy of life insurance, nor does it modify the terms of an existing policy of life insurance. A policy of life insurance is not legally impaired or invalidated in any manner by the withholding or withdrawal of life-sustaining procedures from an insured qualified patient, notwithstanding any term of the policy to the contrary.

(c) A physician, health care facility, or other health care provider, and a health care service plan, insurer issuing disability insurance, self-insured employee welfare benefit plan, or nonprofit hospital plan, may not require a person to execute a declaration as a condition for being insured for, or receiving, health care services.

(d) This chapter creates no presumption concerning the intention of an individual who has not executed a declaration with respect to the use, withholding, or withdrawal of life-sustaining procedures in the event of a terminal condition.

(e) Nothing in this chapter increases or decreases the right of a patient to make decisions regarding use of life-sustaining procedures as long as the patient is able to do so, or impairs or supersedes any right or responsibility that a person has to effect the withholding or withdrawal of medical care in a lawful manner. In that respect, the provisions of this chapter are cumulative.

(f) This chapter does not condone, authorize, or approve mercy killing or euthanasia.

§ 18.12.090. Recognition of declarations executed in other states. A declaration executed in another state or a territory or possession of the United States in compliance with the law of that jurisdiction is effective for purposes of this chapter.

§ 18.12.100. Definitions. In this chapter

(1) "attending physician" means the physician selected by, or assigned to, the patient who has primary responsibility for the treatment and care of the patient;

(2) "declaration" means a document executed in accordance with the requirements of Alaska Statutes 18.12.010;

(3) "health care provider" means a person who is licensed, certified, or otherwise authorized by the law of this state to administer health care in the ordinary course of business or practice of a profession;

(4) "life-sustaining procedure" means a medical procedure or intervention that, when administered to a qualified patient, will serve only to prolong the dying process;

(5) "physician" means a person licensed to practice medicine in this state or an officer in the regular medical service of the armed services of the United States or the United States Public Health Service while in the discharge of their official duties, or while volunteering services without pay or other remuneration to a hospital, clinic, medical office, or other medical facility in the state;

(6) "qualified patient" means a patient who has executed a declaration in accordance with this chapter and who has been determined by the attending physician to be in a terminal condition;

(7) "terminal condition" means a progressive incurable or irreversible condition that, without the administration of life-sustaining procedures, will, in the opinion of two physicians, when available, who have personal-

ly examined the patient, one of whom must be the attending physician, result in death in a relatively short time.

Arizona: Medical Treatment Decision Act

§ 36-3201. Definitions. In this article, unless the context otherwise requires:
1. "Attending physician" means the physician selected by or assigned to the patient who has primary responsibility for the treatment and care of the patient.
2. "Declaration" means a witnessed document in writing which is voluntarily executed by the declarant as provided in § 36-3202.
3. "Guardian" means the guardian of an incapacitated person appointed pursuant to title 14, chapter 5.
4. "Life-sustaining procedure" means any medical procedure or intervention which in the judgment of the attending physician, if applied to a qualified patient, would serve only to prolong the dying process. Life-sustaining procedure does not include the administration of medication, food or fluids or the performance of a medical procedure deemed necessary to provide comfort care.
5. "Qualified patient" means a patient, eighteen years or more of age, who executes a declaration as provided in this article and who is diagnosed and certified in writing to be afflicted with a terminal condition by two physicians who personally examined the patient, one of whom is the attending physician.
6. "Terminal condition" means an incurable or irreversible condition from which, in the opinion of the attending physician, death will occur without the use of life-sustaining procedures.

§ 36-3202. Execution of declaration. A. A person may execute a declaration directing the withholding or withdrawal of life-sustaining procedures in a terminal condition. The declarant must sign the declaration in the presence of two subscribing witnesses who are not:
1. Related to the declarant by blood or marriage.
2. At the time of the declaration, entitled to any portion of the estate of the declarant under a will of the declarant or a codicil to a will then existing or by operation of law then existing.
3. Claimants against any portion of the estate of the declarant at the time of his decease or at the time of the execution of the declaration.
4. Directly financially responsible for the declarant's medical care.

B. The declarant is responsible for providing notification to his attending physician of the existence of the declaration. An attending physician who is notified of the existence of a declaration shall make the declaration, or a copy of the declaration, a part of the declarant's medical records.
C. The declaration shall be substantially in the following form but may include other specific directions. If any of the other specific directions is held invalid, the invalidity does not affect other directions of the declaration which can be given effect without the invalid direction. [*See Appendix A for a copy of this form.*]

§ 36-3203. Revocation of declaration. A. The declarant may revoke a declaration at any time without regard to his mental state or capacity by any of the following methods.
1. Cancellation, defacement, obliteration, burning, tearing or other means of destruction by the declarant or by some person in his presence and by his direction.
2. A written revocation of the declarant expressing his intent to revoke which is signed and dated by the declarant.
3. A verbal expression by the declarant of his intent to revoke the declaration.

B. Upon revoking a declaration, the declarant shall give notice to any physician who has been given notice of the declaration. The physician shall record in the patient's medical records the time and date when he received notification of the revocation. A verbal revocation becomes effective on communication to the attending physician by the declarant or by a person who is reasonably believed to be acting on behalf of the declarant. The attending physician shall record in the patient's medical record the time, date and place of the revocation and the time, date and place, if different, that he received notification of the revocation.

§ 36-3204. Physician's responsibility; written certification; transfer. A. An attending physician who is notified of the existence of a declaration executed as provided in this article shall, without delay after the diagnosis of a terminal condition of the declarant, take the necessary steps to provide for written certification and confirmation of the declarant's terminal condition so that the declarant may be deemed to be a qualified patient.

B. An attending physician who fails to comply with this section is deemed to have refused to comply with the declaration and shall make reasonable efforts to transfer the qualified patient or not hinder the transfer of the patient to another physician who will effectuate the declaration of the qualified patient.

§ 36-3205. Effect of declaration; immunity. A. The desires of a qualified patient who has capacity supersede the effect of a declaration.

B. If the qualified patient lacks capacity at the time of the decision to withhold or withdraw life-sustaining procedures, a declaration executed in accordance with § 36-3202 is presumed to be valid. For the purpose of this article, a physician or health care institution may presume in the absence of actual notice to the contrary that a person who executed a declaration was of sound mind when it was executed. The fact that a person executed a declaration shall not be considered as an indication of a declarant's mental capacity. Age of itself is not a bar to a determination of capacity.

C. No physician, health care institution or licensed health professional who relies in good faith upon a declaration shall be subject to civil or criminal liability or be deemed guilty of unprofessional conduct for withholding or withdrawing life-sustaining procedures from a qualified patient pursuant to a declaration unless that person has actual notice of the revocation of the declaration.

D. The declaration of a qualified patient known to the attending physician to be pregnant shall be given no force or effect as long as the fetus could develop to the point of live birth with continued application of life-sustaining procedures.

§ 36-3206. Guardian's responsibility; notification; revocation. If a guardian is appointed for a person who has previously executed a declaration pursuant to this article, he shall:

1. Observe and honor any declaration or written verbal revocation of a declaration made pursuant to this article.
2. Notify an attending physician of the existence of the declaration and its terms.
3. Verify any indication of revocation by the declarant made to the guardian by a person who claims to be acting on behalf of the declarant.
4. Upon receiving notice from a physician of written certification of a terminal condition, exercise his powers in a manner consistent with the declaration.

§ 36-3207. Insurance and health care services; effect of declaration. A. The making of a declaration as provided in § 36-3202 does not affect in any manner the sale, procurement or issuance of any policy of life insurance, nor is it deemed to modify the terms of an existing policy of life insurance. A policy of life insurance is not legally impaired or invalidated in any manner by the withholding or withdrawal of life-sustaining procedures from an insured qualified patient, notwithstanding any term of the policy.

B. A physician, a health care institution, any other health care provider, a health care service plan, an insurer issuing disability insurance, a self-insured employee welfare benefit plan or a nonprofit hospital plan may not require a person to execute a declaration as a condition for being insured for or receiving health care services.

§ 36-3208. Suicide. The withholding or withdrawal of life-sustaining procedures from a qualified patient in accordance with this article does not, for any purpose, constitute a suicide.

§ 36-3209. Mercy killing and euthanasia prohibited. Nothing in this article shall be construed to condone, authorize or approve mercy killing or euthanasia or to permit any affirmative or deliberate act or omission to end life, other than to permit the natural process of dying.

§ 36-3210. Penalties; violation; classification. A. A person who willfully conceals, cancels, defaces, obliterates or damages the declaration of another without the declarant's consent or who falsifies or forges a revocation of the declaration of another is civilly liable to any person damaged.
B. A person who falsifies or forges the declaration of another, or knowingly conceals or withholds personal knowledge of a revocation as provided in § 36-3203, with the intent to cause a withholding or withdrawal of life-sustaining procedures contrary to the wishes of the declarant and, because of such act, directly causes life-sustaining procedures to be withheld or withdrawn and death to be hastened is guilty of a class 1 felony.

Arkansas: Rights of the Terminally Ill or Permanently Unconscious Act

§ 20-17-201. Definitions. As used in this subchapter, unless the context otherwise requires:
(1) "Attending physician" means the physician who has primary responsibility for the treatment and care of the patient;
(2) "Declaration" means a writing executed in accordance with the requirements of § 20-17-202(a);
(3) "Health care provider" means a person who is licensed, certified, or otherwise authorized by the law of this state to administer health care in the ordinary course of business or practice of a profession;
(4) "Life-sustaining treatment" means any medical procedure or intervention that, when administered to a qualified patient, will serve only to prolong the process of dying or to maintain the patient in a condition of permanent unconsciousness;
(5) "Person" means an individual, corporation, business trust, estate, trust, partnership, association, joint venture, government, governmental subdivision or agency, or any other legal or commercial entity;
(6) "Physician" means an individual licensed to practice medicine in this state;
(7) "Qualified patient" means a patient eighteen (18) or more years of age who has executed a declaration or appointed a health care proxy and who has been determined by the attending physician to be in a terminal condition or in a permanently unconscious state by the attending physician and another qualified physician who has examined the patient;
(8) "State" means a state, territory, or possession of the United States, the District of Columbia, or the Commonwealth of Puerto Rico;
(9) "Terminal condition" means an incurable and irreversible condition that, without the administration of life-sustaining treatment, will, in the opinion of the attending physician, result in death within a relatively short time;
(10) "Health care proxy" is a person eighteen (18) years old or older appointed by the patient as attorney-in-fact to make health care directions including the withholding or withdrawal of life-sustaining treatment if a qualified patient, in the opinion of the attending physician, is permanently unconscious, incompetent, or otherwise mentally or physically incapable of communication.
(11) "Permanently unconscious" means a lasting condition, indefinitely without change in which thought, feeling, sensations, and awareness of self and environment are absent.
§ 20-17-202. Declaration relating to use of life-sustaining treatment. (a) An individual of sound mind and eighteen (18) or more years of age may execute at any time a declaration governing the withholding or withdrawal of life-sustaining treatment. The declaration must be signed by the declarant, or another at the declarant's direction, and witnessed by two (2) individuals.
(b) A declaration may, but need not, be in the following form in the case where the patient has a terminal condition. [*See Appendix A for a copy of this form.*]
§ 20-17-203. When declaration operative. A declaration becomes operative when (i) it is communicated to the attending physician and (ii) the declarant is determined by the attending physician and another physician

in consultation to be in a terminal condition and no longer able to make decisions regarding administration of life-sustaining treatment. When the declaration becomes operative, the attending physician and other health care providers shall act in accordance with its provisions or comply with the transfer provisions of § 20-17-207.

§ 20-17-204. Revocation of declaration. (a) A declaration may be revoked at any time and in any manner by the declarant, without regard to the declarant's mental or physical condition. A revocation is effective upon communication to the attending physician or other health care provider by the declarant or a witness to the revocation.

(b) The attending physician or other health care provider shall make the revocation a part of the declarant's medical record.

§ 20-17-205. Recording determination of terminal condition and declaration. Upon determining that the declarant is in a terminal condition, the attending physician who knows of a declaration shall record the determination and the terms of the declaration in the declarant's medical record.

§ 20-17-206. Treatment of qualified patient. (a) A qualified patient may make decisions regarding life-sustaining treatment as long as the patient is able to do so.

(b) This subchapter does not affect the responsibility of the attending physician or other health care provider to provide treatment, including nutrition and hydration, for a patient's comfort, care, or alleviation of pain.

(c) The declaration of a qualified patient known to the attending physician to be pregnant must not be given effect as long as it is possible that the fetus could develop to the point of live birth with continued application of life-sustaining treatment.

§ 20-17-207. Transfer of patients. An attending physician or other health care provider who is unwilling to comply with this subchapter shall as promptly as practicable take all reasonable steps to transfer care of the declarant to another physician or health care provider.

§ 20-17-208. Immunities. (a) In the absence of knowledge of the revocation of a declaration, a person is not subject to civil or criminal liability or discipline for unprofessional conduct for carrying out the declaration pursuant to the requirements of this subchapter.

(b) A physician or other health care provider, whose actions under this subchapter are in accord with reasonable medical standards is not subject to criminal or civil liability or discipline for unprofessional conduct with respect to those actions.

§ 20-17-209. Penalties. (a) A physician or other health care provider who willfully fails to transfer in accordance with § 20-17-207 is guilty of a Class A misdemeanor.

(b) A physician who willfully fails to record the determination of terminal condition in accordance with § 20-17-205 is guilty of a Class A misdemeanor.

(c) An individual who willfully conceals, cancels, defaces, or obliterates the declaration of another without the declarant's consent or who falsifies or forges a revocation of the declaration of another is guilty of a Class A misdemeanor.

(d) An individual who falsifies or forges the declaration of another, or willfully conceals or withholds personal knowledge of a revocation as provided in § 20-17-204, is guilty of a Class D felony.

(e) An individual who requires or prohibits the execution of a declaration as a condition for being insured for, or receiving, health care services is guilty of a Class D felony.

(f) A person who coerces or fraudulently induces another to execute a declaration under this subchapter is guilty of a Class D felony.

(g) The sanctions provided in this section do not displace any sanction applicable under other law.

§ 20-17-210. Miscellaneous provisions. (a) Death resulting from the withholding or withdrawal of life-sustaining treatment pursuant to a declaration and in accordance with this subchapter does not constitute, for any purpose, a suicide or homicide.

(b) The making of a declaration pursuant to § 20-17-202 does not affect in any manner the sale, procurement, or issuance of any policy of life insurance or annuity, nor does it affect, impair, or modify the terms of an existing policy of life insurance or annuity. A policy of life insurance or annuity is not legally impaired or in-

validated in any manner by the withholding or withdrawal of life-sustaining treatment from an insured qualified patient, notwithstanding any term to the contrary.
(c) A person may not prohibit or require the execution of a declaration as a condition for being insured for, or receiving health care services.
(d) This subchapter creates no presumption concerning the intention of an individual who has revoked or has not executed a declaration with respect to the use, withholding, or withdrawal of life-sustaining treatment in the event of a terminal condition.
(e) This subchapter does not affect the right of a patient to make decisions regarding use of life-sustaining treatment so long as the patient is able to do so, or impair or supersede any right or responsibility that a person has to effect the withholding or withdrawal of medical care.
(f) This subchapter does not require any physician or other health care provider to take any action contrary to reasonable medical standards.
(g) This subchapter does not condone, authorize, or approve mercy killing or euthanasia.
§ 20-17-211. When health care provider may presume validity of declaration. In the absence of knowledge to the contrary, a physician or other health care provider may presume that a declaration complies with this subchapter and is valid.
§ 20-17-212. Recognition of declaration executed in another state. A declaration executed in another state in compliance with the law of that state or of this state is validly executed for purposes of this subchapter.
§ 20-17-213. Effect of previous declaration. An instrument executed before July 20, 1987, which substantially complies with § 20-17-202(a) must be given effect pursuant to this subchapter.
§ 20-17-214. Who may execute written request for another. If any person is a minor, or an adult where a valid declaration does not exist and a health care proxy has not been designated and who, in the opinion of the attending physician, is no longer able to make health care decisions, then such declaration may be executed in the same form on his or her behalf by the first of the following individuals or category of individuals who exist and are reasonably available for consultation:
(1) A legal guardian of the patient, if one has been appointed.
(2) In the case of an unmarried patient under the age of eighteen (18), the parents of the patient;
(3) The patient's spouse;
(4) The patient's adult child, or, if there is more than one (1), then a majority of the patient's adult children participating in the decision;
(5) The parents of a patient over the age of eighteen (18);
(6) The patient's adult sibling, or, if there is more than one (1), then a majority of the patient's adult siblings participating in the decision;
(7) Persons standing in loco parentis to the patient;
(8) A majority of the patient's adult heirs at law who participate in the decision.
§ 20-17-215. Short title. This subchapter may be cited as the "Arkansas Rights of the Terminally Ill or Permanently Unconscious Act."
§ 20-17-216. Severability. If any provision of this subchapter or its application to any person or circumstance is held invalid, the invalidity does not affect other provisions or applications of this subchapter which can be given effect without the invalid provision or application, and to this end, the provisions of this subchapter are severable.
§ 20-17-217. Effective date. This subchapter takes effect on July 20, 1987.
§ 20-17-218. Repeal. The following acts and parts of acts are repealed:
(1) Act 879 of 1977;
(2) All laws and parts of laws in conflict with this subchapter.

California: Natural Death Act

§ 7185. Citation. This act shall be known and may be cited as the Natural Death Act.

§ 7186. Legislative findings and declarations. The Legislature finds that adult persons have the fundamental right to control the decisions relating to the rendering of their own medical care, including the decision to have life-sustaining procedures withheld or withdrawn in instances of a terminal condition.

The Legislature further finds that modern medical technology has made possible the artificial prolongation of human life beyond natural limits.

The Legislature further finds that, in the interest of protecting individual autonomy, such prolongation of life for persons with a terminal condition may cause loss of patient dignity and unnecessary pain and suffering, while providing nothing medically necessary or beneficial to the patient.

The Legislature further finds that there exists considerable uncertainty in the medical and legal professions as to the legality of terminating the use or application of life-sustaining procedures where the patient has voluntarily and in sound mind evidenced a desire that such procedures be withheld or withdrawn.

In recognition of the dignity and privacy which patients have a right to expect, the Legislature hereby declares that the laws of the State of California shall recognize the right of an adult person to make a written directive instructing his physician to withhold or withdraw life-sustaining procedures in the event of a terminal condition.

§ 7187. Definitions. The following definitions shall govern the construction of this chapter: (a) "Attending physician" means the physician selected by, or assigned to, the patient who has primary responsibility for the treatment and care of the patient.

(b) "Directive" means a written document voluntarily executed by the declarant in accordance with the requirements of Section 7188. The directive, or a copy of the directive, shall be made part of the patient's medical records.

(c) "Life-sustaining procedure" means any medical procedure or intervention which utilizes mechanical or other artificial means to sustain, restore, or supplant a vital function, which, when applied to a qualified patient, would serve only to artificially prolong the moment of death and where, in the judgment of the attending physician, death is imminent whether or not such procedures are utilized. "Life-sustaining procedure" shall not include the administration of medication or the performance of any medical procedure deemed necessary to alleviate pain.

(d) "Physician" means a physician and surgeon licensed by the Medical Board of California or the Board of Osteopathic Examiners.

(e) "Qualified patient" means a patient diagnosed and certified in writing to be afflicted with a terminal condition by two physicians, one of whom shall be the attending physician, who have personally examined the patient.

(f) "Terminal condition" means an incurable condition caused by injury, disease, or illness, which, regardless of the application of life-sustaining procedures, would, within reasonable medical judgment, produce death, and where the application of life-sustaining procedures serve only to postpone the moment of death of the patient.

§ 7188. Directive to physicians. Any adult person may execute a directive directing the withholding or withdrawal of life-sustaining procedures in a terminal condition. The directive shall be signed by the declarant in the presence of two witnesses not related to the declarant by blood or marriage and who would not be entitled to any portion of the estate of the declarant upon his decease under any will of the declarant or codicil thereto then existing or, at the time of the directive, by operation of law then existing. In addition, a witness to a directive shall not be the attending physician, an employee of the attending physician or a health facility in which the declarant is a patient, or any person who has a claim against any portion of the estate of the declarant upon his decease at the time of the execution of the directive. The directive shall be in the following form. [*See Appendix A for a copy of this form. The law specifies that the declaration shall be in exactly* *the same form as that listed in Appendix A. The addition of personalized instructions is not expressly forbidden by law.*—**ed. note.**]

§ 7188.5. Directive to physicians: Patient in skilled nursing facility. A directive shall have no force or effect if the declarant is a patient in a skilled nursing facility as defined in subdivision (c) of Section 1250 at the time the directive is executed unless one of the two witnesses to the directive is a patient advocate or ombudsman as may be designated by the State Department of Aging for this purpose pursuant to any other applicable provision of law. The patient advocate or ombudsman shall have the same qualifications as a witness as specified under Section 7188. The intent of this section is to recognize that some patients in skilled nursing facilities may be so insulated from a voluntary decisionmaking role, by virtue of the custodial nature of their care, as to require special assurance that they are capable of willfully and voluntarily executing a directive.

§ 7189. Revocation of directive. (a) A directive may be revoked at any time by the declarant, without regard to his mental state or competency, by any of the following methods:

(1) By being canceled, defaced, obliterated, or burnt, torn, or otherwise destroyed by the declarant or by some person in his presence and by his direction.

(2) By a written revocation of the declarant expressing his intent to revoke, signed and dated by the declarant. Such revocation shall become effective upon communication to the attending physician by the declarant or by a person acting on behalf of the declarant. The attending physician shall record in the patient's medical record the time and date when he received notification of the written revocation.

(3) By a verbal expression by the declarant of his intent to revoke the directive.

Such revocation shall become effective only upon communication to the attending physician by the declarant or by a person acting on behalf of the declarant. The attending physician shall record in the patient's medical record the time, date, and place of the revocation and the time, date, and place, if different, of when he received notification of the revocation.

(b) There shall be no criminal or civil liability on the part of any person for failure to act upon a revocation made pursuant to this section unless that person has actual knowledge of the revocation.

§ 7189.5. Term of directive. A directive shall be effective for five years from the date of execution thereof unless sooner revoked in a manner prescribed in Section 7189. Nothing in this chapter shall be construed to prevent a declarant from reexecuting a directive at any time in accordance with the formalities of Section 7188, including reexecution subsequent to a diagnosis of a terminal condition. If the declarant has executed more than one directive, such time shall be determined from the date of execution of the last directive known to the attending physician. If the declarant becomes comatose or is rendered incapable of communicating with the attending physician, the directive shall remain in effect for the duration of the comatose condition or until such time as the declarant's condition renders him or her able to communicate with the attending physician.

§ 7190. Immunity from civil or criminal liability. No physician or health facility which, acting in accordance with the requirements of this chapter, causes the withholding or withdrawal of life-sustaining procedures from a qualified patient, shall be subject to civil liability therefrom. No licensed health professional, acting under the direction of a physician, who participates in the withholding or withdrawal of life-sustaining procedures in accordance with the provisions of this chapter, shall be subject to any civil liability. No physician, or licensed health professional acting under the direction of a physician, who participates in the withholding or withdrawal of life-sustaining procedures in accordance with the provisions of this chapter shall be guilty of any criminal act or of unprofessional conduct.

§ 7191. Duties of physician. (a) Prior to effecting a withholding or withdrawal of life-sustaining procedures from a qualified patient pursuant to the directive, the attending physician shall determine that the directive complies with Section 7188, and, if the patient is mentally competent, that the directive and all steps proposed by the attending physician to be undertaken are in accord with the desires of the qualified patient.

(b) If the declarant was a qualified patient at least 14 days prior to executing or reexecuting the directive, the directive shall be conclusively presumed, unless revoked, to be the directions of the patient regarding the withholding or withdrawal of life-sustaining procedures. No physician, and no licensed health professional acting under the direction of a physician, shall be criminally or civilly liable for failing to effectuate the directive of the qualified patient pursuant to this subdivision. A failure by a physician to effectuate the directive of a qualified patient pursuant to this division shall constitute unprofessional conduct if the physician refuses to make the necessary arrangements, or fails to take the necessary steps, to effect the transfer of the qualified patient to another physician who will effectuate the directive of the qualified patient.

(c) If the declarant becomes a qualified patient subsequent to executing the directive, and has not subsequently reexecuted the directive, the attending physician may give weight to the directive as evidence of the patient's directions regarding the withholding or withdrawal of life-sustaining procedures and may consider other factors, such as information from the affected family or the nature of the patient's illness, injury, or disease, in determining whether the totality of circumstances known to the attending physician justify effectuating the directive. No physician, and no licensed health professional acting under the direction of a physician, shall be criminally or civilly liable for failing to effectuate the directive of the qualified patient pursuant to this subdivision.

[*In other words, the directive is only legally enforceable under California law if it is executed or reexecuted 14 days or more after the diagnosis of a terminal condition; otherwise, it is only considered advisory of the patient's wishes.*—**ed. note.**]

§ 7192. Suicide : Insurance. (a) The withholding or withdrawal of life-sustaining procedures from a qualified patient in accordance with the provisions of this chapter shall not, for any purpose, constitute a suicide.

(b) The making of a directive pursuant to Section 7188 shall not restrict, inhibit, or impair in any manner the sale, procurement, or issuance of any policy of life insurance, nor shall it be deemed to modify the terms of an existing policy of life insurance. No policy of life insurance shall be legally impaired or invalidated in any manner by the withholding or withdrawal of life-sustaining procedures from an insured qualified patient, notwithstanding any term of the policy to the contrary.

(c) No physician, health facility, or other health provider, and no health care service plan, insurer issuing disability insurance, self-insured employee welfare benefit plan, or nonprofit hospital service plan, shall require any person to execute a directive as a condition for being insured for, or receiving, health care services.

§ 7193. Rights as cumulative. Nothing in this chapter shall impair or supersede any legal right or legal responsibility which any person may have to effect the withholding or withdrawal of life-sustaining procedures in any lawful manner. In such respect the provisions of this act are cumulative.

§ 7194. Criminal penalties. Any person who willfully conceals, cancels, defaces, obliterates, or damages the directive of another without such declarant's consent shall be guilty of a misdemeanor. Any person who, except where justified or excused by law, falsifies or forges the directive of another, or willfully conceals or withholds personal knowledge of a revocation as provided in Section 7189, with the intent to cause a withholding or withdrawal of life-sustaining procedures contrary to the wishes of the declarant, and thereby, because of any such act, directly causes life-sustaining procedures to be withheld or withdrawn and death to thereby be hastened, shall be subject to prosecution for unlawful homicide as provided in Chapter 1 (commencing with Section 187) of Title 8 of Part 1 of the Penal Code.

§ 7195. Construction of chapter. Nothing in this chapter shall be construed to condone, authorize, or approve mercy killing, or to permit any affirmative or deliberate act or omission to end life other than to permit the natural process of dying as provided in this chapter.

Colorado: Medical Treatment Decision Act

§ 15-18-101. Short title. This article shall be known and may be cited as the "Colorado Medical Treatment Decision Act."

§ 15-18-102. Legislative declaration. The general assembly hereby finds, determines, and declares that: (a) Colorado law has traditionally recognized the right of a competent adult to accept or reject medical or surgical treatment affecting his person; (b) Recent advances in medical science have made it possible to prolong dying through the use of artificial, extraordinary, extreme, or radical medical or surgical procedures;
(c) The use of such medical or surgical procedures increasingly involves patients who are unconscious or otherwise incompetent to accept or reject medical or surgical treatment affecting their persons;
(d) The traditional right to accept or reject medical or surgical treatment should be available to an adult while he is competent, notwithstanding the fact that such medical or surgical treatment may be offered or applied when he is suffering from a terminal condition and is either unconscious or otherwise incompetent to decide whether such medical or surgical treatment should be accepted or rejected;
(e) This article affirms the traditional right to accept or reject medical or surgical treatment affecting one's person, and creates a procedure by which a competent adult may make such decisions in advance, before he becomes unconscious or otherwise incompetent to do so;
(f) It is the legislative intent that nothing in this article shall have the effect of modifying or changing currently practiced medical ethics or protocol with respect to any patient in the absence of a declaration as provided for in section 15-18-104;
(g) It is the legislative intent that nothing in this act shall require any person to execute a declaration.
§ 15-18-103. Definitions. As used in this article, unless the context otherwise requires:
(1) "Adult" means any person eighteen years of age or older.
(1.5) "Artificial nourishment" means nourishment supplied through a tube inserted into the stomach or intestines or nutrients injected intravenously into the bloodstream.
(2) "Attending physician" means the physician, whether selected by or assigned to the patient, who has primary responsibility for the treatment and care of said patient.
(3) "Court" means the district court of the county in which a declarant having a terminal condition is located at the time of commencement of a proceeding pursuant to this article or, in the city and county of Denver, the probate court.
(4) "Declarant" means a mentally competent adult who executes a declaration.
(5) "Declaration" means a written document voluntarily executed by a declarant in accordance with the requirements of section 15-18-104.
(6) "Hospital" means an institution holding a license or certificate of compliance as a hospital issued by the department of health of this state and includes hospitals operated by the federal government in Colorado.
(7) "Life-sustaining procedure" means any medical procedure or intervention that, if administered to a qualified patient, would serve only to prolong the dying process. "Life-sustaining procedure" shall not include any medical procedure or intervention for nourishment of the qualified patient or considered necessary by the attending physician to provide comfort or alleviate pain. However, artificial nourishment may be withdrawn or withheld pursuant to section 15-18-104(2.5).
(8) "Physician" means a person duly licensed under the provisions of article 36 of title 12, Colorado Revised Statutes.
(9) "Qualified patient" means a patient who has executed a declaration in accordance with this article and who has been certified by the attending physician and one other physician to be in a terminal condition.
(10) "Terminal condition" means an incurable or irreversible condition for which the administration of life-sustaining procedures will serve only to postpone the moment of death.
§ 15-18-104. Declaration as to medical treatment. (1) Any competent adult may execute a declaration directing that life-sustaining procedures be withheld or withdrawn if, at some future time, he is in a terminal condition and either unconscious or otherwise incompetent to decide whether any medical procedure or intervention should be accepted or rejected. It shall be the responsibility of the declarant or someone acting for him to submit the declaration to the attending physician for entry in the declarant's medical record.
(2) In the case of a declaration of a qualified patient known to the attending physician to be pregnant, a medical evaluation shall be made as to whether the fetus is viable and could with a reasonable degree of medical

certainty develop to live birth with continued application of life-sustaining procedures. If such is the case, the declaration shall be given no force or effect.

(2.5) (a) The declarant may provide in his declaration that, in the event that the only procedure being provided is artificial nourishment, one of the following actions shall be taken:

(I) That artificial nourishment not be continued when it is the only procedure being provided; or

(II) That artificial nourishment be continued for a specified period of time when it is the only procedure being provided; or

(III) That artificial nourishment be continued when it is the only procedure being provided.

(b) A declaration executed prior to March 29, 1989 may be amended by a codicil to include the provisions of this subsection (2.5).

(2.6) Notwithstanding the provisions of subsection (2.5) of this section and section 15-18-103(7), when an attending physician has determined that pain results from a discontinuance of artificial nourishment, he may order that such nourishment be provided but only to the extent necessary to provide comfort and alleviate such pain.

(3) A declaration executed before two witnesses by any competent adult shall be legally effective for the purposes of this article and may, but need not be, in the following form. [*See Appendix A for a copy of this form.*]

§ 15-18-105. Inability of declarant to sign. (1) In the event that the declarant is physically unable to sign the declaration, it may be signed by some other person in the declarant's presence and at his direction. Such other person may not be:

(a) The attending physician or any other physician; or

(b) An employee of the attending physician or health care facility in which the declarant is a patient; or

(c) A person who has a claim against any portion of the estate of the declarant at his death at the time the declaration is signed; or

(d) A person who knows or believes that he is entitled to any portion of the estate of the declarant upon his death either as a beneficiary of a will in existence at the time the declaration is signed or as an heir at law.

§ 15-18-106. Witnesses. (1) The declaration shall be signed by the declarant in the presence of two witnesses. Said witnesses shall not include any person specified in section 15-18-105.

(2) If the declarant is a patient or resident of a health care facility, the witnesses shall not be patients of that facility.

§ 15-18-107. Withdrawal - withholding of life-sustaining procedures. In the event an attending physician is presented with an unrevoked declaration executed by a declarant whom the physician believes has a terminal condition, the attending physician shall cause the declarant to be examined by one other physician. If both physicians find that the declarant has a terminal condition, they shall certify such fact in writing and enter such in the qualified patient's medical record of the hospital in which the withholding or withdrawal of life-sustaining procedures may occur, together with a copy of the declaration. If the attending physician has actual knowledge of the whereabouts of the qualified patient's spouse, any of his adult children, a parent, or attorney-in-fact under a durable power of attorney, the attending physician shall immediately make a reasonable effort to notify at least one of said persons, in the order named, that a certificate of terminal condition has been signed. If no action to challenge the validity of a declaration has been filed within 48 consecutive hours after the certification is made by the physicians, the attending physician shall then withdraw or withhold all life-sustaining procedures pursuant to the terms of the declaration.

§ 15-18-108. Determination of validity. (1) Any person who is the parent, adult child, spouse, or attorney-in-fact under a durable power of attorney of the qualified patient may challenge the validity of a declaration in the appropriate court of the county in which the qualified patient is located. Upon the filing of a petition to challenge the validity of a declaration and notification to the attending physician, a temporary restraining order shall be issued until a final determination as to validity is made.

(2) (a) In proceedings pursuant to this section, the court shall appoint a guardian ad litem for the qualified patient, and the guardian ad litem shall take such action as he deems necessary and prudent in the best interest of the qualified patient and shall present to the court a report of his actions, findings, conclusions, and recommendations.

(b) (I) Unless the court for good cause shown provides for a different method or time of notice, the petitioner, at least five days prior to the hearing, shall cause notice of the time and place of hearing to be given as follows:
(A) To the qualified patient's guardian or conservator, if any, and the court-appointed guardian ad litem; and
(B) To the qualified patient's spouse, if the identity and whereabouts of the spouse are known, to the petitioner, or otherwise to an adult child or parent of the qualified patient.
(II) Notice as required in this paragraph (b) shall be made in accordance with the Colorado rules of civil procedure.
(c) The court may require such evidence, including independent medical evidence, as it deems necessary.
(3) Upon a determination of the validity of the declaration, the court shall enter any appropriate order.
§ 15-18-109. Revocation. A declaration may be revoked by the declarant orally, in writing, or by burning, tearing, cancelling, obliterating, or destroying said declaration.
§ 15-18-110. Liability. (1) With respect to any declaration which appears on its face to have been executed in accordance with the requirements of this article:
(a) Any physician may act in compliance with such declaration in the absence of actual notice of revocation, fraud, misrepresentation, or improper execution;
(b) No physician signing a certificate of terminal condition or withholding or withdrawing life-sustaining procedures in compliance with a declaration shall be subject to civil liability, criminal penalty, or licensing sanctions therefor;
(c) No hospital or person acting under the direction of a physician and participating in the withholding or withdrawal of life-sustaining procedures in compliance with a declaration shall be subject to civil liability, criminal penalty, or licensing sanctions therefor.
§ 15-18-111. Determination of suicide or homicide - effect of declaration on insurance. The withholding or withdrawal of life-sustaining procedures from a qualified patient pursuant to this article shall not, for any purpose, constitute a suicide or homicide. The existence of a declaration shall not affect, impair, or modify any contract of life insurance or annuity or be the basis for any delay in issuing or refusing to issue an annuity or policy of life insurance or any increase of the premium therefor. No insurer or provider of health care shall require any person to execute a declaration as a condition of being insured for or receiving health care services; nor shall the failure to execute a declaration be the basis for any increased or additional premium for a contract or policy for medical or health insurance.
§ 15-18-112. Application of article. (1) Nothing in this article shall be construed as altering or amending the standards of the practice of medicine or establishing any presumption, absent a valid declaration. nor as condoning, authorizing, or approving euthanasia or mercy killing, nor as permitting any affirmative or deliberate act or omission to end life, except to permit natural death as provided in this article.
(2) In the event of any conflict between the provisions of this article, or a declaration executed under this article, and the provisions of section 15-14-501, the provisions of this article and the declaration shall prevail.
§ 15-18-113. Penalties. (1) Any person who willfully conceals, defaces, damages, or destroys a declaration of another, without the knowledge and consent of the declarant, commits a class 1 misdemeanor and shall be punished as provided in section 18-1-106 Colorado Revised Statutes.
(2) Any person who falsifies or forges a declaration of another commits a class 5 felony and shall be punished as provided in section 18-1-105, C.R.S.
(3) Any person who falsifies or forges a declaration of another, and the terms of the declaration are carried out, resulting in the death of the purported declarant, commits a class 2 felony and shall be punished as provided in section 18-1-105, C.R.S.
(4) Any person who willfully withholds information concerning the revocation of the declaration of another commits a class 1 misdemeanor and shall be punished as provided in section 18-1-106, C.R.S.
(5) An attending physician who refuses to comply with the terms of a declaration valid on its face shall transfer the care of the declarant to another physician who is willing to comply with the declaration. Refusal of an attending physician to comply with a declaration and failure to transfer the care of the declarant to another physician shall constitute unprofessional conduct as defined in section 12-36-117, C.R.S.

Connecticut: An Act Concerning Death With Dignity

§ 19a-570. Definitions. For purposes of this section and sections 19a-571 to 19a-575, inclusive:
(1) "Life support system" means any mechanical or electronic device, excluding the provision of nutrition and hydration, utilized by any physician or licensed medical facility in order to replace, assist or supplement the function of any human vital organ or combination of organs and which prolongs the dying process;
(2) "Beneficial medical treatment" includes the use of surgery, treatment, medications and the utilization of artificial technology to sustain life;
(3) "Terminal condition" means the final stage of an incurable or irreversible medical condition which, in the opinion of the attending physician, will result in death.

§ 19a-571. Liability re removal of life support system of incompetent patient. Attending physician must obtain consent of next of kin. Consideration of wishes of patient. Document as expression of wishes. Any physician licensed under Chapter 370 (Section 20-8 et seq.) or any licensed medical facility which removes or causes the removal of a life support system of an incompetent patient shall not be liable for damages in any civil action or subject to prosecution in any criminal proceeding for such removal, provided (1) the decision to remove such life-support system is based on the best medical judgment of the attending physician; (2) the attending physician deems the patient to be in a terminal condition; (3) the attending physician has obtained the informed consent of the next of kin, if known, or legal guardian, if any, of the patient prior to removal; and (4) the attending physician has considered the patient's wishes as expressed by the patient directly, through his next of kin or legal guardian, or in the form of a document executed in accordance with section 19a-575, if any such document is presented to, or in the possession of, the attending physician at the time the decision to terminate a life support system is made. If the attending physician does not deem the patient to be in a terminal condition, beneficial medical treatment and nutrition and hydration must be provided.

§ 19a-572. Failure to execute document creates no presumption re wishes of patient. Sections 19a-571 and 19a-573 to 19a-575, inclusive, create no presumption concerning the wishes of a patient who has not executed a document as described in section 19a-575.

§ 19a-573. Comfort care and pain alleviation to be provided. Notwithstanding the provisions of sections 19a-571, 19a-572, 19a-574 and 19a-575, comfort care and pain alleviation shall be provided in all cases.

§ 19a-574. Nonapplicability to pregnant patient. The provisions of sections 19a-571 to 19a-573, inclusive, and 19a-575 shall not apply to a pregnant patient.

§ 19a-575. Form of document. Any adult person may execute a document in substantially the following form. [*See Appendix A for a copy of this form. The law specifies that the declaration shall be in "substantially" the same form as that listed in Appendix A. The addition of personalized instructions is not expressly forbidden by law.*—**ed. note.**]

Delaware: Death With Dignity Act

§ 2501. Definitions.
(a) "Artificial means" shall mean manufactured or technical contrivances which may be attached to or integrated into the human body, but which are not normally a part of the human body.
(b) "Attending physician" shall mean the physician selected by the patient or someone on his behalf, or assigned by a health care facility to the patient, which physician has primary responsibility for the treatment and care of the patient.

(c) "Declaration" shall mean a witnessed document in writing, voluntarily executed by the declarant in accordance with the requirements of § 2503 of this title.
(d) "Maintenance medical treatment" shall mean any medical or surgical procedure or intervention which utilizes mechanical or other artificial means to sustain, restore or supplant a vital function; and which would serve only to artificially prolong the dying process. The words "maintenance medical treatment" shall not include the administration of medication, nor the performance of any medical procedure necessary to provide comfort care or to alleviate pain.
(e) "Terminal condition" shall means any disease, illness or condition sustained by any human being from which there is no reasonable medical expectation of recovery and which, as a medical probability, will result in the death of such human being regardless of the use or discontinuance of medical treatment implemented for the purpose of sustaining life, or the life processes.
§ 2502. Right of self-determination; appointment of agent. (a) An individual, legally adult, who is competent and of sound mind, has the right to refuse medical or surgical treatment if such refusal is not contrary to existing public health laws. Such individual has the right to make a written, dated declaration instructing any physician, including without limitation the treating physician, to cease or refrain from medical or surgical treatment should the declarant be in a terminal condition, as confirmed in writing by 2 physicians.
(b) An adult person by written declaration may appoint an agent who will act on behalf of such appointor, if, due to a condition resulting from illness or injury and, in the judgment of the attending physician, the appointor becomes incapable of making a decision in the exercise of the right to accept or refuse medical treatment.
(c) An agent appointed in accordance with this section may accept or refuse medical treatment proposed for the appointor if, in the judgment of the attending physician, the appointor is incapable of making that decision. This authority shall include the right to refuse medical treatment which would extend the appointor's life. An agent authorized to make decisions under this chapter has a duty to act in good faith, and with due regard for the benefit and interests of the appointor.
§ 2503. Execution of declaration. (a) Any adult person may execute a declaration directing the withholding or withdrawal of maintenance medical treatment, where the person is in a terminal condition and under such circumstances as may be set forth in the declaration. The declaration made pursuant to this chapter shall be:
(1) In writing;
(2) Signed by the person making the declaration or by another person in the declarant's presence and at the declarant's expressed direction;
(3) Dated; and
(4) Signed in the presence of 2 or more adult witnesses, as set forth in subsection (b) of this section.
(b) The declaration shall be signed by the declarant in the presence of 2 subscribing witnesses, neither of whom:
(1) Is related to the declarant by blood or marriage;
(2) Is entitled to any portion of the estate of the declarant under any will of the declarant or codicil thereto then existing nor, at the time of the declaration, is entitled by operation of law then existing;
(3) Has, at the time of the execution of the declaration, a present or inchoate claim against any portion of the estate of the declarant;
(4) Has a direct financial responsibility for the declarant's medical care; or
(5) Is an employee of the hospital or other health care facility in which the declarant is a patient.
(c) Each witness to the declaration shall state in writing that he is not prohibited under subsection (b) of this section from being a witness under this chapter.
(d) The declaration of a patient diagnosed as pregnant by the attending physician shall be of no effect during the course of the patient's pregnancy. Where a declaration is lacking any requirement under this section and such defect is later corrected by amendment or codicil, whether formally or informally prepared, such declaration shall be valid ab initio, notwithstanding the earlier defect.

[**Form of declaration.** *No particular required or recommended form is given in the Delaware statutes. For a copy of a generic Living Will form which meets the legal requirements of this state, see Appendix B.*—**ed. note.**]

§ 2504. Revocation of declaration. (a) The desires of a declarant who is competent shall at all times supersede the effect of the declaration. A declarant may revoke his declaration at any time, without regard to his mental state or competency. Any of the following methods is sufficient for revocation:

(1) Destruction, cancellation, obliteration, or mutilation of the declaration with an intent to revoke it. If physical disability has rendered the declarant unable to destroy, cancel, obliterate, or mutilate the declaration, he may direct another individual to do so in his presence;

(2) An oral statement made in the presence of 2 persons, each 18 years of age or older, which expresses an intent contrary to that expressed in the declaration;

(3) Either a new declaration, made in the same manner with the same formality as the former declaration, which expresses an intent contrary to that expressed in the prior declaration; or a written revocation signed and dated by the declarant.

(b) There shall be no criminal nor civil liability on the part of any person for failure to act in accordance with a revocation, unless such person has actual or constructive knowledge of the revocation.

(c) If the declarant is incompetent at the time of the decision to withhold or withdraw life-sustaining procedures, a declaration executed in accordance with § 2503 is presumed to be valid. For purposes of this chapter, a physician or a health care facility may presume, in the absence of actual notice to the contrary, that an individual who executed a declaration was of sound mind when it was executed. The fact that an individual executed a declaration shall not be considered as an indication of such individual's mental incompetency.

§ 2505. Immunity of health care personnel from liability. (a) Physicians or nurses who act in reliance on a document executed in accordance with this chapter, where such health care personnel have no actual notice of revocation or contrary indication, by withholding medical procedures for an individual who executed such document shall be presumed to be acting in good faith, and unless negligent shall be immune from civil or criminal liability.

(b) For purposes of this chapter a physician or nurse may presume, in the absence of actual notice to the contrary, that an individual who executed a document under this chapter was of sound mind when it was executed.

§ 2506. Safeguards. (a) Anyone who has good reason to believe that the withdrawal or withholding of a maintenance medical treatment in a particular case: (1) Is contrary to the most recent expressed wishes of a declarant; (2) Is being proposed pursuant to a declaration that has been falsified, forged, or coerced; or (3) Is being considered without the benefit of a revocation which has been unlawfully concealed, destroyed, altered, or cancelled; may petition the Court of Chancery for appointment of a guardian for such declarant.

(b) Upon receipt of a declaration, the hospital or the attending physician shall acknowledge receipt of same, and shall include the declaration as part of the declarant's medical records.

(c) The Division of Aging and the Public Guardian shall have oversight over any declaration executed by a resident of a sanatorium, rest home, nursing home, boarding home, or related institution as the same is defined in § 1101 of this title. Such declaration shall have no force nor effect if the declarant is a resident of a sanatorium, rest home, nursing home, boarding home, or related institution at the time the declaration is executed unless 1 of the witnesses is a person designated as a patient advocate or ombudsman by either the Division of Aging or the Public Guardian. The patient advocate or ombudsman must have the qualifications required of other witnesses under this chapter. [*See § 2503 on "Witnesses" above*—**ed. note.**]

§ 2507. Assumptions and presumptions. (a) Neither the execution of a declaration under this chapter nor the fact that maintenance medical treatment is withheld from a patient in accordance therewith shall, for any purpose, constitute a suicide.

(b) The making of a declaration pursuant to this chapter shall not restrict, inhibit nor impair in any manner the sale, procurement, or issuance of any policy of life insurance, nor shall it be deemed or presumed to modify the terms of an existing policy of life insurance. No policy of life insurance shall be legally impaired

or invalidated in any manner by the withholding or withdrawal of maintenance medical treatment from an insured patient, notwithstanding any term of the policy to the contrary.
(c) No physician, health facility or other health care provider, nor any health care service plan, insurer issuing disability insurance, self-insured employee welfare benefit plan or nonprofit hospital service plan, shall require any person to execute a declaration as a condition to being insured, or for receiving health care services, nor shall the signing of a declaration be a bar.
§ 2508. Penalties. (a) Whoever threatens directly or indirectly, coerces, or intimidates any person to execute a declaration directing the withholding or withdrawal of maintenance medical treatment shall be guilty of a misdemeanor and upon conviction shall be fined not less than $500 nor more than $1000; be imprisoned not less than 30 days nor more than 90 days; or both. The Superior Court shall have jurisdiction over such offenses.
(b) Whoever knowingly conceals, destroys, falsifies, or forges a document with intent to create the false impression that another person has directed that maintenance medical treatment be utilized for the prolongation of his life is guilty of a Class C felony.
(c) The Superior Court shall have jurisdiction over all offenses under this act.
§ 2509. Exemption from liability; defense. Repealed.

District Of Columbia: Uniform Determination of Death Act

§ 6-2401. Standard. An individual who has sustained either: (1) Irreversible cessation of circulatory and respiratory functions; or (2) irreversible cessation of all functions of the entire brain, including the brain stem; is dead. A determination of death must be made in accordance with accepted medical standards.
§ 6-2421. Definitions. For the purposes of this subchapter, the term:
(1) "Attending physician" means the physician selected by, or assigned to, the patient and who has primary responsibility for the treatment and care of the patient.
(2) "Declaration" means a witnessed document in writing, voluntarily executed by the declarant in accordance with the requirements of § 6-2422.
(3) "Life-sustaining procedure" means any medical procedure or intervention, which, when applied to a qualified patient, would serve only to artificially prolong the dying process and where, in the judgment of the attending physician and a second physician, death will occur whether or not such procedure or intervention is utilized. The term "life-sustaining procedure" shall not include the administration of medication or the performance of any medical procedure deemed necessary to provide comfort care or to alleviate pain.
(4) "Physician" means a person authorized to practice medicine in the District of Columbia.
(5) "Qualified patient" means a patient who has executed a declaration in accordance with this subchapter and who has been diagnosed and certified in writing to be afflicted with a terminal condition by 2 physicians who have personally examined the patient, one of whom shall be the attending physician.
(6) "Terminal condition" means an incurable condition caused by injury, disease, or illness, which, regardless of the application of life-sustaining procedures, would, within reasonable medical judgment, produce death, and where the application of life-sustaining procedures serve only to postpone the moment of death of the patient.
§ 6-2422. Declaration—Execution; form. (a) Any person 18 years of age or older may execute a declaration directing the withholding or withdrawal of life-sustaining procedures from themselves should they be in a terminal condition. The declaration made pursuant to this act shall be :
(1) In writing;

(2) Signed by the person making the declaration or by another person in the declarant's presence at the declarant's express direction;
(3) Dated; and
(4) Signed in the presence of 2 or more witnesses at least 18 years of age.
In addition, a witness shall not be:
(A) The person who signed the declaration on behalf of and at the direction of the declarant;
(B) Related to the declarant by blood or marriage;
(C) Entitled to any portion of the estate of the declarant according to the laws of intestate succession of the District of Columbia or under any will of the declarant or codicil thereto;
(D) Directly financially responsible for declarant's medical care; or
(E) The attending physician, an employee of the attending physician, or an employee of the health facility in which the declarant is a patient.
(b) It shall be the responsibility of the declarant to provide for notification to his or her attending physician of the existence of the declaration. An attending physician, when presented with the declaration, shall make the declaration or a copy of the declaration a part of the declarant's medical records.
(c) The declaration shall be substantially in this form, but in addition may include other specific directions not inconsistent with other provisions of this act. [*See Appendix A for a copy of this form*—**ed. note.**] Should any of the other specific directions added to the declaration be held to be invalid, such invalidity shall not affect other directions of the declaration which can be given effect without the invalid direction, and to this end the directions in the declaration are severable.
§ 6-2423. Same—Restrictions. A declaration shall have no effect if the declarant is a patient in an intermediate care or skilled care facility as defined in the Health Care Facilities Regulation, enacted June 14, 1974 (Reg. 74-15; 20 DCR 1423) at the time the declaration is executed unless 1 of the 2 witnesses to the directive is a patient advocate or ombudsman. The patient advocate or ombudsman shall have the same qualifications as a witness under § 6-2422.
§ 6-2424. Same—Revocation. (a) A declaration may be revoked at any time only by the declarant or at the express direction of the declarant, without regard to the declarant's mental state by any of the following methods:
(1) By being obliterated, burnt, torn, or otherwise destroyed or defaced by the declarant or by some person in the declarant's presence and at his or her direction;
(2) By a written revocation of the declaration signed and dated by the declarant or person acting at the direction of the declarant. Such revocation shall become effective only upon communication of the revocation to the attending physician by the declarant or by a person acting on behalf of the declarant. The attending physician shall record in the patient's medical record the time and date when he or she receives notification of the written revocation; or
(3) By a verbal expression of the intent to revoke the declaration, in the presence of a witness 18 years or older who signs and dates a writing confirming that such expression of intent was made. Any verbal revocation shall become effective only upon communication of the revocation to the attending physician by the declarant or by a person acting on behalf of the declarant. The attending physician shall record, in the patient's medical record, the time, date, and place of when he or she receives notification of the revocation.
(b) There shall be no criminal or civil liability on the part of any person for failure to act upon a revocation made pursuant to this section unless that person has actual knowledge of the revocation.
§ 6-2425. Physician's duty to confirm terminal condition. (a) An attending physician who has been notified of the existence of a declaration executed under this subchapter, without delay after the diagnosis of a terminal condition of the declarant, shall take the necessary steps to provide for written certification and confirmation of the declarant's terminal condition, so that the declarant may be deemed to be a qualified patient under this subchapter.
(b) Once written certification and confirmation of the declarant's terminal condition is made a person becomes a qualified patient under this subchapter only if the attending physician verbally or in writing informs the patient of his or her terminal condition and documents such communication in the patient's medical

record. If the patient is diagnosed as unable to comprehend verbal or written communications, such patient shall become a qualified patient as defined in § 6-2421, immediately upon written certification and confirmation of his or her terminal condition by the attending physician.

(c) An attending physician who does not comply with this section shall be considered to have committed an act of unprofessional conduct under § 2-1326.

§ 6-2426. Competency and intent of declarant. (a) The desires of a qualified patient shall at all times supersede the effect of the declaration.

(b) If the qualified patient is incompetent at the time of the decision to withhold or withdraw life-sustaining procedures, a declaration executed in accordance with § 6-2422 is presumed to be valid. For the purpose of this subchapter, a physician or health facility may presume in the absence of actual notice to the contrary that an individual who executed a declaration was of sound mind when it was executed. The fact of an individual's having executed a declaration shall not be considered as an indication of a declarant's mental incompetency.

§ 6-2427. Extent of medical liability; transfer of patient; criminal offenses. (a) No physician, licensed health care professional, health facility, or employee thereof who in good faith and pursuant to reasonable medical standards causes or participates in the withholding or withdrawing of life-sustaining procedures from a qualified patient pursuant to a declaration made in accordance with this subchapter shall, as a result thereof, be subject to criminal or civil liability, or be found to have committed an act of unprofessional conduct.

(b) An attending physician who cannot comply with the declaration of a qualified patient pursuant to this subchapter shall, in conjunction with the next of kin of the patient or other responsible individual, effect the transfer of the qualified patient to another physician who will honor the declaration of the qualified patient. Transfer under these circumstances shall not constitute abandonment. Failure of an attending physician to effect the transfer of the qualified patient according to this section, in the event he or she cannot comply with the directive, shall constitute unprofessional conduct as defined in § 2-1326.

(c) Any person who willfully conceals, cancels, defaces, obliterates, or damages the declaration of another without the declarant's consent or who falsifies or forges a revocation of the declaration of another shall commit an offense, and upon conviction shall be fined an amount not to exceed $5,000 or be imprisoned for a period not to exceed 3 years, or both.

(c) Any person who falsifies or forges the declaration of another, or willfully conceals or withholds personal knowledge of the revocation of a declaration, with the intent to cause a withholding or withdrawal of life-sustaining procedures, contrary to the wishes of the declarant, and thereby, because of such act, directly causes life-sustaining procedures to be withheld or withdrawn and death to be hastened, shall be subject to prosecution for unlawful homicide pursuant to § 22-2401.

§ 6-2428. Exclusion of suicide; effect of declaration upon issuance. (a) The withholding or withdrawal of life-sustaining procedures from a qualified patient in accordance with the provisions of this subchapter shall not, for any purpose, constitute a suicide and shall not constitute the crime of assisting suicide.

(b) The making of a declaration pursuant to § 6-2422 shall not affect in any manner the sale, procurement, or issuance of any policy of life insurance, nor shall it be deemed to modify the terms of an existing policy of life insurance. No policy of life insurance shall be legally impaired or invalidated in any manner by the withholding or withdrawal of life-sustaining procedures from an insured qualified patient, notwithstanding any term of the policy to the contrary.

(c) No physician, health facility, or other health care provider, and no health care service plan, health maintenance organization, insurer issuing disability insurance, self-insured employee welfare benefit plan, nonprofit medical service corporation, or mutual nonprofit hospital service corporation shall require any person to execute a declaration as a condition for being insured for, or receiving, health care services.

§ 6-2429. Preservation of existing rights. (a) Nothing in this subchapter shall impair or supersede any legal right or legal responsibility which any person may have to effect the withholding or withdrawal of life-sustaining procedures in any lawful manner. In such respect the provisions of this act are cumulative.

(b) This act shall create no presumption concerning the intention of an individual who has not executed a declaration to consent to the use or withholding of life-sustaining procedures in the event of a terminal condition.

§ 6-2430. Effect of subchapter. Nothing in this subchapter shall be construed to condone, authorize, or approve mercy killing or to permit any affirmative or deliberate act or omission to end a human life other than to permit the natural process of dying as provided in this subchapter.

Florida: Right to Decline Life-Prolonging Procedures Act

§ 765.01. Life-Prolonging Procedure Act of Florida; short title. Sections 765.01-765.15 may be cited as the "Life-Prolonging Procedure Act of Florida."

§ 765.02. Right to make declaration instructing physician concerning life-prolonging procedures; policy statement. The Legislature finds that every competent adult has the fundamental right to control the decisions relating to his own medical care, including the decision to have provided, withheld, or withdrawn the medical or surgical means or procedures calculated to prolong his life. This right is subject to certain interests of society, such as the protection of human life and the preservation of ethical standards in the medical profession. The Legislature further finds that the artificial prolongation of life for a person with a terminal condition may secure for him only a precarious and burdensome existence, while providing nothing medically necessary or beneficial to the patient. In order that the rights and intentions of a person with such a condition may be respected even after he is no longer able to participate actively in decisions concerning himself, and to encourage communication among such patient, his family, and his physician, the Legislature declares that the laws of this state recognize the right of a competent adult to make an oral or written declaration instructing his physician to provide, withhold, or withdraw life-prolonging procedures, or to designate another to make the treatment decision for him, in the event that such person should be diagnosed as suffering from a terminal condition.

§ 765.03. Definitions. As used in sections 765.01-765.15, the term:

(1) "Attending physician" means the primary physician who has responsibility for the treatment and care of the patient.

(2) "Declaration" means:

(a) A witnessed document in writing, voluntarily executed by the declarant in accordance with the requirements of section 765.04; or

(b) A witnessed oral statement made in accordance with the provisions of section 765.04 by the declarant subsequent to the time he is diagnosed as suffering from a terminal condition.

(3) "Life-prolonging procedure" means any medical procedure, treatment, or intervention which:

(a) Utilizes mechanical or other artificial means to sustain, restore, or supplant a spontaneous vital function; and

(b) When applied to a patient in a terminal condition, serves only to prolong the process of dying.

The term "life-prolonging procedure" does not include the provision of sustenance or the administration of medication or performance of any medical procedure deemed necessary to provide comfort care or to alleviate pain.

(4) "Physician" means a person licensed to practice medicine in the state.

(5) "Qualified patient" means a patient who has made a declaration in accordance with sections 765.01-765.15 and who has been diagnosed and certified in writing by the attending physician, and by one other physician who has examined the patient, to be afflicted with a terminal condition.

(6) "Terminal condition" means a condition caused by injury, disease, or illness from which, to a reasonable degree of medical certainty, there can be no recovery and which makes death imminent.

§ 765.04. Procedure for making a declaration; notice to physician.

(1) Any competent adult may, at any time, make a written declaration directing the withholding or withdrawal of life-prolonging procedures in the event such person should have a terminal condition. A written declaration must be signed by the declarant in the presence of two subscribing witnesses, one of whom is neither a spouse nor a blood relative of the declarant. If the declarant is physically unable to sign the written declaration, his declaration may be given orally, in which event one of the witnesses must subscribe the declarant's signature in the declarant's presence and at the declarant's direction.

(2) It is the responsibility of the declarant to provide for notification to his attending physician that the declaration has been made. In the event the declarant is comatose, incompetent, or otherwise mentally or physically incapable, any other person may notify the physician of the existence of the declaration. An attending physician who is so notified shall promptly make the declaration or a copy of the declaration, if the declaration is written, a part of the declarant's medical records. If the declaration is oral, the physician shall likewise promptly make the fact of such declaration a part of the patient's medical record.

§ 765.05. Suggested form of written declaration. (1) A declaration executed pursuant to section 765.04 may, but need not be, in this form. [*See Appendix A for a copy of the suggested form.*—**ed. note**]

(2) A declaration executed pursuant to section 765.04 may include other specific directions, including, but not limited to, a designation of another person to make the treatment decision for the declarant should he be diagnosed as suffering from a terminal condition and comatose, incompetent, or otherwise mentally or physically incapable of communication. Should any other specific direction be held to be invalid, such invalidity will not affect the declaration.

§ 765.06. Revocation of declaration. A declaration may be revoked at any time by the declarant:

(1) By means of a signed, dated writing;

(2) By means of the physical cancellation or destruction of the declaration by the declarant or by another in the declarant's presence and at the declarant's direction; or

(3) By means of an oral expression of intent to revoke.

Any such revocation will be effective when it is communicated to the attending physician. No civil or criminal liability shall be imposed upon any person for a failure to act upon a revocation unless that person has actual knowledge of such revocation.

§ 765.07. Procedure in absence of declaration; no presumption. (1) Life-prolonging procedures may be withheld or withdrawn from an adult patient with a terminal condition who is comatose, incompetent, or otherwise physically or mentally incapable of communication and has not made a declaration in accordance with section 765.04, if there are a consultation and a written agreement for the withholding or withdrawal of life-prolonging procedures between the attending physician and any of the following individuals, who shall be guided by the express or implied intentions of the patient, in the following order of priority if no individual in a prior class is reasonably available, willing, and competent to act:

(a) The judicially appointed guardian of the person of the patient if such guardian has been appointed. This paragraph shall not be construed to require such appointment before a treatment decision can be made under this section. (

b) The person or persons designated by the patient in writing to make the treatment decision for him should he be diagnosed as suffering from a terminal condition.

(c) The patient's spouse.

(d) An adult child of the patient or, if the patient has more than one adult child, a majority of the adult children who are reasonably available for consultation.

(e) The parents of the patient.

(f) The nearest living relative of the patient.

(2) In any case in which the treatment decision is made, at least two witnesses must be present at the time of the consultation when the treatment decision is made.

(3) The absence of a declaration by an adult patient does not give rise to any presumption as to his intent to consent to, or refuse, life-prolonging procedures.

§ 765.08. Effect of pregnancy on declaration or agreement. The declaration of a qualified patient, or the written agreement for a patient qualified under section 765.07, which patient has been diagnosed as pregnant by the attending physician, shall have no effect during the course of the pregnancy.

§ 765.09. Transfer of a qualified patient. An attending physician who refuses to comply with the declaration of a qualified patient, or the treatment decision of a person designated to make the decision by the declarant in his declaration pursuant to section 765.07, shall make a reasonable effort to transfer the patient to another physician.

§ 765.10. Immunity from liability; weight of proof; presumption.

(1) A health care facility, physician, or other person who acts under the direction of a physician is not subject to criminal prosecution or civil liability, and will not be deemed to have engaged in unprofessional conduct, as a result of the withholding or withdrawal of life-prolonging procedures from a patient with a terminal condition in accordance with sections 765.01-765.15. A person who authorizes the withholding or withdrawal of life-prolonging procedures from a patient with a terminal condition in accordance with a qualified patient's declaration or as provided in section 765.07 is not subject to criminal prosecution or civil liability for such action.

(2) The provisions of this section shall apply unless it is shown by a preponderance of the evidence that the person authorizing or effectuating the withholding or withdrawal of life-prolonging procedures did not, in good faith, comply with the provisions of sections 765.01-765.15. A declaration made in accordance with sections 765.01-765.15 shall be presumed to have been made voluntarily.

§ 765.11. Mercy killing or euthanasia not authorized; suicide distinguished. (1) Nothing in sections 765.01-765.15 shall be construed to condone, authorize, or approve mercy killing or euthanasia, or to permit any affirmative or deliberate act or omission to end life other than to permit the natural process of dying.

(2) The withholding or withdrawal of life-prolonging procedures from a patient in accordance with the provisions of sections 765.01-765.15 does not, for any purpose, constitute a suicide.

§ 765.12. Effect of declaration with respect to insurance. The making of a declaration pursuant to sections 765.01-765.15 shall not affect the sale, procurement, or issuance or any policy of life insurance, nor shall such making of a declaration be deemed to modify the terms of an existing policy of life insurance. No policy of life insurance will be legally impaired or invalidated by the withholding or withdrawal of life-prolonging procedures from an insured patient in accordance with the provisions of sections 765.01-765.15, notwithstanding any term of the policy to the contrary. A person shall not be required to make a declaration as a condition for being insured for, or receiving, health care services.

§ 765.13. Falsification, forgery, or willful concealment, cancellation, or destruction of declaration or revocation; penalties. (1) Any person who willfully conceals, cancels, defaces, obliterates, or damages the declaration of another without the declarant's consent or who falsifies or forges a revocation of the declaration of another, and who thereby causes life-prolonging procedures to be utilized in contravention of the previously expressed intent of the patient, is guilty of a felony of the third degree, punishable as provided in section 775.082, section 775.083, or section 775.084.

(2) Any person who falsifies or forges the declaration of another or who willfully conceals or withholds personal knowledge of the revocation of a declaration, with the intent to cause a withholding or withdrawal of life-prolonging procedures contrary to the wishes of the declarant, and who thereby because of such act directly causes life-prolonging procedures to be withheld or withdrawn and death to be hastened, is guilty of a felony of the second degree, punishable as provided in section 775.082, section 775.083, or section 775.084.

§ 765.14. Existing declarations; how treated. The declaration of any patient made prior to October 1, 1984, shall be given effect as provided in sections 765.01-765.15.

§ 765.15. Preservation of existing rights. The provisions of sections 765.01-765.15 are cumulative to the existing law regarding an individual's right to consent, or refuse to consent, to medical treatment and do not impair any existing rights or responsibilities which a health care provider, a patient, including a minor or incompetent patient, or a patient's family may have in regard to the withholding or withdrawal of life-prolonging medical procedures under the common law or statutes of the state.

Georgia: Living Will Act

§ 31-32-1. Legislative findings. (a) The General Assembly finds that modern medical technology has made possible the artificial prolongation of human life.
(b) The General Assembly further finds that, in the interest of protecting individual autonomy, such prolongation of life for persons with a terminal condition may cause loss of patient dignity and unnecessary pain and suffering, while providing nothing medically necessary or beneficial to the patient.
(c) The General Assembly further finds that there exists considerable uncertainty in the medical and legal professions as to the legality of terminating the use of life-sustaining procedures in certain situations.
(d) In recognition of the dignity and privacy which patients have a right to expect, the General Assembly declares that the laws of the State of Georgia shall recognize the right of a competent adult person to make a written directive, known as a living will, instructing his physician to withhold or withdraw life-sustaining procedures in the event of a terminal condition.
§ 31-32-2. Definitions. As used in this chapter, the term:
(1) "Attending physician" means the physician who has been selected by or assigned to the patient and who has assumed primary responsibility for the treatment and care of the patient; provided, however, that if the physician selected by or assigned to the patient to provide such treatment and care directs another physician to assume primary responsibility for such care and treatment, the physician who has been so directed shall, upon his or her assumption of such responsibility, be the "attending physician."
(2) "Competent adult" means a person of sound mind who is 18 years of age or older.
(3) "Declarant" means a person who has executed a living will authorized by this chapter.
(4) "Hospital" means a facility which has a valid permit or provisional permit issued under Chapter 7 of this title and which is primarily engaged in providing to inpatients, by or under the supervision of physicians, diagnostic services and therapeutic services for medical diagnosis, treatment, and care of injured, disabled, or sick persons.
(5) "Life-sustaining procedures" means any medical procedures or interventions, which, when applied to a patient in a terminal condition, would serve only to prolong the dying process and where, in the judgment of the attending physician and a second physician, death will occur whether or not such procedures or interventions are utilized. The term "life-sustaining procedures" shall not include the following:
(A) Nourishment; or
(B) The administration of medication to alleviate pain or the performance of any medical procedure deemed necessary to alleviate pain.
(6) "Living will" means a written document voluntarily executed by the declarant in accordance with the requirements of Code Section 31-32-3 or 31-32-4.
(7) "Patient" means a person receiving care or treatment from a physician.
(8) "Physician" means a person lawfully licensed in this state to practice medicine and surgery pursuant to Article 2 of Chapter 34 of Title 43.
(9) "Skilled nursing facility" means a facility having a valid permit or provisional permit issued under Chapter 7 of this title and which provides skilled nursing care and supportive care to patients whose primary need is for availability of skilled nursing care on an extended basis.
(10) "Terminal condition" means incurable condition caused by disease, illness, or injury which, regardless of the application of life-sustaining procedures, would produce death. The procedure for establishing a "terminal condition" is as follows: Two physicians, who, after personally examining the declarant, shall certify in writing, based upon conditions found during the course of their examination:
(A) There is no reasonable expectation for improvement in the condition of the declarant; and

(B) Death of the declarant from these conditions is imminent.

§ 31-32-3. Execution; witnesses; form. (a) Any competent adult may execute a document directing that, should the declarant have a terminal condition, life-sustaining procedures be withheld or withdrawn. Such living will shall be signed by the declarant in the presence of at least two competent adults who, at the time of the execution of the living will, to their best of their knowledge:

(1) Are not related to the declarant by blood or marriage;

(2) Would not be entitled to any portion of the estate of the declarant upon the declarant's decease under any testamentary will of the declarant, or codicil thereto, and would not be entitled to any such portion by operation of law under the rules of descent and distribution of this state at the time of the execution of the living will;

(3) Are neither the attending physician nor an employee of the attending physician nor an employee of the hospital or skilled nursing facility in which the declarant is a patient;

(4) Are not directly financially responsible for the declarant's medical care; and

(5) Do not have a claim against any portion of the estate of the declarant.

(b) The declaration shall be a document, separate and self-contained. A declaration executed on or after March 28, 1986, shall be in substantially the form specified in this subsection. A declaration executed on or after March 28, 1986, in substantially the form specified by prior law shall be valid and effective, except that the paragraph limiting the operation of the living will to a seven-year period shall be ineffective. [*See Appendix A for a copy of this form.*—**ed. note**]

§ 31-32-4. Patients in hospitals or skilled nursing facilities. A living will shall have no force or effect if the declarant is a patient in a hospital or skilled nursing facility at the time the living will is executed unless the living will is signed in the presence of the two witnesses as provided in Code Section 31-32-3 and, additionally, is signed in the presence of either the chief of the hospital medical staff, if witnessed in a hospital, or the medical director or any physician on the medical staff who is not participating in the care of the patient, if witnessed in a skilled nursing facility.

§ 31-32-5. Revocation. (a) A living will may be revoked at any time by the declarant, without regard to his mental state or competency, by any of the following methods:

(1) By being canceled, defaced, obliterated, burnt, torn, or otherwise destroyed by the declarant or by some person in his presence and by his direction;

(2) By the declarant or a person acting at the direction of the declarant signing and dating a written revocation expressing the intent of the declarant to revoke. In order to be effective, such a written revocation must clearly express an intention to revoke a living will as opposed to a will or wills relating to the disposition of property after death; and without limiting the generality of the foregoing, it is specifically provided that the revocation clause which is customarily included in a will relating to the disposition of property and which provides for the revocation of "all other wills" of the testator shall not operate to revoke a living will without further evidence of a specific intent to revoke the living will. Such revocation shall become effective only upon communication to the attending physician by the declarant or by a person acting at the direction of the declarant. The attending physician shall record in the patient's medical record the time and date when he received notification of the written revocation; or

(3) By any verbal or nonverbal expression by the declarant of his intent to revoke the living will. In order to be effective, such an oral revocation must clearly express an intention to revoke a living will as opposed to a will relating to the disposition of property after death. Such revocation shall become effective only upon communication to the attending physician by the declarant or by a person acting at the direction of the declarant. The attending physician shall record in the patient's medical record the time, date, and place of the revocation and the time, date, and place, if different, when he received notification of the revocation.

(b) Any person who participates in the withholding or withdrawal of life-sustaining procedures pursuant to a living will, as authorized by this chapter, which person has actual knowledge that such living will has been properly revoked, shall not have any civil or criminal immunity otherwise granted under this chapter for such conduct.

§ 31-32-6. Period of effectiveness. (a) A living will executed on or after the effective date of this subsection (March 28, 1986) shall be effective from the date of execution thereof unless revoked in a manner prescribed in Code Section 31-32-5.
(b) A living will executed prior to the effective date of this subsection (March 28, 1986) in the form specified by prior law shall be effective for a period of seven years from the date of execution thereof, except that, if the declarant crosses through or otherwise marks over the paragraph of such a living will relating to the seven-year period of effectiveness of the living will so as to indicate an intention to defeat the operation of such paragraph, and if the declarant signs or initials the living will in the area of the stricken paragraph, then the living will shall continue in effect until and unless revoked in a manner prescribed in Code Section 31-32-5.
§ 31-32-7. Immunity of participants from liability. (a) No physician nor any person acting under his direction and no hospital, skilled nursing facility, nor any agent or employee thereof who acting in good faith in accordance with the requirements of this chapter causes the withholding or withdrawal of life-sustaining procedures from a patient or who otherwise participates in good faith therein shall be subject to any civil liability therefor. No physician nor any person acting under his direction and no hospital, skilled nursing facility, nor any agent or employee thereof who acting in good faith in accordance with the requirements of this chapter causes the withholding or withdrawal of life-sustaining procedures from a patient or who otherwise participates in good faith therein shall be guilty of any criminal act therefor, nor shall any such person be guilty of unprofessional conduct therefor.
(b) No person who witnesses and attests a living will in good faith and in accordance with Code Section 31-32-3 shall be civilly or criminally liable or guilty of unprofessional conduct for such action.
§ 31-32-8. Conditions precedent to withholding or withdrawal of life-sustaining procedures; transfer of patient upon physician's failure or refusal to comply with living will. (a) Prior to effecting a withholding or withdrawal of life-sustaining procedures from a patient pursuant to a living will, the attending physician:
(1) Shall determine that, to the best of his knowledge, the declarant patient is not pregnant;
(2) Shall, without delay after the diagnosis of a terminal condition of the declarant, take the necessary steps to provide for written certification by said physician of the declarant's terminal condition;
(3) Shall make a reasonable effort to determine that the living will complies with subsection (b) of Code Section 31-32-3; and
(4) Shall make the living will and the written certification of the terminal condition a part of the declarant patient's medical records.
(b) The living will shall be presumed, unless revoked, to be the directions of the declarant regarding the withholding or withdrawal of life-sustaining procedures. No person shall be civilly liable for failing or refusing in good faith to effectuate the living will of the declarant patient. The attending physician who fails or refuses to comply with the declaration of a patient pursuant to this chapter shall endeavor to advise promptly the next of kin or legal guardian of the declarant that such physician is unwilling to effectuate the living will of the declarant patient. The attending physician shall thereafter at the election of the next of kin or the legal guardian of the declarant:
(1) Make a good faith attempt to effect the transfer of the qualified patient to another physician who will effectuate the declaration of the patient; or
(2) Permit the next of kin or legal guardian to obtain another physician who will effectuate the declaration of the patient.
§ 31-32-9. Living will not constituting suicide; effect of living will on insurance; restrictions on health care facilities' preparing living wills. (a) The making of a living will pursuant to this chapter shall not, for any purpose, constitute a suicide.
(b) The making of a living will pursuant to this chapter shall not restrict, inhibit, or impair in any manner the sale, procurement, issuance, or enforceability of any policy of life insurance, nor shall it be deemed to modify the terms of an existing policy of life insurance. No policy of life insurance shall be legally impaired or invalidated in any manner by the making of a living will pursuant to this chapter or by the withholding or withdrawal of life-sustaining procedures from an insured patient, nor shall the making of such a living will

or the withholding or withdrawal of such life-sustaining procedures operate to deny any additional insurance benefits for accidental death of the patient in any case in which the terminal condition of the patient is the result of accident, notwithstanding any term of the policy to the contrary.
(c) No physician, hospital, skilled nursing facility, or other health provider and no health care service plan, insurer issuing disability insurance, self-insured employee welfare benefit plan, or nonprofit hospital service plan shall require any person to execute a living will as a condition for being insured for, or receiving, health care services.
(d) No hospital, skilled nursing facility, or other medical or health care facility shall prepare, offer to prepare, or otherwise provide forms for living wills unless specifically requested to do so by a person desiring to execute a living will.
§ 31-32-10. Concealment or damage of living will; coercion; criminal homicide. Any person who willfully conceals, cancels, defaces, obliterates, alters, or damages the living will of another without such declarant's consent or who witnesses a living will knowing at the time he is not eligible to witness such living will under Code Section 31-32-3 or who coerces or attempts to coerce a person into making a living will shall be guilty of a misdemeanor. Any person who falsifies or forges the living will of another or willfully conceals or withholds personal knowledge of a revocation as provided in Code Section 31-32-5 with the intent to cause a withholding or withdrawal of life-sustaining procedures contrary to the wishes of the declarant and, thereby, because of any such act, directly causes life-sustaining procedures to be withheld or withdrawn and death thereby to be hastened shall be subject to prosecution for criminal homicide as provided in Chapter 5 of Title 16.
§ 31-32-11. Effect of chapter on other legal rights and duties. (a) Nothing in this chapter shall impair or supersede any legal right or legal responsibility which any person may have to effect the withholding or withdrawal of life-sustaining procedures in any lawful manner. In such respect the provisions of this chapter are cumulative.
(b) Nothing in this chapter shall be construed to condone, authorize, or approve mercy killing or to permit any affirmative or deliberate act or omission to end life other than to permit the process of dying as provided in this chapter. Furthermore, nothing in this chapter shall be construed to condone, authorize, or approve abortion.
(c) This chapter shall create no presumption concerning the intention of an individual who has not executed a declaration to consent to the use or withholding of life-sustaining procedures in the event of a terminal condition.
§ 31-32-12. Construction of this act in relation to Title 53. This act is wholly independent of the provisions of Title 53, relating to wills, trusts, and the administration of estates, and nothing in this chapter shall be construed to affect in any way the provisions of said Title 53.

Hawaii: Medical Treatment Decisions Act

§ 327D-1. Purpose. The legislature finds that all competent persons have the fundamental right to control the decisions relating to their own medical care, including the decision to have medical or surgical means or procedures calculated to prolong their lives provided, withheld, or withdrawn. The legislature further finds that the artificial prolongation of life for persons with a terminal condition may secure only a precarious and burdensome existence, while providing nothing medically necessary or beneficial to the patient.
In order that the rights of patients may be respected even after they are no longer able to participate actively in decisions about themselves, the legislature hereby declares that the laws of the State of Hawaii shall recog-

nize the right of an adult person to make a written declaration instructing his or her physician to provide, withhold, or withdraw life-sustaining procedures in the event of a terminal condition.

§ 327D-2. Definitions. Whenever used in this chapter, unless the context otherwise requires:

"Attending physician" means the physician who has primary responsibility for the treatment and care of the patient.

"Declarant" means a person who has executed a declaration in accordance with the requirements of section 327D-3.

"Declaration" means a written document voluntarily executed by the declarant in accordance with the requirements of section 327D-3, regardless of form.

"Health care provider" means a person who is licensed, certified, or otherwise authorized or permitted by law of this State to administer health care in the ordinary course of business or practice of a profession.

"Incompetent person" means any person who is impaired by reason of mental illness, physical illness or disability, chronic use of drugs, chronic intoxication, or other cause to the extent that the person lacks sufficient understanding or capacity to make or communicate responsible decisions concerning that person's health care.

"Life-sustaining procedure" means any medical procedure or intervention except for the provision of fluids, nourishment, medication, or other procedures necessary for patient comfort or pain relief, that when administered to a qualified patient, will serve only to prolong the dying process.

"Physician" means an individual licensed to practice medicine under chapter 453 or chapter 460.

"Qualified patient" means a patient who has executed a declaration in accordance with this chapter, and who has been diagnosed and certified in writing to be in a terminal condition by two physicians who have personally examined the patient, one of whom is the patient's attending physician. Provided, that if there is more than one attending physician, all such attending physicians must certify in writing that the patient is in a terminal condition.

"Terminal condition" means any incurable or irreversible disease, illness, injury or condition which without the administration of life-sustaining procedure will, as a medical probability, result in death in a relatively short time.

§ 327D-3. Execution of declaration. (a) Any competent person who has attained the age of majority may, at any time, execute a written declaration directing the provision, withholding, or withdrawal of life-sustaining procedures in the event such person should have a terminal condition.

(b) The declaration made pursuant to this chapter:

(1) Shall be in writing;

(2) Shall be signed by the person making the declaration, or by another person in the declarant's presence and at the declarant's expressed direction;

(3) Shall be dated;

(4) Shall be signed in the presence of two or more witnesses who:

(A) Are at least 18 years of age;

(B) Are not related to the declarant by blood, marriage, or adoption; and

(C) Are not the attending physician, an employee of the attending physician, or an employee of the medical care facility in which the declarant is a patient;

(5) Shall have all signatures notarized at the same time.

§ 327D-4. Suggested form of written declaration. A declaration executed pursuant to this chapter requesting that medical treatment be withheld or withdrawn may, but need not, be substantially in the following form, and may include other specific directions. Should any of the specific directions be held to be invalid, such invalidity shall not affect other directions of the declaration which can be given effect without the invalid direction, and to this end the directions in a declaration are severable. [*See Appendix A for a copy of this suggested form*—**ed. note.**]

§ 327D-5. Presumed validity of declaration. (a) If the qualified patient is incompetent at the time of the decision to withhold or withdraw life-sustaining procedures, a declaration executed in accordance with section 327D-3 is presumed to be valid.

(b) For the purpose of this chapter, a physician or medical care facility may presume, in the absence of actual notice to the contrary, that an individual who executed a declaration was of sound mind when the declaration was executed.
(c) The fact of an individual's having executed a declaration shall not be considered an indication of a declarant's mental incompetency.
§ 327D-6. Pregnancy. A declaration of a qualified patient diagnosed as pregnant by the attending physician shall be given no force or effect during the course of the pregnancy.
§ 327D-7. Patient's wishes supersede declaration. The desires of a declarant shall at all times supersede the effect of the declaration.
§ 327D-8. Declaration becomes part of medical records. It shall be the responsibility of the declarant to provide for delivery of the notarized declaration to the attending physician. In the event the declarant is comatose, incompetent, or otherwise mentally or physically incapable, any other person may deliver the notarized declaration to the physician. An attending physician who is so notified shall promptly make the declaration a part of the declarant's medical records.
§ 327D-9. Duty to deliver. Any person having a declaration of another in his or her possession and who becomes aware that the declarant is in circumstances under which the terms of the declaration may become applicable, shall deliver the declaration to the declarant's attending physician or to the medical care facility in which the declarant is a patient.
§ 327D-10. Written certification. (a) An attending physician who has been notified of the existence of a declaration executed under this chapter shall make all reasonable efforts to obtain the notarized declaration and, if the declaration so requests, shall without delay after the diagnosis of a terminal condition of the declarant, take the necessary steps to provide for written certification of the declarant's terminal condition by the attending physician and another physician who has examined the declarant, so that the declarant may be deemed to be a qualified patient, as defined in section 327D-2.
(b) Written certification of a declarant's terminal condition should be substantially in the following form:

CERTIFICATION OF INCOMPETENCE AND TERMINAL CONDITION

We hereby certify that.. is not, in our
name of patient
professional opinion, able to participate in decisions concerning medical treatment to be administered and has been diagnosed as having an incurable or irreversible disease, illness, injury or condition, specifically ....(diagnosis), and it is our professional judgment that this terminal condition will result in the death of the patient without the use of life-sustaining procedures.

Signed...(Attending Physician)
Signed... (Second Attending Physician)

(c) All inpatient medical care facilities shall develop a system to visibly identify a qualified patient's chart containing the declaration as set forth in this chapter.
§ 327D-11. Transfer to another physician. (a) An attending physician and any other physician under his or her direction or control, having possession of the patient's declaration or having knowledge that such declaration is part of the patient's record in the medical care facility in which the declarant is receiving care, shall take steps to qualify the patient and shall follow as closely as possible the terms of the declaration.
(b) An attending physician who, because of personal beliefs or conscience, refuses, or is unable, to certify a patient as terminal or to comply with the terms of the patient's declaration shall, without delay, make the necessary arrangements to effect the transfer of the patient, and the appropriate medical records that qualify or would qualify said patient, to another physician chosen by the qualified patient, or by the family of the qualified patient, for effectuation of the terms of the qualified patient's declaration. Such a physician who transfers the patient without delay, or makes a good faith attempt to do so, shall not be subject to criminal

prosecution, subject to civil liability, or found to have committed an act of unprofessional conduct for refusal to comply with the terms of the declaration. Transfer under these circumstances shall not constitute abandonment.

§ 327D-12. Revocation. A declaration may be revoked at any time by the declarant without regard to the declarant's mental state or competency, by any of the following methods:

(1) By being canceled, defaced, obliterated, or burnt, torn, or otherwise destroyed by the declarant or by some person in the declarant's presence and at the declarant's direction.

(2) By a written revocation signed and dated by the declarant expressing his or her intent to revoke. The attending physician shall record in the patient's medical record the time and date when the physician received notification of the written revocation.

(3) By a declarant's verbal expression, in the presence of two adult witnesses, of an intent to revoke the declaration. Such revocation shall become effective upon communication to the attending physician by the declarant or by both witnesses. The attending physician shall record in the patient's medical record the time, date, and place of the revocation and the time, date, and place, if different, of when the attending physician received notification of the revocation.

§ 327D-13. Mercy killing or euthanasia prohibited. Nothing in the chapter shall be construed to condone, authorize, or approve mercy killing or euthanasia.

§ 327D-14. Suicide. Death resulting from the withholding or withdrawal of life-sustaining procedures from a qualified patient under this chapter does not, for any purpose, constitute attempted suicide.

§ 327D-15. Effect on life insurance policies. The execution of a declaration pursuant to section 327D-3 shall not affect the sale, procurement, or issuance of any policy of life insurance, nor shall it be deemed to modify the terms of an existing policy of life insurance. No policy of life insurance shall be legally impaired or invalidated by the withholding or withdrawal of life-sustaining procedures from an insured patient in accordance with the provisions of this chapter, notwithstanding any term of the policy to the contrary.

§ 327D-16. Health care or health insurance. No physician, medical care facility or other health care provider, nor any health care service plan, insurer issuing disability insurance, self-insured employee welfare benefit plan, nonprofit medical service corporation, mutual nonprofit hospital service corporation, or nonprofit hospital service plan shall require any person to execute a declaration as a condition for being insured for, or receiving, health care services.

§ 327D-17. Penalties. (a) Failure of an attending physician to certify a terminal condition in writing according to section 327D-10 or, once a patient is certified as terminal, failure of the physician to transfer according to section 327D-11, constitutes professional misconduct.

(b) Any person who threatens, directly or indirectly, or coerces, or intimidates any person to execute a declaration directing the withholding or withdrawal of life-sustaining procedure shall be guilty of a class C felony.

(c) Any person who wilfully conceals, cancels, defaces, obliterates, or damages another's declaration without the declarant's consent or who falsifies or forges a declarant's revocation of declaration with the intent to create the false impression that the declarant has directed that life-sustaining procedures be utilized for the prolongation of the declarant's life shall be guilty of a misdemeanor.

(d) A physician who wilfully fails to record a statement of revocation according to the requirements of section 327D-12 is guilty of a misdemeanor.

§ 327D-18. Health personnel protections. In the absence of actual notice of the revocation of a declaration, no health care provider, medical care facility, physician, or other person acting under the direction of an attending physician shall be subject to criminal prosecution or civil liability or be deemed to have engaged in unprofessional conduct as a result of the withholding or the withdrawal of life-sustaining procedures from a patient with a terminal condition in accordance with this chapter unless the absence of actual notice resulted from the negligence of the health care provider, physician, or other person.

§ 327D-19. Safeguard provision. Any one who has good reason to believe that the withdrawal or withholding of life-sustaining procedures in a particular case:

(1) Is contrary to the most recent expressed wishes of a declarant;

(2) Is being proposed pursuant to a declaration that has been falsified, forged, or coerced; or

(3) Is being considered without the benefit of a revocation which has been unlawfully concealed, destroyed, altered or cancelled;
may petition the family court for appointment of a guardian for such declarant.
§ 327D-20. Participation in organ transplantation not allowed. No physician participating in a decision to withdraw or withhold life-sustaining procedures from a declarant may participate in transplanting the vital organs of the declarant to another person.
§ 327D-21. Procedure in absence of declaration. (a) In the absence of a declaration, ordinary standards of current medical practice will be followed.
(b) The withholding or withdrawal of life-sustaining procedures pursuant to (a) shall not be considered grounds for any civil or criminal action nor shall it be considered professional misconduct.
§ 327D-22. Preservation of existing rights. Nothing in this chapter shall impair or supersede any legal right or legal responsibility which any person may have to effect the withholding or withdrawal of life-sustaining procedures in any lawful manner. In such respect the provisions of this chapter are cumulative.
§ 327D-23. No presumption. This chapter creates no presumption concerning the intention of an individual who has revoked or has not executed a declaration to consent to the use or withholding or withdrawal of life-sustaining procedures in the event of a terminal condition.
§ 327D-24. Retroactive effect. The declaration of any qualified patient executed prior to June 13, 1986, shall be given effect as provided in this chapter.
§ 327D-25. Recognition of document executed in another state. A document executed in another state will be considered valid for purposes of this chapter if the document and the execution of said document substantially complies with the requirements of this chapter.
§ 327D-26. Effect of multiple documents. In the event a person has one or more valid declarations executed in accordance with this chapter, and/or one or more valid durable powers of attorney executed pursuant to chapter 560, or both, the most recently executed document shall reflect the person's intent.
§ 327D-27. Severability. The provisions of this chapter are severable. If any provision of this chapter or its application to any person or circumstance is held invalid, such invalidity shall not affect other provisions of this chapter which can be given effect without the invalid provision or application.

Idaho: Natural Death Act

§ 39-4501. Short title. This act shall be known and may be cited as the "Natural Death Act."
§ 39-4502. Statement of policy. The legislature finds that adult persons have the fundamental right to control the decisions relating to the rendering of their medical care, including the decision to have life-sustaining procedures withheld or withdrawn.
The legislature further finds that modern medical technology has made possible the artificial prolongation of human life beyond natural limits.
The legislature further finds that patients are sometimes unable to express their desire to withhold or withdraw such artificial life-prolongation procedures which provide nothing medically necessary or beneficial to the patient because of the patient's inability to communicate with the physician. In recognition of the dignity and privacy which patients have a right to expect, the legislature hereby declares that the laws of this state shall recognize the right of a competent person to have his wishes for medical treatment and for the withdrawal of artificial life-sustaining procedures carried out even though that person is no longer able to communicate with the physician.
§ 39-4503. Definitions. The following definitions shall govern the construction of this chapter:
(1) "Attending physician" means the physician licensed by the state board of medicine, selected by, or assigned to, the patient who has primary responsibility for the treatment and care of the patient.
(2) "Competent person" means any emancipated minor or any person eighteen (18) or more years of age who is of sound mind.

(3) "Artificial life-sustaining procedure" means any medical procedure or intervention which utilizes mechanical means to sustain or supplant a vital function which when applied to a qualified patient, would serve only to artificially prolong the moment of death and where, in the judgment of the attending physician, death is imminent whether or not such procedures are utilized, or the patient is diagnosed as being in a persistent vegetative state. Artificial life-sustaining procedures shall not include the administration of medication or the performance of any medical procedure deemed necessary to alleviate pain.
(4) "Durable power of attorney for health care" means a durable power of attorney to the extent that it authorizes an attorney in fact to make health care decisions for the principal.
§ 39-4504. Living will. Any competent person may execute a document known as a "living will." Such document shall be in the following form or in another form that contains the elements set forth in this section. [*See Appendix A for a copy of this form*—**ed. note.**]
§ 39-4505. Durable power of attorney for health care. In order to implement the general desires of a person as expressed in the "living will," a competent person may appoint any adult person to exercise a durable power of attorney for health care. The power shall be effective only when the competent person is unable to communicate rationally. The person granted the durable power of attorney for health care may make health decisions for the person to the same extent that the principal could make such decisions given the capacity to do so.
The durable power of attorney for health care may list alternative holders of the power in the event that the first person named is unable or unwilling to exercise the power.
A durable power of attorney for health care may be in the following form, or in any other form which contains the elements set forth in the following form. [*See Appendix C for a copy of this form.*—**ed. note**]
§ 39-4506. Revocation. (1) A directive may be revoked at any time by the maker thereof, without regard to his mental state or competence, by any of the following methods:
(a) By being cancelled, defaced, obliterated or burned, torn, or otherwise destroyed by the maker thereof or by some person in his presence and by his direction.
(b) By a written, signed revocation of the maker thereof expressing his intent to revoke.
(c) By a verbal expression by the maker thereof of his intent to revoke the directive.
(2) There shall be no criminal or civil liability on the part of any person for failure to act upon a revocation of a directive made pursuant to this section unless that person has actual knowledge of the revocation.
§ 39-4507. Execution of directive. A directive shall be effective from the date of execution unless otherwise revoked. Nothing in this chapter shall be construed to prevent a competent person from reexecuting a directive at any time. If the competent person becomes comatose or is rendered incapable of communicating with the attending physician, the directive shall remain in effect for the duration of the comatose condition or until such time as the patient's condition renders him able to communicate with the attending physician.
§ 39-4508. Immunity. No physician or health facility, which, acting in accordance with the wishes of a patient as expressed by the procedures set forth in this chapter, causes the withholding or withdrawal of artificial life-sustaining procedures from that patient, shall be subject to civil liability or criminal liability therefrom.
Any physician or other health care provider who for ethical or professional reasons is incapable or unwilling to conform to the desires of the patient as expressed by the procedures set forth in this chapter may withdraw without incurring any civil or criminal liability provided the physician or other health care provider makes a good faith effort to assist the patient in obtaining the services of another physician or other health care provider before withdrawal. No person who exercises the responsibilities of a durable power of attorney for health care in good faith shall be subject to civil or criminal liability as a result.
§ 39-4509. General provisions. (1) This chapter shall have no effect or be in any manner construed to apply to persons not executing a directive pursuant to this chapter nor shall it in any manner affect the rights of any such persons or of others acting for or on behalf of such persons to give or refuse to give consent or withhold consent for any medical care; neither shall this chapter be construed to affect chapter 43, title 39, nor chapter 3, title 66, Idaho Code, in any manner.

(2) The making of a directive pursuant to this chapter shall not restrict, inhibit, or impair in any manner the sale, procurement, or issuance of any policy of life insurance, nor shall it be deemed to modify the terms of an existing policy of life insurance. No policy of life insurance shall be legally impaired or invalidated in any manner by the withholding or withdrawal of artificial life-sustaining procedures from an insured qualified patient, notwithstanding any term of the policy to the contrary.
(3) No physician, health facility or other health provider and no health care service plan, insurer issuing disability insurance, self-insured employee welfare benefit plan, or nonprofit hospital service plan, shall require any person to execute a directive as a condition for being insured for, or receiving, health care services.

Illinois: Living Will Act

§ 701. Purpose. The legislature finds that persons have the fundamental right to control the decisions relating to the rendering of their own medical care, including the decision to have death delaying procedures withheld or withdrawn in instances of a terminal condition.
In order that the rights of patients may be respected even after they are no longer able to participate actively in decisions about themselves, the legislature hereby declares that the laws of this State shall recognize the right of a person to make a written declaration instructing his or her physician to withhold or withdraw death delaying procedures in the event of a terminal condition.
§ 702. Definitions. (a) "Attending physician" means the physician selected by, or assigned to, the patient who has primary responsibility for the treatment and care of the patient.
(b) "Declaration" means a witnessed document in writing, voluntarily executed by the declarant in accordance with the requirements of section 703.
(c) "Health-care provider" means a person who is licensed, certified or otherwise authorized by the law of this State to administer health care in the ordinary course of business or practice of a profession.
(d) "Death delaying procedure" means any medical procedure or intervention which, when applied to a qualified patient, in the judgment of the attending physician would serve only to postpone the moment of death. In appropriate circumstances, such procedures include, but are not limited to, assisted ventilation, artificial kidney treatments, intravenous feeding or medication, blood transfusions, tube feeding and other procedures of greater or lesser magnitude that serve only to delay death. However, this Act does not affect the responsibility of the attending physician or other health care provider to provide treatment for a patient's comfort care or alleviation of pain. Nutrition and hydration shall not be withdrawn or withheld from a qualified patient if the withdrawal or withholding would result in death solely from dehydration or starvation rather than from the existing terminal condition.
(e) "Person" means an individual, corporation, business trust, estate, trust, partnership, association, government, governmental subdivision or agency, or any other legal entity.
(f) "Physician" means a person licensed to practice medicine in all its branches.
(g) "Qualified patient" means a patient who has executed a declaration in accordance with this Act and who has been diagnosed and verified in writing to be afflicted with a terminal condition by his or her attending physician who has personally examined the patient. A qualified patient has the right to make decisions regarding death delaying procedures as long as he or she is able to do so.
(h) "Terminal condition" means an incurable and irreversible condition which is such that death is imminent and the application of death delaying procedures serves only to prolong the dying process.
§ 703. Execution of a document. (a) An individual of sound mind and having reached the age of majority or having obtained the status of an emancipated person pursuant to the "Emancipation of Mature Minors Act," as now or hereafter amended, may execute a document directing that if he is suffering from a terminal condition, then death delaying procedures shall not be utilized for the prolongation of his life.
(b) The declaration must be signed by the declarant, or another at the declarant's direction, and witnessed by 2 individuals 18 years of age or older.

(c) The declaration of a qualified patient diagnosed as pregnant by the attending physician shall be given no force and effect as long as in the opinion of the attending physician it is possible that the fetus could develop to the point of live birth with the continued application of death delaying procedures.
(d) If the patient is able, it shall be the responsibility of the patient to provide for notification to his or her attending physician of the existence of a declaration, to provide the declaration to the physician and to ask the attending physician whether he or she is willing to comply with its provisions. An attending physician who is so notified shall make the declaration, or copy of the declaration, a part of the patient's medical records. If the physician is at any time unwilling to comply with its provisions, the physician shall promptly so advise the declarant. If the physician is unwilling to comply with its provisions and the patient is able, it is the patient's responsibility to initiate the transfer to another physician of the patient's choosing. If the physician is unwilling to comply with its provisions and the patient is at any time not able to initiate the transfer, then the attending physician shall without delay notify the person with the highest priority, as set forth in this section, who is available, able, and willing to make arrangements for the transfer of the patient and the appropriate medical records to another physician for the effectuation of the patient's declaration. The order of priority is as follows: (1) any person authorized by the patient to make such arrangements, (2) a guardian of the person of the patient, without the necessity of obtaining a court order to do so, and (3) any member of the patient's family.
(e) The declaration may, but need not, be in the following form, and in addition may include other specific directions. Should any specific direction be determined to be invalid, such invalidity shall not affect other directions of the declaration which can be given effect without the invalid direction, and to this end the directions in the declaration are severable. [*See Appendix A for a copy of the recommended form*—**ed. note.**]
§ 704. Recording of a terminal condition. Upon determining that the declarant has a terminal condition, the attending physician who knows of a declaration shall record the determination and the terms of the declaration in the declarant's medical record. A physician who records in writing a terminal condition under this section is presumed to be acting in good faith. Unless it is alleged and proved that his action violated the standard of reasonable professional care and judgment under the circumstances, he is immune from civil or criminal liability that otherwise might be incurred.
§ 705. Revocation. (a) A declaration may be revoked at any time by the declarant without regard to declarant's mental or physician condition, by any of the following methods:
(1) By being obliterated, burnt, torn, or otherwise destroyed or defaced in a manner indicating intention to cancel;
(2) By a written revocation of the declaration signed and dated by the declarant or person acting at the direction of the declarant;
(3) By an oral or any other expression of the intent to revoke the declaration, in the presence of a witness 18 years of age or older who signs and dates a writing confirming that such expression of intent was made.
(b) A revocation is effective upon communication to the attending physician by the declarant or by another who witnessed the revocation. The attending physician shall record in the patient's medical record the time and date when and the place where he or she received notification of the revocation.
(c) There shall be no criminal or civil liability on the part of any person for failure to act upon a revocation made pursuant to this section unless that person has actual knowledge of the revocation.
§ 706. Physician responsibilities. An attending physician who has been notified of the existence of a declaration executed under this Act, without delay after the diagnosis of a terminal condition of the patient, shall take the necessary steps to provide for written recording of the patient's terminal condition, so that the patient may be deemed to be a qualified patient under this Act, or shall notify the patient or, if the patient is unable to initiate a transfer, the person or persons described in subsection (d) of section 703 in the order of priority stated therein that the physician is unwilling to comply with the provisions of the patient's declaration.
§ 707. Immunity. The desires of a qualified patient shall at all times supersede the effect of the declaration. A physician or other health-care provider may presume, in the absence of knowledge to the contrary, that a declaration complies with this Act and is valid.

No physician, health care provider or employee thereof who in good faith and pursuant to reasonable medical standards causes or participates in the withholding or withdrawing of death delaying procedures from a qualified patient pursuant to a declaration which purports to have been made in accordance with this Act shall, as a result thereof, be subject to criminal or civil liability, or be found to have committed an act of unprofessional conduct.

§ 708. Penalties. (a) Any person who willfully conceals, cancels, defaces, obliterates, or damages the declaration of another without such declarant's consent or who falsifies or forges a revocation of the declaration of another or who willfully fails to comply with section 706 shall be civilly liable.

(b) Any person who coerces or fraudulently induces another to execute a declaration or falsifies or forges the declaration of another, or willfully conceals or withholds personal knowledge of a revocation as provided in section 705 with the intent to cause a withholding or withdrawal of death delaying procedures contrary to the wishes of the qualified patient and thereby, because of such act, directly causes death delaying procedures to be withheld or withdrawn and death to another thereby be hastened, shall be subject to prosecution for involuntary manslaughter.

(c) A physician or other health-care provider who willfully fails to notify the health care facility or fails to comply with section 706 is guilty of engaging in unethical and unprofessional conduct in violation of paragraph 5 of section 4433 of the Medical Practice Act.

(d) A physician who willfully fails to record the determination of terminal condition in accordance with section 704, without giving notice required by section 706 of his unwillingness to comply with the provisions of the patient's declaration, is guilty of willfully omitting to file or record medical reports as required by law in violation of paragraph 22 of section 16 of the Medical Practice Act.

(e) A person who requires or prohibits the execution of a declaration as a condition for being insured for, or receiving, health-care services is guilty of a class A misdemeanor.

(f) The penalties provided in this section do not displace any penalty applicable under other law.

§ 709. General provisions. (a) The withholding or withdrawal of death delaying procedures from a qualified patient in accordance with the provisions of this Act shall not, for any purpose, constitute a suicide.

(b) The making of a declaration pursuant to section 703 shall not affect in any manner the sale, procurement, or issuance of any policy of life insurance, nor shall it be deemed to modify the terms of an existing policy of life insurance. No policy of life insurance shall be legally impaired or invalidated in any manner by the withholding or withdrawal of death delaying procedures from an insured qualified patient, notwithstanding any term of the policy to the contrary.

(c) No physician, health care facility, or other health care provider, and no health care service plan, health maintenance organization, insurer issuing disability insurance, self-insured employee welfare benefit plan, nonprofit medical service corporation, or mutual nonprofit hospital service corporation shall require any person to execute a declaration as a condition for being insured for, or receiving, health care services.

(d) Nothing in this Act shall impair or supersede any legal right or legal responsibility which any person may have to effect the withholding or withdrawal of death delaying procedures in any lawful manner. In such respect the provisions of this Act are cumulative.

(e) This Act shall create no presumption concerning the intention of an individual who has not executed a declaration to consent to the use or withholding of death delaying procedures in the event of a terminal condition.

(f) Nothing in this Act shall be construed to condone, authorize or approve mercy killing or to permit any affirmative or deliberate act or omission to end life other than to permit the natural process of dying as provided in this Act.

(g) An instrument executed before the effective date of this Act that substantially complies with paragraph (e) of section 703 shall be given effect pursuant to the provisions of this Act.

(h) A declaration executed in another state in compliance with the law of that state or this State is validly executed for purposes of this Act, and such declaration shall be applied in accordance with the provisions of this Act.

§ 710. Short title. This Act shall be known and may be cited as the "Illinois Living Will Act."

Indiana: Living Wills And Life-Prolonging Procedures Act

§ 16-8-11-1. Policy. Competent adults have the right to control the decisions relating to their own medical care, including the decision to have medical or surgical means or procedures calculated to prolong their lives provided, withheld, or withdrawn.

§ 16-8-11-2. "Attending physician" defined. As used in this chapter, "attending physician" means the physician who has the primary responsibility for the treatment and care of the patient.

§ 16-8-11-3. "Health care provider" defined. As used in this chapter, "health care provider" has the meaning set forth in Indiana Code 16-9.5-1-1.

§ 16-8-11-4. "Life prolonging procedure" defined. As used in this chapter, "life-prolonging procedure" means any medical procedure, treatment, or intervention that:

(1) uses mechanical or other artificial means to sustain, restore, or supplant a vital function; and

(2) serves to prolong the dying process.

"Life-sustaining procedure" does not include the provision of appropriate nutrition and hydration, the administration of medication, or the performance of any medical procedure necessary to provide comfort care or to alleviate pain.

§ 16-8-11-5. "Life-prolonging procedures will declarant" defined. "Life- prolonging procedures will declarant" means a person who has executed a life-prolonging procedures will under section 12 of this chapter.

§ 16-8-11-6. "Living will declarant" defined. "Living will declarant" means a person who has executed a living will under section 12 of this chapter.

§ 16-8-11-7. "Physician" defined. As used in this chapter, "physician" means a person with an unlimited license to practice medicine in Indiana under Indiana Code 25-22.5.

§ 16-8-11-8. "Qualified patient" defined. As used in this chapter, "qualified patient" means a patient who has been certified as a qualified patient under section 14 of this chapter.

§ 16-8-11-9. "Terminal condition" defined. As used in this chapter, "terminal condition" means a condition caused by injury, disease, or illness from which, to a reasonable degree of medical certainty:

(1) there can be no recovery; and

(2) death will occur from the terminal condition within a short period of time without the provision of life-prolonging procedures.

§ 16-8-11-10. Consent to medical treatment; immunity from liability for failure to treat patient after refusal of treatment. (a) Any competent person may consent to or refuse consent for medical treatment, including life-prolonging procedures.

(b) No health care provider is obligated to provide medical treatment to a patient who has refused medical treatment under this section.

(c) No civil or criminal liability is imposed upon a health care provider for the failure to provide medical treatment to a patient who has refused the treatment in accordance with this section.

§ 16-8-11-11. Life-prolonging procedures will declarations; living will declarations. (a) A person who is of sound mind and is at least 18 years of age may execute a life-prolonging procedures will declaration [*to have life-sustaining procedures administered and continued*—**ed. note**], under section 12 of this chapter, or a living will declaration [to *have life-sustaining procedures withheld or withdrawn*—**ed. note**], under section 12 of this chapter.

(b) A declaration under section 12 of this chapter must be:

(1) voluntary;

(2) in writing;

(3) signed by the person making the declaration or by another person in the declarant's presence and at the declarant's express direction;
(4) dated; and
(5) signed in the presence of at least 2 competent witnesses who are at least 18 years of age.
(c) A witness to a living will declaration under subsection (b)(5) may not be:
(1) the person who signed the declaration on behalf of and at the direction of the declarant;
(2) a parent, spouse, or child of the declarant;
(3) entitled to any part of the declarant's estate whether the declarant dies testate or intestate, including whether the witness could take from the declarant's estate if the declarant's will is declared invalid; or
(4) directly financially responsible for the declarant's medical care. **Note:** For the purposes of subdivision (3), a person is not considered to be entitled to any part of the declarant's estate solely by virtue of being nominated as a personal representative or as the attorney for the estate in the declarant's will.
(d) The living will declaration of a person diagnosed as pregnant by the attending physician has no effect during the person's pregnancy.
(e) The life-prolonging procedures will declarant or the living will declarant shall notify the declarant's attending physician of the existence of the declaration. An attending physician who is so notified shall make the declaration or a copy of the declaration a part of the declarant's medical records.
(f) A living will declaration under section 12 of this chapter:
(1) does not obligate the physician to use, withhold, or withdraw life-prolonging procedures but is presumptive evidence of the patient's desires concerning the use, withholding, or withdrawal of life-prolonging procedures under this chapter, and
(2) shall be given great weight by the physician in determining the intent of the patient who is mentally incompetent.
(g) A life-prolonging procedures will declaration under section 12 does obligate the physician to use life-prolonging procedures as requested.
§ 16-8-11-12. Form of declaration. A declaration must be substantially in the form set forth below, but the declaration may include additional specific directions. The invalidity of any additional, specific directions does not affect the validity of the declaration. [*See Appendix A for the recommended form of each declaration, the living will declaration and the life-prolonging procedures declaration.*—**ed. note.**]
§ 16-8-11-13. Revocation of living will declaration or life-prolonging procedures will declaration. (a) A living will declaration or a life-prolonging procedures will declaration may be revoked at any time by the declarant by:
(1) A signed, dated writing;
(2) physical cancellation or destruction of the declaration by the declarant or another in the declarant's presence and at the declarant's direction; or
(3) an oral expression of the intent to revoke.
(b) A revocation is effective when communicated to the attending physician.
(c) No civil or criminal liability is imposed upon a person for failure to act upon a revocation unless the person had actual knowledge of the revocation.
(d) The revocation of a life-prolonging procedures will declaration is not evidence that the declarant desires to have life-prolonging procedures withheld or withdrawn.
§ 16-8-11-14. Certification as qualified patient; procedure where physician refuses to honor declaration. (a) The attending physician shall immediately certify in writing that a person is a qualified patient, if:
(1) the attending physician has:
(A) diagnosed the patient as having a terminal condition; and
(B) determined that the patient's death will occur from the terminal condition whether or not life-prolonging procedures are used; and
(2) the patient has executed a living will declaration or a life-prolonging procedures will declaration in accordance with this chapter and was of sound mind at the time of the execution.
(b) The attending physician shall include a copy of the certificate in the patient's medical records.

(c) It is lawful for the attending physician to withhold or withdraw life-prolonging procedures from a qualified patient if that patient properly executed a living will declaration under this act.
(d) A health care provider or an employee under the direction of a health care provider who:
(1) in good faith; and
(2) in accordance with reasonable medical standards;
participates in the withholding or withdrawal of life-prolonging procedures from a qualified patient who has executed a living will declaration in accordance with this chapter is not subject to criminal or civil liability and may not be found to have committed an act of unprofessional conduct.
(e) An attending physician who refuses to use, withhold, or withdraw life-prolonging procedures from a qualified patient shall transfer the qualified patient to another physician who will honor the patient's living will declaration or life-prolonging procedures will declaration unless:
(1) the physician has reason to believe the declaration was not validly executed or there is evidence that the patient no longer intends the declaration to be enforced; and
(2) the patient is presently unable to validate the declaration.
(f) If the attending physician, after reasonable investigation, finds no other physician willing to honor the patient's declaration, the attending physician may refuse to withhold or withdraw life-prolonging procedures.
(g) If the attending physician does not transfer a patient for the reason set forth in subsection (e), the physician shall attempt to ascertain the patient's intention and attempt to determine the validity of the declaration by consulting with any of the following individuals who are reasonably available, willing, and competent to act:
(1) The judicially appointed guardian of the person of the patient if one has been appointed. This subdivision shall not be construed to require the appointment of a guardian in order that a treatment decision can be made under this section.
(2) The person or persons designated by the patient in writing to make the treatment decision for the patient should the patient be diagnosed as suffering from a terminal condition.
(3) The patient's spouse.
(4) An adult child of the patient or, if the patient has more than 1 adult child, by a majority of the children who are reasonably available for consultation.
(5) The parents of the patient.
(6) An adult sibling of the patient or, if the patient has more than 1 adult sibling, by a majority of the siblings who are reasonably available for consultation.
(7) The patient's clergy or others with firsthand knowledge of the patient's intention.
The individuals described in subdivisions (1) through (7) shall act in the best interest of the patient and shall be guided by the patient's express or implied intentions, if known.
(h) The physician shall list the names in the patient's medical records of the individuals described in the subsection (g) who were consulted and the information received.
(i) If the attending physician determines from the information received under subsection (g) that the qualified patient intended to execute a valid living will declaration, the physician may either:
(1) withhold or withdraw life-prolonging procedures, with the concurrence of 1 other physician, as documented in the patient's medical records; or
(2) request a court of competent jurisdiction to appoint a guardian for the patient to make the consent decision on behalf of the patient.
§ 16-8-11-15. Presumptions. If the qualified patient who executed a living will declaration is incompetent at the time of the decision to withhold or withdraw life-prolonging procedures, a living will declaration executed in accordance with this chapter is presumed to be valid. For purposes of this chapter, a health care provider may presume in the absence of actual notice to the contrary that the declarant was of sound mind when it was executed. The fact that the declarant executed a declaration may not be considered as an indication of a declarant's mental incompetency.
§ 16-8-11-16. Cancellation or destruction of declaration; falsification or forgery of revocation; offense. A person who knowingly or intentionally:

(1) physically cancels or destroys a living will declaration or a life-prolonging procedures will declaration without the declarant's consent; or (2) falsifies or forges a revocation of another person's living will declaration or life-prolonging procedures will declaration;
commits a Class D felony.

§ 16-8-11-17. Falsification or forgery of declaration; concealment or withholding of revocation of declaration; offense. A person who knowingly or intentionally:
(1) falsifies or forges the living will declaration of another person with intent to cause withholding or withdrawal of life-prolonging procedures; or (2) conceals or withholds personal knowledge of the revocation of a living will declaration with intent to cause a withholding or withdrawal of life-prolonging procedures;
commits a Class C felony.

§ 16-8-11-18. Suicide; effect of living will declaration or life-prolonging procedures will declaration.
(a) A death caused by the withholding or withdrawal of life-prolonging procedures in accordance with this chapter does not constitute a suicide.
(b) The execution of a living will declaration or a life-prolonging procedures will declaration under this chapter does not:
(1) affect the sale or issuance of any life insurance policy; or
(2) modify the terms of a policy in force when the declaration is executed.
(c) A policy of life insurance is not legally impaired or invalidated by the withholding or withdrawal of life-prolonging procedures from an insured qualified patient, notwithstanding any term of the policy to the contrary.
(d) A person may not require another person to execute a living will declaration or a life-prolonging procedures will declaration as a condition for being insured for, or receiving, health care services.
(e) This chapter does not impair or supersede any legal right or legal responsibility that any person may have to effect the withholding or withdrawal of life-prolonging procedures in any lawful manner.
(f) A person who has been found guilty, or guilty but mentally ill, of an offense described in section 17 of this chapter is subject to Indiana Code 29-1-2-12.1.

§ 16-8-11-19. Presumption of intent to consent to withholding or withdrawal of life-prolonging procedures. This chapter creates no presumption concerning the intention of a person who has not executed a living will declaration to consent to the withholding or withdrawal of life-prolonging procedures in the event of a terminal condition.

§ 16-8-11-20. Limitations. Nothing in this chapter shall be construed to authorize euthanasia or to authorize any affirmative or deliberate act or omission to end life other than to permit the natural process of dying, including the withholding or withdrawing of life-prolonging procedures under this chapter.

§ 16-8-11-21. Intervening forces; proximate causation. The act of withholding or withdrawing life-prolonging procedures, when done pursuant to: (1) a living will declaration made under this chapter;
(2) a court order or decision of a court-appointed guardian; or
(3) a good faith medical decision by the attending physician that the patient has a terminal condition;
shall not be construed to be an intervening force or to affect the chain of proximate cause between the conduct of any person that placed the patient in a terminal condition and the patient's death.

§ 16-8-11-22. Violation by physician; discipline. A physician who knowingly violates this chapter is subject to disciplinary sanctions under Indiana Code 25-1-9 as if the physician had knowingly violated a rule adopted by the medical licensing board under Indiana Code 25-22.5-2-7.

Iowa: Life-Sustaining Procedures Act

Policy statement. The legislature finds that all adults have the fundamental right to control the decisions relating to their own medical care, including the decision to have medical or surgical means or procedures calculated to prolong their lives provided, withheld, or withdrawn. This right is subject to certain interests of society, such as the protection of human life and the preservation of ethical standards in the medical profession. The legislature further finds that the artificial prolongation of life for persons with a terminal condition may secure only a precarious and burdensome existence, while providing nothing medically necessary or beneficial to the patient. In order that the rights and intentions of persons with such conditions may be respected even after they are no longer able to participate actively in decisions concerning themselves, and to encourage communications between these patients, their families, and their physicians, the legislature declares that the laws of Iowa shall recognize the right of an adult to make a written declaration instructing the adult's physician to provide, withhold, or withdraw life-sustaining procedures or to designate another to make treatment decisions, in the event the person is diagnosed as suffering from a terminal condition.

§ 144A.1. Short title. This chapter may be cited as the "Life-sustaining Procedures Act."

§ 144A.2. Definitions. Except as otherwise provided, as used in this chapter:

1. "Adult" means an individual eighteen years of age or older.
2. "Attending physician" means the physician selected by, or assigned to, the patient who has primary responsibility for the treatment and care of the patient.
3. "Declaration" means a document executed in accordance with the requirements of section 144A.3.
4. "Health care provider" means a health care facility licensed pursuant to chapter 135C, a hospice program licensed pursuant to chapter 135, or a hospital licensed pursuant to chapter 135B.
5. "Life-sustaining procedure" means any medical procedure, treatment or intervention which meets both of the following requirements:

a. Utilizes mechanical or artificial means to sustain, restore, or supplant spontaneous vital function.

b. When applied to a patient in a terminal condition, would serve only to prolong the dying process.

"Life-sustaining procedure" does not include the provision of sustenance or the administration of medication or performance of any medical procedure deemed necessary to provide comfort care or to alleviate pain.

6. "Physician" means a person licensed to practice medicine and surgery, osteopathy or osteopathic medicine and surgery in this state.
7. "Qualified patient" means a patient who has executed a declaration in accordance with this chapter and who has been determined by the attending physician to be in a terminal condition.
8. "Terminal condition" means an incurable or irreversible condition that, without the administration of life-sustaining procedures, will, in the opinion of the attending physician, result in death within a relatively short time.

§ 144A.3. Declaration relating to use of life-sustaining procedures. 1. Any competent adult may execute a declaration at any time directing that life-sustaining procedures be withheld or withdrawn. The declaration may be given operative effect only if the declarant's condition is determined to be terminal and the declarant is not able to make treatment decisions. The declaration must be signed by the declarant or another at the declarant's direction in the presence of two persons who shall sign the declaration as witnesses. An attending physician or health care provider may presume, in the absence of actual notice to the contrary, that the declaration complies with this act and is valid.

2. It is the responsibility of the declarant to provide the declarant's attending physician with the declaration.

3. A declaration executed pursuant to this chapter may, but need not, be in the following form. [*See Appendix A for a copy of this form*—**ed. note.**]

§ 144A.4. Revocation of declaration. 1. A declaration may be revoked at any time and in any manner by which the declarant is able to communicate the declarant's intent to revoke, without regard to mental or physical condition. A revocation is only effective as to the attending physician upon communication to such physician by the declarant or by another to whom the revocation was communicated.

2. The attending physician shall make the revocation a part of the declarant's medical record.

§ 144A.5. Determination of terminal condition. When an attending physician who has been provided with a declaration determines that the declarant is in a terminal condition, this decision must be confirmed by another physician. The attending physician must record that determination in the declarant's medical record.

§ 144A.6. Treatment of qualified patients. 1. A qualified patient has the right to make decisions regarding use of life-sustaining procedures as long as the qualified patient is able to do so. If a qualified patient is not able to make such decisions, the declaration shall govern decisions regarding use of life-sustaining procedures.

2. The declaration of a qualified patient known to the attending physician to be pregnant shall not be in effect as long as the fetus could develop to the point of live birth with continued application of life-sustaining procedures. However, the provisions of this subsection do not impair any existing rights or responsibilities that any person may have in regard to the withholding or withdrawal of life-sustaining procedures

§ 144A.7. Procedure in absence of declaration. 1. Life-sustaining procedures may be withheld or withdrawn from a patient who is in a terminal condition and who is comatose, incompetent, or otherwise physically or mentally incapable of communication and has not made a declaration in accordance with this chapter if there is consultation and written agreement for the withholding or withdrawal of life-sustaining procedures between the attending physician and any of the following individuals, who shall be guided by the express or implied intentions of the patient, in the following order of priority if no individual in a prior class is reasonably available, willing, and competent to act:

a. The attorney-in-fact designated to make treatment decisions for the patient should such person be diagnosed as suffering from a terminal condition, if the designation is in writing and complies with section 633.705.

b. The guardian of the person of the patient if one has been appointed, provided court approval is obtained in accordance with section 633.635, subsection 2, paragraph "c". This paragraph does not require the appointment of a guardian in order for a treatment decision to be made under this section.

c. The patient's spouse.

d. An adult child of the patient or, if the patient has more than one adult child, a majority of the adult children who are reasonably available for consultation.

e. A parent of the patient, or parents if both are reasonably available.

f. An adult sibling.

2. When a decision is made pursuant to this section to withhold or withdraw life-sustaining procedures, there shall be a witness present at the time of the consultation when that decision is made.

3. Subsections 1 and 2 shall not be in effect for a patient who is known to the attending physician to be pregnant with a fetus that could develop to the point of live birth with continued application of life-sustaining procedures. However, the provisions of this subsection do not impair any existing rights or responsibilities that any person may have in regard to the withholding or withdrawal of life-sustaining procedures.

§ 144A.8. Transfer of patients. 1. An attending physician who is unwilling to comply with the requirements of section 144A.5 or who is unwilling to comply with the declaration of a qualified patient in accordance with section 144A.6 or who is unwilling to comply with the provisions of section 144A.7 shall take all reasonable steps to effect the transfer of the patient to another physician.

2. If the policies of a health care provider preclude compliance with the declaration of a qualified patient under this chapter or preclude compliance with the provisions of section 144A.7, the provider shall take all reasonable steps to effect the transfer of the patient to a facility in which the provisions of this chapter can be carried out.

§ 144A.9. Immunities. 1. In the absence of actual notice of the revocation of a declaration, the following, while acting in accordance with the requirements of this chapter, are not subject to civil or criminal liability or guilty of unprofessional conduct:

a. A physician who causes the withholding or withdrawal of life-sustaining procedures from a qualified patient.

b. The health care provider in which such withholding or withdrawal occurs.

c. A person who participates in the withholding or withdrawal of life-sustaining procedures under the direction of or with the authorization of a physician.
2. A physician is not subject to civil or criminal liability for actions under this chapter which are in accord with reasonable medical standards.
3. Any person, institution, or facility against whom criminal or civil liability is asserted because of conduct in compliance with this chapter may interpose this chapter as an absolute defense.
§ 144A.10. Penalties. 1. Any person who willfully conceals, withholds, cancels, destroys, alters, defaces, or obliterates the declaration of another without the declarant's consent or who falsifies or forges a revocation of the declaration of another is guilty of a serious misdemeanor.
2. Any person who falsifies or forges the declaration of another, or willfully conceals or withholds personal knowledge of or delivery of a revocation as provided in section 144A.4, with the intent to cause a withholding or withdrawal of life-sustaining procedures, is guilty of a serious misdemeanor.
§ 144A.11. General provisions. 1. Death resulting from the withholding or withdrawal of life-sustaining procedures pursuant to a declaration and in accordance with this chapter does not, for any purpose, constitute a suicide or homicide.
2. The making of a declaration pursuant to section 144A.3 does not affect in any manner the sale, procurement, or issuance of any policy of life insurance, nor shall it be deemed to modify the terms of an existing policy of life insurance. No policy of life insurance is legally impaired or invalidated in any manner by the withholding or withdrawal of life-sustaining procedures pursuant to this chapter, notwithstanding any term of the policy to the contrary.
3. A physician, health care provider, health care service plan, insurer issuing disability insurance, self-insured employee welfare benefit plan, or nonprofit hospital plan shall not require any person to execute a declaration as a condition for being insured for, or receiving, health care services.
4. This chapter creates no presumption concerning the intention of an individual who has not executed a declaration with respect to the use, withholding, or withdrawal of life-sustaining procedures in the event of a terminal condition.
5. This chapter shall not be interpreted to increase or decrease the right of a patient to make decisions regarding use of life-sustaining procedures as long as the patient is able to do so, nor to impair or supersede any right or responsibility that any person has to effect the withholding or withdrawal of medical care in any lawful manner. In that respect, the provisions of this act are cumulative.
6. This chapter shall not be construed to condone, authorize, or approve mercy killing or euthanasia, or to permit any affirmative or deliberate act or omission to end life other than to permit the natural process of dying.

Kansas: Natural Death Act

§ 65-28, 101. Withholding or withdrawal of life-sustaining procedures; legislative finding and declaration. The legislature finds that adult persons have the fundamental right to control the decisions relating to the rendering of their own medical care, including the decision to have life-sustaining procedures withheld or withdrawn in instances of a terminal condition.
In order that the rights of patients may be respected even after they are no longer able to participate actively in decisions about themselves, the legislature hereby declares that the laws of this state shall recognize the right of an adult person to make a written declaration instructing his or her physician to withhold or withdraw life-sustaining procedures in the event of a terminal condition.
§ 65-28, 102. Same; definitions. As used in this act:
(a) "Attending physician" means the physician selected by, or assigned to, the patient who has primary responsibility for the treatment and care of the patient.

(b) "Declaration" means a witnessed document in writing, voluntarily executed by the declarant in accordance with the requirements of Kansas Statutes Annotated 65-28,103.
(c) "Life-sustaining procedure" means any medical procedure or intervention which, when applied to a qualified patient, would serve only to prolong the dying process and where, in the judgment of the attending physician, death will occur whether or not such procedure or intervention is utilized. "Life-sustaining procedure" shall not include the administration of medication or the performance of any medical procedure deemed necessary to provide comfort care or to alleviate pain.
(d) "Physician" means a person licensed to practice medicine and surgery by the state board of healing arts.
(e) "Qualified patient" means a patient who has executed a declaration in accordance with this act and who has been diagnosed and certified in writing to be afflicted with a terminal condition by two physicians who have personally examined the patient, one of whom shall be the attending physician.
§ 65-28,103. Same; declaration authorizing; effect during pregnancy of qualified patient; duty to notify attending physician; form of declaration; severability of directions. (a) Any adult person may execute a declaration directing the withholding or withdrawal of life-sustaining procedures in a terminal condition. The declaration made pursuant to this act shall be: (1) In writing; (2) signed by the person making the declaration, or by another person in the declarant's presence and by the declarant's expressed direction; (3) dated; and (4) signed in the presence of two or more witnesses at least eighteen (18) years of age neither of whom shall be the person who signed the declaration on behalf of and at the direction of the person making the declaration, related to the declarant by blood or marriage, entitled to any portion of the estate of the declarant according to the laws of intestate succession of this state or under any will of the declarant or codicil thereto, or directly financially responsible for declarant's medical care. The declaration of a qualified patient diagnosed as pregnant by the attending physician shall have no effect during the course of a qualified patient's pregnancy.
(b) It shall be the responsibility of the declarant to provide for notification to his or her attending physician of the existence of the declaration. An attending physician who is so notified shall make the declaration, or a copy of the declaration, a part of the declarant's medical records.
(c) The declaration shall be substantially in the following form, but in addition may include other specific directions. [*See Appendix A for a copy of the recommended form.*—**ed. note.**] Should any of the other specific directions be held to be invalid, such invalidity shall not affect other directions of the declaration which can be given effect without the invalid direction, and to this end the directions in the declaration are severable.
§ 65-28,104. Same; revocation of declaration. (a) A declaration may be revoked at any time by the declarant by any of the following methods:
(1) By being obliterated, burnt, torn, or otherwise destroyed or defaced in a manner indicating intention to cancel;
(2) by a written revocation of the declaration signed and dated by the declarant or person acting at the direction of the declarant; or
(3) by a verbal expression of the intent to revoke the declaration, in the presence of a witness eighteen (18) years of age or older who signs and dates a writing confirming that such expression of intent was made. Any verbal revocation shall become effective upon receipt by the attending physician of the above mentioned writing. The attending physician shall record in the patient's medical record the time, date, and place of when he or she received notification of the revocation.
(b) There shall be no criminal or civil liability on the part of any person for failure to act upon a revocation made pursuant to this section unless that person has actual knowledge of the revocation.
§ 65-28,105. Same; written certification and confirmation of declarant's terminal condition; effect of failure to comply. An attending physician who has been notified of the existence of a declaration executed under this act, without delay after the diagnosis of a terminal condition of the declarant, shall take the necessary steps to provide for written certification and confirmation of the declarant's terminal condition, so that the declarant may be deemed to be a qualified patient under this act. An attending physician who fails to comply with this section shall be deemed to have refused to comply with the declaration and shall be subject to subsection (a) of Kansas Statutes Annotated 65-28,107.

§ 65-28,106. Same; desires of qualified patient supersede declaration; presumptions relating to declaration; immunity from civil or criminal liability for persons acting pursuant to declaration. The desires of a qualified patient shall at all times supersede the effect of the declaration.

If the qualified patient is incompetent at the time of the decision to withhold or withdraw life-sustaining procedures, a declaration executed in accordance with Kansas Statutes Annotated 65-28,103 is presumed to be valid.

For the purpose of this act, a physician or medical care facility may presume in the absence of actual notice to the contrary that an individual who executed a declaration was of sound mind when it was executed. The fact of an individual's having executed a declaration shall not be considered as an indication of a declarant's mental incompetency. Age of itself shall not be a bar to a determination of competency.

No physician, licensed health care professional, medical care facility or employee thereof who in good faith and pursuant to reasonable medical standards causes or participates in the withholding or withdrawal of life-sustaining procedures from a qualified patient pursuant to a declaration made in accordance with this act shall, as a result thereof, be subject to criminal or civil liability, or be found to have committed an act of unprofessional conduct.

§ 65-28,107. Same; attending physician's refusal to comply with declaration of qualified patient; transfer of patient; unprofessional conduct; unlawful acts. (a) An attending physician who refuses to comply with the declaration of a qualified patient pursuant to this act shall effect the transfer of the qualified patient to another physician. Failure of an attending physician to comply with the declaration of a qualified patient and to effect the transfer of the qualified patient shall constitute unprofessional conduct as defined in Kansas Statutes Annotated 65-2837.

(b) Any person who willfully conceals, cancels, defaces, obliterates, or damages the declaration of another without such declarant's consent or who falsifies or forges a revocation of the declaration of another shall be guilty of a class A misdemeanor.

(c) Any person who falsifies or forges the declaration of another, or willfully conceals or withholds personal knowledge of the revocation of a declaration, with the intent to cause a withholding or withdrawal of life-sustaining procedures contrary to the wishes of the declarant, and thereby, because of such act, directly causes life-sustaining procedures to be withheld or withdrawn and death to be hastened, shall be guilty of a class E felony.

§ 65-28,108. Same; construction and effect of act. (a) The withholding or withdrawal of life-sustaining procedures from a qualified patient in accordance with the provisions of this act shall not, for any purpose, constitute a suicide and shall not constitute the crime of assisting suicide as defined by Kansas Statutes Annotated 21-3406.

(b) The making of a declaration pursuant to Kansas Statutes Annotated 65-28,103 shall not affect in any manner the sale, procurement, or issuance of any policy of life insurance, nor shall it be deemed to modify the terms of an existing policy of life insurance. No policy of life insurance shall be legally impaired or invalidated in any manner by the withholding or withdrawal of life-sustaining procedures from an insured qualified patient, notwithstanding any term of the policy to the contrary.

(c) No physician, medical care facility, or other health care provider, and no health care service plan, health maintenance organization, insurer issuing disability insurance, self-insured employee welfare benefit plan, nonprofit medical service corporation or mutual nonprofit hospital service corporation shall require any person to execute a declaration as a condition for being insured for, or receiving, health care services.

(d) Nothing in this act shall impair or supersede any legal right or legal responsibility which any person may have to effect the withholding or withdrawal of life-sustaining procedures in any lawful manner. In such respect the provisions of this act are cumulative.

(e) This act shall create no presumption concerning the intention of an individual who has not executed a declaration to consent to the use or withholding of life-sustaining procedures in the event of a terminal condition.

§ 65-28,109. Same; act not to be construed to condone or approve mercy killing or to permit other than natural process of dying. Nothing in this act shall be construed to condone, authorize or approve mercy

killing or to permit any affirmative or deliberate act or omission to end life other than to permit the natural process of dying as provided in this act.
§ 65-28,110 to 65-28,120. Reserved.

Kentucky: Living Will Act

§ 311.622. Legislative finding. (1) The General Assembly finds that all adults have the fundamental right to control the decisions relating to their own medical care, including the decision to have medical or surgical means or procedures calculated to prolong their lives provided, withheld, or withdrawn.
(2) In order that the dignity, privacy, and sanctity of adults with terminal conditions may be respected even after they are no longer able to participate actively in decisions concerning their medical care, the General Assembly hereby declares that the laws of the Commonwealth of Kentucky shall recognize the right of an adult to make a written declaration pursuant to the provisions of Kentucky Revised Statutes 311.626, instructing the adult's physician to withhold or withdraw life-prolonging treatment in the event such person is diagnosed as having a terminal condition.
§ 311.624. Definitions for Kentucky Revised Statutes 311.622 to 311.644. As used in Kentucky Revised Statutes 311.622 to 311.644:
(1) "Adult" means a person eighteen (18) years of age or older and who is of sound mind.
(2) "Attending physician" means the physician who has primary responsibility for the treatment and care of the patient.
(3) "Declaration" means a witnessed document in writing, voluntarily made by the declarant in accordance with the requirements of Kentucky Revised Statutes 311.626.
(4) "Health care facility" means any institution, place, building, agency, or portion thereof, public or private, whether organized for profit or not, used, operated, or designed to provide medical diagnosis, treatment, nursing, rehabilitative, or preventive care, and licensed pursuant to Kentucky Revised Statutes Chapter 216B.
(5) "Life-prolonging treatment" means any medical procedure, treatment, or intervention which:
(a) Utilizes mechanical or other artificial means to sustain, prolong, restore, or supplant a spontaneous vital function or is otherwise of such a nature as to afford a patient no reasonable expectation of recovery from a terminal condition; and
(b) When applied to a patient in a terminal condition, would serve only to prolong the dying process. "Life-prolonging treatment" shall not include the administration of medication or the performance of any medical procedure deemed necessary to alleviate pain or for nutrition or hydration.
(6) "Physician" means a person licensed to practice medicine in the Commonwealth of Kentucky.
(7) "Qualified patient" means an adult patient of sound mind who has:
(a) Made a declaration in accordance with Kentucky Revised Statutes 311.626;
(b) Been diagnosed by the attending physician and one (1) other physician as having a terminal condition, with said condition noted by both in the patient's medical record; and
(c) Who is not known to be pregnant, provided that for any adult woman of child-bearing age who has made a declaration and been diagnosed in writing as having a terminal condition, the attending physician shall cause a test to be made to determine if the woman is pregnant.
(8) "Terminal condition" means a condition caused by injury, disease, or illness which, to a reasonable degree of medical probability, as determined solely by the qualified patient's attending physician and one (1) other physician, is incurable and irreversible and will result in death within a relatively short time, and where the application of life-prolonging treatment would serve only to artificially prolong the dying process.
§ 311.626. Declaration—Witness. (1) An adult may, prior to or after having been diagnosed as having a terminal condition, make a written declaration directing the withholding or withdrawal of life-prolonging treatment.

(2) Except as provided in Kentucky Revised Statutes 311.634, a declaration made pursuant to this section shall be honored by a declarant's family, regular family physician or attending physician, and any health care facility of or in which the declarant is a patient. A declaration made pursuant to this section shall be substantially in the following form, and may include other specific directions. Should any other specific directions be held by a court of appropriate jurisdiction to be invalid, such invalidity shall not affect the declaration. [*See Appendix A for a copy of the recommended form*—**ed. note.**]

(3) A written declaration shall be signed by the declarant in the presence of two (2) subscribing witnesses. In no instance shall any of the following be a witness to any declaration made under this section:

(a) A blood relative who would be a beneficiary of the declarant; or

(b) A beneficiary of the declarant under descent and distribution statutes of the Commonwealth; or

(c) An employee of a health care facility in which the declarant is a patient; or

(d) An attending physician of the declarant; or

(e) Any person directly financially responsible for the declarant's health care.

§ 311.628. Notification of declarant's attending physician of existence of declaration. It shall be the responsibility of the declarant to provide for notification to the declarant's attending physician that a declaration has been made. In the event that declarant is comatose, incompetent, or otherwise mentally or physically incapable, any other person may notify the attending physician of the existence of a declaration. An attending physician who is so notified shall promptly make the declaration or a copy of the declaration a part of the declarant's medical records.

§ 311.630. Revocation procedures. (1) A declaration may be revoked by:

(a) A writing declaring an intention to revoke, which writing shall be signed and dated by the declarant; or

(b) An oral statement by the declarant of an intent to revoke; or

(c) The declarant or by some other person in the declarant's presence and at the declarant's direction, by cutting, tearing, burning, obliterating, canceling, or destroying the declaration, or the signature thereto, with the intent to revoke.

(2) An oral statement by the declarant to revoke a declaration shall override any previous written declaration made.

(3) Any such revocation shall become effective immediately. An attending physician or health care facility shall not be required to administer treatment in accordance with the revocation until such time as notice of the revocation is received. Upon receiving notice of the revocation, the attending physician or health care facility shall record, in the declarant's medical record, the time, date, and place of such notice receipt. No physician or health care facility shall be subject to any liability for acting in good faith upon the knowledge, or lack thereof, of the existence or revocation of a declaration.

§311.632. Exemption of health care facility or physician from criminal prosecution or civil lability for actions. (1) A health care facility, physician, or other person acting under the direction of a physician shall not be subject to criminal prosecution or civil liability or be deemed to have engaged in unprofessional conduct as a result of the withholding or withdrawal of life-prolonging treatment from a patient in a terminal condition in accordance with Kentucky Revised Statutes 311.622 to 311.644. A person who authorizes the withholding or withdrawal of life-prolonging treatment from a patient in a terminal condition in accordance with a declaration shall not be subject to criminal prosecution or civil liability for such action.

(2) The provisions of this section shall apply unless it is shown by a preponderance of the evidence that the person authorizing or effectuating the withholding or withdrawal of life-prolonging treatment did not, in good faith, comply with the provisions of Kentucky Revised Statutes 311.622 to 311.644. A declaration made in accordance with Kentucky Revised Statutes 311.626 shall be presumed to have been made voluntarily and validly executed unless the attending physician or health care facility has actual knowledge to the contrary.

§ 311.634. Notification of patient when attending physician or health care facility refuses to comply—Transfer of patient. (1) Where an individual has been diagnosed as having a terminal condition and has executed a declaration, prior to or at the time of admission to a health care facility, the individual or the family or guardian of the individual shall inform the attending physician and health care facility of the existence of a declaration. An attending physician or health care facility which refuses to comply with the declaration of a qualified patient shall immediately inform the patient and the family or guardian of the patient of such refusal. No physician or health care facility which refuses to comply with the declaration of a qualified patient shall impede the transfer of such patient to another physician or health care facility which will comply with the declaration. In cases where the patient, the family, or the guardian of the patient, has requested and authorized a transfer, the transferring attending physician and health care facility shall supply the patient's medical records and other information or assistance, as may be medically necessary for the continued care of the patient, to the receiving physician and health care facility.

(2) No physician, nurse staff member or employee of a public or private hospital, or employee of a public or private health care facility, who shall state in writing to such hospital or health care facility the person's objection to complying with the declaration of a qualified patient on moral, religious, or professional grounds, shall be required to or held liable for refusal to comply with the declaration of a qualified patient as long as the physician, nurse staff member, or employee complies with the requirements of subsection (1) of this section regarding patient notification and patient transfer.

(3) It shall be unlawful discriminatory practice for any person to impose penalties or take disciplinary action against or deny or limit licenses, certifications, degrees, or other approvals or documents of qualification to any physician, nurse staff member, or employee who refuses to comply with the declaration of a qualified patient and provided the person complies with the provisions of subsections (1) and (2) of this section.

§ 311.636. Construction of Kentucky Revised Statutes 311.622 to 311.644. Nothing in Kentucky Revised Statutes 311.622 to 311.644 shall be construed to condone, authorize, or approve mercy killing or euthanasia, or to permit any affirmative or deliberate act to end life other than to permit the natural process of dying.

§ 311.638. Withholding or withdrawal of life-prolonging treatment not to constitute suicide—Effect of declaration on life insurance. (1) The withholding or withdrawal of life-prolonging treatment from a qualified patient in accordance with the provisions of Kentucky Revised Statutes 311.622 to 311.644 shall not, for any purpose, constitute a suicide. Nor shall the making of a declaration pursuant to Kentucky Revised Statutes 311.626 affect the sale, procurement, or issuance of any policy of life insurance, nor shall it be deemed to modify the terms of an existing policy of life insurance. No policy of life insurance shall be legally impaired or invalidated by the withholding or withdrawal of life-prolonging treatment from an insured qualified patient, notwithstanding any term of the policy to the contrary.

(2) No physician, health care facility, or other health care provider shall require any person to make a declaration as a condition of receiving health care services. No contract for health insurance, or disability insurance, or credit health insurance or insurance under any nonprofit hospital, medical-surgical, dental and health service corporation, or any self-insured private employer group plan, or any health maintenance organization as provided under Kentucky Revised Statutes Chapter 304 shall require any person to make a declaration as a condition of being insured for health care services; neither shall any of the aforementioned health insurance contracts or plans be legally impaired or invalidated in any manner by the making of a declaration or the withholding or withdrawal of life-prolonging treatment from an insured qualified patient, notwithstanding any term of the policy to the contrary.

§ 311.640. Effect of Kentucky Revised Statutes 311.622 to 311.644 on intention or right of adult. (1) Kentucky Revised Statutes 311.622 to 311.644 creates no presumption concerning the intention of an adult who has revoked or has not executed a declaration with respect to the use, withholding, or withdrawal of life-prolonging treatment in the event of a terminal condition.

(2) Kentucky Revised Statutes 311.622 to 311.644 shall not affect the common law or statutory right of an adult to make decisions regarding the use of life-prolonging treatment, so long as the adult is able to do so, or impair or supersede any common law or statutory right that an adult has to effect the withholding or withdrawal of medical care.

§ 311.642. Civil liability—Penalty. (1) Any person who willfully conceals, cancels, defaces, obliterates, or damages the declaration of another without the declarant's consent or who falsifies or forges a revocation of the declaration of another, thereby causing life-prolonging treatment to be utilized in contravention of the previously expressed intent of the patient shall be civilly liable.

(2) Any person who falsifies or forges the declaration of another, or willfully conceals or withholds personal knowledge of the revocation of a declaration, with the intent to cause a withholding or withdrawal of life-prolonging treatment, contrary to the wishes of the declarant, and thereby, because of such act, directly causes life-prolonging treatment to be withheld or withdrawn and death to be hastened, shall be guilty of a Class B felony.

§ 311.644. Short title. Kentucky Revised Statutes 311.622 to 311.642 may be cited as the "Kentucky Living Will Act."

Louisiana: Declarations Concerning Life-Sustaining Procedures Act

§ 1299.58.1. Legislative purpose, findings and intent.

A. Purpose and findings. (1) The legislature finds that all persons have the fundamental right to control the decisions relating to their own medical care, including the decision to have life-sustaining procedures withheld or withdrawn in instances where such persons are diagnosed as having a terminal and irreversible condition.

(2) The legislature further finds that the artificial prolongation of life for a person diagnosed as having a terminal and irreversible condition may cause loss of individual and personal dignity and secure only a precarious and burdensome existence while providing nothing medically necessary or beneficial to the person.

(3) In order that the rights of such persons may be respected even after they are no longer able to participate actively in decisions concerning themselves, the legislature hereby declares that the laws of the state of Louisiana shall recognize:

(a) The right of such a person to make a declaration instructing his physician to withhold or withdraw life-sustaining procedures or designating another to make the treatment decision and make such a declaration for him, in the event he is diagnosed as having a terminal and irreversible condition; and

(b) The right of certain individuals to make a declaration pursuant to which life-sustaining procedures may be withheld or withdrawn from an adult patient who is comatose, incompetent, or otherwise physically or mentally incapable of communication, or from a minor, in the event such adult patient or minor is diagnosed and certified as having a terminal and irreversible condition.

(4) In furtherance of the rights of such persons, the legislature finds and declares that nothing in this Part shall be construed to be the exclusive means by which life-sustaining procedures may be withheld or withdrawn, nor shall this Part be construed to require the application of medically inappropriate treatment or life-sustaining procedures to any patient or to interfere with medical judgment with respect to the application of medical treatment or life-sustaining procedures.

B. Intent. (1) The legislature intends that the provisions of this Part are permissive and voluntary. The legislature further intends that the making of a declaration pursuant to this Part merely illustrates a means of documenting a patient's decision relative to withholding or withdrawal of medical treatment or life-sustaining procedures.

(2) It is the intent of the legislature that nothing in this Part shall be construed to require the making of a declaration pursuant to this Part.

(3) It is the intent of the legislature that nothing in this Part shall be construed to be the exclusive means by which life-sustaining procedures may be withheld or withdrawn, nor shall this Part be construed to require the application of medically inappropriate treatment or life-sustaining procedures to any patient or to interfere with medical judgment with respect to the application of medical treatment or life-sustaining procedures.

§ 1299.58.2. Definitions. As used in this Part, the following words shall have the meanings ascribed to them unless the context clearly states otherwise:

(1) "Attending physician" means the physician who has primary responsibility for the treatment and care of the patient.

(2) "Declaration" means a witnessed document, statement, or expression voluntarily made by the declarant, authorizing the withholding or withdrawal of life-sustaining procedures in accordance with the requirements of this Part. A declaration may be made in writing, orally, or by other means of nonverbal communication.

(3) "Declarant" means a person who has executed a declaration as defined herein.

(4) "Life-sustaining procedure" means any medical procedure or intervention which, within reasonable medical judgment, would serve only to prolong the dying process for a person diagnosed as having a terminal and irreversible condition. A "life-sustaining procedure" shall not include any measure deemed necessary to provide comfort care.

(5) "Minor" means a person who has not reached the age of majority.

(6) "Physician" means a physician or surgeon licensed by the Louisiana State Board of Medical Examiners.

(7) "Qualified patient" means a patient diagnosed and certified in writing as having a terminal and irreversible condition by two physicians who have personally examined the patient, one of whom shall be the attending physician.

(8) "Terminal and irreversible condition" means a condition caused by injury, disease, or illness which, within reasonable medical judgment, would produce death and for which the application of life-sustaining procedures would serve only to postpone the moment of death.

(9) "Witness" means a competent adult who is not related to the declarant or qualified patient, whichever is applicable, by blood or marriage and who would not be entitled to any portion of the estate of the person from whom life-sustaining procedures are to be withheld or withdrawn upon his decease.

§ 1299.58.3. Making of declaration; notification; illustrative form.

A. (1) Any adult person may, at any time, make a written declaration directing the withholding or withdrawal of life-sustaining procedures in the event such person should have a terminal and medically irreversible condition.

(2) A written declaration shall be signed by the declarant in the presence of two witnesses.

(3) An oral or nonverbal declaration may be made by an adult in the presence of two witnesses by any nonwritten means of communication at any time subsequent to the diagnosis of a terminal and irreversible condition.

B.(1) It shall be the responsibility of the declarant to notify his attending physician that a declaration has been made.

(2) In the event the declarant is comatose, incompetent, or otherwise mentally or physically incapable of communication, any other person may notify the physician of the existence of the declaration.

(3) Any attending physician who is so notified shall promptly make the declaration or copy of the declaration, if written, a part of the declarant's medical record.

(4) If the declaration is oral or nonverbal, the physician shall promptly make a recitation of the reasons the declarant could not make a written declaration and make the recitation a part of the patient's medical records.

C.(1) The declaration may, but need not, be in the following illustrative form and may include other specific directions including but not limited to a designation of another person to make the treatment decision for the declarant should he be diagnosed as having a terminal and irreversible condition and be comatose, incompetent, or otherwise mentally or physically incapable of communications. [*See Appendix A for a copy of the illustrative form*—**ed. note.**]

§ 1299.58.4. Revocation. A declaration may be revoked at any time by the declarant without regard to his or her mental state or competency by any of the following methods:

(1) By being cancelled, defaced, obliterated, burned, torn, or otherwise destroyed by the declarant or by some person in the presence of and at the direction of the declarant.

(2)(a) By a written revocation of the declarant expressing the intent to revoke, signed and dated by the declarant.

(b) The attending physician shall record in the patient's medical record the time and date when notification of the written revocation was received.
(3)(a) By an oral or nonverbal expression by the declarant of the intent to revoke the declaration.
(b) Such revocation by any method enumerated in this Section shall become effective upon communication to the attending physician.
(c) The attending physician shall record in the patient's medical records the time and date when notification of the revocation was received.

§ 1299.58.5. Procedure for making a declaration for a qualified patient who has not previously made a declaration.

A.(1) Nothing in this Part shall be construed in any manner to prevent the withholding or the withdrawal of life-sustaining procedures from a qualified patient with a terminal and irreversible condition who is comatose, incompetent, or otherwise physically or mentally incapable of communication and has not made a prior declaration in accordance with this Part.
(2) When a comatose or incompetent person or a person who is physically or mentally incapable of communication has been certified as a qualified patient and has not previously made a declaration, any of the following individuals in the following order of priority, if there is no individual in a prior class who is reasonably available, willing, and competent to act, may make a declaration on the qualified patient's behalf:
(a) The judicially appointed tutor or curator of the patient if one has been appointed. This Subparagraph shall not be construed to require such appointment in order that a declaration can be made under this Section.
(b) The patient's spouse not judicially separated.
(c) An adult child of the patient.
(d) The parents of the patient.
(e) The patient's sibling.
(f) The patient's other ascendants or descendants.
(3) If there is more than one person within the above named class in Subparagraphs (c) through (f), then the declaration shall be made by all of that class available for consultation upon good faith efforts to secure participation of all of that class.
B. In any case where the declaration is made by a person specified in Subparagraphs (A)(2)(b), (c), (d), (e), or (f), there shall be at least two witnesses present at the time the declaration is made.
C. The absence of a declaration by an adult patient shall not give rise to any presumption as to the intent to consent to or to refuse life-sustaining procedures.

§ 1299.58.6. Making a declaration for the benefit of a terminally ill minor.

A. If a minor has been certified as a qualified patient, the following individuals may voluntarily make a declaration to document the decision relative to withholding or withdrawal of medical treatment or life-sustaining procedures on a minor's behalf:
(1) The spouse if he has reached the age of majority; or
(2) If there is no spouse, or if the spouse is not available, or is a minor, or is otherwise unable to act, then either the parent or guardian of the minor.
B. An individual named in Subsection A of this Section may not make a declaration:
(1) If he has actual notice of contrary indications by the minor who is terminally ill; or
(2) If, as a parent or guardian, he has actual notice of opposition by either another parent, or guardian, or a spouse who has attained the age of majority.
C. Nothing in this Section shall be construed to require the making of a declaration for a terminally ill minor. The legislature intends that the provisions of this Part are permissive and voluntary. The legislature further intends that the making of a declaration pursuant to this Part merely illustrates a means of documenting the decision relative to withholding or withdrawal of medical treatment or life-sustaining procedures on behalf of a minor.

§ 1299.58.7. Physician responsibility.

A. Any attending physician who has been notified of the existence of a declaration made under this Part or at the request of the proper person as provided in Revised Statutes 40: 1299.58.5 or 40: 1299.58.6 upon diagnosis of a terminal and irreversible condition of the patient, shall take necessary steps to provide for written certification of the patient's terminal and irreversible condition, so that the patient may be deemed to be a qualified patient as defined in Revised Statutes 40: 1299.58.2.

B. Any attending physician who refuses to comply with the declaration of a qualified patient or declaration otherwise made pursuant to this Part shall make a reasonable effort to transfer the patient to another physician.

§ 1299.58.8. Immunity from liability.

A. Any health care facility, physician, or other person acting under the direction of a physician shall not be subject to criminal prosecution or civil liability or be deemed to have engaged in unprofessional conduct as a result of the withholding or withdrawing of life-sustaining procedures from a qualified patient with a terminal and irreversible condition in accordance with the provisions of this Part.

B. In instances where a patient diagnosed as having a terminal and irreversible condition or his representative utilized means other than those in accordance with the provisions of this Part to document or manifest the patient's intention and desire that medical treatment or life-sustaining procedures be withheld or withdrawn, any health care facility, physician, or other person acting under the direction of a physician shall not be subject to criminal prosecution or civil liability or be deemed to have engaged in unprofessional conduct as a result of the withholding or withdrawal of life-sustaining procedures when the health care facility, physician, or other person acting under the direction of a physician has acted in good faith reliance on patient's or his representative's manifestations that medical treatment or life-sustaining procedures be withheld or withdrawn and the continued utilization of life-sustaining procedures would, within reasonable medical judgment, serve only to prolong the dying process.

C. (1) Inasmuch as the provisions of this Part are declared by the legislature to provide an alternative nonexclusive means by which life-sustaining procedures may be withheld or withdrawn, the provisions of this Section shall apply to any case in which life-sustaining procedures are withheld or withdrawn unless it is shown by a preponderance of the evidence that the person authorizing or effectuating the withholding or withdrawal of life-sustaining procedures did not, in good faith, comply with the provisions of this Part or did not act in good faith compliance with the intention of the terminal and irreversible patient that medical treatment or life-sustaining procedures be withheld or withdrawn.

(2) A declaration made in accordance with this Part shall be presumed to have been made voluntarily.

§ 1299.58.9. Penalties.

A. Any person who willfully conceals, cancels, defaces, obliterates, or damages the declaration of another without such declarant's consent or who falsifies or forges a revocation of the declaration of another shall be civilly liable.

B. Any person who falsifies or forges the declaration of another or willfully conceals or withholds personal knowledge of a revocation of a declaration with the intent to cause the withholding or withdrawal of life-sustaining procedures contrary to the wishes of the declarant, and thereby because of such act directly causes life-sustaining procedures to be withheld or withdrawn and death thereby to be hastened may be subject to prosecution under Title 14 of the Louisiana Revised Statutes of 1950.

§ 1299.58.10. General application.

A. Nothing in this Part shall be construed to condone, authorize, or approve mercy killing or euthanasia or to permit any affirmative or deliberate act or omission to end life other than to permit the natural process of dying.

B. (1) The withholding or withdrawal of life-sustaining procedures from a qualified patient in accordance with the provisions of this Part shall not, for any purpose, constitute a suicide.

(2) Nor shall the making of a declaration pursuant to this Part affect the sale, procurement, or issuance of any life insurance policy, nor shall it be deemed to modify the terms of an existing policy.

(3) No policy shall be legally impaired or invalidated by the withholding or withdrawal of life-sustaining procedures from an insured, qualified patient, notwithstanding any term of the policy to the contrary.

(4) A person shall not be required to make a declaration as a condition for being insured or for receiving health care services.

(5) The removal of life support systems under this Part shall not be deemed the cause of death for purposes of insurance coverage.
(6) The provisions of this Part are cumulative with existing law pertaining to an individual's right to consent or refuse to consent to medical or surgical treatment.

Maine: Living Will Act

§ 2921. Definitions. As used in this chapter, unless the context otherwise indicates, the following terms have the following meanings.
1. Attending physician. "Attending physician" means the physician who has primary responsibility for the treatment and care of the patient.
2. Declaration. "Declaration" means a document executed in accordance with the requirements of section 2922.
3. Health care provider. "Health care provider" means a person who is licensed, certified or otherwise authorized by the law of this State to administer health care in the ordinary course of business or practice of a profession.
4. Life-sustaining procedure. "Life-sustaining procedure" means any medical procedure or intervention that, when administered to a qualified patient, will serve only to prolong the dying process and shall not include nutrition and hydration.
5. Person. "Person" means an individual, corporation, business trust, estate, trust, partnership, association, government, government subdivision or agency or any other legal entity.
6. Physician. "Physician" means an individual licensed to practice medicine in this State.
7. Qualified patient. "Qualified patient" means a patient who has executed a declaration in accordance with this chapter.
8. Terminal condition. "Terminal condition" means an incurable or irreversible condition that, without the administration of life-sustaining procedures, will, in the opinion of the attending physician, result in death within a short time.
§ 2922. Declaration relating to use of life-sustaining procedures.
1. Declaration; execution. A competent individual 18 years of age or older may execute a declaration at any time directing that life-sustaining procedures be withheld or withdrawn. The declaration must be signed by the declarant, or another at the declarant's direction, in the presence of 2 subscribing witnesses.
2. Incorporation in medical record. A physician or other health care provider who is provided a copy of the declaration shall make it a part of the declarant's medical record.
3. Operative effect. A declaration has operative effect only when:
A. The declaration is communicated to the attending physician;
B. The declarant is determined by the attending physician to be in a terminal condition; and
C. The declarant is unable to make treatment decisions.
4. Suggested form. A declaration may, but need not, be in the following form. [*See Appendix A for a copy of this recommended form*—**ed. note.**]
§ 2923. Revocation of declaration.
1. Revocation; communication. A declaration may be revoked at any time and in any manner by which the declarant is able to communicate an intent to revoke, without regard to mental or physical condition. A revocation is only effective as to the attending physician or any health care provider upon communication to the physician by the declarant or by another who witnessed the communication of the intent to revoke.
2. Revocation part of medical record. The attending physician or health care provider shall make the revocation a part of the declarant's medical record.
§ 2924. Recording determination of terminal condition and contents of declaration. Upon determining that the declarant is in a terminal condition, the attending physician who has been notified of the existence

and contents of a declaration shall record the determination and the substance of the declaration in the declarant's medical record.

§ 2925. Treatment of qualified patients.

1. Decisions regarding use of life-sustaining procedures. A qualified patient has the right to make decisions regarding use of life-sustaining procedures as long as the patient is able to do so. If a qualified patient is not able to make those decisions, the declaration shall govern decisions regarding use of life-sustaining procedures.

2. Comfort care; alleviation of pain. This chapter does not prohibit any action considered necessary by the attending physician to provide for comfort care or the alleviation of pain.

§ 2926. Transfer of patients. An attending physician or health care provider who is unwilling to comply with this chapter shall take all reasonable steps to effect the transfer of the declarant to another physician or health care provider in order to comply with this chapter.

§ 2927. Immunities.

1. Actions in the absence of actual notice of revocation of declaration. In the absence of actual notice of the revocation of a declaration, the following, while acting in accordance with the requirements of this chapter, are not subject to civil or criminal liability or charges of unprofessional conduct:

A. A physician who causes the withholding or withdrawal of life-sustaining procedures from a qualified patient; and

B. A person who participates in the withholding or withdrawal of life-sustaining procedures under the direction or with the authorization of a physician.

§ 2928. Penalties.

1. Willful failure to transfer. A physician or health care provider who willfully fails to transfer in accordance with section 2926 is guilty of a Class E crime.

2. Failure to record determination of terminal condition. A physician who willfully fails to record the determination of a terminal condition in accordance with section 2924 is guilty of a Class E crime.

3. Concealing, canceling, defacing, or obliterating declaration. Any person who willfully conceals, cancels, defaces or obliterates the declaration of another without the declarant's consent or who falsifies or forges a revocation of the declaration of another is guilty of a Class E crime.

4. Falsification or forgery of declaration. Any person who falsifies or forges the declaration of another or willfully conceals or withholds personal knowledge of a revocation as provided in section 2923, with the intent to cause a withholding or withdrawal of life-sustaining procedures, is guilty of a Class B crime.

§ 2929. General provisions.

1. Death not suicide or homicide. Death resulting from the withholding or withdrawal of life-sustaining procedures pursuant to a declaration and in accordance with this chapter does not, for any purpose, constitute a suicide or homicide.

2. Declaration not to affect insurance. The making of a declaration pursuant to section 2922 does not affect in any manner the sale, procurement or issuance of any policy of life insurance, nor is it deemed to modify the terms of an existing policy of life insurance. A policy of life insurance is not legally impaired or invalidated in any manner by the withholding or withdrawal of life-sustaining procedures from an insured qualified patient, notwithstanding any term of the policy to the contrary.

3. Requirement of declaration as condition for insurance or health care services. A person may not prohibit or require the execution of a declaration by any individual as a condition for being insured for or receiving health care services.

4. Presumption concerning life-sustaining procedure. This chapter creates no presumption concerning the intention of an individual who has not executed or who has revoked a declaration with respect to the use, withholding or withdrawal of life-sustaining procedures in the event of a terminal condition.

5. Patient's right concerning withholding or withdrawal of medical care. Nothing in this chapter may be interpreted to increase or decrease the right of a patient to make decisions regarding use of life-sustaining procedures as long as the patient is able to do so, or to impair or supersede any right or responsibility that

any person has to effect the withholding or withdrawal of medical care in any lawful manner. In that respect, the provisions of this chapter are cumulative.
6. Mercy killing, euthanasia or suicide. This chapter does not condone, authorize or approve mercy killing, euthanasia or suicide.
§ 2930. Recognition of declarations executed in other states. A declaration executed in another state in compliance with the laws of that state or this state is validly executed for purposes of this chapter.
§ 2931. Presumption of validity. A physician or health care provider may presume in the absence of actual notice to the contrary that a declaration executed in this State or another state complies with this chapter and is valid.

Maryland: Life-Sustaining Procedures Act

§ 5-601. Definitions. (a) *In general.*—In this subtitle the following words have the meanings indicated.
(b) *Attending physician.*—"Attending physician" means a physician who has been selected by or assigned to, and has primary responsibility for the treatment and care of, a declarant.
(c) *Declarant.*—"Declarant" means an individual who has executed a declaration.
(d) *Declaration.*—"Declaration" means a document that is executed under § 5-602 or § 5-611 of this subtitle.
(e) *Life-sustaining procedure.*—"Life-sustaining procedure" means any medical procedure, treatment, or intervention which uses mechanical or other artificial means to sustain, restore, or supplant a spontaneous vital function or is otherwise of such a nature as to afford a patient no reasonable expectation of recovery from a terminal condition and which, when applied to a patient in a terminal condition, would serve to secure only a precarious and burdensome prolongation of life.
(f) *Qualified patient.*—"Qualified patient" means a declarant diagnosed, within a reasonable degree of medical certainty, to be in a terminal condition as certified in writing by 2 physicians, both of whom have personally examined the declarant, and at least 1 of whom is an attending physician of the declarant.
(g) *Terminal condition.*—"Terminal condition" means an incurable condition of a patient caused by injury, disease, or illness which, to a reasonable degree of medical certainty, makes death imminent and from which, despite the application of life-sustaining procedures, there can be no recovery.
§ 5-602. Declaration—In general. (a) *Requirements.*—Any individual qualified to make a will under § 4-101 of the Estates and Trusts Article may execute a declaration, as provided in subsection (c) of this section, directing the withholding or withdrawal of life-sustaining procedures under this subtitle. The declaration shall be:
(1) Voluntary;
(2) Dated and in writing;
(3) Signed by the declarant or, if at the declarant's expressed direction and in the declarant's presence, by another individual on behalf of the declarant;
(4) Executed in the presence of and attested by at least 2 witnesses, each of whom at the time of execution, is at least 18 years old and is not:
(i) An individual who signed the declaration at the direction and on behalf of the declarant under paragraph (3) of this subsection;
(ii) Related to the declarant by blood or marriage within a degree listed under § 2-202 of the Family Law Article;

(iii) Either a creditor of the declarant or knowingly entitled to any portion of the estate of the declarant under any existing testamentary instrument of the declarant or knowingly entitled to any financial benefit by reason of the death of the declarant; or
(iv) Financially or otherwise responsible for the declarant's medical care or an employee of any such person or institution.
(b) *Notice to physician.*— (1) A declarant is responsible for notifying the attending physician of the existence of the declaration either directly or through another individual.
(2) Notice may be given by delivery of the declaration or a copy of the declaration to the attending physician.
(3) The attending physician shall make the declaration or other written documents containing a declaration in conformance with the provisions of subsection (c)(1) of this section a part of the declarant's medical records.
(c) *Form.*—(1) The declaration shall be substantially in the following form. [*See Appendix A for a copy of the recommended form*—**ed. note.**]
(2) The declaration may include additional provisions on this or other subjects that are not inconsistent with other provisions of this subtitle. If any additional provisions are declared invalid, the invalidity does not affect the validity of the declaration or of other provisions which can be given effect without the invalid provision, and to this end the provisions in the declaration are severable.
§ 5-603. Same—Revocation. A declarant may revoke a declaration at any time by: (1) A written statement to that effect:
(i) Signed and dated by the declarant; or
(ii) If the statement so indicates, signed and dated by a person acting at the direction of the declarant.
(2) An expression to that effect, after the declarant knows of the disease, illness, or injury involved in any question regarding the existence of a terminal condition;
(3) Destroying the declaration;
(4) Marking, burning, tearing, or otherwise altering, defacing, or damaging the declaration in a manner indicating the intention to revoke it.
§ 5-604. Required actions by attending physician. (a) *Attending physicians of declarants in terminal condition.*—Subject to the provisions of subsections (b) and (c) of this section and if the declarant is unable to give directions regarding the use of life-sustaining procedures, the attending physician of a declarant in a terminal condition shall promptly:
(1) Take the actions necessary to provide for the certification required for the declarant to become a qualified patient; and
(2) Upon certification, implement the declaration.
(b) *Transfer of declarant to other physician.*—An attending physician who does not comply with subsection (a) of this section shall make every reasonable effort to transfer the declarant to another physician.
(c) *Revoked declarations.*—Subsection (a) of this section does not apply if the attending physician knows that the declaration has been revoked or for so long as the physician has a reasonable basis for believing that the declaration may have been revoked.
(d) *Basis for physician's conclusion placed in medical records.*—The attending physician shall place in the declarant's medical records the evidentiary basis for the physician's conclusion:
(1) That a valid and unrevoked declaration exists if the physician acts under subsection (a) of this section; or
(2) That the declaration has been revoked or may have been revoked if the physician acts under subsection (c) of this section.
§ 5-605. When declaration may not be implemented. The declaration of a qualified patient to withhold or withdraw life-sustaining procedures may not be implemented: (1) By the denial of food, water, or of such medication and medical procedures as are necessary to provide comfort care and to alleviate pain; or
(2) If the qualified patient is pregnant.
§ 5-606. Declaration presumed valid. In the absence of evidence to the contrary, a declaration which, on its face, satisfies the requirements of § 5-602 or § 5-611 of this subtitle is presumed to be valid.
§ 5-607. Withholding or withdrawing of life-sustaining procedures.

(a) *Civil liability.*—Except as provided in subsection (b) or subsection (c) of this section, on notification of the existence of a valid declaration any person who causes a failure to comply with the provisions of § 5-604 may be held civilly liable.
(b) *Certain health care providers not liable.*—A paid or volunteer fire fighter, paramedic, or member of an ambulance or rescue squad is not subject to criminal or civil liability for aid, care, or assistance rendered in good faith and under reasonable standards to a qualified patient, even if that aid, care, or assistance is contrary to the provisions of that qualified patient's declaration.
(c) *Liability of nonprofessionals.*— (1) A person who in good faith, pursuant to reasonable medical standards, and in accordance with the requirements of this subtitle, causes or participates in the withholding or withdrawal of life-sustaining procedures from a qualified patient:
(i) Is not subject to civil or criminal liability; and
(ii) May not be found to have committed professional misconduct.
(2) The provisions of paragraph (1) of this subsection do not:
(i) Apply to any acts or omissions prior to the time a declarant becomes a qualified patient; or
(ii) Exempt any person from liability or professional responsibility for willful or wanton misconduct or for negligence.
§ 5-608. Conditional execution of declaration. A person or other legal entity may not require execution of a declaration as a condition for providing shelter, insurance coverage, or health care benefits or services.
§ 5-609. Prohibited actions by life insurers. A life insurer, as defined in Article 48A of the Code, because of the execution or implementation of a declaration under this act, may not:
(1) Decline to provide or continue coverage to the declarant;
(2) Consider the terms of an existing policy of life insurance to have been breached or modified; or
(3) Invoke any suicide or intentional death exemption or exclusion in any policy covering the declarant.
§ 5-610. Provisions cumulative; presumption of intent for individuals not executing declaration; construction of provisions. The provisions of this subtitle: (1) Are cumulative and may not be construed to impair or supersede any legal right or responsibility that any person may have to effect the initiation, continuation, withholding, or withdrawal of life-sustaining procedures;
(2) Do not create a presumption concerning the intention of an individual who is in a terminal condition and who has not executed a declaration regarding the initiation, continuation, withholding, or withdrawal of life-sustaining procedures; and
(3) May not be construed to permit any affirmative or deliberate act or omission to end life other than to permit the withholding or withdrawing of life-sustaining procedures from a declarant in a terminal condition.
§ 5-611. Declaration for initiation or continuation of life-sustaining procedures. An individual who is qualified to make a will under § 4-101 of the Estates and Trusts Article, in lieu of a declaration directing the withholding or withdrawal of life-sustaining procedures, may execute a declaration directing the initiation or continuation of life-sustaining procedures in accordance with standard medical practice.
§ 5-612. Execution of more than one declaration; declaration executed outside State. (a) *Only last executed declaration given effect.*—If an individual validly executes more than 1 declaration under this subtitle, only the last executed declaration shall be given effect.
(b) *Declarations executed outside State by nonresidents.*—A declaration that is executed outside of this State by a nonresident shall be given effect in this State if that declaration is in compliance with the provisions of this subtitle.
§ 5-613. Acts authorized by subtitle not considered suicide, violation of criminal law, or standard of professional practice. An act authorized by this subtitle may not, for any purpose, be considered to be a suicide or a violation of any criminal law or standard of professional conduct.
§ 5-614. Forgeries and other prohibited acts. Any person who forges a revocation or a declaration, or who willfully purports by any of the other methods set forth in § 5-603 of this subtitle to revoke a declaration without the consent of the declarant, or who willfully conceals or withholds personal knowledge of a revocation is guilty of a misdemeanor and on conviction is subject to a fine not exceeding $1,000.

Minnesota: Adult Health Care Decisions Act

§ 145B.01. Citation. This chapter may be cited as the "adult health care decisions act."

§ 145B.02. Definitions

Subdivision 1. Applicability. The definitions in this section apply to this chapter.

Subd. 2. Declaration. "Declaration" means a writing made according to section 145B.03.

Subd. 3. Health care. "Health care" means care, treatment, services, or procedures to maintain, diagnose, or treat an individual's physical condition when the individual is in a terminal condition.

Subd. 4. Health care decision. "Health care decision" means a decision to begin, continue, increase, limit, discontinue, or not begin any health care.

Subd. 5. Health care facility. "Health care facility" means a hospital or other entity licensed under sections 144.50 to 144.58; a nursing home licensed to serve adults under section 144A.02; or a home care provider licensed under sections 144A.43 to 144A.49.

Subd. 6. Health care provider. "Health care provider" means a person, health care facility, organization, or corporation licensed, certified, or otherwise authorized or permitted by the laws of this state to administer health care directly or through an arrangement with other health care providers.

Subd. 7. HMO. "HMO" means an organization licensed under sections 62D.01 to 62D.30.

Subd. 8. Terminal condition. "Terminal condition" means an incurable or irreversible condition for which the administration of medical treatment will serve only to prolong the dying process.

§ 145B.03. Declaration

Subdivision 1. Scope. A competent adult may make a declaration of preferences or instructions regarding health care. These preferences or instructions may include, but are not limited to, consent to or refusal of any health care, treatment, service, procedure, or placement. A declaration may include preferences or instructions regarding health care, the designation of a proxy to make health care decisions on behalf of the declarant, or both.

Subd. 2. Requirements for executing a declaration. (a) A declaration is effective only if it is signed by the declarant and two witnesses or a notary public.

(b) A declaration must state:

(1) the declarant's preferences regarding whether the declarant wishes to receive or not receive artificial administration of nutrition and hydration; or

(2) that the declarant wishes the proxy, if any, to make decisions regarding the administering of artificially administered nutrition and hydration for the declarant if the declarant is unable to make health care decisions and the declaration becomes operative. If the declaration does not state the declarant's preferences regarding artificial administration of nutrition and hydration, the declaration shall be enforceable as to all other preferences or instructions regarding health care, and a decision to administer, withhold, or withdraw nutrition and hydration artificially shall be made pursuant to section 145B.13. However, the mere existence of a declaration or appointment of a proxy does not, by itself, create a presumption that the declarant wanted the withholding or withdrawing of artificially administered nutrition or hydration.

(c) The declaration may be communicated to and then transcribed by one of the witnesses. If the declarant is physically unable to sign the document, one of the witnesses shall sign the document at the declarant's direction.

(d) Neither of the witnesses can be someone who is entitled to any part of the estate of the declarant under a will then existing or by operation of law. Neither of the witnesses nor the notary may be named as a proxy in the declaration. Each witness shall substantially make the following declaration on the document:

"I certify that the declarant voluntarily signed this declaration in my presence and that the declarant is personally known to me. I am not named as a proxy by the declaration."

Subd. 3. Guardian or conservator. Except as otherwise provided in the declaration, designation of a proxy is considered a nomination of a guardian or conservator of the person for purposes of section 525.544.

§ 145B.04. Suggested form

A declaration executed after August 1, 1989, under this chapter must be substantially in the form in this section. Forms printed for public distribution must be substantially in the form in this section. [*See Appendix A for a copy of this form*—**ed. note.**]

§ 145B.05. When operative

A declaration becomes operative when it is delivered to the declarant's physician or other health care provider. The physician or provider must comply with it to the fullest extent possible, consistent with reasonable medical practice and other applicable law, or comply with the notice and transfer provisions of sections 145B.06 and 145B.07. The physician or health care provider shall continue to obtain the declarant's informed consent to all health care decisions if the declarant is capable of informed consent.

§ 145B.06. Compliance with declaration

Subdivision 1. By health care provider. (a) A physician or other health care provider shall make the declaration a part of the declarant's medical record. If the physician or other health care provider is unwilling at any time to comply with the declaration, the physician or health care provider must promptly notify the declarant and document the notification in the declarant's medical record. After notification, if a competent declarant fails to transfer to a different physician or provider, the physician or provider has no duty to transfer the patient.

(b) If a physician or other health care provider receives a declaration from a competent declarant and does not advise the declarant of unwillingness to comply, and if the declarant then becomes incompetent or otherwise unable to seek transfer to a different physician or provider, the physician or other health care provider who is unwilling to comply with the declaration shall promptly take all reasonable steps to transfer care of the declarant to a physician or other health care provider who is willing to comply with the declaration.

Subd. 2. By proxy. A proxy designated to make health care decisions and who agrees to serve as proxy may make health care decisions on behalf of a declarant to the same extent that the declarant could make the decision, subject to limitations or conditions stated in the declaration. In exercising this authority, the proxy shall act consistently with any desires the declarant expresses in the declaration or otherwise makes known to the proxy. If the declarant's desires are unknown, the proxy shall act in the best interests of the declarant.

§ 145B.07. Transfer of care

If a declaration is delivered to a physician or other health care provider who transfers care of patients to other health care providers, or if a declaration is delivered to a health care provider, including a health care facility or HMO that delivers patient care through an arrangement with individual providers, the physician or other health care provider receiving a declaration shall make reasonable efforts:

(1) to ensure that an agreement with the patient to comply with the declaration will be honored by others who provide health care to that patient; or

(2) to identify and deliver the declaration to the individual providers and facilitate the declarant's discussion with those individuals whose agreement to comply with the declaration is required.

§ 145B.08. Access to medical information by proxy

Unless a declaration under this chapter provides otherwise, a proxy has the same rights as the declarant to receive information regarding proposed health care, to receive and review medical records, and to consent to the disclosure of medical records for purposes related to the declarant's health care or insurance.

§ 145B.09. Revocation

Subdivision 1. General. A declaration under this chapter may be revoked in whole or in part at any time and in any manner by the declarant, without regard to the declarant's physical or mental condition. A revocation is effective when the declarant communicates it to the attending physician or other health care provider. The attending physician or other health care provider shall note the revocation as part of the declarant's medical record.

Subd. 2. Effect of marriage dissolution or annulment on designation of proxy. Unless a declaration under this chapter expressly provides otherwise, if after executing a declaration the declarant's marriage is dissolved or annulled, the dissolution or annulment revokes any designation of the former spouse as a proxy to make health care decisions for the declarant.

§ 145B.10. Penalties

Subdivision 1. Concealing or changing declaration. An individual who willfully conceals, cancels, defaces, or obliterates a declaration of another under this chapter without the declarant's consent or who falsifies or forges a revocation of the declaration of another is guilty of a gross misdemeanor.

Subd. 2. Forging a declaration. An individual who falsifies or forges the declaration of another under this chapter, or who willfully conceals or withholds personal knowledge of a revocation, is guilty of aggravated forgery under section 609.625, subdivision 1.

Subd. 3. Forced execution of a declaration. A person who coerces or fraudulently induces another to execute a declaration under this chapter is guilty of a felony.

Subd. 4. Required or prohibited execution. A person who requires or prohibits the execution of a declaration under this chapter as a condition for being insured for or receiving all or some health care services is guilty of a misdemeanor.

Subd. 5. Other sanctions preserved. The sanctions provided in this section do not displace any sanction applicable under other law.

§ 145B.11. Effect on insurance

The making or effectuation of a declaration under this chapter does not affect the sale, procurement, issuance or validity of a policy of life insurance or annuity, nor does it affect, impair, or modify the terms of an existing policy of life insurance or annuity or the liability of the party issuing the policy or annuity contract.

§ 145B.12. What if there is no declaration or proxy?

No presumption created. Subdivision 1. If an individual has not executed or has revoked a declaration under this chapter, a presumption is not created with respect to:

(1) the individual's intentions concerning the provision of health care; or

(2) the appropriate health care to be provided.

Nutrition or hydration. Subd. 2. Nothing in this chapter shall be construed to authorize or justify the withholding or withdrawal of artificially administered nutrition or hydration from any person who has not issued a declaration or designated a proxy under this chapter.

§ 145B.13. Reasonable medical practice required

In reliance on a patient's declaration, a decision to administer, withhold, or withdraw medical treatment after the patient has been diagnosed by the attending physician to be in a terminal condition must always be based on reasonable medical practice, including:

(1) continuation of appropriate care to maintain the patient's comfort, hygiene, and human dignity and to alleviate pain;

(2) oral administration of food or water to a patient who accepts it, except for clearly documented medical reasons; and

(3) in the case of a declaration of a patient that the attending physician knows is pregnant, the declaration must not be given effect as long as it is possible that the fetus could develop to the point of live birth with continued application of life-sustaining treatment.

§ 145B.14. Certain practices not condoned

Nothing in this chapter may be construed to condone, authorize, or approve mercy killing, euthanasia, suicide, or assisted suicide.

§ 145B.15. Recognition of previously executed declaration

A declaration that substantially complies with section 145B.03, but is made before August 1, 1989, is an effective declaration under this chapter.

§ 145B.16. Recognition of document executed in another state

A declaration executed in another state is effective if it substantially complies with this chapter.

§ 145B.17. Existing rights

Nothing in this chapter impairs or supersedes the existing rights of any patient or any other legal right or legal responsibility a person may have to begin, continue, withhold, or withdraw health care. Nothing in this chapter prohibits lawful treatment by spiritual means through prayer in lieu of medical or surgical treatment when treatment by spiritual means has been authorized by the declarant.

Mississippi: Withdrawal of Life-Saving Mechanisms Act

§ 41-41-101. Legislative purpose. The purpose of this act is to allow a person to authorize the withdrawal of life-sustaining mechanisms from his body under the conditions provided by sections 41-41-103 et seq.

§ 41-41-103. Definitions.

For purposes of §§ 41-41-101 et seq., the following words shall have the meaning ascribed herein unless the context otherwise requires:

(a) "Physician" shall mean a person licensed to practice medicine in any state in the United States of America.

(b) "Withdrawal of life-sustaining mechanisms" shall means the cessation of use of extraordinary techniques and applications, including mechanical devices, which prolong life through artificial means.

§ 41-41-105. Age requirement; mental competency. Any person of the age of eighteen (18) years or older who is mentally competent may authorize withdrawal of life-sustaining mechanisms.

§ 41-41-107. Declaration of intent; form. (1) The authorization for withdrawal of life-sustaining mechanisms must be a declaration signed by at least two (2) persons who witnessed the execution of the declaration by the declarant which shall be in substantially the following form. [*See Appendix A for a copy of the recommended form*—**ed. note.**]

(2) The declaration shall be filed with the bureau of vital statistics of the state board of health.

§ 41-41-109. Revocation. (1) A declaration executed as provided in section 41-41-107 may be revoked by a revocation signed by the declarant and at least two (2) persons who witnessed the declarant's execution of the revocation which shall be in substantially the following form. [*See Appendix A for a copy of the recommended form of the revocation*—**ed. note.**]

(2) The revocation shall be filed with the bureau of vital statistics of the state board of health.

(3) If a declarant wishes to revoke the authorization for withdrawal of life-sustaining mechanisms but is unable physically to execute a revocation as provided in this section, a clear expression by the declarant, oral or otherwise, of the declarant's wish to revoke the authorization is effective as a revocation of authorization.

(4) An attending physician having actual knowledge or reason to believe that his patient has executed a declaration in conformance with sections 41-41-101 et seq. may ask the declarant, prior to procedures which might reasonably be expected to cause the declarant to become permanently unconscious or unable to make his wishes known, if said declarant revokes his declaration. The physician's determination of declarant's response in such situations shall be final.

§ 41-41-111. Signature of declarant or maker of revocation; witnesses. A declaration made pursuant to section 41-41-107 and a revocation made pursuant to section 41-41-109, except for the type of revocation provided by section 41-41-109(3), are valid only if signed by the declarant or maker of the revocation in the presence of at least two (2) attesting witnesses who, at the time the declaration or revocation is executed, are not: (a) Related to the declarant or maker of the revocation by blood or marriage; or

(b) Entitled to any portion of the estate of the declarant or maker of the revocation upon his decease under any will or codicil of the declarant or maker of the revocation or by operation of law at the time of the execution of the declaration or revocation; or

(c) The attending physician or an employee of the attending physician or of a health facility in which the declarant or maker of the revocation is a patient; or

(d) Persons who at the time of the execution of the declaration or revocation have a claim against any portion of the estate of the declarant or maker of the revocation upon the death of the declarant or maker of the revocation.

§ 41-41-113. Withdrawal of life-sustaining mechanisms. A declaration executed and filed in the manner required by sections 41-41-101 et seq. shall be honored when the declarant suffers a terminal physical condition causing severe distress or unconsciousness and the declarant's physician and two (2) other physicians concur that there is no expectation that the declarant will regain consciousness or a state of health that is meaningful to the declarant and that but for the use of life-sustaining mechanisms the declarant would immediately die.

§ 41-41-115. Responsibility of physician in charge; transfer of patient to another physician or medical facility; transplants. (1) Before withdrawing life-sustaining mechanisms from a patient, the physician in charge must be satisfied that the patient has authorized the action as provided in sections 41-41-105 et seq. and, in particular, such physician shall request and receive a certified copy of the declaration and a certificate that no revocation has been filed of record with the bureau of vital statistics of the state board of health.

(2) No physician or medical facility has a duty to participate in the withdrawal of life-sustaining mechanisms authorized by sections 41-41-101 et seq., but a physician or medical facility not honoring a patient's authorization has a duty to cooperate in the transfer of the patient to another physician or medical facility that will give effect to an authorization made in accordance with sections 41-41-101 et seq.

(3) No physician participating in a decision to withdraw life-sustaining mechanisms from a declarant may participate in transplanting the vital organs of the declarant to another person.

§ 41-41-117. Exemption of physician from criminal prosecution or civil liability. (1) A physician who in good faith and in accordance with the provisions of sections 41-41-101 et seq. causes withdrawal of life-sustaining mechanisms is not guilty of a criminal offense or subject to civil liability for his action and is not in breach of a professional oath, affirmation, or standard of care.

(2) Nothing in sections 41-41-101 et seq. shall be construed to condone, authorize, or approve the taking of life for merciful reasons, or to permit any affirmative or deliberate act or omission to end life other than to permit the natural process of dying as provided in sections 41-41-101 et seq.

§ 41-41-119. Presumption as to suicide; life insurance; medical insurance. (1) The authorization of withdrawal of life-sustaining mechanisms under the provisions of sections 41-41-101 et seq. may not for any purpose be considered suicide.

(2) An authorization of withdrawal of life-sustaining mechanisms or the actual withdrawal of life-sustaining mechanisms made or performed under the provisions of sections 41-41-101 et seq. may not modify in any manner the terms of a life insurance policy nor shall it restrict, inhibit or impair in any manner the sale, procurement or issuance of any life insurance policy.

(3) No provision of a life insurance policy purporting to restrict, limit, negate, or alter in any manner the benefits, conditions or terms of the policy on account of an authorization of withdrawal of life-sustaining mechanisms or the actual withdrawal of life-sustaining mechanisms under the provisions of sections 41-41-101 et seq. is valid.

(4) No physician, medical facility or other health care provider, and no health care service plan, insurer issuing disability insurance, self-insured employee welfare benefit plan or nonprofit hospital service plan shall require any person to execute a declaration or revocation pursuant to sections 41-41-101 et seq. as a condition for being insured for, or receiving, health care service.

§ 41-41-121. Criminal offenses. Any person who falsifies or forces the declaration of another, or willfully conceals or withholds personal knowledge of a revocation as provided in section 41-41-109, with the intent to cause a withholding or withdrawal of life-sustaining procedures contrary to the wishes of the declarant, and thereby, because of any such act, directly causes life-sustaining procedures to be withheld or withdrawn and death to thereby be hastened, shall be guilty of a felony and upon conviction shall be sentenced to the custody of the department of corrections for not more than twenty (20) years.

Missouri: Uniform Rights of the Terminally Ill Act

§ 459.010. Definitions. As used in sections 459.010 to 459.055, the following terms mean:
(1) **"Attending physician"**, the physician selected by, or assigned to, the patient who has primary responsibility for the treatment and care of the patient;
(2) **"Competent person"**, a person eighteen years of age or older of sound mind who is able to receive and evaluate information and to communicate a decision;
(3) **"Death-prolonging procedure"**, any medical procedure or intervention which, when applied to a patient, would serve only to prolong artificially the dying process and where, in the judgment of the attending physician pursuant to usual and customary medical standards, death will occur within a short time whether or not such procedure or intervention is utilized. Death-prolonging procedure shall not include the administration of medication or the performance of medical procedure deemed necessary to provide comfort care or to alleviate pain nor the performance of any procedure to provide nutrition or hydration.
(4) **"Declaration"**, a document executed in accordance with the requirements of section 459.015;
(5) **"Physician"**, a person licensed to practice medicine and surgery by the state board of registration for the healing arts;
(6) **"Terminal condition"**, an incurable and irreversible condition which, in the opinion of the attending physician, is such that death will occur within a short time regardless of the application of medical procedures.

§ 459.015. Declaration, who may execute requirements of declaration; form; witnesses required, when; notice to physician; filed; where
1. Any competent person may execute a declaration directing the withholding or withdrawal of death-prolonging procedures. The declaration made pursuant to sections 459.010 to 459.055 shall be:
(1) In writing;
(2) Signed by the person making the declaration, or by another person in the declarant's presence and by the declarant's expressed direction;
(3) Dated; and
(4) If not wholly in the declarant's handwriting, signed in the presence of two or more witnesses at least eighteen years of age neither of whom shall be the person who signed the declaration on behalf of and at the direction of the person making the declaration.
2. It shall be the responsibility of the declarant to provide for notification to his attending physician of the existence of the declaration. Upon the request of the patient, the declaration shall be placed in the declarant's medical records as maintained by his attending physician and the medical records of any health facility of which he is a patient.
3. The declaration may be in the following form, but it shall not be necessary to use this sample form. [*See Appendix A for a copy of this sample form*—**ed. note.**] In addition, the declaration may include other specific directions. Should any of the other specific directions be held to be invalid, such invalidity shall not affect other directions of the declaration which can be given effect without the invalid declaration, and to this end the directions in the declaration are severable.

§ 459.020. Revocation; mental or physical condition not considered part of medical records; liability for failure to act, when. 1. A declaration may be revoked at any time and in any manner by which the declarant is able to communicate his intent to revoke, without regard to physical or mental condition.
2. The attending physician or health care provider shall make the revocation a part of the declarant's medical record.

3. There shall be no criminal or civil liability on the part of any person for failure to act upon a revocation made pursuant to this section unless the revocation is in the patient's medical record or unless that person has actual knowledge of the revocation.

§ 459.025. Declaration operative, when. The directions of a declarant able to make treatment decisions shall at all times supersede the declaration. The declaration shall be given operative effect only if the declarant's condition is determined to be terminal and the declarant is not able to make treatment decisions. Such determinations shall be recorded in the declarant's medical record. A physician, health care professional or facility or other person shall not act contrary to the declarant's expressed intent to withhold or withdraw death-prolonging procedures without serious reason therefor consistent with the best interest of the declarant. Such reason shall be recorded in the declarant's medical record. The declaration to withdraw or withhold treatment by a patient diagnosed as pregnant by the attending physician shall have no effect during the course of the declarant's pregnancy.

§ 459.030. Physician or health facility unwilling to comply to transfer declarant. 1. An attending physician who is unwilling to comply with the requirements of section 459.025 or who is unwilling to comply with the declaration of a patient in accordance with section 459.015 shall take all reasonable steps to effect the transfer of the declarant to another physician.

2. If the policies of a health care facility preclude compliance with the declaration of a patient under sections 459.010 to 459.055, that facility shall take all reasonable steps to effect the transfer of the declarant to a facility in which the provisions of sections 459.010 to 459.055 can be carried out.

§ 459.035. Declarant presumed to be competent. For the purpose of sections 459.010 to 459.055, a physician or medical care facility may presume in the absence of actual notice to the contrary than an individual who executed a declaration was competent when it was executed. The fact of an individual having executed a declaration shall not be considered as an indication of a declarant's mental incapacity. Advanced age of itself shall not be a bar to a determination of capacity.

§ 459.040. Physicians not liable, when. A physician, licensed health care professional, medical care facility or employee thereof or other person who, in good faith and pursuant to usual and customary medical standards, causes or participates in the withholding or withdrawal of death-prolonging procedures, which acts are not otherwise unlawful, from a patient pursuant to a declaration made in accordance with sections 459.010 to 459.055 shall not, as a result thereof, be subject to criminal or civil liability or be found to have committed an act of unprofessional conduct.

§ 459.045. Unprofessional conduct by physician, when; inheritance rights forfeited, when; destroying or forging declaration, penalties. 1. It shall constitute unprofessional conduct if a physician or other licensed health care professional or facility with actual knowledge of a declaration acts, when the declarant is in a terminal condition and unable to make treatment decisions, contrary to the expressed intention of the declarant as stated in his declaration, without serious reason thereof consistent with the best interest of the declarant.

2. Any person with actual knowledge of a declaration who acts, when the declarant is in a terminal condition and unable to make treatment decisions, contrary to the expressed intention of the patient as stated in his declaration, without serious reason thereof consistent with the best interests of the patient, shall lose such rights of inheritance to the extent such loss is provided for by the patient's last will and testament.

3. Any person who willfully conceals, cancels, defaces, obliterates, or destroys the declaration of another without such declarant's consent or who falsifies or forges a revocation of the declaration of another shall be guilty of a class A misdemeanor.

4. Any person who falsifies or forges the declaration of another, or who willfully conceals or withholds personal knowledge of the revocation of a declaration, with the purpose of causing withholding or withdrawal of medical procedures contrary to the wishes of the declarant, and thereby, because of such act, directly causes medical procedures to be withheld or withdrawn, causing death or causing death to be hastened, shall be guilty of a class B felony.

§ 459.050. Life insurance, declaration not to affect. 1. The making of a declaration pursuant to sections 459.010 to 459.055 shall not affect in any manner the sale, procurement, or issuance of any policy of life insurance, nor shall it be deemed to modify the terms of an existing policy of life insurance. No policy of life

insurance shall be legally impaired or invalidated in any manner by the withholding or withdrawal of death-prolonging procedures from an insured declarant, notwithstanding any term of the policy to the contrary.
2. No person, corporation, or governmental agency shall require or induce any person to execute a declaration as a condition for a contract or for the provision of any service or benefit whatsoever.
§ 459.055. Purposes of declaration. Sections 459.010 to 459.055 shall be interpreted consistent with the following:
(1) Each person has the primary right to request or refuse medical treatment subject to the state's interest in protecting innocent third parties, preventing homicide and suicide and preserving good ethical standards in the medical profession;
(2) Nothing in sections 459.010 to 459.055 shall be interpreted to increase or decrease the right of a patient to make decisions regarding use of medical procedures so long as the patient is able to do so, nor to impair or supersede any right or responsibility that any person has to effect the withholding or withdrawal of medical care in any lawful manner. In that respect, the provisions of sections 459.010 to 459.055 are cumulative;
(3) Sections 459.010 to 459.055 shall create no presumption concerning the intention of an individual who has not executed a declaration to consent to the use or withholding of medical procedures;
(4) Communication regarding treatment decisions among patients, the families and physicians is encouraged;
(5) Sections 459.010 to 459.055 do not condone, authorize or approve mercy killing or euthanasia nor permit any affirmative or deliberate act or omission to shorten or end life.

Montana: Living Will Act

Part 1: General

§ 50-9-101. Short title. This chapter may be cited as the "Montana Living Will Act."
§ 50-9-102. Definitions. As used in this chapter, the following definitions apply:
(1) "Attending physician" means the physician selected by or assigned to the patient, who has primary responsibility for the treatment and care of the patient.
(2) "Board" means the Montana state board of medical examiners.
(3) "Declaration" means a document executed in accordance with the requirements of 50-9-103.
(4) "Department" means the department of health and environmental sciences.
(5) "Emergency medical services personnel" means paid or volunteer firefighters, law enforcement officers, first responders, emergency medical technicians, or other emergency services personnel acting within the ordinary course of their professions.
(6) "Health care provider" means a person who is licensed or otherwise authorized by the law of this state to administer health care in the ordinary course of business or practice of a profession.
(7) "Life-sustaining procedure" means any medical procedure or intervention that, when administered to a qualified patient, will serve only to prolong the dying process.
(8) "Living will protocol" means a locally developed, community-wide method or a standardized, state-wide method developed by the department and approved by the board, of providing palliative care to and withholding life-sustaining procedures from a qualified patient under 50-9-202 by emergency medical service personnel.
(9) "Physician" means a person licensed under Title 37, chapter 3, to practice medicine in this state.
(10) "Qualified patient" means a patient who has executed a declaration in accordance with this chapter and who has been determined by the attending physician to be in a terminal condition.
(11) "Reliable documentation" means a standardized, state-wide identification card or form or a necklace or bracelet of uniform design, adopted by a written, formal understanding of the local community emergency medical services agencies and licensed hospice and home health agencies, that signifies and certifies that a valid and current declaration is on file and that the individual is a qualified patient.

(12) "Terminal condition" means an incurable or irreversible condition that, without the administration of life-sustaining procedures, will, in the opinion of the attending physician, result in death within a relatively short time.

§ 50-9-103. Declaration relating to use of life-sustaining procedures. (1) Any competent adult may execute a declaration at any time directing that life-sustaining procedures be withheld or withdrawn. However, The declaration is effective only if the declarant's condition is determined to be terminal and the declarant is not able to make treatment decisions. The declaration must be signed by the declarant, or another at the declarant's direction, in the presence of two witnesses. A physician or health care provider may presume, in the absence of actual notice to the contrary, that the declaration complies with this chapter and is valid.

(2) It is the responsibility of the declarant to notify his physician of the declaration. A physician or other health care provider who is provided a copy of the declaration shall make it a part of the declarant's medical records.

(3) A declaration may, but need not be, in the following form. [*See Appendix A for a copy of the suggested form*—**ed. note.**]

§ 50-9-104. Revocation of declaration. (1) A declaration may be revoked at any time and in any manner by which the declarant is able to communicate his intent to revoke, without regard to mental or physical condition. A revocation is effective only as to the attending physician or any health care provider acting under the guidance of that physician upon communication to the physician or health care provider by the declarant or by another to whom the revocation is communicated. A health care provider or emergency medical services personnel witnessing a revocation shall act upon the revocation and shall communicate the revocation to the attending physician at the earliest opportunity. A revocation communicated to a person other than the attending physician, emergency medical services personnel, or a health care provider is not effective unless the attending physician is informed of it before the qualified patient is in need of life-sustaining procedures.

(2) The attending physician or health care provider shall make the revocation a part of the declarant's medical record.

§ 50-9-105 through 50-9-109 reserved.

§ 50-9-110. Authority to adopt rules. The department may adopt rules to implement this chapter.

§ 50-9-111. Recognition of declarations executed in other states. A declaration executed in a manner substantially similar to 50-9-103 in another state and in compliance with the law of that state is effective for purposes of this chapter.

Part 2: Effect on Health Care—Rights and Duties

§ 50-9-201. Recording determination of terminal condition and content of declaration. When an attending physician who has been notified of the existence and content of a declaration determines that the declarant is in a terminal condition, the physician shall record that determination and the content of the declaration in the declarant's medical record.

§ 50-9-202. Treatment of qualified patients. (1) A qualified patient has the right to make decisions regarding use of life-sustaining procedures if the patient is able to do so. If a qualified patient is not able to make such decisions, the declaration governs decisions regarding use of life-sustaining procedures.

(2) This chapter does not prohibit the application of any medical procedure or intervention, including the provision of nutrition and hydration, considered necessary to provide comfort care or alleviate pain.

(3) The declaration of a qualified patient known to the attending physician to be pregnant must be given no effect if it is probable that the fetus could develop to the point of live birth with continued application of life-sustaining procedures.

§ 50-9-203. Transfer of patients. (1) An attending physician who is unwilling to comply with the requirements of 50-9-201 or who is unwilling to comply with the declaration of a qualified patient in accordance with 50-9-202 shall take all reasonable steps to transfer the declarant to another physician.

(2) If the policies of a health care facility preclude compliance with the declaration of a qualified patient under this chapter, that facility shall take all reasonable steps to transfer the patient to a facility in which the provisions of this chapter can be carried out.

§ 50-9-204. Immunities. (1) In the absence of actual notice of the revocation of a declaration, the following, while acting in accordance with the requirements of this chapter, are not subject to civil or criminal liability or guilty of unprofessional conduct:

(a) a physician who causes the withholding or withdrawal of life-sustaining procedures from a qualified patient;

(b) a person who participates in the withholding or withdrawal of life-sustaining procedures under the direction or with the authorization of a physician;

(c) emergency medical services personnel who cause or participate in the withholding or withdrawal of life-sustaining procedures under the direction of or with the authorization of a physician or who on receipt of reliable documentation follow a living will protocol;

(d) emergency medical services personnel who proceed to provide life-sustaining treatment to a qualified patient pursuant to a revocation communicated to them; and

(e) a health care facility in which withholding or withdrawal occurs.

(2) A physician is not subject to civil or criminal liability for actions under this chapter that are in accord with reasonable medical standards.

§ 50-9-205. Effect on insurance—patient's decision. (1) Death resulting from the withholding or withdrawal of life-sustaining procedures pursuant to a declaration and in accordance with this chapter is not, for any purpose, a suicide or homicide.

(2) The making of a declaration pursuant to 50-9-103 does not affect in any manner the sale, procurement, or issuance of any policy of life insurance, nor does it modify the terms of an existing policy of life insurance. No policy of life insurance is legally impaired or invalidated in any manner by the withholding or withdrawal of life-sustaining procedures from an insured qualified patient, notwithstanding any term of the policy to the contrary.

(3) No physician, health care facility, or other health care provider and no health care service plan, insurer issuing disability insurance, self-insured employee welfare benefit plan, or nonprofit hospital plan may require any person to execute a declaration as a condition for being insured for or receiving health care services.

(4) This chapter creates no presumption concerning the intention of an individual who has not executed a declaration with respect to the use, withholding, or withdrawal of life-sustaining procedures in the event of a terminal condition.

(5) Nothing in this chapter increases or decreases the right of a patient to make decisions regarding use of life-sustaining procedures if the patient is able to do so or impairs or supersedes any right or responsibility that any person has to effect the withholding or withdrawal of medical care in any lawful manner. In that respect, the provisions of this chapter are cumulative.

(6) This chapter does not authorize or approve mercy killing.

§ 50-9-206. Penalties. (1) A physician who willfully fails to transfer in accordance with 50-9-203 is guilty of a misdemeanor punishable by a fine not to exceed $500 or imprisonment in the county jail for a term not to exceed 1 year, or both.

(2) A physician who willfully fails to record the determination of terminal condition in accordance with 50-9-201 is guilty of a misdemeanor punishable by a fine not to exceed $500 or imprisonment in the county jail for a term not to exceed 1 year, or both.

(3) A person who purposely conceals, cancels, defaces, or obliterates the declaration of another without the declarant's consent or who falsifies or forges a revocation of the declaration of another is guilty of a misdemeanor punishable by a fine not to exceed $500 or imprisonment in the county jail for a term not to exceed 1 year, or both.

(4) A person who falsifies or forges the declaration of another or purposely conceals or withholds personal knowledge of a revocation as provided in 50-9-104, with the intent to cause a withholding or withdrawal of

life-sustaining procedures, is guilty of a misdemeanor punishable by a fine not to exceed $500 or imprisonment in the county jail for a term not to exceed 1 year, or both.

Nevada: Withholding or Withdrawal of Life-Sustaining Procedures

§ 449.540. Definitions. As used in Nevada Revised Statutes 449.540 to 449.680, inclusive, unless the context otherwise requires, the words and terms defined in NRS 449.550 to 449.590, inclusive, have the meanings ascribed to them in those sections.

§ 449.550. "Attending physician" defined. "Attending physician" means the physician, selected by or assigned to a patient, who has primary responsibility for the treatment and care of the patient.

§ 449.560. "Declaration" defined. "Declaration" means a written document executed by an adult person directing that when he is in a terminal condition and becomes comatose or is otherwise rendered incapable of communicating with his attending physician, life-sustaining procedures shall not be applied.

§ 449.570. "Life-sustaining procedure" defined. "Life-sustaining procedure" means a medical procedure which utilizes mechanical or other artificial methods to sustain, restore or supplant a vital function. The term does not include medication or procedures necessary to alleviate pain.

§ 449.580. "Physician" defined. Repealed.

§ 449.590. "Terminal condition" defined. "Terminal condition" means an incurable condition which is such that the application of life-sustaining procedures serves only to postpone the moment of death.

§ 449.600. Execution of declaration. Any adult person may execute a declaration directing that when he is in a terminal condition and becomes comatose or is otherwise rendered incapable of communicating with his attending physician, life-sustaining procedures be withheld or withdrawn from him. The person must execute the declaration in the same manner in which a will is executed [in the presence of 2 subscribing witnesses] except that a witness may not be:

1. Related to the declarant by blood or marriage.
2. The attending physician.
3. An employee of the attending physician or of the hospital or other medical facility in which the declarant is a patient.
4. A person who has a claim against any portion of the estate of the declarant.

§ 449.610. Form of declaration; entry and removal of declaration from medical records. The declaration shall be in substantially the following form. [*See Appendix A for a copy of the recommended form. No specific provision is made for personalized instructions, but neither are they expressly forbidden*—**ed. note.**] The executed declaration, or a copy thereof signed by the declarant and the witnesses, shall be placed in the medical record of the declarant and a notation made of its presence and the date of its execution. A notation of the circumstances and date of removal of a declaration shall be entered in the medical record if the declaration is removed for any reason.

§ 449.620. Revocation of declaration; immunity when revocation of declaration not followed. 1. A declaration may be revoked at any time by the declarant in the same way in which a will may be revoked [by a signed and dated written revocation in the presence of 2 subscribing witnesses], or by an oral expression of intent to revoke. An oral revocation is effective upon communication to the attending physician by the declarant or another person communicating it on behalf of the declarant. The attending physician shall record the oral revocation and the date on which he received it in the medical record of the declarant.

2. No person is liable in a civil or criminal action for failure to act upon a revocation of a declaration unless the person had actual knowledge of the revocation.

§ 449.630. Immunity when life-sustaining procedures are withheld or withdrawn. No hospital or other medical facility, physician, or person working under the direction of a physician who causes the withholding or withdrawal of life-sustaining procedures from a patient in a terminal condition who has a declaration in effect and has become comatose or has otherwise been rendered incapable of communicating with his attending physician is subject to criminal or civil liability or to a charge of unprofessional conduct or malpractice as a result of an action taken in accordance with Nevada Revised Statutes 449.600 to 449.660, inclusive.

§ 449.640. Immunity when declaration of patient not followed. 1. If a patient in a terminal condition has a declaration in effect and becomes comatose or is otherwise rendered incapable of communicating with his attending physician, the physician must give weight to the declaration as evidence of the patient's directions regarding the application of life-sustaining procedures, but the attending physician may also consider other factors in determining whether the circumstances warrant following the directions.

2. No hospital or other medical facility, physician or person working under the direction of a physician is subject to criminal or civil liability for failure to follow the directions of the patient to withhold or withdraw life-sustaining procedures.

§ 449.650. Effect of declaration concerning suicide and insurance policies; execution of declaration prohibited as condition for insurance or receipt of health care. 1. A person does not commit suicide by executing a declaration.

2. The execution of a declaration does not restrict, inhibit or impair the sale, procurement or issuance of any policy of insurance, nor shall it be deemed to modify any term of an existing policy of insurance. No policy of life insurance is impaired or invalidated in whole or in part by the withholding or withdrawal of life-sustaining procedures from an insured person, regardless of any term of the policy.

3. No person may require another person to execute a declaration as a condition for being insured for or receiving health care services.

§ 449.660. Penalties. 1. Any person who willfully conceals, cancels, defaces, obliterates or damages the declaration of another without the consent of the declarant is guilty of a misdemeanor.

2. Any person who falsifies or forges a document purporting to be the declaration of another, or who willfully conceals or withholds personal knowledge of a revocation, with the intent to cause a withholding or withdrawal of life-sustaining procedures contrary to the wishes of the declarant and thereby directly causes life-sustaining procedures to be withheld or withdrawn and death to be hastened is guilty of murder.

§ 449.670. Termination of life. Nothing in Nevada Revised Statutes 449.600 to 449.620, inclusive, permits any affirmative or deliberate act or omission which ends life other than to permit the natural process of dying.

§ 449.680. Other right or responsibility to withhold or withdraw life-sustaining procedures not limited. Nothing in Nevada Revised Statutes 449.610 to 449.660, inclusive, limits the right or responsibility which a person may otherwise have to withhold or withdraw life-sustaining procedures.

§ 449.690. Effect of instrument executed before July 1, 1977. An instrument executed before July 1, 1977, which clearly expresses the intent of the declarant to direct the withholding or withdrawal of life-sustaining procedures from him when he is in a terminal condition and becomes comatose or is otherwise rendered incapable of communicating with his attending physician shall, if executed in a manner which attests voluntary execution and not subsequently revoked, be given the same effect as a declaration prepared and executed in accordance with Nevada Revised Statutes 449.540 to 449.680, inclusive.

New Hampshire: Terminal Care Document

§ 137-H:1. Purpose and policy. The state of New Hampshire recognizes that a person has a right, founded in the autonomy and sanctity of the person, to control the decisions relating to the rendering of his own medical care. In order that the rights of persons may be respected even after they are no longer able to participate actively in decisions about themselves, and to encourage communication between patients and their physicians, the legislature hereby declares that the laws of this state shall recognize the right of a competent person to make a written declaration instructing his physician to provide, withhold, or withdraw life-sustaining procedures in the event of a terminal condition.

§ 137-H:2. Definitions. In this chapter:

I. "Attending physician" means the physician selected by or assigned to the patient who has primary responsibility for the treatment and care of the patient.

II. "Life-sustaining procedures" means any medical procedure or intervention which utilizes mechanical or other artificial means to sustain, restore, or supplant a vital function, which, in the written judgment of the attending physician and a consulting physician, when applied to the qualified patient, would serve only to artificially postpone the moment of death, and where, in the written judgment of the attending physician and the consulting physician, the patient is in a terminal condition. "Life-sustaining procedures" shall not include the administration of medication, sustenance, or the performance of any medical procedure deemed necessary to provide comfort care or to alleviate pain.

III. "Terminal care document" means a document which, when duly executed, contains the express direction that no life-sustaining procedures be taken when the person executing the document is in a terminal condition, without hope of recovery from such condition and is unable to actively participate in the decision-making process.

IV. "Physician" means a medical doctor licensed to practice in the state of New Hampshire pursuant to Revised Statutes Annotated 329.

V. "Qualified patient" means a patient who has executed a declaration in accordance with this chapter and who has been diagnosed and certified in writing to be in a terminal condition by 2 physicians who have personally examined the patient, one of whom shall be attending physician.

VI. "Terminal condition" means an incurable condition caused by injury, disease, or illness which is such that death is imminent and the application of life-sustaining measures would, within the reasonable medical judgment of the attending physician and a consulting physician, only postpone the moment of death.

§ 137-H: 3. Terminal Care Document. A person of sound mind who is 18 years of age or older may execute at any time a document commonly known as a terminal care document, directing that no life-sustaining procedures be used to prolong his life when he is in a terminal condition. The document shall only be effective if the person is permanently incapable of participating in decisions about his care, and it may be, but need not be, in form and substance substantially as follows. [*See Appendix A for a copy of the recommended form. The declaration is to be witnessed by two witnesses and notarized by a notary public or justice of the peace or other official authorized to administer oaths*—**ed. note.**]

§ 137-H: 4. Execution and Witness. The document set forth in Revised Statutes Annotated 137-H: 3 shall be executed by the person making the same in the presence of 2 or more subscribing witnesses, none of whom shall be the person's spouse, heir at law, attending physician or person acting under the direction or control of the attending physician or any other person who has at the time of the witnessing thereof any claims against the estate of the person, and shall be acknowledged pursuant to the provisions of Revised Statutes Annotated 456 or Revised Statutes Annotated 456-A.

§ 137-H: 5. Notification; Medical Record. An attending physician who is requested to do so by the person executing the terminal care document shall make the document or a copy of the document a part of that person's permanent medical record.

§ 137-H: 6. Physician Responsibilities.

I. An attending physician and any other physician under his direction or control, having in his possession his patient's terminal care document, or having knowledge that such a duly executed document is part of the patient's record in the institution in which he is receiving care, or who has been notified of the existence of a declaration executed under this chapter, shall follow as closely as possible within the bounds of responsible medical practice, the dictates of said document. In addition, the attending physician or any other physician under his control or direction who becomes aware, pursuant to this section, of such a document shall, without delay, take the necessary steps to provide for written verification of the patient's terminal condition, so that the patient may be deemed to be a qualified patient under this chapter, however if a physician, because of his personal beliefs or conscience, is unable to comply with the terms of the declaration, he or she shall forthwith so inform the patient or the patient's family. The qualified patient may, or the family of the qualified patient shall, then request that the case be referred to another physician.

II. An attending physician who, because of personal beliefs or conscience, is unable to comply with the declaration pursuant to this chapter shall, without delay, make the necessary arrangements to effect the transfer of the qualified patient and the appropriate medical records that qualify said patient to another physician who has been chosen by the qualified patient or by the family of the qualified patient.

§ 137-H: 7. Revocation.

I. A person who has validly executed a terminal care document consistent with the provisions of Revised Statutes Annotated 137-H: 3 and Revised Statutes Annotated 137-H: 4 may revoke the document in the following manner:

(a) By burning, tearing, or obliterating the same or causing the same to be done by some other person at his direction and in his presence;

(b) By oral revocation in the presence of 2 or more witnesses, none of whom shall be the person's spouse or heir at law; or

(c) By written revocation, to be signed and dated in the presence of 2 or more witnesses, none of whom shall be the person's spouse or heir at law, expressing the intent to revoke.

II. Revocation shall become effective upon communication to the attending physician who shall record in the patient's medical record the time and date when he received notification.

§ 137-H: 8. Duty to Deliver. Any person having in his possession a duly executed terminal care document or a revocation thereof, if it becomes known to him that the person executing the same is in such circumstances that the terms of the terminal care document might become applicable, shall forthwith deliver the same to the physician attending the person executing said document or to the medical facility in which said person is a patient.

§ 137-H: 9. Immunity. An attending physician, other physician, nurse, health care professional or any other person acting for him or under his control, or hospital or other medical facility within which the person may be, shall be immune from any civil or criminal liability for any act or intentional failure to act if said act or intentional failure to act is done in good faith and in keeping with reasonable medical standards pursuant to the terminal care document and in accordance with this chapter.

§ 137-H: 10. Suicide.

I. The withholding or withdrawal of life-sustaining procedures from a patient who has executed a document consistent with the purposes of Revised Statutes Annotated 137-H: 3 shall at no time be construed as a suicide for any legal purpose.

II. Nothing in this chapter shall be construed to constitute, condone, authorize, or approve suicide or permit any affirmative or deliberate act or omission to end one's own life other than to permit the natural process of dying as provided in this chapter.

§ 137-H: 11. Freedom from Influence.

I. No physician, health facility, or other health provider, and no health care service plan, insurer issuing disability insurance, self-insured employee welfare benefit plan, or nonprofit hospital service plan shall require any person to execute a terminal care document as a condition for being insured for or receiving health care services; nor shall health care services be refused because a person is known to have executed a terminal care document.

II. The execution of a terminal care document pursuant to Revised Statutes Annotated 137-H: 3 shall not affect in any manner the sale, procurement, or issuance of any policy of life insurance, nor shall it be deemed to modify the terms of an existing policy of life insurance. No policy of life insurance shall be legally impaired or invalidated in any manner by the withholding or withdrawal of life-sustaining procedures from an insured qualified patient, notwithstanding any term of the policy to the contrary.

§ 137-H: 12. No presumption. This chapter shall not be construed to create a presumption that in the absence of a terminal care document, a person wants life-sustaining procedures to be either taken or withdrawn. Nor shall this chapter be construed to supplant any existing rights and responsibilities under the law of this state governing the conduct of physicians in consultation with patients or their families or legal guardians in the absence of a terminal care document.

§ 137-H: 13. Assisted Suicide, Mercy Killing, Euthanasia. Nothing in this chapter shall be construed to constitute, condone, authorize, or approve assisted suicide, mercy killing, or euthanasia, or permit any affirmative or deliberate act or omission to end life other than to permit the natural process of dying of those in a terminal condition as provided in this chapter.

§ 137-H: 14. Exceptions.

I. Nothing in this chapter shall be construed to condone, authorize, or approve the withholding of life-sustaining procedures from or to permit any affirmative or deliberate act or omission to end the life of a pregnant woman by an attending physician when such physician has knowledge of the woman's pregnant condition.

II. Nothing in this chapter shall be construed to condone, authorize, or approve of the arbitrary withholding or withdrawing of life-sustaining procedures from mentally incompetent or developmentally disabled persons.

III. A terminal care document shall have no force or effect if the declarant at the time of the execution of the document is a patient in a hospital or a skilled nursing facility, unless the document is signed pursuant to the requirements of Revised Statutes Annotated 551:2 and is signed in the presence of either the chief of the hospital medical staff, if witnessed in a hospital, or the medical director, if witnessed in a skilled nursing facility.

§ 137-H: 15. Penalty. A person who knowingly and falsely makes, alters, forges, or counterfeits, or knowingly and falsely causes to be made, altered, forged, or counterfeited, or procures, aids, or counsels the making, altering, forging, or counterfeiting, of a terminal care document or revocation with the intent to injure or defraud a person shall be guilty of a class B felony, notwithstanding any provisions in Title LXII.

§ 137-H: 16. Existing Rights. Repealed.

New Mexico: Right to Die Act

§ 24-7-1. Short title. This act [24-7-1 to 24-7-11 New Mexico Statutes Annotated 1978] may be cited as the "Right to Die Act."

§ 24-7-2. Definitions. As used in the Right to Die Act:

A. "family members" means either the incompetent person's spouse and children over the age of eighteen or, if the incompetent person has no spouse and no children over the age of eighteen, the incompetent person's parents or, if neither parent is alive, the incompetent person's adult siblings;

B. "irreversible coma" means that state in which brainstem functions remain but the major components of the cerebrum are irreversibly destroyed;

C. "maintenance medical treatment" means medical treatment designed solely to sustain the life processes;

D. "minor" means a person who has not reached the age of majority;

E. "physician" means an individual licensed to practice medicine in New Mexico; and

F. "terminal illness" means an illness that will result in death as defined in Section 12-2-4 NMSA 1978, regardless of the use or discontinuance of maintenance medical treatment.

§ 24-7-3. Execution of a document. A. An individual of sound mind and having reached the age of majority may execute a document directing that if he is ever certified under the New Mexico Right to Die Act as suffering from a terminal illness or being in an irreversible coma, maintenance medical treatment shall not be utilized for the prolongation of his life.

B. A document described in Subsection A of this section is not valid unless it has been executed with the same formalities as required of a valid will pursuant to the provisions of the Probate Code.

§ 24-7-4. Execution of a document for the benefit of a terminally ill minor or a minor in an irreversible coma. A. If a minor has been certified under the Right to Die Act as suffering a terminal illness or irreversible coma, the following individual may execute the document on his behalf:

(1) the spouse, if he or she has reached the age of majority; or

(2) if there is no spouse, or if the spouse is not available at the time of the certification or is otherwise unable to act, then either the parent or guardian of the minor.

B. An individual named in Subsection A of this section may not execute a document:

(1) if he has actual notice of contrary indications by the minor who is terminally ill or is in an irreversible coma; or

(2) when executing as a parent or guardian, if he has actual notice of opposition by either another parent or guardian or a spouse who has attained the age of majority.

C. A document described in Subsection A of this section is not valid unless it has been executed with the same formalities as required of a valid will under the Probate Code and has been certified upon its face by a district court judge pursuant to Subsection D of this section.

D. Any person executing a document pursuant to the provisions of this section shall petition the district court of the county in which the minor is domiciled, or the county in which the minor is being maintained, for certification upon the face of the document. The court shall appoint a guardian ad litem to represent the minor and may hold an evidentiary hearing before certification. All costs shall be charged to the petitioner. If the district court judge is satisfied that all requirements of the Right to Die Act have been satisfied, that the document was executed in good faith and that the certification of the terminal illness or irreversible coma was in good faith, he shall certify the document.

§ 24-7-5. Certification of a terminal illness or irreversible coma. A. For purposes of the Right to Die Act, certification of a terminal illness or irreversible coma may be rendered only in writing by two physicians, one of whom is the physician in charge of the individual who is terminally ill or in an irreversible coma. A copy of any such certification shall be kept in the records of the medical facility where the patient is being maintained. If the patient is not being maintained in a medical facility, a copy shall be retained by the physician in charge in his own case records.

B. Individual attending physicians may decline to participate in the withholding or withdrawal of maintenance medical treatment and be immune from civil or criminal liability. In exercising this right, however, the attending physician must take appropriate steps to transfer the patient to another qualified physician.

C. A physician who certifies a terminal illness or irreversible coma under this section is presumed to be acting in good faith. Unless it is alleged and proved that his action violated the standard of reasonable professional care and judgment under the circumstances, he is immune from civil or criminal liability that otherwise might be incurred.

§ 24-7-6. Revocation of a document. A. An individual who has executed a document under the Right to Die Act may, at any time thereafter, revoke the document. Revocation may be accomplished by destroying the document, or by contrary indication expressed in the presence of one witness who has reached the age of majority.

B. A minor may revoke the document in the manner provided under Subsection A of this section. During the remainder of his terminal illness, any such revocation may constitute actual notice of his contrary indication.

§ 24-7-7. Physician's immunity from liability. A. After certification of a terminal illness or irreversible coma under the Right to Die Act, a physician who relies on a document executed under this act, of which he has no actual notice of revocation or contrary indication, and who withholds maintenance medical treatment from a terminally ill individual or an individual in an irreversible coma who executed the document is presumed to be acting in good faith. Unless it is alleged and proved that the physician's actions violated the standard of reasonable professional care and judgment under the circumstances, he is immune from civil or criminal liability that otherwise might be incurred.

B. A physician who relies on a document executed on behalf of a terminally ill minor or a minor in an irreversible coma under the Right to Die Act and certified on its face by a district court judge pursuant to Section 24-7-4 New Mexico Statutes Annotated 1978 and who withholds maintenance medical treatment from the terminally ill minor on whose behalf the document was executed is presumed to be acting in good faith if he has no actual notice of revocation or contrary indication. Unless it is alleged and proved that the physician's actions violated the standard of reasonable professional care and judgment under the circumstances, he is immune from civil or criminal liability that otherwise might be incurred.

C. In the absence of actual notice to the contrary, a physician might presume that an individual who executed a document under the Right to Die Act was of sound mind when the document was executed.

D. Any hospital or medical institution or its employees who act or refrain from acting in reasonable reliance on and in compliance with a document executed under the Right to Die Act are immune from civil or criminal liability that otherwise might be incurred.

§ 24-7-8. Insurance. A. The withholding of maintenance medical treatment from any individual pursuant to the provisions of the Right to Die Act shall not, for any purpose, constitute a suicide.

B. The execution of a document pursuant to the Right to Die Act shall not restrict, inhibit, or impair in any manner the sale, procurement or issuance of any policy of life insurance, nor shall it be deemed to modify the terms of an existing policy of life insurance. No policy of life insurance shall be legally impaired or invalidated in any manner by the withholding of maintenance medical treatment under the Right to Die Act from an insured individual, notwithstanding any term of the policy to the contrary.

C. No physician, health facility or other health care provider, and no health care service plan, insurer issuing disability insurance, self-insured employee welfare benefit plan or nonprofit hospital service plan shall require any person to execute a document pursuant to the Right to Die Act as a condition for being insured for, or receiving, health care service.

§ 24-7-8.1 Substituted consent. A. When an incompetent person who has not executed a document under the Right to Die Act is certified as terminally ill or in an irreversible coma under the procedures described in Section 24-7-5, a physician may remove maintenance medical treatment from that person when all family members who can be contacted through reasonable diligence agree in good faith that the patient, if competent, would choose to forgo that treatment. This provision is not intended to limit existing authority in the family to consent to other forms of medical care for incompetent family members.

B. A physician who removes maintenance medical treatment from a patient under the provisions of this section is presumed to be acting in good faith. Unless it is alleged and proved that the physician's actions violated the standard of reasonable professional care and judgment under the circumstances, he is immune from civil or criminal judgment liability that otherwise might be incurred.

§ 24-7-9. Cumulative provisions. Nothing in the Right to Die Act shall impair or supersede any existing legal right or legal responsibility which any person may have to effect the withholding or nonutilization of any maintenance medical treatment in any lawful manner. In such respect the provisions of the Right to Die Act are cumulative.

§ 24-7-10. Penalties. A. Whoever knowingly and willfully conceals, destroys, falsifies or forges a document with intent to create the false impression that another person has directed that no maintenance medical treatment be utilized for the prolongation of his life or the life of a minor, or whoever knowingly and willfully conceals evidence of revocation of a document executed pursuant to the Right to Die Act is guilty of a second degree felony, punishable by imprisonment in the penitentiary for a period of not less than ten years nor more than fifty years or a fine of not more than $10,000 or both.

B. Whoever knowingly and willfully conceals, destroys, falsifies or forges a document with intent to create the false impression that another person has not directed that maintenance medical treatment not be utilized for the prolongation of his life is guilty of a third degree felony, punishable by imprisonment in the penitentiary for a term of not less than two years nor more than ten years or a fine of not more than $5,000 or both.

C. Whoever executes a document under the Right to Die Act for the benefit of a terminally ill minor or a

minor in an irreversible coma and who either has actual notice of contrary indications by the minor or, when executing as a parent or guardian, has actual notice of opposition by either another parent or guardian or a spouse, is guilty of a second degree felony, punishable by imprisonment in the penitentiary for a period of not less than ten years nor more than fifty years, or by a fine of not more than $10,000 or both.
§ 24-7-11. Application. [The Right to Die Act applies to all persons executing documents in conformity with that act on or after the effective date of the Right to Die Act (March 17, 1977).] **REPEALED.**
[**Recommended or required form.** *None specified by legislature. It is suggested that you use the uniform Living Will form in Appendix B*—**ed. note.**]

New York: Orders Not To Resuscitate[1]

§ 2960. Legislative findings and purpose. The legislature finds that, although cardiopulmonary resuscitation has proved invaluable in the prevention of sudden, unexpected death, it is appropriate for an attending physician, in certain circumstances, to issue an order not to attempt cardiopulmonary resuscitation of a patient where appropriate consent has been obtained. The legislature further finds that there is a need to clarify and establish the rights and obligations of patients, their families, and health care providers regarding cardiopulmonary resuscitation and the issuance of orders not to resuscitate.
§ 2961. Definitions. The following words or phrases, as used in this article, shall have the following meanings unless the context otherwise requires:
1. "Adult" means any person who is eighteen years of age or older, or is the parent of a child, or has married.
2. "Attending physician" means the physician selected by or assigned to a patient in a hospital, who has primary responsibility for the treatment and care of the patient. Where more than one physician shares such responsibility, any such physician may act as the attending physician pursuant to this article.
3. "Capacity" means the ability to understand and appreciate the nature and consequences of an order not to resuscitate, including the benefits and disadvantages of such an order, and to reach an informed decision regarding the order.
4. "Cardiopulmonary resuscitation" means measures, as specified in regulations promulgated by the commissioner, to restore cardiac function or to support ventilation in the event of a cardiac or respiratory arrest. Cardiopulmonary resuscitation shall not include measures to improve ventilation and cardiac functions in the absence of an arrest.
5. "Close friend" means any person, eighteen years of age or older, who presents an affidavit to an attending physician stating that he is a close friend of the patient and that he has maintained such regular contact with the patient as to be familiar with the patient's activities, health, and religious or moral beliefs and stating the facts and circumstances that demonstrate such familiarity.
6. "Developmental disability" means a developmental disability as defined in subdivision twenty-two of section 1.03 of the mental hygiene law.
7. "Hospital" means a general hospital as defined in subdivision ten of section twenty-eight hundred one of this chapter and a residential health care facility as defined in subdivision three of section twenty-eight hundred one of this chapter or a hospital as defined in subdivision ten of section 1.03 of the mental hygiene law or a school named in section 13.17 of the mental hygiene law.

1 This act is more narrow than the Living Will laws of other states, focusing only on do not resuscitate orders.

8. "Hospitalization" means the period during which a person is a patient in, or a resident of, a hospital.
9. "Medically futile" means that cardiopulmonary resuscitation will be unsuccessful in restoring cardiac and respiratory function or that the patient will experience repeated arrest in a short time period before death occurs.
10. "Mental hygiene facility" means a residential facility operated or licensed by the office of mental health or the office of mental retardation and developmental disabilities.
11. "Mental illness" means a mental illness as defined in subdivision twenty of section 1.03 of the mental hygiene law.
12. "Minor" means any person who is not an adult.
13. "Order not to resuscitate" means an order not to attempt cardiopulmonary resuscitation in the event a patient suffers cardiac or respiratory arrest.
14. "Parent" means a parent who has custody of a minor.
15. "Patient" means a person admitted to a hospital.
16. "Reasonably available" means that a person to be contacted can be contacted with diligent efforts by an attending physician or another person acting on behalf of the attending physician or the hospital.
17. "Surrogate" means the person selected to make a decision regarding resuscitation on behalf of another person pursuant to section twenty-nine hundred sixty-five of this article.
18. "Surrogate list" means the list set forth in subdivision four of section twenty-nine hundred sixty-five of this article.
19. "Terminal condition" means an illness or injury from which there is no recovery and which reasonably can be expected to cause death within one year.

§ 2962. Presumption in favor of resuscitation; lawfulness of order; effectiveness of order; duty to provide information; no duty to expand equipment.

1. Every person admitted to a hospital shall be presumed to consent to the administration of cardiopulmonary resuscitation in the event of cardiac or respiratory arrest, unless there is consent to the issuance of an order not to resuscitate as provided in this article.
2. It shall be lawful for the attending physician to issue an order not to resuscitate a patient, provided that the order has been issued pursuant to the requirements of this article. The order shall be included in writing in the patient's chart. An order not to resuscitate shall be effective upon issuance.
3. Before obtaining, pursuant to this article, the consent of the patient, or of the surrogate of the patient, or parent or legal guardian of the minor patient, to an order not to resuscitate, the attending physician shall provide to the person giving consent information about the patient's diagnosis and prognosis, the reasonably foreseeable risks and benefits of cardiopulmonary resuscitation for the patient, and the consequences of an order not to resuscitate.
4. Nothing in this article shall require a hospital to expand its existing equipment and facilities to provide cardiopulmonary resuscitation.

§ 2963. Determination of capacity to make a decision regarding cardiopulmonary resuscitation.

1. Every adult shall be presumed to have the capacity to make a decision regarding cardiopulmonary resuscitation unless determined otherwise pursuant to this section or pursuant to a court order. A lack of capacity shall not be presumed from the fact that a committee of the property or conservator has been appointed for the adult pursuant to article seventy-seven or seventy-eight of the mental hygiene law, or that a guardian has been appointed pursuant to article seventeen-A of the surrogate's court procedure act.
2. A determination that an adult patient lacks capacity shall be made by the attending physician to a reasonable degree of medical certainty. The determination shall be made in writing and shall contain such attending physician's opinion regarding the cause and nature of the patient's incapacity as well as its extent and probable duration. The determination shall be included in the patient's medical chart.
3. (a) At least one other physician, selected by a person authorized by the hospital to make such selection, must concur in the determination that an adult lacks capacity. The concurring determination shall be made in writing after personal examination of the patient and shall contain the physician's opinion regarding the

cause and nature of the patient's incapacity as well as its extent and probable duration. Each concurring determination shall be included in the patient's medical chart.
(b) If the attending physician of a patient in a general hospital determines that a patient lacks capacity because of mental illness, the concurring determination required by paragraph (a) of this subdivision shall be provided by a physician certified or eligible to be certified by the American Board of Psychiatry and Neurology.
(c) If the attending physician determines that a patient lacks capacity because of a developmental disability, the concurring determination required by paragraph (a) of this subdivision shall be provided by a physician or psychologist employed by a school named in section 13.17 of the mental hygiene law, or who has been employed for a minimum of two years to render care and service in a facility operated or licensed by the office of mental retardation and developmental disabilities, or who has been approved by the commissioner of mental retardation and developmental disabilities in accordance with regulations promulgated by such commissioner. Such regulations shall require that a physician or psychologist possess specialized training or three years experience in treating developmental disabilities.
4. Notice of a determination that the patient lacks capacity shall promptly be given (a) to the patient, where there is any indication of the patient's ability to comprehend such notice, together with a copy of a statement prepared in accordance with section twenty-nine hundred seventy-eight of this article, (b) to the person on the surrogate list highest in order of priority listed, when persons in prior subparagraphs are not reasonably available, and (c) if the patient is in or is transferred from a mental hygiene facility, to the facility director. Nothing in this subdivision shall preclude or require notice to more than one person on the surrogate list.
5. A determination that a patient lacks capacity to make a decision regarding an order not to resuscitate pursuant to this section shall not be construed as a finding that the patient lacks capacity for any other purpose.
§ 2964. Decision-making by an adult with capacity.
1. (a) The consent of an adult with capacity must be obtained prior to issuing an order not to resuscitate, except as provided in subdivision three of this section.
(b) If the adult has capacity at the time the order is issued, the consent must be obtained at or about such time, notwithstanding any prior oral or written consent.
2. (a) During hospitalization, an adult with capacity may express a decision consenting to an order not to resuscitate orally in the presence of at least two witnesses eighteen years of age or older, one of whom is a physician affiliated with the hospital in which the patient is being treated. Any such decision shall be recorded in the patient's medical chart.
(b) Prior to or during hospitalization, an adult with capacity may express a decision consenting to an order not to resuscitate in writing, dated and signed in the presence of at least two witnesses eighteen years of age or older who shall sign the decision.
(c) An attending physician who is provided with or informed of a decision pursuant to this subdivision shall record or include the decision in the patient's medical chart if the decision has not been recorded or included, and either:
(i) promptly issue an order not to resuscitate the patient or issue an order at such time as the conditions, if any, specified in the decision are met, and inform the hospital staff responsible for the patient's care of the order; or
(ii) promptly make his or her objection to the issuance of such an order and the reasons therefor known to the patient and either make all reasonable efforts to arrange for the transfer of the patient to another physician, if necessary, or promptly submit the matter to the dispute mediation system.
(d) Prior to issuing an order not to resuscitate a patient who has expressed a decision consenting to an order not to resuscitate under specified medical conditions, the attending physician must make a determination, to a reasonable degree of medical certainty, that such conditions exist, and include the determination in the patient's medical chart.
3.(a) In the event that the attending physician determines, in writing, that, to a reasonable degree of medical certainty, an adult patient who has capacity would suffer immediate and severe injury from a discussion of

cardiopulmonary resuscitation, the attending physician may issue an order not to resuscitate without obtaining the patient's consent, but only after:
(i) consulting with and obtaining the written concurrence of another physician selected by a person authorized by the hospital to make such selection, given after personal examination of the patient, concerning the assessment of immediate and severe injury to the patient from a discussion of cardiopulmonary resuscitation;
(ii) ascertaining the wishes of the patient to the extent possible without subjecting the patient to a risk of immediate and severe injury;
(iii) including the reasons for not consulting the patient in the patient's chart; and
(iv) obtaining the consent of a surrogate pursuant to section twenty-nine hundred sixty-five of this article, provided, however, that the consent of a surrogate shall not be required if the patient has previously consented to an order not to resuscitate pursuant to subdivision two of this section.
(b) Where the provisions of this subdivision have been invoked, the attending physician shall reassess the patient's risk of injury from a discussion of cardiopulmonary resuscitation on a regular basis and shall consult the patient regarding resuscitation as soon as the medical basis for not consulting the patient no longer exists.
4. If the patient is in or is transferred from a mental hygiene facility, notice of the patient's consent to an order not to resuscitate shall be given to the facility director prior to the issuance pursuant to this section of an order not to resuscitate. Notification to the facility director shall not delay issuance of an order not to resuscitate. If the facility director concludes that the patient lacks capacity or that issuance of an order not to resuscitate may be inconsistent with the patient's wishes, the facility director shall submit the matter to the dispute mediation system of this article.

§ 2965. Surrogate decision-making.

1.(a) The consent of a surrogate acting on behalf of an adult patient who lacks capacity or on behalf of an adult patient for whom consent by a surrogate is authorized by subdivision three of section twenty-nine hundred sixty-four of this article must be obtained prior to issuing an order not to resuscitate the patient, except as provided in paragraph (b) of this subdivision or section twenty-nine hundred sixty-six of this article.
(b) The consent of a surrogate shall not be required where the adult had, prior to losing capacity, consented to an order not to resuscitate pursuant to subdivision two of section twenty-nine hundred sixty-four of this article.
2. An adult with capacity has the right to designate a surrogate for the purpose of making a decision regarding cardiopulmonary resuscitation in the event the adult is subsequently determined to lack capacity.
3. An adult with capacity may designate a surrogate either (a) in writing, dated, and signed in the presence of two witnesses eighteen years of age or older who shall sign the designation or (b) during the time the adult is a patient, orally in the presence of two witnesses eighteen years of age or older. The two witnesses shall promptly inform an attending physician of the patient's designation of a surrogate. A designation may be revoked in the same manner as that provided in section twenty-nine hundred sixty-nine of this article for the revocation of consent to the issuance of an order not to resuscitate.
4.(a) One person from the following list, to be chosen in order of priority listed, when persons in the prior subparagraphs are not reasonably available, willing to make a decision regarding issuance of an order not to resuscitate, and competent to make a decision regarding issuance of an order not to resuscitate, shall have the authority to act as surrogate on behalf of the patient:
(i) a person designated by the adult pursuant to subdivision three of this section;
(ii) a committee of the person or a guardian appointed pursuant to article seventeen-A of the surrogate's court procedure act, provided that this paragraph shall not be construed to require the appointment of a committee of the person or guardian for the purpose of making the resuscitation decision;
(iii) the spouse;
(iv) a son or daughter eighteen years of age or older;
(v) a parent;
(vi) a brother or sister eighteen years of age or older; and
(vii) a close friend.

(b) After the surrogate has been identified, the name of such person shall be included in the patient's medical chart.
5.(a) The surrogate shall make a decision regarding cardiopulmonary resuscitation on the basis of the adult patient's wishes including a consideration of the patient's religious and moral beliefs, or, if the patient's wishes are unknown and cannot be ascertained, on the basis of the patient's best interests.
(b) Notwithstanding any law to the contrary, the surrogate shall have the same right as the patient to receive medical information and medical records.
(c) A surrogate may consent to an order not to resuscitate on behalf of an adult patient only if there has been a determination by an attending physician with the concurrence of another physician selected by a person authorized by the hospital to make such selection, given after personal examination of the patient that, to a reasonable degree of medical certainty:
(i) the patient has a terminal condition; or
(ii) the patient is permanently unconscious; or
(iii) resuscitation would be medically futile; or
(iv) resuscitation would impose an extraordinary burden on the patient in light of the patient's medical condition and the expected outcome of resuscitation for the patient.
Each determination shall be included in the patient's medical chart.
(d) If a physician is designated by the patient to act as the patient's surrogate pursuant to this section, the physician shall not make the determination of the patient's medical condition required by paragraph (c) of this subdivision.
6.(a) A surrogate shall express a decision consenting to an order not to resuscitate in writing, dated, and signed in the presence of one witness eighteen years of age or older who shall sign the decision.
(b) The attending physician who is provided with the decision of a surrogate shall include the decision in the patient's medical chart and, if the surrogate has consented to the issuance of an order not to resuscitate, shall either:
(i) promptly issue an order not to resuscitate the patient and inform the hospital staff responsible for the patient's care of the order; or
(ii) promptly make the attending physician's objection to the issuance of such an order known to the surrogate and either make all reasonable efforts to arrange for the transfer of the patient to another physician, if necessary, or promptly refer the matter to the dispute mediation system.
(c) If the patient is in or is transferred from a mental hygiene facility, notice of a surrogate's consent to an order not to resuscitate shall be given to the facility director prior to the issuance pursuant to this section of an order not to resuscitate. Notification to the facility director shall not delay issuance of an order not to resuscitate. If the facility director concludes that the patient has capacity or that issuance of an order not to resuscitate is otherwise inconsistent with this article, the facility director shall submit the matter to the dispute mediation system of this article.
(d) If the attending physician has actual notice of opposition to a surrogate's consent to an order not to resuscitate by any person on the surrogate list, or, if the patient is in or is transferred from a mental hygiene facility, by the facility director, the physician shall submit the matter to the dispute mediation system and such order shall not be issued or shall be revoked in accordance with the provisions of subdivision three of section twenty-nine hundred seventy-two of this article.
7. If a surrogate has consented to an order not to resuscitate, notice of the surrogate's decision shall be given to the patient where there is any indication of the patient's ability to comprehend such notice, except if a determination has been made pursuant to subdivision three of section twenty-nine hundred sixty-four of this article. If the patient objects, an order not to resuscitate shall not be issued.
§ 2966. Decision-making on behalf of an adult patient without capacity for whom no surrogate is available.
1. If no surrogate is reasonably available, willing to make a decision regarding issuance of an order not to resuscitate, and competent to make a decision regarding issuance of an order not to resuscitate on behalf of an adult patient who lacks capacity and who has not previously expressed a decision regarding cardiopul-

monary resuscitation, an attending physician (a) may issue an order not to resuscitate the patient, provided that the attending physician determines, in writing, that, to a reasonable degree of medical certainty, resuscitation would be medically futile, and another physician selected by a person authorized by the hospital to make such selection, after personal examination of the patient, reviews and concurs in writing with such determination, or (b) shall issue an order not to resuscitate the patient, provided that, pursuant to subdivision one of section twenty-nine hundred seventy-six of this article, a court has granted a judgment directing the issuance of such an order.

2. If the patient is in or is transferred from a mental hygiene facility, prior to issuance of an order not to resuscitate pursuant to subdivision one of this section, notice of such order shall be given to the facility director. Notification to the facility director shall not delay issuance of an order not to resuscitate. If the facility director concludes that the patient has capacity or that issuance of an order not to resuscitate is otherwise inconsistent with this article, the facility director shall submit the matter to the dispute mediation system of this article.

3. Notwithstanding any other provisions of this section, where a decision to consent to an order not to resuscitate has been made, notice of the decision shall be given to the patient, where there is any indication of the patient's ability to comprehend such notice, except where a determination has been made pursuant to subdivision three of section twenty-nine hundred sixty-four of this article. If the patient objects, an order not to resuscitate shall not be issued.

§ 2967. Decision-making on behalf of a minor patient.

1. An attending physician, in consultation with a minor's parent or legal guardian, shall determine whether a minor has the capacity to make a decision regarding resuscitation.

2.(a) The consent of a minor's parent or legal guardian and the consent of the minor, if the minor has capacity, must be obtained prior to issuing an order not to resuscitate the minor.

(b) Where the attending physician has reason to believe that there is another parent or a non-custodial parent who has not been informed of a decision to issue an order not to resuscitate the minor, the attending physician shall make diligent efforts to notify that parent or noncustodial parent of the decision prior to issuing the order.

(c) If the minor is in or is transferred from a mental hygiene facility, notice of a decision to issue an order not to resuscitate the minor shall be given to the facility director prior to issuance of an order not to resuscitate. Notification to the facility director shall not delay issuance of an order not to resuscitate. If the facility director concludes that issuance of an order not to resuscitate is inconsistent with this article, the facility director shall submit the matter to the dispute mediation system of this article.

3. A parent or legal guardian may consent to an order not to resuscitate on behalf of a minor only if there has been a written determination by the attending physician, with the written concurrence of another physician selected by a person authorized by the hospital to make such selections given after personal examination of the patient, that, to a reasonable degree of medical certainty, the minor suffers from one of the medical conditions set forth in paragraph (c) of subdivision five of section twenty-nine hundred sixty-five of this article. Each determination shall be included in the patient's medical chart.

4.(a) A parent or legal guardian of a minor, in making a decision regarding cardiopulmonary resuscitation, shall consider the minor patient's wishes, including a consideration of the minor patient's religious and moral beliefs, and shall express a decision consenting to issuance of an order not to resuscitate in writing, dated and signed in the presence of one witness eighteen years of age or older who shall sign the decision.

(b) The attending physician who is provided with the decision of a minor's parent or legal guardian, expressed pursuant to this subdivision, and of the minor if the minor has capacity, shall include such decision or decisions in the minor's medical chart and shall comply with the provisions of paragraph (b) of subdivision six of section twenty-nine hundred sixty-five of this article.

(c) If the attending physician has actual notice of the opposition of a parent or non-custodial parent to consent by another parent to an order not to resuscitate a minor, the physician shall submit the matter to the dispute mediation system and such order shall not be issued or shall be revoked in accordance with the provisions of subdivision three of section twenty-nine hundred seventy-two of this article.

§ 2968. Effect of order not to resuscitate on other treatment. Consent to the issuance of an order not to resuscitate shall not constitute consent to withhold or withdraw medical treatment other than cardiopulmonary resuscitation.

§ 2969. Revocation of consent to order not to resuscitate.

1. A person may, at any time, revoke his or her consent to an order not to resuscitate himself or herself by making either a written or an oral declaration to a physician or member of the nursing staff at the hospital where he or she is being treated, or by any other act evidencing a specific intent to revoke such consent.
2. Any surrogate, parent, or legal guardian may at any time revoke his or her consent to an order not to resuscitate a patient by (a) notifying a physician or member of the nursing staff of the revocation of consent in writing, dated and signed, or (b) orally notifying the attending physician, in the presence of a witness eighteen years of age or older.
3. Any physician who is informed of or provided with a revocation of consent pursuant to this section shall immediately include the revocation in the patient's chart, cancel the order, and notify the hospital staff responsible for the patient's care of the revocation and cancellation. Any member of the nursing staff who is informed of or provided with a revocation of consent pursuant to this section shall immediately notify a physician of such revocation.

§ 2970. Physician review of the order not to resuscitate.

1. For each patient for whom an order not to resuscitate has been issued, the attending physician shall review the patient's chart to determine if the order is still appropriate in light of the patient's condition and shall indicate on the patient's chart that the order has been reviewed (a) for the patient in a hospital, other than a residential health care facility, at least every three days; (b) for a patient in a residential health care facility, each time the patient is required to be seen by a physician but in no case less often than every sixty days. Failure to comply with this subdivision shall not render an order not to resuscitate ineffective.

2.(a) If the attending physician determines at any time that an order not to resuscitate is no longer appropriate because the patient's medical condition has improved, the physician shall immediately notify the person who consented to the order. Except as provided in paragraph (b) of this subdivision, if such person declines to revoke consent to the order, the physician shall promptly (i) make reasonable efforts to arrange for the transfer of the patient to another physician or (ii) submit the matter to the dispute mediation system.

(b) If the order not to resuscitate was entered upon the consent of a surrogate, parent, or legal guardian and the attending physician who issued the order, or, if unavailable, another attending physician at any time determines that the patient does not suffer from one of the medical conditions set forth in paragraph (c) of subdivision five of section twenty-nine hundred sixty-five of this article, the attending physician shall immediately include such determination in the patient's chart, cancel the order, and notify the person who consented to the order and all hospital staff responsible for the patient's care of the cancellation.

(c) If an order not to resuscitate was entered upon the consent of a surrogate and the patient at any time gains or regains capacity, the attending physician who issued the order, or, if unavailable, another attending physician shall immediately cancel the order and notify the person who consented to the order and all hospital staff directly responsible for the patient's care of the cancellation.

§ 2971. Interinstitutional transfers. If a patient for whom an order not to resuscitate has been issued is transferred from a hospital to a different hospital the order shall be effective upon receipt until:

1. a physician at the transferee hospital cancels the order; or
2. twenty-four hours have elapsed from the time of the patient's admission to the transferee hospital, whichever shall occur first, except that if the order has not been cancelled by a physician at the transferee hospital an attending physician at the transferee hospital, upon receipt of a copy of or written notice of the order, may presume that the order was validly issued and may issue an order not to resuscitate continuing the prior order.

§ 2972. Dispute mediation system.

1.(a) Each hospital shall establish a mediation system for the purpose of mediating disputes regarding the issuance of orders not to resuscitate.

(b) The dispute mediation system shall be described in writing and adopted by the hospital's governing authority. It may utilize existing hospital resources, such as a patient advocate's office or hospital chaplain's office, or it may utilize a body created specifically for this purpose, but, in the event a dispute involves a patient deemed to lack capacity pursuant to (i) paragraph (b) of subdivision three of section twenty-nine hundred sixty-three of this article, the system must include a physician or psychologist eligible to provide a concurring determination pursuant to such subdivision, or a family member or guardian of the person of a person with a mental illness of the same or similar nature, or (ii) paragraph (c) of subdivision three of section twenty-nine hundred sixty-three of this article, the system must include a physician or psychologist eligible to provide a concurring determination pursuant to such subdivision, or a family member or guardian of the person of a person with a developmental disability of the same or similar nature.

2. The dispute mediation system shall be authorized to mediate (a) any dispute challenging consent to the issuance of an order not to resuscitate, including disputes regarding the determination of the patient's capacity, arising under this article between the patient and an attending physician or the hospital that is caring for the patient and, if the patient is a minor, the patient's parent, or among an attending physician, a parent, non-custodial parent, or legal guardian of a minor patient, any person on the surrogate list, the hospital that is caring for the patient and, where the dispute involves a patient who is in or is transferred from a mental hygiene facility, the facility director, and (b) any dispute submitted by a person on the surrogate list, challenging a decision by a surrogate not to consent to issuance of an order not to resuscitate.

3. After a dispute regarding the issuance of an order not to resuscitate has been submitted to the dispute mediation system, an order not to resuscitate shall not be issued or shall be revoked and may not be reissued until (a) the dispute has been resolved or the system has concluded its effort to resolve the dispute or (b) seventy-two hours have elapsed from the time of the submission of the dispute, whichever shall occur first. Persons participating in the dispute mediation system shall be informed of their right to judicial review.

4. If a dispute between a patient who has expressed a decision rejecting cardiopulmonary resuscitation and an attending physician or the hospital that is caring for the patient is submitted to the dispute mediation system, and either:

(a) the dispute mediation system has concluded its efforts to resolve the dispute, or

(b) seventy-two hours have elapsed from the time of submission without resolution of the dispute, whichever shall occur first, the attending physician shall either: (i) promptly issue an order not to resuscitate the patient or issue the order at such time as the conditions, if any, specified in the decision are met, and inform the hospital staff responsible for the patient's care of the order; or (ii) promptly arrange for the transfer of the patient to another physician or hospital.

5. Persons appointed pursuant to this section to participate in the dispute mediation system shall not have authority to determine whether a do not resuscitate order shall be issued.

§ 2973. Judicial review.

1. The patient, an attending physician, a parent, non-custodial parent, or legal guardian of a minor patient, any person on the surrogate list, the hospital that is caring for the patient and, in disputes involving a patient who is in or is transferred from a mental hygiene facility, the facility director, may commence a special proceeding pursuant to article four of the civil practice laws and rules, in a court of competent jurisdiction, with respect to any dispute arising under this article, except that the decision of a patient not to consent to issuance of an order not to resuscitate may not be subjected to judicial review. In any proceeding brought pursuant to this subdivision challenging a decision regarding issuance of an order not to resuscitate on the ground that the decision is contrary to the patient's wishes or best interests, the person or entity challenging the decision must show, by clear and convincing evidence, that the decision is contrary to the patient's wishes including consideration of the patient's religious and moral beliefs, or, in the absence of evidence of the patient's wishes, that the decision is contrary to the patient's best interests. In any other proceeding brought pursuant to this subdivision, the court shall make its determination based upon the applicable substantive standards and procedures set forth in this article.

2. In any proceeding brought pursuant to this section, the court may issue an order, pursuant to the standards applicable to the issuance of a temporary restraining order according to section six thousand three hundred

thirteen of the civil practice law and rules, which shall suspend the order not to resuscitate to permit review of the matter by the court.
3. Where a person or entity may invoke the dispute mediation system, no such proceeding shall be commenced until the dispute mediation system has concluded its efforts to resolve the dispute or seventy-two hours have elapsed from the submission of the dispute to the dispute mediation system, whichever shall occur first, provided, however, that the patient may commence an action for relief with respect to any dispute under this article at any time and provided further that the department of health or any other duly authorized state agency may commence an action or proceeding to enjoin a violation of this article at any time.
§ 2974. Immunity.
1. No physician, health care professional, nurse's aide, hospital or person employed by or under contract with the hospital shall be subject to criminal prosecution, civil liability, or be deemed to have engaged in unprofessional conduct for carrying out in good faith pursuant to this article a decision regarding cardiopulmonary resuscitation by or on behalf of a patient or for those actions taken in compliance with the standards and procedures set forth in this article.
2. No physician, health care professional, nurse's aide, hospital, or person employed by or under contract with the hospital shall be subjected to criminal prosecution, civil liability, or be deemed to have engaged in unprofessional conduct for providing cardiopulmonary resuscitation to a patient for whom an order not to resuscitate has been issued, provided such physician or person:
(a) reasonably and in good faith was unaware of the issuance of an order not to resuscitate; or
(b) reasonably and in good faith believed that consent to the order not to resuscitate had been revoked or cancelled.
3. No person shall be subject to criminal prosecution or civil liability for consenting or declining to consent in good faith, on behalf of a patient, to the issuance of an order not to resuscitate pursuant to this article.
4. No person shall be subject to criminal prosecution or civil liability or be deemed to have engaged in unprofessional conduct for acts performed in good faith as a mediator in the dispute mediation system established by this article.
§ 2975. Effect of order not to resuscitate on insurance and health care services.
1. No policy of life insurance shall be legally impaired, modified, or invalidated in any manner by the issuance of an order not to resuscitate notwithstanding any term of the policy to the contrary.
2. A person may not prohibit or require the issuance of an order not to resuscitate for an individual as a condition for such individual's being insured or for receiving health care services.
§ 2976. Judicially approved order not to resuscitate.
1. If no surrogate is reasonably available, willing to make a decision regarding issuance of an order not to resuscitate, and competent to make a decision regarding issuance of an order not to resuscitate on behalf of an adult patient who lacks capacity and who had not previously expressed a decision regarding cardiopulmonary resuscitation pursuant to this article, an attending physician or hospital may commence a special proceeding pursuant to article four of the civil practice law and rules, in a court of competent jurisdiction, for a judgment directing the physician to issue an order not to resuscitate where the patient has a terminal condition, is permanently unconscious, or resuscitation would impose an extraordinary burden on the patient in light of the patient's medical condition and the expected outcome of resuscitation for the patient, and issuance of an order not to resuscitate is consistent with the patient's wishes including a consideration of the patient's religious and moral beliefs or, in the absence of evidence of the patient's wishes, the patient's best interests.
2. Nothing in this article shall be construed to preclude a court of competent jurisdiction from approving the issuance of an order not to resuscitate under circumstances other than those under which such an order may be issued pursuant to this article.
§ 2977. Regulations.
1. Except as provided in subdivision two of this section, the commissioner of health (a) subject to the approval of the state hospital review and planning council by a majority vote of its members, shall establish such regulations as may be necessary for the implementation of this article and (b) may provide suggested

forms that may be used for the purpose of expressing a decision regarding cardiopulmonary resuscitation or for the purpose of designating a surrogate, pursuant to this article.
2. The commissioners of mental health and mental retardation and developmental disabilities, in consultation with the commissioner of health, shall establish such regulations as may be necessary for implementation of this article with respect to those persons in mental hygiene facilities.
§ 2978. Rights to be publicized.
1. The commissioner of health, after consultation with the commissioners of mental health and mental retardation and developmental disabilities, shall prepare a statement summarizing the rights, duties, and requirements of this article and shall require that a copy of such statement:
(a) be furnished by the hospital to patients or to persons on the surrogate list known to the hospital at or prior to the time of admission to the hospital, and at the time of the first decision made pursuant to sections twenty-nine hundred sixty-four, twenty-nine hundred sixty-five, twenty-nine hundred sixty-six, or twenty-nine hundred sixty-seven of this article or as soon thereafter as practicable and to each member of the hospital's staff involved in the provision of medical care; and
(b) is posted in a public place in each hospital.
2. The statement of rights required by this section may be included in any other statement of patient's rights required by other provisions of this chapter.
[**Recommended or required form.** *None specified by legislature. It is suggested that you use the uniform Living Will form in Appendix B, specifying under "Additional specific instructions" that cardiopulmonary resuscitation is not to be performed . Other treatments you do or do not want may be specified in this same space on the form as well*—**ed. note.**]

North Carolina: Right to Natural Death Act

§ 90-320. General purpose of Article. (a) The General Assembly recognizes as a matter of public policy that an individual's rights include the right to a peaceful and natural death and that a patient or his representative has the fundamental right to control the decisions relating to the rendering of his own medical care, including the decision to have extraordinary means withheld or withdrawn in instances of a terminal condition. This Article is to establish an optional and nonexclusive procedure by which a patient or his representative may exercise these rights.
(b) Nothing in this Article shall be construed to authorize any affirmative or deliberate act or omission to end life other than to permit the natural process of dying. Nothing in this Article shall impair or supersede any legal right or legal responsibility which any person may have to effect the withholding or withdrawal of life-sustaining procedures in any lawful manner. In such respect the provisions of this Article are cumulative.
§ 90-321. Right to a natural death. (a) As used in this Article the term:
(1) "Declarant" means a person who has signed a declaration in accordance with subsection (c);
(2) "Extraordinary means" is defined as any medical procedure or intervention which in the judgment of the attending physician would serve only to postpone artificially the moment of death by sustaining, restoring, or supplanting a vital function;
(3) "Physician" means any person licensed to practice medicine under Article 1 of Chapter 90 of the laws of the State of North Carolina.
(b) If a person has declared, in accordance with subsection (c) below, a desire that his life not be prolonged by extraordinary means; and the declaration has not been revoked in accordance with subsection (e); and
(1) It is determined by the attending physician that the declarant's present condition is
a. Terminal; and

b. incurable; and

(2) There is confirmation of the declarant's present condition as set out above in subdivision (b)(1) by a physician other than the attending physician;

then extraordinary means may be withheld or discontinued upon the direction and under the supervision of the attending physician.

(c) The attending physician may rely upon a signed, witnessed, dated, and proved declaration:

(1) Which expresses a desire of the declarant that no extraordinary means be used to prolong his life if his condition is determined to be terminal and incurable; and

(2) Which states that the declarant is aware that the declaration authorizes a physician to withhold or discontinue the extraordinary means; and (

(3) Which has been signed by the declarant in the presence of two witnesses who believe the declarant to be of sound mind and who state that they (i) are not related within the third degree to the declarant or the declarant's spouse, (ii) do not know or have a reasonable expectation that they would be entitled to any portion of the estate of the declarant upon his death under any will of the declarant or codicil thereto then existing or under the Intestate Succession Act as it then provides, (iii) are not the attending physician, or an employee of the attending physician, or an employee of a health facility in which the declarant is a patient, or an employee of a nursing home or any group-care home in which the declarant resides, and (iv) do not have a claim against any portion of the estate of the declarant at the time of the declaration.

(4) Which has been proved before a clerk or assistant clerk of superior court, or a notary public who certifies substantially as set out in the model form set out in subsection (d) below.

(d) The following form is specifically determined to meet the requirements above. [*See Appendix A for a copy of the recommended form. This form is specifically determined to meet the requirements of this act. The addition of personalized instructions is not specifically forbidden*—**ed. note.**]

(e) The declaration may be revoked by the declarant, in any manner by which he is able to communicate his intent to revoke, without regard to his mental or physical condition. Such revocation shall become effective only upon communication to the attending physician by the declarant or by an individual acting on behalf of the declarant.

(f) The execution and consummation of declarations made in accordance with subsection (c) shall not constitute suicide for any purpose.

(g) No person shall be required to sign a declaration in accordance with subsection (c) as a condition for becoming insured under any insurance contract or for receiving any medical treatment.

(h) The withholding or discontinuance of extraordinary means in accordance with this section shall not be considered the cause of death for any civil or criminal purposes nor shall it be considered unprofessional conduct. Any person, institution or facility against whom criminal or civil liability is asserted because of conduct in compliance with this section may interpose this section as a defense.

(i) Any certificate in the form provided by this section prior to July 1, 1979, shall continue to be valid.

§ 90-322. Procedures for natural death in the absence of a declaration. (a) If a person is comatose and there is no reasonable possibility that he will return to a cognitive sapient state or is mentally incapacitated, and

(1) It is determined by the attending physician that the person's present condition is:

a. Terminal;

b. Incurable; and

c. Irreversible; and

(2) There is confirmation of the person's present condition as set out above in this subsection, in writing by a physician other than the attending physician; and

(3) A vital function of the person could be restored by extraordinary means or a vital function of the person is being sustained by extraordinary means;

then, extraordinary means may be withheld or discontinued in accordance with subsection (b).

(b) If a person's condition has been determined to meet the conditions set forth in subsection (a) and no instrument has been executed as provided in section 90-321, the extraordinary means to prolong life may be

withheld or discontinued upon the direction and under the supervision of the attending physician with the concurrence (i) of the person's spouse, or (ii) of a guardian of the person, or (iii) of a majority of the relatives of the first degree, in that order. If none of the above is available then at the discretion of the attending physician the extraordinary means may be withheld or discontinued upon the direction and under the supervision of the attending physician.
(c) Repealed by Session Laws 1979.
(d) The withholding or discontinuance of such extraordinary means shall not be considered the cause of death for any civil or criminal purpose nor shall it be considered unprofessional conduct. Any person, institution, or facility against whom criminal or civil liability is asserted because of conduct in compliance with this section may interpose this section as a defense.
§ 90-323. Death; determination by physician. The determination that a person is dead shall be made by a physician licensed to practice medicine applying ordinary and accepted standards of medical practice. Brain death, defined as irreversible cessation of total brain function, may be used as a sole basis for the determination that a person has died, particularly when brain death occurs in the presence of artificially maintained respiratory and circulatory functions. This specific recognition of brain death as a criterion of death of the person shall not preclude the use of other medically recognized criteria for determining whether and when a person has died.

North Dakota: Uniform Rights of Terminally Ill Act

§ 23-06.4.01. Legislative intent. Every competent adult has the right and the responsibility to control the decisions relating to the adult's own medical care, including the decision to have medical or surgical means or procedures calculated to prolong the adult's life provided, withheld, or withdrawn. Communication about such matters is encouraged between each person and the person's family, the physician, and other health care providers. This chapter does not condone, authorize, approve, or permit mercy killing, euthanasia, or assisted suicide or permit any affirmative or deliberate act or omission to end life other than to permit the natural process of dying.
§ 23-06.4-02. Definitions. In this chapter, unless the context otherwise requires:
1. "Attending physician" means the physician who has primary responsibility for the treatment and care of the patient.
2. "Declaration" means a writing executed in accordance with the requirements of subsection 1 of section 23-06.4-03.
3. "Health care provider" means a person who is licensed, certified, or otherwise authorized by the law of this state to administer health care in the ordinary course of business or practice of a profession.
4. "Life-prolonging treatment" means any medical procedure, treatment, or intervention that, when administered to a qualified patient, will serve only to prolong the process of dying and where, in the judgment of the attending physician, death will occur whether or not the treatment is utilized. The term does not include the provision of appropriate nutrition and hydration or the performance of any medical procedure necessary to provide comfort, care, or alleviate pain.
5. "Physician" means an individual licensed to practice medicine in this state pursuant to chapter 43-17.
6. "Qualified patient" means a patient eighteen or more years of age who has executed a declaration and who has been determined by the attending physician and another physician who has personally examined the patient to be in a terminal condition.
7. "Terminal condition" means an incurable or irreversible condition that, without administration of life-prolonging treatment, will result, in the opinion of the attending physician, in imminent death. The term does

not include any form of senility, Alzheimer's disease, mental retardation, mental illness, or chronic mental or physical impairment, including comatose conditions that will not result in imminent death.

§ 23-06.4.03. Declaration relating to use of life-prolonging treatment.

1. An individual of sound mind and eighteen or more years of age may execute at any time a declaration governing the use, withholding, or withdrawal of life-prolonging treatment. The declaration must be signed by the declarant, or another at the declarant's direction, and witnessed by two individuals who are not:

a. Related to the declarant by blood or marriage;

b. Entitled to any portion of the estate of the declarant under any will of the declarant or codicil to the will existing by operation of law or otherwise, at the time of the declaration;

c. Claimants against any portion of the estate of the declarant at the time of the execution of the declaration;

d. Directly financially responsible for the declarant's medical care;

e. Attending physicians of the declarant.

2. If the declarant is a resident of a long-term care facility, as defined in section 50-10.1-01, at the time the declaration is executed, one of the two witnesses to the declaration must be a regional long-term care ombudsman as provided in section 50-10.1.02.

3. A declaration must be substantially in the form set forth below in subdivision a or b, as applicable, but the declaration may include additional specific directives. The invalidity of any additional specific directives does not affect the validity of the declaration. [*See Appendix A for a copy of the recommended forms, (1) a declaration to withdraw or withhold life-prolonging treatment and (2) a declaration to direct the use of life-prolonging treatment*—**ed. note.**]

4. A physician or other health care provider who is furnished a copy of the declaration shall make it a part of the declarant's medical record and, if unwilling to comply with the declaration, promptly so advise the declarant.

§ 23-06.4-04. When declaration operative. A declaration becomes operative when it is communicated to the attending physician, and the declarant is determined by the attending physician and another physician to be in a terminal condition and no longer able to make decisions regarding administration of life-prolonging treatment. A declaration made under section 23-06.4-03 does not obligate the physician to use, withhold, or withdraw life-prolonging treatment but is presumptive evidence of the declarant's desires concerning the use, withholding, or withdrawal of such treatment and must be given great weight by the physician in determining the intent of the incompetent declarant.

§ 23-06.4-05. Revocation of declaration.

1. A declaration may be revoked at any time and in any manner by the declarant, provided the declarant is competent, including by:

a. A signed, dated writing;

b. Physical cancellation or destruction of the declaration by the declarant or another in the declarant's presence and at the declarant's direction; or

c. An oral expression of intent to revoke.

2. A revocation is effective upon communication to the attending physician or other health care provider by the declarant or a witness to the revocation.

3. The attending physician or other health care provider shall make the revocation a part of the declarant's medical record.

§ 23-06.4-06. Recording determination of terminal condition and declaration. Upon determining that the declarant is in a terminal condition, the attending physician who knows of a declaration shall record the determination and the terms of the declaration in the declarant's medical record.

§ 23-06.4-07. Management of qualified patients.

1. A qualified patient may make decisions regarding life-prolonging treatment as long as the patient is competent.

2. This chapter does not affect the responsibility of the attending physician or other health care provider to provide treatment for a patient's comfort care or alleviation of pain.

3. This chapter does not affect the responsibility of the attending physician or other health care provider to provide nutrition and hydration. Nutrition and hydration may be withheld from a patient with a terminal condition if the nutrition and hydration could not be physically assimilated by the patient or would be physically harmful or unreasonably painful to the patient.
4. Notwithstanding a declaration executed under this chapter, medical treatment must be provided to a pregnant patient with a terminal condition unless, to a reasonable degree of medical certainty as certified on the patient's medical chart by the attending physician and an obstetrician who has examined the patient, such medical treatment will not maintain the patient in such a way as to permit the continuing development and live birth of the unborn child or will be physically harmful or unreasonably painful to the patient or will prolong severe pain that cannot be alleviated by medication.
§ 23-06.4-08. Transfer of patients. An attending physician or other health care provider who is unwilling to comply with this chapter shall take, as promptly as practicable, all reasonable steps to transfer care of the declarant to another physician or health care provider who is willing to comply with this chapter.
§ 23-06.4-09. Immunities.
1. In the absence of knowledge of the revocation of a declaration, a person is not subject to civil or criminal liability or discipline for unprofessional conduct for carrying out the declaration pursuant to the requirements of this chapter.
2. A physician or other health care provider, whose actions are authorized by this chapter, is not subject to criminal or civil liability or discipline for unprofessional conduct with respect to those actions unless done in a grossly negligent manner.
§ 23-06.4-10. Penalties.
1. An individual who willfully conceals, cancels, defaces, or obliterates the declaration of another without the declarant's consent or who falsifies or forges a revocation of the declaration of another is guilty of a class A misdemeanor.
2. An individual who falsifies or forges the declaration of another, or willfully conceals or withholds personal knowledge of a revocation as provided in section 23-06.4-05, is guilty of a class C felony.
3. A person who requires or prohibits the execution of a declaration as a condition for being insured for, or receiving, health care services is guilty of a class A misdemeanor.
4. A person who coerces or fraudulently induces another to execute a declaration under this chapter is guilty of a class C felony.
5. The sanctions provided in this section do not displace any sanction applicable under other law.
§ 23-06.4-11. Miscellaneous provisions.
1. Death resulting from the withholding or withdrawal of life-prolonging treatment pursuant to a declaration and in accordance with this chapter does not constitute, for any purpose, a suicide or homicide.
2. The making of a declaration under section 23-06.4-03 does not affect in any manner the sale, procurement, or issuance of any policy of life insurance or annuity, nor does it affect, impair, or modify the terms of an existing policy of life insurance or annuity. A policy of life insurance or annuity is not legally impaired or invalidated in any manner by the withholding or withdrawal of life-prolonging treatment from an insured qualified patient, notwithstanding any term to the contrary.
3. A person may not prohibit or require the execution of a declaration as a condition for being insured for, or receiving, health care services.
4. This chapter creates no presumption concerning the intention of an individual who has revoked or has not executed a declaration with respect to the use, withholding, or withdrawal of life-prolonging treatment in the event of a terminal condition.
5. This chapter does not affect the right of a patient to make decisions regarding use of life-prolonging treatment, so long as the patient is able to do so, or impair or supersede any right or responsibility that a person has to effect the provision, withholding, or withdrawal of medical care.
6. This chapter does not require any physician or other health care provider to take any action contrary to reasonable medical standards.

§ 23-06.4-12. When health care provider may presume validity of declaration. In the absence of knowledge to the contrary, a physician or other health care provider may presume that a declaration complies with this chapter and is valid.
§ 23-06.4-13. Recognition of declaration executed in another state. A declaration executed in another state by a resident of that state in compliance with the law of that state or of this state is validly executed for purposes of this chapter.
§ 23-06.4-14. Effect of previous declaration. An instrument executed before July 10, 1989, which basically complies with the intent of subsection 1 of section 23-06.4-03, must be given effect pursuant to this chapter. A previously executed instrument that purports to comply with the intent of this chapter is valid for five years from July 10, 1989, unless the declarant becomes incompetent within five years after the execution of the declaration and remains incompetent at the time of the determination of a terminal condition under section 23-06.4-04, in which case the declaration continues in effect. When the declaration expires, a new declaration must be executed if the declarant wishes to make a written declaration under this chapter.

Oklahoma: Natural Death Act

§ 3101. Short title. Sections 1 through 11 of this act shall be known and may be cited as the "Oklahoma Natural Death Act."
§ 3102. Definitions. As used in the Oklahoma Natural Death Act:
1. "Attending physician" means the physician who has primary responsibility for the treatment and care of the patient. The attending physician may be selected by the patient or assigned by the physician selected by the patient;
2. "Declarant" means any person who has issued a directive according to the procedure provided for in Section 3103 of this title in contemplation of death;
3. "Directive" means a written document voluntarily executed by the declarant in accordance with the requirements of Section 3103 of this title. The directive or a copy shall be made part of the medical records of the patient;
4. "Life-sustaining procedure" means an extraordinary medical procedure or intervention which utilizes mechanical or other artificial means to sustain, restore, or supplant a vital bodily function. When applied to a qualified patient, a life-sustaining procedure would serve only to artificially prolong the moment of death when in the judgment of the attending physician, as noted in the medical records of the qualified patient, death is imminent whether or not such procedures are utilized. "Life-sustaining procedure" shall not include the administration of nourishment, hydration and medication or the performance of any medical procedure deemed necessary to alleviate pain.
5. "Person" means any individual twenty-one (21) years of age or older;
6. "Physician" means a physician or surgeon licensed by the State Board of Medical Licensure and Supervision or State Board of Osteopathy.
7. "Qualified patient" means a patient twenty-one (21) years of age or older who has been personally diagnosed and certified in writing by two physicians to be afflicted with a terminal condition. Said written determination shall be signed and dated and filed with the patient's chart and one copy with the hospital or nursing home, where said patient is located. One physician shall be the attending physician and the other shall be chosen by the patient or the attending physician; and
8. "Terminal condition" means an incurable irreversible condition caused by injury, disease, or illness, which within reasonable medical judgment would produce death regardless of the application of life-sustaining procedures, and when the application of life-sustaining procedures serves only to postpone the moment of the death of the patient.
§ 3103. Directive for withholding or withdrawal of life-sustaining procedures; execution; witnesses; declarant's signature; form. A. Any person may execute a directive for the withholding or withdrawal of

life-sustaining procedures in the event of a terminal condition. The directive shall be signed by the declarant in the presence of two witnesses.

B. Witnesses to the execution of the directive shall not be:

1. Under twenty-one (21) years of age;
2. Related to the declarant by blood or marriage;
3. Financially responsible for the medical care of the declarant;
4. Entitled to any portion of the estate of the declarant pursuant to any will of the declarant, any codicil thereto, or by operation of law;
5. The attending physician;
6. An employee of the attending physician or an employee of a health care facility in which the declarant is a patient;
7. A patient in a health care facility in which the declarant is a patient; or
8. A person who, at the time of the execution of the directive, has a claim against any portion of the estate of the declarant.

C. The signature of the declarant shall be acknowledged. Witnesses shall subscribe and swear to the directive before a notary public.

D. The directive shall be substantially in this form. [*See Appendix A for a copy of the recommended form. Personalized instructions are not specifically forbidden*—**ed. note.**]

§ 3104. Revocation of directive; methods; liability for failure to act on revocation. A. A directive may be revoked at any time by the declarant without regard to his mental state or competency by any of the following methods:

1. Being canceled, defaced, obliterated, burnt, torn, or otherwise destroyed by the declarant or by some person in his presence and by his direction;
2. A written revocation of the declarant expressing his intent to revoke, signed and dated by the declarant. Such revocation shall become effective only on the receipt of said revocation by the attending physician provided by the declarant or by a person acting on behalf of the declarant. The attending physician or his designee shall record in the medical record of the patient the time and date the notification of the written revocation was received and shall enter the word "VOID" on each page of the directive in the medical records of the patient; or
3. A verbal expression by the declarant of his intent to revoke the directive made in the presence of a witness twenty-one (21) years of age or older who signs and dates a written confirmation that such expression of intent was made. Any verbal revocation shall become effective upon receipt of the above-mentioned writing by the attending physician. The attending physician or his designee shall record in the medical record of the patient the time, date, and place of revocation and the time, date, and place of receipt of the notification of the revocation, if different, and shall enter the word "VOID" on each page of the directive in the medical records of the patient.

B. Except as otherwise provided for in the Oklahoma Natural Death Act, there shall be no criminal or civil liability on the part of any person for failure to act on a revocation made pursuant to this section unless that person has actual knowledge of the revocation.

§ 3105. Term of directive; re-execution. A directive shall be effective until it is revoked in a manner prescribed in the provisions of section 3104 of the Oklahoma Natural Death Act. Nothing in the Oklahoma Natural Death Act shall be construed to prevent a declarant from re-executing a directive at any time in accordance with the formalities of section 3103 of the Oklahoma Natural Death Act, including re-execution subsequent to a diagnosis of a terminal condition. If the declarant becomes comatose or is rendered incapable of communicating with the attending physician, the directive shall remain in effect for the duration of the condition or until such time as the declarant revokes the directive pursuant to the provisions of the Oklahoma Natural Death Act.

§ 3106. Civil and criminal liability for withholding or withdrawing life-sustaining procedures. The withholding or withdrawal of life-sustaining procedures by any physician, health facility or other health care professionals from a qualified patient in accordance with the provisions of the Oklahoma Natural Death Act shall not constitute negligence. Further, the withholding or withdrawal of life-sustaining procedures by any physician, health facility or other health care professionals from a qualified patient in accordance with the provisions of the Oklahoma Natural Death Act shall not constitute an offense pursuant to Sections 813 through 818 of Title 21 of the Oklahoma Statutes. Further, the withholding or withdrawal of life-sustaining procedures shall not be considered the cause of death for any civil or criminal purpose nor shall it be considered unprofessional conduct. Any person, institution or facility against whom criminal or civil liability is asserted because of conduct in compliance with the Oklahoma Natural Death Act may interpose this section as a defense.

No physician or health care facility which, in accordance with the Oklahoma Natural Death Act, causes the withholding or withdrawal of life-sustaining procedures from a qualified patient shall be subject to civil liability unless negligent. No health care professional can use this act as a reason to withhold food, nourishment or water to effectuate death under this act. No health care professional who participates under the direction of a physician in the withholding or withdrawal of life-sustaining procedures in accordance with the provisions of the Oklahoma Natural Death Act shall be subject to any civil liability unless negligent. No physician or health care professional acting under the direction of a physician who participates in the withholding or withdrawal of life-sustaining procedures in accordance with the Oklahoma Natural Death Act shall be guilty of any criminal act or unprofessional conduct unless negligent. No physician shall be civilly or criminally liable for failure to act pursuant to the directive of the declarant when such physician, health care facility, or health care professional had no knowledge of such directive.

§ 3107. Qualified patients; verification of directive; presumptions; failure or refusal to comply with directive; subsequently qualified patients; certification and confirmation of terminal condition. A. Prior to the withholding or withdrawal of life-sustaining procedures from a qualified patient pursuant to the directive, the attending physician shall verify with the patient the execution of his directive and, if the patient is mentally competent, that the directive and all steps proposed by the attending physician to be undertaken are in accord with the existing desires of the qualified patient and are communicated to the patient.

B. If the declarant was a qualified patient prior to executing or re-executing the directive, the directive shall be conclusively presumed, unless revoked, to be the directions of the patient regarding the withholding or withdrawal of life-sustaining procedures. No physician or health care professional acting under the direction of a physician shall be civilly or criminally liable for failing to comply with the directive of a qualified patient pursuant to this subsection. An attending physician who refuses to comply with the directive of a qualified patient shall transfer the qualified patient to another physician. A failure by a physician to comply with the directive of a qualified patient pursuant to this subsection may constitute unprofessional conduct if the physician refuses to make the necessary arrangements or fails to transfer the qualified patient to another physician who will comply with the directive of the qualified patient.

C. If the declarant becomes a qualified patient subsequent to executing the directive and has not subsequently re-executed the directive, the attending physician may give weight to the directive as evidence of the directions of the patient regarding the withholding or withdrawal of life-sustaining procedures and may consider other factors such as information from the affected family or the nature of the illness, injury, or disease of the patient in determining whether the totality of circumstances known to the attending physician justifies effectuating the directive. No physician and no health care professional acting under the direction of a physician shall be civilly or criminally liable for failing to effectuate the directive of the qualified patient pursuant to this subsection.

[*Only directives executed or re-executed after the diagnosis and certification of a terminal condition are legally enforceable, in other words; those executed before such a terminal diagnosis will be regarded as merely advisory of the patient's wishes*—**ed. note.**]

D. Without delay after the diagnosis of a terminal condition of the declarant, an attending physician who has been notified of the existence of a directive shall take the necessary steps to provide for written certification and confirmation of the terminal condition of the declarant so that the declarant may be deemed a qualified patient pursuant to the Oklahoma Natural Death Act. The failure of a physician to provide written certifica-

tion of the terminal condition of the declarant pursuant to this subsection or to transfer the declarant to another physician who will so certify the condition of the declarant may constitute unprofessional conduct.
§ 3108. Insurance policies. A. The making of a directive pursuant to section 3103 of the Oklahoma Natural Death Act shall not restrict, inhibit, or impair in any manner the sale, procurement, or issuance of any policy of life insurance, nor shall it be deemed to modify the terms of an existing policy of life insurance. No policy of life insurance shall be legally impaired or invalidated in any manner by the withholding or withdrawal of life-sustaining procedures from an insured qualified patient, notwithstanding any term to the contrary in any policy in effect prior to the effective date of the Oklahoma Natural Death Act.
B. No physician, health care facility, or other health care professional and no health care service plan or insurer issuing insurance shall require any person to execute a directive as a condition for being insured for or receiving health care services. The execution or failure to execute a directive shall not be considered in any way in establishing the premiums for insurance.
§ 3109. Tampering with directive; criminal homicide. The concealment, cancellation, defacement, obliteration, or damage of the directive of another without the consent of the declarant, upon conviction, shall be a misdemeanor. The falsification or forgery of a directive of another or the willful concealment or the withholding of personal knowledge of a revocation as provided for in the Oklahoma Natural Death Act with the intent to cause a withholding or withdrawal of life-sustaining procedures contrary to the wishes of the declarant thereby, because of any such act, directly causing life-sustaining procedures to be withheld or withdrawn and death to thereby be hastened, shall be criminal homicide.
§ 3110. Failure of qualified patient to execute directive. The failure of a qualified patient to execute a directive under the provisions of section 3103 of the Oklahoma Natural Death Act shall create no presumption as to the patient's wishes regarding life-sustaining procedures.
§ 3111. Construction of act. Nothing in the Oklahoma Natural Death Act shall be construed to condone, authorize, approve, or permit any affirmative or deliberate act or omission of an act to end life, other than to permit the natural process of dying as provided for in the Oklahoma Natural Death Act.

Oregon: Rights with Respect to Terminal Illness

§ 127.605. Definitions of Oregon Revised Statutes 127.605 to 127.650. As used in ORS 127.605 to 127.650:
(1) "Attending physician" means the physician with primary responsibility for the care and treatment of the patient.
(2) "Directive" means a written document voluntarily executed by a declarant in accordance with the requirements set forth in ORS 127.610.
(3) "Life-sustaining procedure" means any medical procedure or intervention that utilizes mechanical or other artificial means to sustain, restore or supplant a vital function of a qualified patient that is used to maintain the life of a person suffering from a terminal condition and serves only to artificially prolong the moment of death or when death is imminent whether or not such procedures are used. "Life-sustaining procedure" does not include the usual care provided to individuals who are in facilities defined in ORS 442.015 (13)(a), which would include routine care necessary to sustain patient comfort and the usual and typical provision of nutrition which in the medical judgment of the attending physician a patient can tolerate.
(4) "Physician" means an individual licensed to practice medicine by the Board of Medical Examiners for the State of Oregon.
(5) "Qualified patient" means an individual 18 years of age or older, whom the attending physician and one other physician, upon diagnostic examination of the patient, certify to be suffering from a terminal condition.

(6) "Terminal condition" means an incurable condition caused by injury, disease or illness which, regardless of the application of life-sustaining procedures would within reasonable medical judgment produce death, and where the application of life-sustaining procedures serve only to postpone the moment of death of the patient.

§ 127.610. Execution and revocation of directive; form; witness qualifications and responsibility. (1) An individual of sound mind and 18 years of age or older may at any time execute or re-execute a directive directing the withholding or withdrawal of life-sustaining procedures should the declarant become a qualified patient. The directive shall be in exactly the following form. [*See Appendix A for a copy of the required form; no allowance for personalized instructions is made*—**ed. note.**]

(2) A directive made pursuant to subsection (1) of this section is only valid if signed by the declarant in the presence of two attesting witnesses who, at the time the directive is executed, are not:

(a) Related to the declarant by blood or marriage;

(b) Entitled to any portion of the estate of the declarant upon the decease thereof under any will or codicil of the declarant or by operation of law at the time of the execution of the directive;

(c) The attending physician or an employee of the attending physician or of a health facility in which the declarant is a patient; or

(d) Persons who at the time of the execution of the directive have a claim against any portion of the estate of the declarant upon the declarant's decease.

(3) One of the witnesses, if the declarant is a patient in a long-term care facility at the time the directive is executed, shall be an individual designated by the Department of Human Resources for the purpose of determining that the declarant is not so insulated from the voluntary decision-making role that the declarant is not capable of wilfully and voluntarily executing a directive.

(4) A witness who does not attest a directive in good faith shall be liable for any damages that arise from giving effect to an invalid directive.

(5) A directive made pursuant to Oregon Revised Statutes 127.605 to 127.650 and 97.990 (5) to (7) may be revoked at any time by the declarant without regard to mental state or competency by any of the following methods:

(a) By being burned, torn, canceled, obliterated, or otherwise destroyed by the declarant or by some person in the declarant's presence and by direction of the declarant.

(b) By a written revocation of the declarant expressing intent to revoke, signed and dated by the declarant.

(c) By a verbal expression by the declarant of intent to revoke the directive.

(6) Unless revoked, a directive shall be effective from the date of execution. If the declarant has executed more than one directive, the last directive to be executed shall control. If the declarant becomes comatose or is rendered incapable of communicating with the attending physician, the directive shall remain in effect for the duration of the comatose condition or until such time as the declarant's condition renders the declarant able to communicate with the attending physician.

§ 127.615. Validity of directive as to physician. A directive that is valid on its face is valid as to any physician for the purposes of Oregon Revised Statutes 127.605 to 127.650 and 97.990 (5) to (7) unless the physician has actual knowledge of facts that render the directive invalid or is under the direction of a court not to give effect to the directive.

§ 127.620. Effect on directive. (1) It shall be lawful for an attending physician or a licensed health professional under the direction of an attending physician, acting in good faith and in accordance with the requirements of Oregon Revised Statutes 127.605 to 127.650 and 97.990 (5) to (7), to withhold or withdraw life-sustaining procedures from a qualified patient who has properly executed a directive in accordance with the requirements of ORS 127.605 to 127.650 and 97.990 (5) to (7).

(2) A physician or licensed health professional or health facility under the direction of a physician who, acting in good faith and in accordance with the requirements of Oregon Revised Statutes 127.605 to 127.650 and 97.990 (5) to (7), causes the withholding or withdrawal of life-sustaining procedures shall not be guilty of any criminal offense, shall not be subject to civil liability and shall not be in violation of any professional oath, affirmation or standard of care.

(3) A physician or licensed health professional or health facility shall not be guilty of any criminal offense, shall not be subject to civil liability and shall not be in violation of any professional oath, affirmation or standard of care for failing to assume the duties created by or for failing to give effect to any directive or revocation made pursuant to Oregon Revised Statutes 127.605 to 127.650 and 97.990 (5) to (7) unless that physician has actual knowledge of the directive or revocation.

§ 127.625. Duties created by directive. (1) Except as provided in this section, no physician, licensed health professional or medical facility shall be under any duty, whether by contract, by statute or by any other legal requirement to participate in the withholding or withdrawal of life-sustaining procedures.

(2)(a) An attending physician shall make a directive or a copy of a directive made pursuant to Oregon Revised Statutes 127.605 to 127.650 and 97.990 (5) to (7) part of the patient's medical record.

(b) An attending physician shall record in the patient's medical record the time, date, place and manner of a revocation and the time, date, place and manner, if different, of when the physician received notification of the revocation. If the revocation is written, the attending physician shall make the revocation or a copy of the revocation a part of the patient's medical record.

(3) A physician or medical facility electing for any reason not to participate in the withholding or withdrawal of life-sustaining procedures in accord with a directive made pursuant to Oregon Revised Statutes 127.605 to 127.650 and 97.990 (5) to (7) shall:

(a) Make a reasonable effort to locate a physician or medical facility that will give effect to a qualified patient's directive and shall have a duty to transfer the qualified patient to that physician or facility; or

(b) At the request of a patient or of the patient's family, a physician or medical facility shall transfer the patient to another physician or medical facility that will reconsider circumstances which might make Oregon Revised Statutes 127.605 to 127.650 and 97.990 (5) to (7) applicable to the patient.

§ 127.630. Effect of directive on insurance. (1) Except as provided in subsection (2) of this section, the making of a directive pursuant to Oregon Revised Statutes 127.605 to 127.650 and 97.990 (5) to (7) shall not restrict, inhibit or impair in any manner the sale, procurement or issuance of any policy of insurance, nor shall it be deemed to modify the terms of an existing policy of insurance.

(2) No physician, health facility, health care service plan, insurer issuing disability insurance, self-insured employee welfare benefit plan, nonprofit hospital service plan or other direct or indirect health service provider shall require any person to execute a directive as a condition for being insured for, or receiving, health care services.

(3) No policy of insurance shall be legally impaired or invalidated in any manner by the withholding or withdrawal of life-sustaining procedures from an insured qualified patient.

§ 127.635. Withdrawal of life-sustaining procedures; conditions; physician's liability; effect on insurance policy. (1) Life-sustaining procedures as defined in Oregon Revised Statutes 127.605 (3) which would otherwise be applied to a qualified patient may be withdrawn in accordance with subsections (2) and (3) of this section if a person is comatose and there is no reasonable possibility that the person will return to a cognitive sapient state and:

(a) It is determined by the attending physician that the person has a terminal condition as defined in Oregon Revised Statutes 127.605 (6) ; and

(b) There is confirmation of the person's condition by a committee of physicians, not including the attending physician, appointed by the medical staff of the health facility or, if none, by the health facility in which the person is confined.

(2) If a person's condition has been determined to meet the conditions set forth in subsection (1) of this section and no directive has been executed as provided in Oregon Revised Statutes 127.610, life-sustaining procedures may be withdrawn upon the direction and under the supervision of the attending physician at the request of the first of the following, in the following order, who can be located upon reasonable effort by the health care facility:

(a) The person's spouse;

(b) A guardian of the person, if any;

(c) A majority of the adult children of the person who can be so located; or

(d) Either parent of the person.
(3) If none of the persons described in subsection (2) of this section is available, then life-sustaining procedures may be withdrawn upon the direction and under the supervision of the attending physician.
(4) A physician or licensed health professional or health facility under the direction of a physician who, acting in good faith and in accordance with the requirements of this section and Oregon Revised Statutes 127.640, causes the withdrawal of life-sustaining procedures shall not be guilty of any criminal offense, shall not be subject to civil liability and shall not be in violation of any professional oath, affirmation or standard of care.
(5) No policy of insurance shall be legally impaired or invalidated in any manner by the withdrawal of life-sustaining procedures pursuant to this section.
§ 127.640. Withdrawal of life-sustaining procedures from comatose patient who has not executed directive. Before withdrawing life-sustaining procedures from a patient who is comatose but who has executed no directive, the attending physician shall determine that the conditions of Oregon Revised Statutes 127.635 (1) to (3) of the previous section have been met.
§ 127.645. Construction of ORS 127.605 to 127.650 concerning mercy killing, exclusiveness and suicide. (1) Nothing in Oregon Revised Statutes 127.605 to 127.650 and 97.990 (5) to (7) shall be construed to condone, authorize or approve mercy killing, or to permit any affirmative or deliberate act or omission to end life other than to permit the natural process of dying as provided in Oregon Revised Statutes 127.605 to 127.650 and 97.990 (5) to (7).
(2) Nothing in Oregon Revised Statutes 127.605 to 127.650 and 97.990 (5) to (7) shall impair or supersede any legal right or legal responsibility which any person may have to effect the withholding or withdrawal of life-sustaining procedures in any lawful manner. In such respect the provisions of Oregon Revised Statutes 127.605 to 127.650 and 97.990 (5) to (7) are cumulative.
(3) The withholding or withdrawal of life-sustaining procedures from a qualified patient in accordance with the provisions of Oregon Revised Statutes 127.605 to 127.650 and 97.990 (5) to (7) shall not, for any purpose, constitute a suicide.
§ 127.650. Prohibited acts. (1) No person shall by wilfully concealing or destroying a revocation or by wilfully falsifying or forging a directive cause the withdrawal or withholding of life-sustaining procedures.
(2) No person shall by wilfully concealing or destroying a directive or by wilfully falsifying or forging a revocation cause an individual's intent with respect to the withholding or withdrawal of life-sustaining procedures not to be given effect.

South Carolina: Death with Dignity Act

§ 44-77-10. Short title. This chapter may be cited as the Death With Dignity Act.
§ 44-77-20. Definitions. As used in this chapter:
(1) "Declarant" means a person who has signed a declaration in accordance with Sections 44-77-40 and 44-77-50, in accordance with earlier versions of this chapter, or in accordance with the law of another state if the declaration provided for by the law expresses an intent that is substantially the same as the intent of the declaration provided in Section 44-77-40.
(2) "Life-sustaining procedures" means any medical procedures or intervention which would serve only to prolong the dying process and where, in the judgment of the attending physician, death will occur whether or not the procedures are utilized. Life-sustaining procedures do not include the administration of medication or the provision of treatment, nutrition, and hydration for comfort care or alleviation of pain.
(3) "Physician" means any person licensed to practice medicine.

(4) "Terminal condition" means an incurable or irreversible condition that, without the use of life-sustaining procedures, will result in death within a relatively short period of time.
(5) "Active treatment" means the standard of reasonable professional care that would be rendered by a physician to a patient in the absence of a declaration including but not limited to, hospitalization and medication.
(6) "Person" means an individual, partnership, committee, association, corporation, hospital, or any other organization or group.
§ 44-77-30. When life-sustaining procedures may be withheld. If any person eighteen years of age or older adopts a declaration that is substantially in the form provided in Section 44-77-50 and that on its face is duly executed, witnessed, and authenticated as provided in Section 44-77-40 or on its face is in compliance with the law of the state of the declarant's domicile at the time that the declaration is adopted, if the declaration provided for by the law expresses an intent that is substantially the same as the intent of the declaration provided in Section 44-77-40, and the person's present condition is certified to be terminal by two physicians who personally have examined the declarant, one of whom is the declarant's attending physician, and the other of whom is a physician other than the attending physician, then life-sustaining procedures may be withheld or withdrawn upon the direction and under the supervision of the attending physician.
All patients with life-threatening illnesses that are diagnosed as terminal must be administered active treatment for at least six hours before the physician may give effect to a declaration.
§ 44-77-40. Validity of declaration. A declaration is valid:
(1) which expresses substantially in the form set forth in Section 44-77-50 a desire of the declarant that no life-sustaining procedures be used to prolong dying if his condition is terminal and states that the declarant is aware that the declaration authorizes a physician to withhold or withdraw life-sustaining procedures; and
(2) which has been dated and signed by the declarant in the presence of an officer authorized to administer oaths under the laws of the state where the signing occurs and in the presence of two witnesses who state in an affidavit as set forth in Section 44-77-50 that, to the extent that they have knowledge of their status, they are not related to the declarant by blood or marriage, either as a spouse, lineal ancestor, descendant of the parents of the declarant, or spouse of any of them, not directly financially responsible for the person's medical care, not entitled to any portion of the estate of the declarant upon his decease under any will of the declarant then existing or as an heir by intestate succession, and not a beneficiary of a life insurance policy of the declarant, and who state that no more than one witness is an employee of a health facility in which the declarant is a patient and that no witness to the declaration is the attending physician or an employee of the attending physician or any person who has a claim against any portion of the estate of the declarant upon his decease at the time of the execution of the declaration.
(3) which, if the declarant is a patient in a hospital or skilled or intermediate care nursing facility at the time the declaration is executed, has been witnessed by an ombudsman as designated by the State Ombudsman, Office of the Governor, with the ombudsman acting as one of the two witnesses and having the same qualifications as a witness as provided in this section. The intent of this section is to recognize that some patients in skilled or intermediate care nursing facilities may be so insulated from a voluntary decision-making role, by virtue of the custodial nature of their care, as to require special assurance that they are capable of willfully and voluntarily executing a declaration.
(4) which accompanying affidavit has been subscribed and sworn to by the two witnesses in the presence of the declarant, and of each other, and of an officer authorized to administer oaths under the laws of the state where the signing occurs.
§ 44-77-50. Form of declaration. The declaration must be substantially in the following form with the procedure and requirements for revocation of the declaration appearing either in boldface print or in all upper case letters, the characters in either case being of at least the same size as used in the rest of the declaration.
[See Appendix A for a copy of this form. The addition of personalized instructions is not specifically forbidden. The declaration must be notarized. Each Living Will prepared in accordance with the provisions of this act shall state the procedure and requirements for revocation of the declaration. The law states that requirements for revocation of the declaration must be set forth in bold-face print or in all capital letters, and the

characters in this section must be at least the same size as those used in the rest of the declaration, as shown in the model—**ed. note.**]

§ 44-77-60. Repealed.

§ 44-77-70. Ineffectiveness of declaration during course of declarant's pregnancy. If a declarant has been diagnosed as pregnant, the Declaration is not effective during the course of the declarant's pregnancy.

§ 44-77-80. Revocation of declaration. The Declaration may be revoked:

(1) by being defaced, torn, obliterated, or otherwise destroyed in expression of the declarant's intent to revoke by the declarant or by some person in the presence of and by the direction of the declarant. Revocation by destruction of one or more of multiple original declarations revokes all of the original declarations. The revocation of the original declarations actually not destroyed becomes effective only upon communication to the attending physician. The attending physician shall record in the declarant's medical record the time and date when the physician received notification of the revocation;

(2) by a written revocation signed and dated by the declarant expressing his intent to revoke. The revocation becomes effective only upon communication to the attending physician. The attending physician shall record in the declarant's medical record the time and date when the physician received notification of the written revocation.

(3) by an oral expression by the declarant of his intent to revoke the Declaration. The revocation becomes effective only upon communication to the attending physician by the declarant. However, an oral revocation made by the declarant becomes effective upon communication to the attending physician by a person other than the declarant if:

(a) the person was present when the oral revocation was made;

(b) the revocation was communicated to the physician within a reasonable time;

(c) the physical or mental condition of the declarant makes it impossible for the physician to confirm through subsequent conversation with the declarant that the revocation has occurred. The attending physician shall record in the declarant's medical record the time, date, and place of the revocation and the time, date, and place, if different, of when the physician received notification of the revocation. To be effective as a revocation, the oral expression clearly must indicate the declarant's desire that the declaration not be given effect or that life-sustaining procedures be administered;

(4) by a written, signed, and dated revocation or by an oral revocation by the declarant's designee, the designee's name and address being supplied in the declaration, expressing the designee's intent to permanently or temporarily revoke the declaration. The revocation becomes effective only upon communication to the attending physician by the designee. The attending physician shall record in the declarant's medical record the time, date, and place of the revocation and the time, date, and place, if different, of when the physician received notification of the revocation. A designee may revoke only if the declarant is incompetent to do so.

§ 44-77-90. Reliance on declaration; presumption of good faith; immunity from liability. After certification of a terminal condition, a physician who relies on a declaration which on its face appears to have been executed in accordance with the provisions of this chapter, of which he has no actual notice of revocation and who withholds or withdraws or participates in the withholding or withdrawal of life-sustaining procedures from the terminally ill patient who executed the declaration, is presumed to be acting in good faith. Any person who in good faith and in accordance with the provisions of this chapter participates in the withholding or withdrawal of life-sustaining procedures from the patient is not subject to criminal or civil liability on account of the withholding or withdrawal. The immunity from civil liability does not extend to cases of provable malpractice committed in connection with the withholding or withdrawal.

§ 44-77-100. Circumstances in which physician's failure to effectuate declaration constitutes unprofessional conduct. A physician or health care facility electing for any reason not to participate in the withholding or withdrawal of life-sustaining procedures in accordance with a declaration executed under this chapter shall make a reasonable effort to locate a physician or health care facility that will effectuate the declaration and has a duty to transfer the patient to that physician or facility. A failure by a physician to effectuate the declaration of a terminal patient constitutes unprofessional conduct if the physician fails or refuses to make reasonable efforts to effect the transfer of the patient to another physician who will effectuate the declaration.

§ 44-77-110. Execution and consummation of declaration as not constituting suicide. The execution and consummation of declarations made in accordance with Sections 44-77-40 and 44-77-50 do not constitute suicide for any purpose.

§ 44-77-120. Declaration as a condition for insurance; receipt of medical treatment, or admission to hospital or nursing home. No person may be required to sign a declaration in accordance with Sections 44-77-40 and 44-77-50 as a condition for becoming insured under any insurance contract or for receiving any medical treatment or as a condition of being admitted to a hospital or nursing home facility.

§ 44-77-130. Chapter not to be construed to authorize or approve mercy killing. Nothing in this chapter may be construed to authorize or approve mercy killing, or to permit any affirmative or deliberate act or omission to end life other than to permit the natural process of dying.

§ 44-77-140. No presumption as to intent to arise from absence of declaration; other legal rights not impaired. The absence of a declaration by an adult patient does not give rise to any presumption as to his intent to consent to or refuse death-prolonging procedures. Nothing in this chapter impairs any other legal right or legal responsibility which any person may have to effect the withholding or withdrawal of life-sustaining procedures in any lawful manner.

§ 44-77-150. Repealed by implication.

§ 44-77-160. Penalties.

(A) Any person who coerces or fraudulently induces another person to execute a declaration under this chapter, falsifies or forges a declaration, or wilfully conceals, cancels, obliterates, or destroys a revocation of a declaration, and the declarant dies as a result of the withdrawal of treatment or nontreatment in reliance on the declaration, that person is subject to prosecution in accordance with the criminal laws of this State.

(B) Nothing in this chapter prohibits any person from informing another person of the existence of this chapter, delivering to another person a copy of this chapter or a form of declaration, or counseling another person in good faith concerning the execution of a declaration.

(C) If any person wilfully conceals, cancels, defaces, obliterates, or damages the declaration of another without the declarant's consent or falsifies or forges a revocation of the declaration of another, that person breaches a duty owed to the declarant and is responsible for payment of any expenses or other damages incurred as a result of the wrongful act.

Tennessee: Right to Natural Death Act

§ 32-11-101. Short title. This chapter shall be known and cited as the "Tennessee Right to Natural Death Act."

§ 32-11-102. Legislative intent. (a) The general assembly declares it to be the law of the state of Tennessee that every person has the fundamental and inherent right to die naturally with as much dignity as circumstances permit and to accept, refuse, withdraw from, or otherwise control decisions relating to the rendering of his or her own medical care, specifically including palliative care and the use of extraordinary procedures and treatment.

(b) The general assembly does further empower the exercise of this right by written declaration, called a "living will", as hereinafter provided.

§ 32-11-103. Definitions. The following definitions shall govern the construction and operation of this chapter:

(1) "Competent person" means an individual who is able to understand and appreciate the nature and consequences of a decision to accept or refuse treatment;
(2) "Declarant" means an individual who declares a living will under the provisions of this chapter;
(3) "Health care provider," "health care facility," or "health facility" means a person, facility, or institution licensed or authorized to provide health or medical care;
(4) "Living will" means a written declaration, pursuant to this chapter, stating declarant's desires for medical care or noncare, including palliative care, and other related matters such as organ donation and bodily disposal;
(5) "Medical care" includes any procedure or treatment rendered by a physician or health care provider designed to diagnose, assess, or treat a disease, illness or injury. These include, but are not limited to, surgery, drugs, transfusions, mechanical ventilation, dialysis, cardiopulmonary resuscitation, artificial or forced feeding, radiation therapy, or any other medical act designed for diagnosis, assessment, or treatment or to sustain, restore, or supplant vital body function. Provided, however, that in no case shall this section be interpreted to allow the withholding of simple nourishment or fluids so as to condone death by starvation or dehydration.
(6) "Palliative care" includes any measure taken by a physician or health care provider designed primarily to maintain the patient's comfort. These also include, but are not limited to, sedatives and pain-killing drugs, nonartificial oral feeding, suction, hydration, and hygienic care;
(7) "Physician" means any person licensed or permitted to practice medical care under title 63, chapters 6 and 9;
(8) "Qualified patient" means a patient who has executed a declaration in accordance with this chapter and who has been diagnosed and certified in writing to be afflicted with a terminal condition by two (2) physicians who have personally examined the patient, one (1) of whom shall be the attending physician; and
(9) "Terminal condition" means any disease, illness, injury, or condition sustained by any human being from which there is no reasonable medical expectation of recovery and which, as a medical probability, will result in the death of such human being within a short period of time regardless of the use or discontinuance of medical treatment implemented for the purpose of sustaining life, or the life processes.
§ 32-11-104. Execution of declaration. (a) Any competent adult person may execute a declaration directing the withholding or withdrawal of medical care to his person, to become effective on loss of competency, which declaration shall be acknowledged and signed by the declarant in the presence of two (2) witnesses who shall verify in such declaration that they are not related to the declarant by blood or marriage and that they would not be entitled to any portion of the estate of the declarant upon his demise under any will or codicil thereto made by the declarant. In addition, the witnesses shall verify that neither of them is the attending physician nor an employee of the attending physician nor an employee of a health care facility in which the declarant is a patient, and neither of them has a claim against any portion of the estate of the declarant. The declaration shall be substantially in the form established in § 32-11-105.
(b) It shall be the responsibility of the declarant or someone acting on his behalf to deliver a copy of such living will or declaration to the attending physician and/or other concerned health care provider. An attending physician who is so notified shall make the declaration, or a copy of it, part of the declarant's medical record.
§ 32-11-105. Form of declaration. The declaration may be substantially in this form, but not to the exclusion of other written and clear expressions of intent to accept, refuse, or withdraw medical care. [*See Appendix A for a copy of this form; personalized instructions are allowed to be added, in other words*—**ed. note.**]
§ 32-11-106. Revocation of declaration. A declaration may be revoked at any time by the declarant, without regard to his or her mental state or competency, by any of the following methods, effectively communicated by the declarant to the attending physician or other concerned health care provider:
(1) Written revocation by the declarant, dated and signed by the declarant and at least one (1) witness, or notarized.

(2) By oral statement or revocation made by the declarant to the attending physician. Such revocation shall be made a part of the declarant's medical record by the attending physician.

§ 32-11-107. Effective date of declaration; subsequent declarations; incapacitated declarants. A declaration shall be effective from the date of its execution until revoked in a manner prescribed by this chapter. Nothing in this chapter shall be construed to prevent a declarant from reexecuting a declaration at any time in accordance with the formalities of this chapter, including reexecution after a diagnosis of a terminal condition. If the declarant has executed more than one (1) declaration, then the latest declaration known to the attending physician shall take precedence. If the declarant becomes comatose or if his condition renders him incapable of communicating with the attending physician, the declaration shall remain in effect during the comatose condition or until the declarant's condition renders him able to communicate with the attending physician.

§ 32-11-108. Compliance with declaration; failure to comply; liability and penalties. (a) Any physician or other individual health care provider who cannot in good conscience comply with the provisions of such living will, on being informed of the declaration, shall so inform the declarant, or if the declarant is not competent, his next of kin or a legal guardian, and at their option make every reasonable effort to assist in the transfer of the patient to another physician who will comply with the declaration. Any health care provider who fails to make good faith reasonable efforts to comply with the preceding procedure as prescribed by the attending physician shall be civilly liable and subject to professional disciplinary action, including revocation or suspension of license. Provided that the health care provider shall not be subject to civil liability for medical care provided during the interim period until transfer is effectuated.

(b) A physician or other health care provider who by no fault of his own has not received notice of such declaration, revocation, or other change shall not suffer civil, administrative, or criminal penalties under this chapter.

§ 32-11-109. Willful misconduct; penalty. Any person who willfully conceals, cancels, defaces, obliterates, or damages the declaration or revocation of another without such declarant's consent, or who falsifies or forges same shall be civilly liable and subject to criminal prosecution for a misdemeanor and if a provider, subject to administrative and professional discipline.

§ 32-11-110. Construction and effect of chapter; signatures; severability; liability for complying with chapter. (a) The withholding or withdrawal of medical care from a declarant in accordance with the provisions of this chapter shall not, for any purpose, constitute a suicide, euthanasia, or homicide.

(b) The making of a declaration pursuant to § 32-11-104 shall not affect in any manner the sale, procurement, or issuance of any policy of life insurance, nor shall it be deemed to modify the terms of an existing policy of life insurance. No policy of life insurance shall be legally impaired or invalidated in any manner by withholding or withdrawal of medical care from an insured declarant.

(c) No physician, health care facility, or other health care provider, and no health care service plan, insurer issuing disability insurance, self-insured employee welfare benefit plan, or nonprofit hospital plan, shall require any person to execute a declaration as a condition for being insured for, or receiving, health care services.

(d) Nothing in this chapter shall impair or supersede any legal right or legal responsibility which any person may have to effect the withholding or withdrawal of medical care in any lawful manner. In such respect, the provisions of this chapter are cumulative.

(e) This chapter shall create no presumption concerning the intention of an individual who has not executed a declaration to consent to the use, withholding, or withdrawal of medical care.

(f) A competent declarant, unable to sign his or her declaration, may make a signature as provided in section 1-3-105.

(g) If any provision of this chapter or the application thereof to any person or circumstances is held invalid, such invalidity shall not affect other provisions or applications of the chapter which can be given effect without the invalid provision or application, and to this end the provisions of this chapter are severable.

(h) No physician or health facility which, acting in accordance with the requirements of this chapter, causes the withholding or withdrawal of life-sustaining procedures from a patient, shall be subject to civil liability

therefrom. No health care provider, acting under the direction of a physician, who participates in the withholding or withdrawal of life-sustaining procedures in accordance with the provisions of this chapter shall be subject to any civil liability. No physician, or health care provider acting under the direction of a physician, who participates in the withholding or withdrawal of life-sustaining procedures in accordance with the provisions of this chapter shall be guilty of any criminal act or of unprofessional conduct.
(i) No physician or health care provider shall be subject to civil or criminal liability or considered guilty of unprofessional conduct as a result of actions under this chapter which are in accord with reasonable medical standards or as a result of another physician's or health care provider's actions or failure to act in accordance with the provisions of this chapter.

Texas: Natural Death Act

§ 672.001. Short title. This chapter may be cited as the Natural Death Act.
§ 672.002. Definitions. In this chapter:
(1) "Attending physician" means the physician who has primary responsibility for a patient's treatment and care.
(2) "Declarant" means a person who has executed or issued a directive under this chapter.
(3) "Directive" means an instruction made under Section 672.003, 672.005, or 672.006 to withhold or withdraw life-sustaining procedures in the event of a terminal condition.
(4) "Life-sustaining procedure" means a medical procedure or intervention that uses mechanical or other artificial means to sustain, restore, or supplant a vital function, and only artificially postpones the moment of death of a patient in a terminal condition whose death is imminent. The term does not include the administration of medication or the performance of a medical procedure considered necessary to provide comfort or care or to alleviate pain.
(5) "Physician" means a physician licensed by the Texas State Board of Medical Examiners or a properly credentialed physician who holds a commission in the United States armed forces and who is serving on active duty in this state.
(6) "Qualified patient" means a patient with a terminal condition that has been diagnosed and certified in writing by the attending physician and one other physician who have personally examined the patient.
(7) "Terminal condition" means an incurable condition caused by injury, disease, or illness that would produce death regardless of the application of life-sustaining procedures, according to reasonable medical judgment, and in which the application of life-sustaining procedures serves only to postpone the moment of the patient's death.
§ 672.003. Written directive by Competent Adult; Notice to Physician. (a) A competent adult may at any time execute a written directive.
(b) The declarant must sign the directive in the presence of two witnesses, and those witnesses must sign the directive.
(c) A witness may not be:
(1) related to the declarant by blood or marriage;
(2) entitled to any portion of the declarant's estate after the declarant's death under a will or codicil executed by the declarant or by operation of law;
(3) the attending physician;
(4) an employee of the attending physician or health care facility in which the declarant is a patient;
(5) a patient in a health care facility in which the declarant is a patient;
(6) a person who, at the time the directive is executed, has a claim against any part of the declarant's estate after the declarant's death.

(d) A declarant may include in a directive directions other than those provided by Section 672.004 and may designate in a directive a person to make a treatment decision for the declarant in the event the declarant becomes comatose, incompetent, or otherwise mentally or physically incapable of communication.
(e) A declarant shall notify the attending physician of the existence of a written directive. If the declarant is comatose, incompetent, or otherwise mentally or physically incapable of communication, another person may notify the attending physician of the existence of the written directive. The attending physician shall make the directive a part of the declarant's medical record.
§ 672.004. Form of Written Directive. A written directive may be in the following form. [*See Appendix A for a copy of the suggested form*—**ed. note.**]
§ 672.005. Issuance of Nonwritten Directive by Competent Adult Qualified Patient. (a) A competent qualified patient who is an adult may issue a directive by a nonwritten means of communication.
(b) A declarant must issue the nonwritten directive in the presence of the attending physician and two witnesses. The witnesses must possess the same qualifications as are required by Section 672.003(c).
(c) The physician shall make the fact of the existence of the directive a part of the declarant's medical record and the witnesses shall sign the entry in the medical record.
§ 672.006. Execution of Directive on Behalf of Patient Younger Than 18 Years of Age. The following persons may execute a directive on behalf of a qualified patient who is younger than 18 years of age:
(1) the patient's spouse, if the spouse is an adult;
(2) the patient's parents; or
(3) the patient's legal guardian.
§ 672.007. Patient Desire Supersedes Directive. The desire of a competent qualified patient, including a competent qualified patient younger than 18 years of age, supersedes the effect of a directive.
§ 672.008. Procedure When Declarant Is Incompetent or Incapable of Communication. (a) This section apples when an adult qualified patient has executed or issued a directive and is comatose, incompetent, or otherwise mentally or physically incapable of communication.
(b) If the adult qualified patient has designated a person to make a treatment decision as authorized by Section 672.003(d), the attending physician and the designated person may make a treatment decision to withhold or withdraw life-sustaining procedures from the patient.
(c) If the adult qualified patient has not designated a person to make a treatment decision, the attending physician shall comply with the directive unless the physician believes that the directive does not reflect the patient's present desire.
§ 672.009. Procedure When Person Has not Executed or Issued a Directive and is Incompetent or Incapable of Communication. (a) If an adult qualified patient has not executed or issued a directive and is comatose, incompetent, or otherwise mentally or physically incapable of communication, the attending physician and the patient's legal guardian may make a treatment decision that may include a decision to withhold or withdraw life-sustaining procedures from the patient.
(b) If the patient does not have a legal guardian, the attending physician and at least two persons, if available, of the following categories, in the following priority, may make a treatment decision that may include a decision to withhold or withdraw life-sustaining procedures:
(1) the patient's spouse;
(2) a majority of the patient's reasonably available adult children;
(3) the patient's parents; or
(4) the patient's nearest living relative.
(c) A treatment decision made under Subsection (a) or (b) must be based on knowledge of what the patient would desire, if known.
(d) A treatment decision made under Subsection (b) must be made in the presence of at least two witnesses who possess the same qualifications as are required by Section 672.003(c).
(e) The fact that an adult qualified patient has not executed or issued a directive does not create a presumption that the patient does not want a treatment decision to be made to withhold or withdraw life-sustaining procedures.

§ 672.010. Patient Certification and Prerequisites for Complying With Directive. (a) An attending physician who has been notified of the existence of a directive shall provide for the declarant's certification as a qualified patient on diagnosis of a terminal condition.
(b) Before withholding or withdrawing life-sustaining procedures from a qualified patient under this chapter, the attending physician must:
(1) determine that the patient's death is imminent, regardless of the application of life-sustaining procedures;
(2) note that determination in the patient's medical record; and
(3) determine that the steps proposed to be taken are in accord with this chapter and the patient's existing desires.
§ 672.011. Duration of Directive. A directive is effective until it is revoked as prescribed by Section 672.012.
§ 672.012. Revocation of Directive. (a) A declarant may revoke a directive at any time without regard to the declarant's mental state or competency. A directive may be revoked by:
(1) the declarant or someone in the declarant's presence and at the declarant's direction canceling, defacing, obliterating, burning, tearing, or otherwise destroying the directive;
(2) the declarant signing and dating a written revocation that expresses the declarant's intent to revoke the directive; or
(3) the declarant orally stating the declarant's intent to revoke the directive.
(b) A written revocation executed as prescribed by Subsection (a)(2) takes effect only when the declarant or a person acting on behalf of the declarant notifies the attending physician of its existence or mails the revocation to the attending physician. The attending physician or the physician's designee shall record in the patient's medical record the time and date when the physician received notice of the written revocation and shall enter the word "VOID" on each page of the copy of the directive in the patient's medical record.
(c) An oral revocation issued as prescribed by Subsection (a)(3) takes effect only when the declarant or a person acting on behalf of the declarant notifies the attending physician of the revocation. The attending physician or the physician's designee shall record in the patient's medical record the time, date, and place of the revocation and, if different, the time, date, and place that the physician received notice of the revocation. The attending physician or the physician's designees shall enter the word "VOID" on each page of the copy of the directive in the patient's medical records.
(d) Except as otherwise provided by this chapter, a person is not civilly or criminally liable for failure to act on a revocation made under this section unless the person has actual knowledge of the revocation.
§ 672.013. Reexecution of Directive. A declarant may at any time reexecute a directive in accordance with the procedures prescribed by Section 672.003, including reexecution after the declarant is diagnosed as having a terminal condition.
§ 672.014. Effect of Directive on Insurance Policy and Premiums. (a) The fact that a person has executed or issued a directive under this chapter does not:
(1) restrict, inhibit, or impair in any manner the sale, procurement, or issuance of a life insurance policy to that person; or
(2) modify the terms of an existing life insurance policy.
(b) Notwithstanding the terms of any life insurance policy, the fact that life-sustaining procedures are withheld or withdrawn from an insured qualified patient under this chapter does not legally impair or invalidate that person's life insurance policy.
(c) A physician, health facility, health provider, insurer, or health care service plan may not require a person to execute or issue a directive as a condition for obtaining insurance for health care services or receiving health care services.
(d) The fact that a person has executed or issued or failed to execute or issue a directive under this chapter may not be considered in any way in establishing insurance premiums.
§ 672.015. Limitation of Liability for Withholding or Withdrawing Life-Sustaining Procedures. (a) A physician or health facility that causes life-sustaining procedures to be withheld or withdrawn from a qualified patient in accordance with this chapter is not civilly liable for that action unless negligent.

(b) A health professional, acting under the direction of a physician, who participates in withholding or withdrawing life-sustaining procedures from a qualified patient in accordance with this chapter is not civilly liable for that action unless negligent.
(c) A physician, or a health professional acting under the direction of a physician, who participates in withholding or withdrawing life-sustaining procedures from a qualified patient in accordance with this chapter is not criminally liable or guilty of unprofessional conduct as a result of that action unless negligent.
§ 672.016. Limitation of Liability for Failure to Effectuate Directive. (a) A physician, health care facility, or health care professional who has no knowledge of a directive is not civilly or criminally liable for failing to act in accordance with the directive.
(b) A physician, or a health professional acting under the direction of a physician, is not civilly or criminally liable for failing to effectuate a qualified patient's directive.
(c) If an attending physician refuses to comply with a directive or treatment decision, the physician shall make a reasonable effort to transfer the patient to another physician.
§ 672.017. Honoring Directive Does not Constitute Offense of Aiding Suicide. A person does not commit an offense under Section 22.08, Penal Code, by withholding or withdrawing life-sustaining procedures from a qualified patient in accordance with this chapter.
§ 672.018. Criminal Penalty; Prosecution. (a) A person commits an offense if the person intentionally conceals, cancels, defaces, obliterates, or damages another person's directive without that person's consent. An offense under this subsection is a Class A misdemeanor.
(b) A person is subject to prosecution for criminal homicide under Chapter 19, Penal Code, if the person, with the intent to cause life-sustaining procedures to be withheld or withdrawn from another person contrary to the other person's desires, falsifies or forges a directive or intentionally conceals or withholds personal knowledge of a revocation and thereby directly causes life-sustaining procedures to be withheld or withdrawn from the other person with the result that the other person's death is hastened.
§ 672.019. Pregnant Patients. A person may not withdraw or withhold life-sustaining procedures under this chapter from a pregnant patient.
§ 672.020. Mercy killing not Condoned. This chapter does not condone, authorize, or approve mercy killing or permit an affirmative or deliberate act or omission to end life except to permit the natural process of dying as provided by this chapter.
§ 672.021. Legal Right or Responsibility not Affected. This chapter does not impair or supersede any legal right or responsibility a person may have to effect the withholding or withdrawal of life-sustaining procedures in a lawful manner.

Utah: Personal Choice and Living Will Act

§ 75-2-1101. Short title. This part is known as the "Personal Choice and Living Will Act."
§ 75-2-1102. Intent statement. (1) The legislature finds:
(a) developments in medical technology make possible many alternatives for treating medical conditions and make possible the unnatural prolongation of death;
(b) terminally ill persons should have the clear legal choice to be spared unwanted life-sustaining procedures, and be permitted to die with a maximum of dignity and a minimum of pain; and
(c) considerable uncertainty exists in the medical and legal professions as to the legality of terminating the use or application of life-sustaining procedures, even when a person in a terminal condition has evidenced a desire that the procedures be withheld or withdrawn.

(2) In recognition of the dignity and privacy which all persons are entitled to expect, and to protect the right of individuals to refuse to be touched or treated in any manner without their willing consent, the Legislature declares that this state recognizes the right to make binding written directives instructing physicians and other providers of medical services to withhold or withdraw, or to provide only to the extent set forth in a directive, life-sustaining and other medical procedures.

§ 75-2-1103. Definitions. As used in this part:

(1) "Agent" means any director, officer, employee, or other person authorized to act on behalf of a provider of medical services.

(2) "Attending physician" means the physician selected by or assigned to a person, who has primary responsibility for the treatment and care of the person.

(3) "Declarant" means a person 18 years of age or older who has signed or directed the signing of any directive, or for whom a directive has been signed under this part.

(4) "Directive" means a written document voluntarily executed by or on behalf of a person in accordance with the requirements of this part.

(5) "Provider of medical services" includes all persons licensed to provide medical services and all health care facilities, including hospitals, psychiatric hospitals, home health agencies, hospices, skilled nursing facilities, intermediate care facilities, intermediate care facilities for the mentally retarded, residential health care facilities, and facilities owned or operated by health maintenance organizations.

(6)(a) "Life-sustaining procedure" means any medical procedure or intervention which, when applied to a person who has been found under this part to have a terminal condition, would in the judgment of the attending physician serve only to prolong the dying process.

(b) Life-sustaining procedure does not include the administration of medication or sustenance, or the performance of any medical procedure deemed necessary to provide comfort care, or to alleviate pain.

(7) "Terminal condition" means a condition caused by injury, disease, or illness, which regardless of the application of life-sustaining procedures, would within reasonable medical judgment produce death, and where the application of life-sustaining procedures serves only to postpone the moment of death of the person.

(8) "In writing" means any printed or handwritten directive.

§ 75-2-1104. Directive for medical services. (1) A person 18 years of age or older may execute a directive under this part. The directive is binding upon attending physicians and all other providers of medical services.

(2) The directive shall be:

(a) in writing;

(b) signed by the declarant or by another person in the declarant's presence and by the declarant's expressed direction;

(c) dated; and

(d) signed in the presence of two or more witnesses 18 years of age or older.

(3) Neither of the witnesses may be:

(a) the person who signed the directive on behalf of the declarant;

(b) related to the declarant by blood or marriage;

(c) entitled to any portion of the estate of the declarant according to the laws of intestate succession of this state or under any will or codicil of the declarant;

(d) directly financially responsible for the declarant's medical care; or

(e) any agent of any health care facility in which the declarant is a patient at the time the directive is executed.

(4) The directive shall be in substantially this form. [*See Appendix A for a copy of the recommended form. The addition of personalized instructions is not forbidden by law*—**ed. note.**]

§ 75-2-1105. Directive for medical services after injury or illness is incurred. (1) (a) A person 18 years of age or older may, after incurring an injury, disease, or illness, direct his care by means of a directive made under this section, which is binding upon attending physicians and other providers of medical services.

(b) When a declarant has executed a directive under Section 75-2-1104 and is in a terminal condition, that directive takes precedence over a nonconflicting directive executed under this section. A directive executed by an attorney-in-fact appointed under Section 75-2-1106 takes precedence over all earlier signed directives.
(2) A directive made under this section shall be:
(a) in writing;
(b) signed by the declarant or by another person in the declarant's presence and by the declarant's expressed direction, or if the declarant does not have the ability to give current directions concerning his care and treatment, by the following persons, as proxy, in the following order of priority if no person in a prior class is available, willing, and competent to act:
(i) An attorney-in-fact appointed under Section 75-2-1106;
(ii) any previously appointed legal guardian of the declarant;
(iii) the person's spouse if not legally separated;
(iv) the parents or surviving parent;
(v) the person's child 18 years of age or older, or if the person has more than one child, by a majority of the children 18 years of age or older who are reasonably available for consultation upon good faith efforts to secure participation of all those children;
(vi) by the declarant's nearest reasonably available living relative 18 years of age or older if the declarant has no parent or child living;
(vii) by a legal guardian appointed for the purposes of this section;
(c) dated;
(d) signed, completed, and certified by the declarant's attending physician; and
(e) signed pursuant to Subsection (b) above in the presence of two or more witnesses 18 years of age or older.
(3) Neither of the witnesses may be:
(a) the person who signed the directive on behalf of the declarant;
(b) related to the declarant by blood or marriage;
(c) entitled to any portion of the declarant's estate according to the laws of intestate succession of this state or under any will or codicil of the declarant;
(d) directly financially responsible for declarant's medical care; or
(e) an agent of any health care facility in which the declarant is a patient or resident at the time of executing the directive.
(4) A directive executed under this section shall be in substantially the following form and shall contain a description by the attending physician of the declarant's injury, disease, or illness. It shall include specific directions for care and treatment or withholding of treatment. [*See Appendix A for a copy of this recommended form, a directive for medical services* after *injury or illness is incurred*—**ed. note.**]
§ 75-2-1106. Special power of attorney. (1) A person 18 years of age or older, the "principal," may designate any other person 18 years of age or older to execute a directive under Section 75-2-1105 on behalf of the principal after the principal incurs an injury, disease, or illness which renders him unable to make a directive, by executing a special power of attorney before a notary public, which shall be in substantially the following form. [*See Appendix C for a copy of this recommended form*—**ed. note.**]
(2) A directive executed by an attorney-in-fact appointed under this section takes precedence over all previously signed directives.
§ 75-2-1107. Medical services for terminally ill persons without a directive. (1) If a person 18 years of age or older has not executed a directive or power of attorney under this part and is unable to communicate, and the attending physician has determined that the person is in a terminal condition, life-sustaining procedures may be withheld or withdrawn under the supervision of the attending physician as provided in Subsections (2) and (3).
(2) The attending physician shall consult with and obtain written concurrence in writing of:
(a) another physician, that the person's condition is as described in Subsection (1); and
(b) any of the following persons in the following order of priority who is available, willing, and competent to act:

(i) a legal guardian, or the person's spouse;
(ii) a parent; or
(iii) the person's children 18 years of age or older.
(3) If a treatment decision is made by any of the parties named in Subsection (2) other than the legal guardian, at least two witnesses who are adults shall be present at the time of the decision and shall sign the document required in Subsection (2) recording the decision.
§ 75-2-1108. Current desires of declarant. The desires of a competent declarant, which can be determined directly or indirectly, at all times take precedence over and supersede any contrary directions contained in earlier signed directives.
§ 75-2-1109. Pregnancy. A directive which provides for the withholding or withdrawal of life-sustaining procedures has no force during the course of a declarant's pregnancy.
§ 75-2-1110. Notification to physician. It is the responsibility of the declarant or other signer of a directive to notify or provide for notification to attending physicians of the existence of a directive made under this part. Attending physicians who are notified shall make the directive or a copy of it a part of the declarant's medical records.
§ 75-2-1111. Revocation of directive. (1) A directive may be revoked at any time by the declarant if the declarant has signed it personally, or by the person or persons who signed a directive on behalf of a declarant, based on changed circumstances or conditions or a change of mind, and by:
(a) being obliterated, burned, torn, or otherwise destroyed or defaced in any manner indicating an intention to effect revocation;
(b) a written revocation of the directive signed and dated by the declarant or by a person signing on behalf of the declarant or acting at the direction of the declarant;
(c) oral expression of an intent to revoke the directive in the presence of a witness 18 years of age or older who signs and dates a written instrument confirming that the expression of intent was made.
(2) Any oral revocation not otherwise known to the attending physician becomes binding only upon receipt by the attending physician and other providers of medical services of a written revocation under Subsection 75-2-1111(b) or (c). The attending physician shall record in the declarant's medical record the time, date, and place when notice of a written revocation was received.
(3) There is no criminal or civil liability on the part of any person for failing to act upon a revocation made under this part unless that person has actual knowledge of the revocation.
§ 75-2-1112. Physician compliance with directive. (1) Attending physicians and other providers of medical services have a duty to cooperate with those authorized under the circumstances set forth in this part to make written directives concerning the administering or withholding of care and treatment and shall cooperate in making good faith medical certifications as provided in this part.
(2) Attending physicians and other providers of medical services who fail to comply with this part reasonably and without undue delay, or refuse or decline to comply with directives executed under this part shall promptly effect a transfer of the declarant to another physician or provider of medical services.
(3) Failure of an attending physician or other provider of medical services to comply with a directive executed under this part or to effect the transfer of the declarant to another physician or provider of medical services constitutes unprofessional conduct.
§ 75-2-1113. Presumption of validity of directive. A directive executed under this part is presumed valid and binding and physicians and other providers of medical services shall presume, in the absence of actual notice to the contrary, that a person who executes a directive, whether or not in the presence of the physician or other provider of medical services, is of sound mind and exercised discretion in the matter. The fact a person executed a directive is not to be construed as an indication that the person was suffering from any mental incompetency.
§ 75-2-1114. Physician liability for compliance with directive. Physicians, other providers of medical services, and their agents, who in good faith participate in the withholding or withdrawing of life-sustaining procedures or administer medical care or treatment in conformity with a directive, and persons who sign directives under this part or exercise rights on behalf of a declarant in signing a directive under this part, are

not subject to any criminal or civil proceeding or penalty and are not deemed to have committed an act of unprofessional conduct.

§ 75-2-1115. Illegal destruction or falsification of directive. (1) A person who willfully conceals, cancels, defaces, obliterates, or damages a directive of another without the declarant's consent or who falsifies or forges a revocation of the directive of another is guilty of a class A misdemeanor.

(2) A person who falsifies or forges the directive of another or willfully conceals or withholds personal knowledge of the revocation of a directive with the intent to cause a withholding or withdrawal of life-sustaining procedures contrary to the wishes of a declarant, and because of this action directly causes life-sustaining procedures to be withheld or withdrawn and death to be hastened is guilty of criminal homicide.

§ 75-2-1116. Compliance with directive is not suicide. Neither the withholding nor the withdrawal of life-sustaining procedures in the administration of medical treatment, nor the implementation of medical treatment choices expressed in directives executed under this part constitutes suicide nor the crime of assisting suicide.

§ 75-2-1117. No insurance or health care may require a directive. (1) The making of a directive under this part does not affect in any manner:

(a) the obligation of any life or medical insurance company regarding any policy of life or medical insurance;

(b) the sale, procurement, or issuance of any policy of life or health insurance; or

(c) the terms of any existing policy.

(2) A policy is not legally impaired or invalidated in any manner by the withholding or withdrawing of life-sustaining procedures or by the following of any directions in a directive executed as provided in this part, notwithstanding any terms of any policy to the contrary. Following procedures directed in a directive does not constitute legal cause for failing to promptly pay life insurance or health insurance benefits.

(3) A physician or other provider of medical services, a health care service, a planned health maintenance organization, an insurer issuing disability, health, or life insurance, a self-insured employee welfare or benefit plan, a nonprofit medical service corporation or mutual nonprofit hospital service corporation or any other person, firm, or entity may not require a person to execute a directive under this part as a condition for being insured for or receiving health care or life insurance contract services. However, nothing in this part may be construed to require any insurer to insure risks otherwise deemed unsuitable.

(4) Nothing in this part is intended to impair or supersede any other legal right or legal responsibility which a person may have to effect the withholding or withdrawal of life-sustaining procedures in any lawful manner.

(5) This part creates no presumption concerning the intention of a person who has not executed a directive to consent to or refuse the use or withholding of life-sustaining or other medical procedures.

§ 75-2-1118. Directive not mercy killing. Nothing in this part may be construed to condone, authorize, or approve mercy killing, euthanasia, or suicide.

Vermont: Terminal Care Document

§ 5251. Purpose and policy. The state of Vermont recognizes that a person as a matter of right may rationally make an election as to the extent of medical treatment he will receive in the event that his physical state reaches such a point of deterioration that he is in a terminal state and there is no reasonable expectation that life can be continued with dignity and without pain. A person has a fundamental right to determine whether or not life-sustaining procedures which would cause prolongation of life beyond natural limits should be used or withdrawn.

§ 5252. Definitions. The following definitions shall be applicable in the construction of this chapter:

(1) "Attending physician" means the physician selected by, or assigned to the patient, who has primary responsibility for the treatment and care of the patient.

(2) "Extraordinary measures" means any medical procedure or intervention which utilizes mechanical or other artificial means to sustain, restore, or supplant a vital function which, in the judgment of the attending physician, when applied to the patient, would serve only to artificially postpone the moment of death and where, in the judgment of the attending physician, the patient is in a terminal state.
(3) "Terminal care document" means a document which, when duly executed, contains the express direction that no extraordinary measures be taken when the person executing said document is in a terminal state, without hope of recovery from such state and is unable to actively participate in the decision-making process.
(4) "Physician" means a medical doctor licensed to practice in the state of Vermont.
(5) "Terminal state" means an incurable condition caused by injury, disease or illness which regardless of the application of life-saving procedures would, within reasonable medical judgment, produce death and where application of life-sustaining procedures would only postpone the moment of death.
§ 5253. Terminal care document. A person of sound mind who is 18 years of age or older may execute at any time a document commonly known as a terminal care document, directing that no extraordinary measures be used to prolong his life when he is in a terminal state. The document shall only be effective in the event that the person is incapable of participating in decisions about his care and may, but need not, be in form and substance substantially as follows. [*See Appendix A for a copy of the suggested form*—**ed. note.**]
§ 5254. Execution and witnesses. The document set forth in section 5253 of this title shall be executed by the person making the same in the presence of two or more subscribing witnesses, none of whom shall be the person's spouse, heir, attending physician or person acting under the direction or control of the attending physician, or any other person who has at the time of the witnessing thereof any claims against the estate of the person.
§ 5255. Reserved for future use.
§ 5256. Action by physician. An attending physician and any other physician under his direction or control, having in his possession his patient's terminal care document, or having knowledge that such a duly executed document is part of the patient's record in the institution in which he is receiving care, shall be bound to follow as closely as possible the dictates of said document. However, if because of moral conflict with the spirit of this act, a physician finds it impossible to follow his patient's directions, he shall forthwith have a duty to so inform his patient or actively assist in selecting another physician who is willing to honor the patient's directions, or both.
§ 5257. Revocation. A person who has validly executed a document consistent with the provisions of sections 5253 and 5254 may revoke the same orally in the presence of two or more witnesses, at least one of whom shall not be a spouse or a relative (as specified in 15 Vermont Statutes Annotated subsection 1 or 2), or by burning, tearing, or obliterating the same or by causing the same to be done by some other person at his direction and in his presence. A terminal care document may be revoked only as provided herein.
§ 5258. Duty to deliver. Any person having in his possession a duly executed terminal care document, if it becomes known to him that the person executing the same is in such circumstances that the terms of the terminal care document might become applicable, shall forthwith deliver the same to the physician attending the person executing said document or to the hospital in which said person is a patient.
§ 5259. Immunity. An attending physician, other physician, nurse, health professional or any other person acting for him or under his control, or hospital within which the person may be, shall forever be immune from any civil or criminal liability for any act or intentional failure to act if said act or intentional failure to act is done pursuant to the terminal care document.
§ 5260. Suicide. The withholding or withdrawal of life-sustaining procedures from a patient who has executed a document consistent with the purposes of section 5253 of this title shall at no time be construed as a suicide for any legal purpose.
§ 5261. Freedom from influence. No physician, health facility, or other health provider, and no health care service plan, insurer issuing disability insurance, self-insured employee welfare benefit plan, or nonprofit hospital service plan, shall require any person to execute a terminal care document as a condition for being insured for, or receiving, health care services; nor can health care or services be refused except as is hereinbefore provided because a person is known to have executed a terminal care document.

§ 5262. Presumptions. This chapter shall not be construed to create a presumption that in the absence of a terminal care document a person wants extraordinary measures to be taken.

Virginia: Natural Death Act

§ 54.1-2981. Short title. The provisions of this article shall be known and may be cited as the "Natural Death Act of Virginia."

§ 54.1-2982. Definitions. As used in this article:

"Attending physician" means the primary physician who has responsibility for the treatment and care of the patient.

"Declaration" means (i) a witnessed document in writing, voluntarily executed by the declarant in accordance with the requirements of § 54.1-2983 or (ii) a witnessed oral statement, made by the declarant subsequent to the time he is diagnosed as suffering from a terminal condition and in accordance with the provisions of § 54.1-2983.

"Life-prolonging procedure" means any medical procedure, treatment or intervention which (i) utilizes mechanical or other artificial means to sustain, restore or supplant a spontaneous vital function or is otherwise of such a nature as to afford a patient no reasonable expectation of recovery from a terminal condition and (ii) when applied to a patient in a terminal condition, would serve only to prolong the dying process; however, nothing in this act shall prohibit the administration of medication or the performance of any medical procedure deemed necessary to provide comfort care or to alleviate pain.

"Physician" means a person licensed to practice medicine in the Commonwealth of Virginia.

"Qualified patient" means a patient who has (i) made a declaration in accordance with this article and (ii) been diagnosed and certified in writing by the attending physician, (and, in any case where the patient is comatose, incompetent or otherwise physically or mentally incapable of communication, by one other physician who has examined the patient) to be afflicted with a terminal condition.

"Terminal condition" means a condition caused by injury, disease or illness from which, to a reasonable degree of medical certainty, (i) there can be no recovery, and (ii) death is imminent.

"Witness" means a person who is not a spouse or blood relative of the patient.

§ 54.1-2983. Procedure for making declaration; notice to physician. Any competent adult may, at any time, make a written declaration directing the withholding or withdrawal of life-prolonging procedures in the event such person should have a terminal condition. A written declaration shall be signed by the declarant in the presence of two subscribing witnesses. An oral declaration may be made by a competent adult in the presence of a physician and two witnesses by any nonwritten means of communication at any time subsequent to the diagnosis of a terminal condition.

It shall be the responsibility of the declarant to provide for notification to his attending physician that a declaration has been made. In the event the declarant is comatose, incompetent or otherwise mentally or physically incapable, any other person may notify the physician of the existence of a declaration. An attending physician who is so notified shall promptly make the declaration or a copy of the declaration, if written, a part of the declarant's medical records. If the declaration is oral, the physician shall likewise promptly make the fact of such declaration a part of the patient's medical record.

§ 54.1-2984. Suggested form of written declaration. A declaration executed pursuant to this article may, but need not, be in one of the following forms, and may include other specific directions including, but not limited to, a designation of another person to make the treatment decision for the declarant should he be (i) diagnosed as suffering from a terminal condition and (ii) comatose, incompetent or otherwise mentally or physically incapable of communication. Should any other specific directions be held to be invalid, such invalidity shall not affect the declaration. [*See Appendix A for a copy of the two suggested forms, the first of which gives the individual the option of delegating someone else to make the treatment decision for oneself in the event of a terminal condition and the second of which is a standard Living Will*—**ed. note.**]

§ 54.1-2985. Revocation of declaration. A declaration may be revoked at any time by the declarant (i) by a signed, dated writing; (ii) by physical cancellation or destruction of the declaration by the declarant or another in his presence and at his direction; or (iii) by oral expression of intent to revoke. Any such revocation shall be effective when communicated to the attending physician. No civil or criminal liability shall be imposed upon any person for a failure to act upon a revocation unless that person has actual knowledge of such revocation.

§ 54.1-2986. Procedure in absence of declaration; no presumption. Life-prolonging procedures may be withheld or withdrawn from an adult patient with a terminal condition who (i) is comatose, incompetent or otherwise physically or mentally incapable of communication and (ii) has not made a declaration in accordance with this article, provided there is consultation and agreement for the withholding or withdrawal of life-prolonging procedures between the attending physician and any of the following individuals, in the following order of priority if no individual in a prior class is reasonably available, willing and competent to act:

1. The judicially appointed guardian or committee of the person of the patient if one has been appointed. This subdivision shall not be construed to require such appointment in order that a treatment decision can be made under this section; or
2. The person or persons designated by the patient in writing to make the treatment decision for him should he be diagnosed as suffering from a terminal condition; or
3. The patient's spouse; or
4. An adult child of the patient or, if the patient has more than one adult child, by a majority of the children who are reasonably available for consultation; or
5. The parents of the patient; or
6. The nearest living relative of the patient.

In any case where the treatment decision is made by a person specified in subdivision 3, 4, 5 or 6, there shall be at least two witnesses present at the time of the consultation when the treatment decision is made, and life-prolonging procedures shall not be withdrawn or withheld pursuant to subdivision 3, 4, 5 or 6 herein without the consent of at least two of those persons set forth in such subdivisions, provided they are reasonably available.

The absence of a declaration by an adult patient shall not give rise to any presumption as to his intent to consent or to refuse life-prolonging procedures.

§ 54.1-2987. Transfer of patient by physician who refuses to comply with declaration or treatment decision. An attending physician who refuses to comply with the declaration of a qualified patient or the treatment decision of a person designated to make the decision (i) by the declarant in his declaration or (ii) pursuant to § 54.1-2986 shall make a reasonable effort to transfer the patient to another physician.

§ 54.1-2988. Immunity from liability; burden of proof; presumption. A health care facility, physician or other person acting under the direction of a physician shall not be subject to criminal prosecution or civil liability or be deemed to have engaged in unprofessional conduct as a result of the withholding or withdrawal of life-prolonging procedures from a patient with a terminal condition in accordance with this article. A person who authorizes the withholding or withdrawal of life-prolonging procedures from a patient with a terminal condition in accordance with a qualified patient's declaration or as provided in § 54.1-2986 shall not be subject to criminal prosecution or civil liability for such action.

The provisions of this section shall apply unless it is shown by a preponderance of the evidence that the person authorizing or effectuating the withholding or withdrawal of life-prolonging procedures did not, in good faith, comply with the provisions of this article. A declaration made in accordance with this article shall be presumed to have been made voluntarily.

§ 54.1-2989. Willful destruction, concealment, etc., of declaration or revocation; penalties. Any person who willfully conceals, cancels, defaces, obliterates, or damages the declaration of another without the declarant's consent or who falsifies or forges a revocation of the declaration of another, thereby causing life-prolonging procedures to be utilized in contravention of the previously expressed intent of the patient shall be guilty of a Class 6 felony.

Any person who falsifies or forges the declaration of another, or willfully conceals or withholds personal knowledge of the revocation of a declaration, with the intent to cause a withholding or withdrawal of life-prolonging procedures, contrary to the wishes of the declarant, and thereby, because of such act, directly causes life-prolonging procedures to be withheld or withdrawn and death to be hastened, shall be guilty of a Class 2 felony.

§ 54.1-2990. Mercy killing or euthanasia prohibited. Nothing in this article shall be construed to condone, authorize or approve mercy killing or euthanasia, or to permit any affirmative or deliberate act or omission to end life other than to permit the natural process of dying.

§ 54.1-2991. Effect of declaration; suicide; insurance; declarations executed prior to effective date. The withholding or withdrawal of life-prolonging procedures from a qualified patient in accordance with the provisions of this article shall not, for any purpose, constitute a suicide.

Nor shall the making of a declaration pursuant to this article affect the sale, procurement or issuance of any policy of life insurance, nor shall it be deemed to modify the terms of an existing policy of life insurance. No policy of life insurance shall be legally impaired or invalidated by the withholding or withdrawal of life-prolonging procedures from an insured qualified patient, notwithstanding any term of the policy to the contrary. A person shall not be required to make a declaration as a condition for being insured for, or receiving, health care services.

The declaration of any qualified patient made prior to July 1, 1983, shall be given effect as provided in this article.

§ 54.1-2992. Preservation of existing rights. The provisions of this article are cumulative with existing law regarding an individual's right to consent or refuse to consent to medical treatment and shall not impair any existing rights or responsibilities which a health care provider, a patient, including a minor or incompetent patient, or a patient's family may have in regard to the withholding or withdrawal of life-prolonging medical procedures under the common law or statutes of the Commonwealth.

Washington: Natural Death Act

§ 70.122.010. Legislative findings. The legislature finds that adult persons have the fundamental right to control the decisions relating to the rendering of their own medical care, including the decision to have life-sustaining procedures withheld or withdrawn in instances of a terminal condition.

The legislature further finds that modern medical technology has made possible the artificial prolongation of human life beyond natural limits.

The legislature further finds that, in the interest of protecting individual autonomy, such prolongation of life for persons with a terminal condition may cause loss of personal dignity, and unnecessary pain and suffering, while providing nothing medically necessary or beneficial to the patient.

The legislature further finds that there exists considerable uncertainty in the medical and legal professions as to the legality of terminating the use or application of life-sustaining procedures where the patient has voluntarily and in sound mind evidenced a desire that such procedures be withheld or withdrawn.

In recognition of the dignity and privacy which patients have a right to expect, the legislature hereby declares that the laws of the state of Washington shall recognize the right of an adult person to make a written directive instructing such person's physician to withhold or withdraw life-sustaining procedures in the event of a terminal illness.

§ 70.122.020. Definitions. Unless the context clearly requires otherwise, the definitions contained in this section shall apply throughout this chapter.

(1) "Attending physician" means the physician selected by, or assigned to, the patient who has primary responsibility for the treatment and care of the patient.

(2) "Directive" means a written document voluntarily executed by the declarer in accordance with the requirements of the Revised Code of Washington 70.122.030.

(3) "Health facility" means a hospital as defined in RCW 70.38.020(7) or a nursing home as defined in RCW 70.38.020(8).
(4) "Life-sustaining procedure" means any medical or surgical procedure or intervention which utilizes mechanical or other artificial means to sustain, restore, or supplant a vital function, which, when applied to a qualified patient, would serve only to artificially prolong the moment of death and where, in the judgment of the attending physician, death is imminent whether or not such procedures are utilized. "Life-sustaining procedure" shall not include the administration of medication or the performance of any medical procedure deemed necessary to alleviate pain.
(5) "Physician" means a person licensed under chapters 18.71 or 18.57 RCW.
(6) "Qualified patient" means a patient diagnosed and certified in writing to be afflicted with a terminal condition by two physicians one of whom shall be the attending physician, who have personally examined the patient.
(7) "Terminal condition" means an incurable condition caused by injury, disease, or illness, which, regardless of the application of life-sustaining procedures, would, within reasonable medical judgment, produce death, and where the application of life-sustaining procedures serve only to postpone the moment of death of the patient.
(8) "Adult person" means a person attaining the age of majority as defined in RCW 26.28.010 and 26.28.015.
§ 70.122.030. Directive to withhold or withdraw life-sustaining procedures. (1) Any adult person may execute a directive directing the withholding or withdrawal of life-sustaining procedures in a terminal condition. The directive shall be signed by the declarer in the presence of two witnesses not related to the declarer by blood or marriage and who would not be entitled to any portion of the estate of the declarer upon declarer's decease under any will of the declarer or codicil thereto then existing or, at the time of the directive, by operation of law then existing. In addition, a witness to a directive shall not be the attending physician, an employee of the attending physician or a health facility in which the declarer is a patient, or any person who has a claim against any portion of the estate of the declarer upon declarer's decease at the time of the execution of the directive. The directive, or a copy thereof, shall be made part of the patient's medical records retained by the attending physician, a copy of which shall be forwarded to the health facility upon the withdrawal of life-sustaining procedures. The directive shall be essentially in the following form, but in addition may include other specific directions. [*See Appendix A for a copy of the suggested form*—**ed. note.**]
(2) Prior to effectuating a directive the diagnosis of a terminal condition by two physicians shall be verified in writing, attached to the directive, and made a permanent part of the patient's medical records.
§ 70.122.040. Revocation of directive. (1) A directive may be revoked at any time by the declarer, without regard to declarer's mental state or competency, by any of the following methods:
(a) By being canceled, defaced, obliterated, burned, torn, or otherwise destroyed by the declarer or by some person in declarer's presence and by declarer's direction.
(b) By a written revocation of the declarer expressing declarer's intent to revoke, signed, and dated by the declarer. Such revocation shall become effective only upon communication to the attending physician by the declarer or by a person acting on behalf of the declarer. The attending physician shall record in the patient's medical record the time and date when said physician received notification of the revocation.
(c) By a verbal expression by the declarer of declarer's intent to revoke the directive. Such revocation shall become effective only upon communication to the attending physician by the declarer or by a person acting on behalf of the declarer. The attending physician shall record in the patient's medical record the time, date, and place of the revocation and the time, date, and place, if different, of when said physician received notification of the revocation.
(2) There shall be no criminal or civil liability on the part of any person for failure to act upon a revocation made pursuant to this section unless that person has actual or constructive knowledge of the revocation.
(3) If the declarer becomes comatose or is rendered incapable of communicating with the attending physician, the directive shall remain in effect for the duration of the comatose condition or until such time as the declarer's condition renders declarer able to communicate with the attending physician.

§ 70.122.050. Liability of health personnel, facilities. No physician or health facility which, acting in good faith in accordance with the requirements of this chapter, causes the withholding or withdrawal of life-sustaining procedures from a qualified patient, shall be subject to civil liability therefrom. No licensed health personnel, acting under the direction of a physician, who participates in good faith in the withholding or withdrawal of life-sustaining procedures in accordance with the provisions of this chapter shall be subject to any civil liability. No physician, or licensed health personnel acting under the direction of a physician, who participates in good faith in the withholding or withdrawal of life-sustaining procedures in accordance with the provisions of this chapter shall be guilty of any criminal act or of unprofessional conduct.

§ 70.122.060. Procedures by physician. (1) Prior to effectuating a withholding or withdrawal of life-sustaining procedures from a qualified patient pursuant to the directive, the attending physician shall make a reasonable effort to determine that the directive complies with the Revised Code of Washington 70.122.030 and, if the patient is mentally competent, that the directive and all steps proposed by the attending physician to be undertaken are currently in accord with the desires of the qualified patient.

(2) The directive shall be conclusively presumed, unless revoked, to be the directions of the patient regarding the withholding or withdrawal of life-sustaining procedures. No physician, and no licensed health personnel acting in good faith under the direction of a physician, shall be criminally or civilly liable for failing to effectuate the directive of the qualified patient pursuant to this subsection. If the physician refuses to effectuate the directive, such physician shall make a good faith effort to transfer the qualified patient to another physician who will effectuate the directive of the qualified patient.

§ 70.122.070. Effects of carrying out directive—Insurance. (1) The withholding or withdrawal of life-sustaining procedures from a qualified patient pursuant to the patient's directive in accordance with the provisions of this chapter shall not, for any purpose, constitute a suicide.

(2) The making of a directive pursuant to the Revised Code of Washington 70.122.030 shall not restrict, inhibit, or impair in any manner the sale, procurement, or issuance of any policy of life insurance, nor shall it be deemed to modify the terms of an existing policy of life insurance. No policy of life insurance shall be legally impaired or invalidated in any manner by the withholding or withdrawal of life-sustaining procedures from an insured qualified patient, notwithstanding any term of the policy to the contrary.

(3) No physician, health facility, or other health provider, and no health care service plan, insurer issuing disability insurance, self-insured employee welfare benefit plan, or nonprofit hospital service plan, shall require any person to execute a directive as a condition for being insured for, or receiving, health care services.

§ 70.122.080. Effects of carrying out directive on cause of death. The act of withholding or withdrawing life-sustaining procedures when done pursuant to a directive described in the Revised Code of Washington 70.122.030 and which causes the death of the declarer, shall not be construed to be an intervening force or to affect the chain of proximate cause between the conduct of any person that placed the declarer in a terminal condition and the death of the declarer.

§ 70.122.090. Criminal conduct—penalties. Any person who wilfully conceals, cancels, defaces, obliterates, or damages the directive of another without such declarer's consent shall be guilty of a gross misdemeanor. Any person who falsifies or forges the directive of another, or wilfully conceals or withholds personal knowledge of a revocation as provided in the Revised Code of Washington 70.122.040 with the intent to cause withholding or withdrawal of life-sustaining procedures contrary to the wishes of the declarer, and thereby, because of any such act, directly causes life-sustaining procedures to be withheld or withdrawn and death to thereby be hastened, shall be subject to prosecution for murder in the first degree as defined in RCW 9A.32.030.

§ 70.122.100. Mercy killing not authorized. Nothing in this chapter shall be construed to condone, authorize, or approve mercy killing, or to permit any affirmative or deliberate act or omission to end life other than to permit the natural process of dying.

§ 70.122.900. Short title. This act shall be known and may be cited as the "Natural Death Act."

§ 70.122.905. Severability. If any provision of this act or the application thereof to any person or circumstances is held invalid, such invalidity shall not affect other provisions or applications of the act which can be given effect without the invalid provisions or application, and to this end the provisions of this act are severable.

West Virginia: Natural Death Act

§ 16-30-1. Short title. This article shall be known and may be cited as the "West Virginia Natural Death Act."

§ 16-30-2. Definitions. For the purposes of this article, the terms:

(1) "Attending physician" means the physician selected by, or assigned to, the patient who has primary responsibility for the treatment and care of the patient;

(2) "Declaration" means a witnessed document in writing, voluntarily executed by the declarant in accordance with the requirements of section three [§ 16-30-3] of this article;

(3) "Life-sustaining procedure" means any medical procedure or intervention which, when applied to a qualified patient, would serve only to artificially prolong the dying process and where, in the judgment of the attending physician and a second physician, death will occur whether or not such procedure or intervention is utilized. The term "life-sustaining procedure" does not include the administration of medication or the performance of any medical procedure deemed necessary to provide comfort, care or alleviate pain;

(4) "Physician" means a person authorized to practice medicine in the State of West Virginia;

(5) "Qualified patient" means a patient who has executed a declaration in accordance with this article and who has been diagnosed and certified in writing to be afflicted with a terminal condition by two physicians who have personally examined the patient, one of whom is the attending physician: Provided, that if there be more than one attending physician, all such attending physicians must certify in writing that the patient is afflicted with a terminal condition; and

(6) "Terminal condition" means an incurable condition caused by injury, disease or illness, which, regardless of the application of life-sustaining procedures, would, within reasonable medical judgment, cause natural death and where the application of life-sustaining procedures serves only to postpone the moment of death.

§ 16-30-3. Executing a declaration. (a) Any person eighteen years of age or older may execute a declaration directing the withholding or withdrawal of life-sustaining procedures from themselves should they be in a terminal condition. The declaration made pursuant to this article shall be:

(1) In writing;

(2) signed by the person making the declaration or by another person in the declarant's presence at the declarant's express direction;

(3) dated;

(4) signed in the presence of two or more witnesses at least eighteen years of age; and

(5) signed and attested by such witnesses whose signatures and attestations shall be notarized.

(b) In addition, a witness may not be:

(1) The person who signed the declaration on behalf of and at the direction of the declarant;

(2) Related to the declarant by blood or marriage;

(3) Entitled to any portion of the estate of the declarant according to the laws of intestate succession of the State of West Virginia or under any will of the declarant or codicil thereto: Provided, that the validity of the declaration shall not be affected when a witness at the time of witnessing such declaration was unaware that he was a named beneficiary of the declarant's will;

(4) Directly financially responsible for declarant's medical care; or

(5) The attending physician, an employee of the attending physician or an employee of the health facility in which the declarant is a patient.

(c) It shall be the responsibility of the declarant to provide for notification to his or her attending physician of the existence of the declaration. An attending physician, when presented with the declaration, shall make the declaration or a copy of the declaration a part of the declarant's medical records.
(d) The declaration shall be substantially in the following form, but in addition may include other specific directions not inconsistent with other provisions of this article. Should any of the other specific directions be held to be invalid, such invalidity shall not affect other directions of the declaration which can be given effect without the invalid direction and to this end the directions in the declaration are severable. [*See Appendix A for a copy of the recommended form*—**ed. note.**]
§ 16-30-4. Revocation. (a) A declaration may be revoked at any time only by the declarant or at the express direction of the declarant, without regard to the declarant's mental state by any of the following methods:
(1) By being destroyed by the declarant or by some person in the declarant's presence and at his direction;
(2) By a written revocation of the declaration signed and dated by the declarant or person acting at the direction of the declarant. Such revocation shall become effective only upon communication of the revocation to the attending physician by the declarant or by a person acting on behalf of the declarant. The attending physician shall record in the patient's medical record the time and date when he or she receives notification of the written revocation; or
(3) By a verbal expression of the intent to revoke the declaration in the presence of a witness eighteen years of age or older who signs and dates a writing confirming that such expression of intent was made. Any verbal revocation shall become effective only upon communication of the revocation to the attending physician by the declarant or by a person acting on behalf of the declarant. The attending physician shall record, in the patient's medical record, the time, date and place of when he or she receives notification of the revocation.
(b) There is no criminal or civil liability on the part of any person for failure to act upon a revocation made pursuant to this section unless that person has actual knowledge of the revocation.
§ 16-30-5. Physician's duty to confirm terminal condition; chart identification. (a) An attending physician who has been notified of the existence of a declaration executed under this article, without delay after the diagnosis of a terminal condition of the declarant, shall take the necessary steps to provide for written certification and confirmation of the declarant's terminal condition so that the declarant may be deemed to be a qualified patient under this article.
(b) Once written certification and confirmation of the declarant's terminal condition is made, a person becomes a qualified patient under this article only if the attending physician verbally or in writing informs the patient of his or her terminal condition and documents such communication in the patient's medical record. If the patient is diagnosed as unable to comprehend verbal or written communications, such patient becomes a qualified patient as defined in section two [§ 16-30-2] of this article, immediately upon written certification and confirmation of his terminal condition by the attending physician.
(c) All inpatient health care facilities shall develop a system to visibly identify a qualified patient's chart which contains a declaration as set forth in this article.
§ 16-30-6. Competency and intent of declarant. (a) The desires of a qualified patient at all times supersede the effect of the declaration.
(b) If the qualified patient is incompetent at the time of the decision to withhold or withdraw life-sustaining procedures, a declaration executed in accordance with section three [§ 16-30-3] of this article is presumed to be valid. For the purposes of this article, a physician or health facility may presume in the absence of actual notice to the contrary that an individual who executed a declaration was of sound mind when it was executed. The fact that an individual executed a declaration is not an indication of a declarant's mental incompetency.
§ 16-30-7. Liability and protection of declaration; penalties. (a) No physician, licensed health care professional, health facility, or employee thereof who in good faith and pursuant to reasonable medical standards causes or participates in the withholding or withdrawing of life-sustaining procedures from a qualified patient pursuant to a declaration made in accordance with this article may, as a result thereof, be subject to criminal or civil liability.

(b) An attending physician who cannot comply with the declaration of a qualified patient pursuant to this article shall, in conjunction with the next of kin of the patient or other responsible individual, effect the transfer of the qualified patient to another physician who will honor the declaration of the qualified patient. Transfer under these circumstances does not constitute abandonment.
(c) Any person who willfully conceals, cancels, defaces, obliterates or damages the declaration of another without the declarant's consent or who falsifies or forges a revocation of the declaration of another is guilty of a felony, and, upon conviction thereof, shall be fined an amount not to exceed five thousand dollars or be imprisoned in the penitentiary for a period not to exceed three years, or both fined and imprisoned.
(d) Any person who falsifies or forges the declaration of another or willfully conceals or withholds personal knowledge of the revocation of a declaration with the intent to cause a withholding or withdrawal of life-sustaining procedures, contrary to the wishes of the declarant and, thereby, because of such act, directly causes life-sustaining procedures to be withheld or withdrawn and death to be hastened is guilty of a felony, and, upon conviction thereof, shall be imprisoned in the penitentiary not less than one nor more than five years.
§ 16-30-8. Insurance. (a) The withholding or withdrawal of life-sustaining procedures from a qualified patient in accordance with the provisions of this article does not, for any purpose, constitute a suicide and does not constitute the crime of assisting suicide.
(b) The making of a declaration pursuant to section three [§ 16-30-3] of this article does not affect in any manner the sale, procurement or issuance of any policy of life insurance, nor does it modify the terms of an existing policy of life insurance. No policy of life insurance may be legally impaired or invalidated in any manner by the withholding or withdrawal of life-sustaining procedures from an insured qualified patient, notwithstanding any term of the policy to the contrary.
(c) No physician, health facility or other health care provider and no health care service plan, health maintenance organization, insurer issuing disability insurance, self-insured employee welfare benefit plan, nonprofit medical service corporation or mutual nonprofit hospital service corporation may require any person to execute a declaration as a condition for being insured for or receiving health care services.
§ 16-30-9. Preservation of existing rights. (a) Nothing in this article impairs or supersedes any legal right or legal responsibility which any person may have to effect the withholding or withdrawal of life-sustaining procedures in any lawful manner. In such respect the provisions of this article are cumulative.
(b) This act creates no presumption concerning the intention of an individual who has not executed a declaration to consent to the use or withholding of life-sustaining procedures in the event of a terminal condition.
§ 16-30-10. Prohibition. Nothing in this article may be construed to condone, authorize or approve mercy killing or to permit any affirmative or deliberate act or omission to end a human life other than to permit the natural process of dying as provided in this article.

Wisconsin: Natural Death Act

§ 154.01. Definitions. In this chapter:
(1) "Attending physician" means a physician licensed under chapter 448 who has primary responsibility for the treatment and care of the patient.
(2) "Declaration" means a written, witnessed document voluntarily executed by the declarant under section 154.03(1), but is not limited in form or substance to that provided in section 154.03(2). Only the original declaration is a valid instrument.
(3) "Health care professional" means a person licensed, certified or registered under chapter 441, 448 or 455.
(4) "Inpatient health care facility" has the meaning provided under section 140.86(1) and includes community-based residential facilities, as defined in section 50.01(1g).
(5) "Life-sustaining procedure" means any medical procedure or intervention that, in the judgment of the attending physician, would serve only to prolong the dying process but not avert death when applied to a qualified patient. "Life-sustaining procedure" includes assistance in respiration, artificial maintenance of

blood pressure and heart rate, blood transfusion, kidney dialysis and other similar procedures, but does not include:

(a) The alleviation of pain by administering medication or by performing any medical procedure.

(b) The provision of fluid maintenance and nutritional support.

(6) "Qualified patient" means a declarant who has been diagnosed and certified in writing to be afflicted with a terminal condition by 2 physicians, one of whom is the attending physician, who have personally examined the declarant.

(7) "Responsible person" means the attending physician, a health care professional working with the declarant, an inpatient health care facility in which the declarant is located or the declarant's spouse, child, parent, brother, sister, grandparent or grandchild.

(8) "Terminal condition" means an incurable condition caused by injury or illness that reasonable medical judgment finds would cause death imminently, so that the application of life-sustaining procedures serves only to postpone the moment of death.

§ 154.03. Declaration to physicians. (1) Any person of sound mind and 18 years of age or older may at any time voluntarily execute a declaration authorizing the withholding or withdrawal of life-sustaining procedures when the person is in a terminal condition, which shall take effect on the date of execution. A declaration must be signed by the declarant in the presence of 2 witnesses. If the declarant is physically unable to sign a declaration, the declaration must be signed in the declarant's name by one of the witnesses or some other person at the declarant's express direction and in his or her presence; such a proxy signing shall either take place or be acknowledged by the declarant in the presence of 2 witnesses. Witnesses may not be related to the declarant by blood or marriage or entitled to any portion of the estate of the declarant upon his or her decease under any will of the declarant. The attending physician, the attending nurse or the attending medical staff, an employee of the attending physician or an employee of the inpatient health care facility in which the declarant is a patient who is a health care provider under section 146.81(1) and is involved in the medical care of the patient or any person with a claim against any portion of the estate of the declarant upon his or her death at the time of the execution of the declaration may not be a witness to a declaration. The declarant is responsible for notifying his or her attending physician of the existence of the declaration. An attending physician who is so notified shall make the original declaration a part of the declarant's medical record.

(1m) Notwithstanding subsection (1), an employee of the inpatient health care facility in which the declarant is a patient but who is not involved in the medical care or treatment of that patient may be a witness to the declaration, regardless of whether or not the inpatient health care facility may have a claim against the estate of the declarant.

(2) The department of health and social services shall prepare and provide copies of the declaration for distribution in quantities to health care professionals, hospitals, nursing homes, county clerks and local bar associations and individually to private persons. The department of health and social services may charge a reasonable fee for the cost of preparation and distribution. The declaration distributed by the department of health and social services shall be in the following form. [*See Appendix A for a copy of the required form. The law does not specifically prohibit the addition of personalized instructions*—**ed. note.**]

§ 154.05. Revocation of declaration.

(1) Method of revocation. A declaration may be revoked at any time by the declarant by any of the following methods:

(a) By being canceled, defaced, obliterated, burned, torn, or otherwise destroyed by the declarant or by some person who is directed by the declarant and who acts in the presence of the declarant.

(b) By a written revocation of the declarant expressing the intent to revoke, signed and dated by the declarant.

(c) By a verbal expression by the declarant of his or her intent to revoke the declaration. This revocation becomes effective only if the declarant or a person who is acting on behalf of the declarant notifies the attending physician of the revocation.

(2) Recording the revocation. The attending physician shall record in the patient's medical record the time, date and place of the revocation and the time, date and place, if different, that he or she was notified of the revocation.

§ 154.07. Duties and immunities.
(1) Liability. No physician, inpatient health care facility or health care professional acting under the direction of a physician may be held criminally or civilly liable, or charged with unprofessional conduct, for any of the following:
(a) Participating in the withholding or withdrawal of life-sustaining procedures under this chapter.
(b) Failing to act upon a revocation unless the person or facility has actual knowledge of the revocation.
(c) Failing to comply with a declaration, except that failure by a physician to comply with a declaration of a qualified patient constitutes unprofessional conduct if the physician refuses or fails to make a good faith attempt to transfer the qualified patient to another physician who will comply with the declaration.
(2) Effect of declaration. The desires of a qualified patient who is competent supersede the effect of the declaration at all times. If a qualified patient is incompetent at the time of the decision to withhold or withdraw life-sustaining procedures, a declaration executed under this chapter is presumed to be valid. The declaration of a qualified patient who is diagnosed as pregnant by the attending physician has no effect during the course of the qualified patient's pregnancy. For the purposes of this chapter, a physician or inpatient health care facility may presume in the absence of actual notice to the contrary that a person who executed a declaration was of sound mind at the time.
§ 154.11 General provisions.
(1) Suicide. The withholding or withdrawal of life-sustaining procedures from a qualified patient under this chapter does not, for any purpose, constitute suicide. Execution of a declaration under this chapter does not, for any purpose, constitute attempted suicide.
(2) Life insurance. Making a declaration under section 154.03 may not be used to impair in any manner the procurement of any policy of life insurance, and may not be used to modify the terms of an existing policy of life insurance. No policy of life insurance may be impaired in any manner by the withholding or withdrawal of life-sustaining procedures from an insured qualified patient.
(3) Health insurance. No person may be required to execute a declaration as a condition prior to being insured for, or receiving, health care services.
(4) Other rights. This chapter does not impair or supersede any person's legal right or responsibility to withhold or withdraw life-sustaining procedures.
(5) Intent. Failure to execute a declaration under this chapter creates no presumption that the person consents to the use or withholding of life-sustaining procedures in the event of a terminal condition.
(6) Construction. Nothing in this chapter condones, authorizes or permits any affirmative or deliberate act to end life other than to permit the natural process of dying.
(7) Applicability. (a) A declaration under section 154.03(2), 1983 statutes, that is executed before April 22, 1986, and that is not subsequently revoked or has not subsequently expired is governed by the provisions of chapter 154, 1983 statutes.
(b) A declaration under section 154.03(2), 1983 statutes, that is executed after April 22, 1986, is void.
§ 154.15. Penalties. (1) Any person who wilfully conceals, cancels, defaces, obliterates, or damages the declaration of another without the declarant's consent may be fined not more than $500 or imprisoned not more than 30 days or both.
(2) Any person who, with the intent to cause a withholding or withdrawal of life-sustaining procedures contrary to the wishes of the declarant, illegally falsifies or forges the declaration of another or conceals a declaration revoked under section 154.05(1)(a) or (b) or any responsible person who withholds personal knowledge of a revocation under section 154.05 shall be fined not more than $10,000 or imprisoned not more than 10 years or both.

Wyoming: Living Will Act

§ 35-22-101. Definitions. (a) As used in this act:

(i) "Attending physician" means the physician selected by, or assigned to, the patient who has primary responsibility for the treatment and care of the patient;
(ii) "Declaration" means a witnessed document in writing, voluntarily executed by the declarant in accordance with the requirements of Wyoming Statutes 35-22-102;
(iii) "Life-sustaining procedure" means any medical procedure or intervention which, when applied to a qualified patient, would serve only to prolong the dying process and where in the judgment of the attending physician, death will occur whether or not the procedure or intervention is utilized. Life-sustaining procedure does not include the administration of nourishment, medication or the performance of any medical procedure deemed necessary to provide comfort care or to alleviate pain;
(iv) "Physician" means a person licensed to practice medicine and surgery by the state board of medical examiners;
(v) "Qualified patient" means a patient who has executed a declaration in accordance with this act and who has been diagnosed and certified in writing to be afflicted with a terminal condition by two (2) physicians who have personally examined the patient, one (1) of whom shall be the attending physician;
(vi) "Terminal condition" means a condition caused by injury, disease or illness from which, to a reasonable degree of medical certainty, there can be no recovery and death is imminent;
(vii) "This act" means Wyoming Statutes 35-22-102 through 35-22-108.
§ 35-22-102. Declaration concerning life-sustaining procedures in terminal condition. (a) Any adult may execute a declaration directing the withholding or withdrawal of life-sustaining procedures in a terminal condition. The declaration made pursuant to this act shall be in writing, dated and signed by the person making the declaration, or by another person in the declarant's presence and by the declarant's expressed direction, and in the presence of two (2) or more adult witnesses. The witnesses shall not be:
(i) The person who signed the declaration on behalf of and at the direction of the person making the declaration;
(ii) Related to the declarant by blood or marriage;
(iii) Entitled to any portion of the estate of the declarant according to laws of intestate succession of this state or under any will of the declarant or codicil thereto; or
(iv) Directly financially responsible for the declarant's medical care.
(b) The declaration of a qualified patient diagnosed as pregnant by the attending physician shall have no effect during the course of the qualified patient's pregnancy.
(c) The declarant shall provide for notification to his or her attending physician of the existence of the declaration. An attending physician who is so notified shall make the declaration, or a copy of the declaration, a part of the declarant's medical records.
(d) The declaration may be substantially in the following form, but in addition may include other specific directions and need not include the designation of another person to make treatment decisions for the declarant. If any of the other specific directions are held to be invalid, the invalidity shall not affect other directions of the declaration which can be given effect without the invalid direction and to this end the directions in the declaration are severable. [*See Appendix A for a copy of the suggested form*—**ed. note.**]
§ 35-22-103. Revocation of declaration. (a) A declaration may be revoked at any time by the declarant by:
(i) Being obliterated, burned, torn or otherwise destroyed or defaced in a manner indicating intention to cancel; or
(ii) A written revocation of the declaration signed and dated by the declarant or person acting at the direction of the declarant; or
(iii) A verbal expression of the intent to revoke the declaration, in the presence of an adult witness who signs and dates a writing confirming that the expression of intent was made. Any verbal revocation is effective upon receipt by the attending physician of the above mentioned writing. The attending physician shall record in the patient's medical record the time, date and place of when he or she received a notification of the revocation.
(b) The desires of a qualified patient shall at all times supersede the effect of the declaration.

(c) There is no criminal or civil liability on the part of any person for failure to act upon a revocation made pursuant to this section unless that person has actual knowledge of this revocation.

§ 35-22-104. Duties of attending physician. (a) An attending physician who has been notified of the existence of a declaration executed under this act, without delay after the diagnosis of a terminal condition of the declarant, shall take the necessary steps to provide for written certification and confirmation of the declarant's terminal condition, so that declarant may be deemed to be a qualified patient under this act.

(b) An attending physician who refuses to comply with the declaration of a qualified patient pursuant to this act shall attempt to effect the transfer of the qualified patient to another physician.

§ 35-22-105. Effect of incompetency. If the qualified patient is incompetent at the time of the decision to withhold or withdraw life-sustaining procedures, a declaration executed in accordance with Wyoming Statutes 35-22-102 is presumed to be valid. For the purpose of this act, a physician or medical care facility may presume in the absence of actual notice to the contrary that an individual who executed a declaration was of sound mind when it was executed. The fact of an individual's having executed a declaration shall not be considered as an indication of a declarant's mental incompetency. Age of itself is not a bar to a determination of competency.

§ 35-22-106. Liability of medical personnel. No physician, licensed health care professional, medical care facility or employee thereof who in good faith and pursuant to reasonable medical standards causes or participates in the withholding or withdrawing of life-sustaining procedures from a qualified patient pursuant to a declaration made in accordance with this act shall, as a result thereof, be subjected to criminal or civil liability.

§ 35-22-107. Offenses; penalties. (a) Any person who willfully conceals, cancels, defaces, obliterates or damages the declaration of another without the declarant's consent or who falsifies or forges a revocation of the declaration of another is guilty of a misdemeanor punishable by imprisonment for six (6) months in county jail, a fine of seven hundred fifty dollars ($750.00), or both.

(b) Any person who falsifies or forges the declaration of another, or willfully conceals or withholds personal knowledge of the revocation of a declaration, with the intent to cause a withholding or withdrawal of life-sustaining procedures contrary to the wishes of the declarant, and thereby, because of that act, directly causes life-sustaining procedures to be withheld or withdrawn and death to be hastened, is guilty of a felony punishable by imprisonment for not to exceed twenty (20) years.

§ 35-22-108. Effect of declaration. (a) The withholding or withdrawal of life-sustaining procedures from a qualified patient in accordance with this act shall not, for any purpose, constitute a crime.

(b) The making of a declaration pursuant to Wyoming Statutes 35-22-102 shall not affect in any manner the sale, procurement or issuance of any policy of life insurance, nor shall it be deemed to modify the terms of an existing policy of life insurance. No policy of life insurance shall be legally impaired or invalidated in any manner by the withholding or withdrawal of life-sustaining procedures from an insured qualified patient, notwithstanding any term of the policy to the contrary.

(c) No physician, medical care facility or other health care provider and no health care service plan, health maintenance organization, insurer issuing disability insurance, self-insured employee welfare benefit plan, nonprofit medical service corporation or mutual nonprofit hospital service corporation shall require any person to execute a declaration as a condition for being insured for, or receiving, health care services.

(d) The provisions of this act are cumulative and nothing in this act impairs or supersedes any legal right or legal responsibility which any person may have to effect the withholding or withdrawal of life-sustaining procedures in any lawful manner.

(e) This act creates no presumption concerning the intention of an individual who has not executed a declaration to consent to the use or withholding of life-sustaining procedures in the event of a terminal condition.

§ 35-22-109. Construction of provisions. Nothing in this act shall be construed to condone, authorize or approve mercy killing or to permit any affirmative or deliberate act or omission to end life other than to permit the natural process of dying as provided in this act.

Appendix A

State-Mandated Living Will Forms

STATE OF ALABAMA

DECLARATION

Declaration made this .... day of ....(Month, year). I,.................................(Name), being of sound mind, willfully and voluntarily make known my desires that my dying shall not be artificially prolonged under the circumstances set forth below, do hereby declare:

If at any time I should have an incurable injury, disease, or illness certified to be a terminal condition by two physicians who have personally examined me, one of whom shall be my attending physician, and the physicians have determined that my death will occur whether or not life-sustaining procedures are utilized and where the application of life-sustaining procedures would serve only to artificially prolong the dying process, I direct that such procedures be withheld or withdrawn, and that I be permitted to die naturally with only the administration of medication or the performance of any medical procedure deemed necessary to provide me with comfort care.

In the absence of my ability to give directions regarding the use of such life-sustaining procedures, it is my intention that this declaration shall be honored by my family and physician(s) as the final expression of my legal right to refuse medical or surgical treatment and accept the consequences from such refusal.

I understand the full import of this declaration and I am emotionally and mentally competent to make this declaration.

Signed.......................................

City, County and State of Residence...

Date..

The declarant has been personally known to me and I believe him or her to be of sound mind. I did not sign the declarant's signature above for or at the direction of the declarant. I am not related to the declarant by blood or marriage, entitled to any portion of the estate of the declarant according to the laws of intestate succession or under any will of declarant or codicil thereto, or directly financially responsible for declarant's medical care.

Witness....................................

Witness....................................
Date..

STATE OF ALASKA

DECLARATION

If I should have an incurable or irreversible condition that will cause my death within a relatively short time, it is my desire that my life not be prolonged by administration of life-sustaining procedures.
If my condition is terminal and I am unable to participate in decisions regarding my medical treatment, I direct my attending physician to withhold or withdraw procedures that merely prolong the dying process and are not necessary to my comfort or to alleviate pain.
I [ ] do [ ] do not desire that nutrition or hydration (food and water) be provided by gastric tube or intravenously if necessary.
Signed this ....day of ...., ...

Signature......................................
Place...

The declarant is known to me and voluntarily signed or voluntarily directed another to sign this document in my presence.

Witness..

Address...

Witness..

Address...

State of...

......................................Judicial District

The foregoing instrument was acknowledged before me this ....(date) by ....(name of person acknowledged).

....
Signature of Person Taking Acknowledgment

....
Title or Rank

....
Serial Number, if any

THIS DECLARATION MUST EITHER BE WITNESSED BY TWO PERSONS OR ACKNOWLEDGED BY A PERSON QUALIFIED TO TAKE ACKNOWLEDGMENTS UNDER ALASKA STATUTES 09.63.010.

STATE OF ARIZONA

DECLARATION

Declaration made this ....day of ....(month, year).
I,.................................(name), being of sound mind, willfully and voluntarily make known my desire that my dying not be artificially prolonged under the circumstances set forth below and declare that:

If at any time I should have an incurable injury, disease or illness certified to be a terminal condition by two physicians who have personally examined me, one of whom is my attending physician, and the physicians have determined that my death will occur unless life-sustaining procedures are used and if the application of life-sustaining procedures would serve only to artificially prolong the dying process, I direct that life-sustaining procedures be withheld or withdrawn and that I be permitted to die naturally with only the administration of medication, food or fluids or the performance of medical procedures deemed necessary to provide me with comfort care.

In the absence of my ability to give directions regarding the use of life-sustaining procedures, it is my intention that this declaration be honored by my family and attending physician as the final expression of my legal right to refuse medical or surgical treatment and accept the consequences from such refusal.

I understand the full import of this declaration and I have emotional and mental capacity to make this declaration.

signed..

city, county, and state of residence...

The declarant is personally known to me and I believe him to be of sound mind.

witness...

witness...

STATE OF ARKANSAS

DECLARATION*

(*In the case of a patient who has a terminal condition.)

If I should have an incurable or irreversible condition that will cause my death within a relatively short time, and I am no longer able to make decisions regarding my medical treatment, I direct my attending physician, pursuant to the Arkansas Rights of the Terminally Ill or Permanently Unconscious Act, to [withhold or withdraw treatment that only prolongs the process of dying and is not necessary to my comfort or to alleviate pain] [follow the instructions of .... whom I appoint as my Health Care Proxy to decide whether life-sustaining treatment should be withheld or withdrawn].
Signed this ....day of.............., ...

Signature....................................
Address......................................

The declarant voluntarily signed this writing in my presence.
Witness......................................
Address......................................
Witness......................................
Address......................................

STATE OF ARKANSAS

DECLARATION**

(**In the case of a patient who is permanently unconscious)

If I should become permanently unconscious I direct my attending physician, pursuant to the Arkansas Rights of the Terminally Ill or Permanently Unconscious Act, to [withhold or withdraw life-sustaining treatments that are no longer necessary to my comfort or to alleviate pain] [follow the instructions of................................ whom I appoint as my health care proxy to decide whether life-sustaining treatment should be withheld or withdrawn].

Signed this ....day of........................, 19 ......
Signature...................................
Address.....................................

The declarant voluntarily signed this writing in my presence.
Witness.....................................
Address.....................................
Witness.....................................
Address.....................................

STATE OF CALIFORNIA

DIRECTIVE TO PHYSICIANS

Directive made this ....day of ....(month, year).

I, ..., being of sound mind, willfully, and voluntarily make known my desire that my life shall not be artificially prolonged under the circumstances set forth below, do hereby declare:

1. If at any time I should have an incurable injury, disease, or illness certified to be a terminal condition by two physicians, and where the application of life-sustaining procedures would serve only to artificially prolong the moment of my death and where my physician determines that my death is imminent whether or not life-sustaining procedures are utilized, I direct that such procedures be withheld or withdrawn, and that I be permitted to die naturally.

2. In the absence of my ability to give directions regarding the use of such life-sustaining procedures, it is my intention that this directive shall be honored by my family and physician(s) as the final expression of my legal right to refuse medical or surgical treatment and accept the consequences from such refusal.

3. If I have been diagnosed as pregnant and that diagnosis is known to my physician, this directive shall have no force or effect during the course of my pregnancy.

4. I have been diagnosed and notified at least 14 days ago as having a terminal condition by ....,M.D., whose address is ...., and whose telephone number is .... I understand that if I have not filled in the physician's name and address, it shall be presumed that I did not have a terminal condition when I made out this directive.

5. This directive shall have no force or effect five years from the date filled in above.

6. I understand the full import of this directive and I am emotionally and mentally competent to make this directive.

Signed...................................

City, County and State of Residence...

The declarant has been personally known to me and I believe him or her to be of sound mind.

Witness.................................

Witness.................................

STATE OF COLORADO

DECLARATION AS TO MEDICAL OR SURGICAL TREATMENT

I,....................................(name of declarant), being of sound mind and at least eighteen years of age, direct that my life shall not be artificially prolonged under the circumstances set forth below and hereby declare that:

1. If at any time my attending physician and one other physician certify in writing that:

a. I have an injury, disease, or illness which is not curable or reversible and which, in their judgment, is a terminal condition, and

b. For a period of seven consecutive days or more, I have been unconscious, comatose, or otherwise incompetent so as to be unable to make or communicate responsible decisions concerning my person, then

I direct that, in accordance with Colorado law, life-sustaining procedures shall be withdrawn and withheld pursuant to the terms of this declaration, it being understood that life-sustaining procedures shall not include any medical procedure or intervention for nourishment considered necessary by the attending physician to provide comfort or alleviate pain. However, I may specifically direct, in accordance with Colorado law, that artificial nourishment be withdrawn or withheld pursuant to the terms of this declaration.

2. In the event that the only procedure I am being provided is artificial nourishment, I direct that **one** of the following actions be taken:

(initials of declarant) a. Artificial nourishment shall not be continued when it is the only procedure being provided; or

(initials of declarant) b. Artificial nourishment shall be continued for ____ days when it is the only procedure being provided; or

(initials of declarant) c. Artificial nourishment shall be continued when it is the only procedure being provided.

3. I execute this declaration, as my free and voluntary act this............day of...................... 19......

By......................................
Declarant

The foregoing instrument was signed and declared by ....
to be his declaration, in the presence of us, who, in his presence, in the presence of each other, and at his request, have signed our names below as witnesses, and we declare that, at the time of the execution of this instrument, the declarant, according to our best knowledge and belief, was of sound mind and under no constraint or undue influence.

Dated at...................., Colorado, this............day of....................,19...

....
Name and Address

....
Name and Address

STATE OF COLORADO)
) ss.
County of________________)

SUBSCRIBED and sworn to before me by ....,
the declarant, and..and
...., witnesses, as the voluntary act and deed of the declarant, this.............day of
..............................., 19........

My commission expires:

....
Notary Public

STATE OF CONNECTICUT

LIVING WILL DOCUMENT

If the time comes when I am incapacitated to the point when I can no longer actively take part in decisions for my own life, and am unable to direct my physician as to my own medical care, I wish this statement to stand as a testament of my wishes. I..(name) request that I be allowed to die and not be kept alive through life support systems if my condition is deemed terminal. I do not intend any direct taking of my life, but only that my dying not be unreasonably prolonged. This request is made, after careful reflection, while I am of sound mind.

....(Signature)

....(Date)

....(Witness)

....(Witness)

DISTRICT OF COLUMBIA

DECLARATION

Declaration made this ......day of ....(month, year).

I, ...(name), being of sound mind, willfully and voluntarily make known my desires that my dying shall not be artificially prolonged under the circumstances set forth below, do declare:
If at any time I should have an incurable injury, disease, or illness certified to be a terminal condition by 2 physicians who have personally examined me, one of whom shall be my attending physician, and the physicians have determined that my death will occur whether or not life-sustaining procedures are utilized and where the application of life-sustaining procedures would serve only to artificially prolong the dying process, I direct that such procedures be withheld or withdrawn, and that I be permitted to die naturally with only the administration of medication or the performance of any medical procedure deemed necessary to provide me with comfort care or to alleviate pain.
In the absence of my ability to give directions regarding the use of such life-sustaining procedures, it is my intention that this declaration shall be honored by my family and physician(s) as the final expression of my legal right to refuse medical or surgical treatment and accept the consequences from such refusal.
I understand the full import of this declaration and I am emotionally and mentally competent to make this declaration.

Signed.......................................
Address.......................................

I believe the declarant to be of sound mind. I did not sign the declarant's signature above for or at the direction of the declarant. I am at least 18 years of age and am not related to the declarant by blood or marriage, entitled to any portion of the estate of the declarant according to the laws of intestate succession of the District of Columbia or under any will of the declarant or codicil thereto, or directly financially responsible for declarant's medical care. I am not the declarant's attending physician, an employee of the attending physician, or an employee of the health facility in which the declarant is a patient.

Witness.....................................

Witness.....................................

STATE OF FLORIDA

DECLARATION

Declaration made this........day of........................(month, year).

I, ...(name), willfully and voluntarily make known my desire that my dying not be artificially prolonged under the circumstances set forth below, and I do hereby declare:

If at any time I should have a terminal condition and if my attending physician has determined that there can be no recovery from such condition and that my death is imminent, I direct that life-prolonging procedures be withheld or withdrawn when the application of such procedures would serve only to prolong artificially the process of dying, and that I be permitted to die naturally with only the administration of medication or the performance of any medical procedure deemed necessary to provide me with comfort care or to alleviate pain.

In the absence of my ability to give directions regarding the use of such life-prolonging procedures, it is my intention that this declaration be honored by my family and physician as the final expression of my legal right to refuse medical or surgical treatment and to accept the consequences for such refusal.

If I have been diagnosed as pregnant and that diagnosis is known to my physician, this declaration shall have no force or effect during the course of my pregnancy.

I understand the full import of this declaration, and I am emotionally and mentally competent to make this declaration.

Signed.......................................

The declarant is known to me, and I believe him or her to be of sound mind.

Witness.....................................

Witness.....................................

STATE OF GEORGIA

"LIVING WILL

Living will made this.......day of.........................(month, year).

I,..................................., being of sound mind, willfully and voluntarily make known my desire that my life shall not be prolonged under the circumstances set forth below and do declare:

1. If at any time I should have a terminal condition as defined in and established in accordance with the procedures set forth in paragraph (10) of Code Section 31-32-2 of the Official Code of Georgia Annotated, I direct that the application of life-sustaining procedures to my body be withheld or withdrawn and that I be permitted to die;

2. In the absence of my ability to give directions regarding the use of such life-sustaining procedures, it is my intention that this living will shall be honored by my family and physician(s) as the final expression of my legal right to refuse medical or surgical treatment and accept the consequences from such refusal;

3. I understand that I may revoke this living will at any time;

4. I understand the full import of this living will, and I am at least 18 years of age and am emotionally and mentally competent to make this living will; and

5 If I am female and I have been diagnosed as pregnant, this living will shall have no force and effect during the course of my pregnancy.

Signed................................

.......................(City),............................(County), and

............................(State of Residence).

I hereby witness this living will and attest that:

(1) The declarant is personally known to me and I believe the declarant to be at least 18 years of age and of sound mind;

(2) I am at least 18 years of age;

(3) To the best of my knowledge, at the time of the execution of this living will, I:

(A) Am not related to the declarant by blood or marriage;

(B) Would not be entitled to any portion of the declarant's estate by any will or by operation of law under the rules of descent and distribution of this state;

(C) Am not the attending physician of declarant or an employee of the attending physician or an employee of the hospital or skilled nursing facility in which declarant is a patient;
(D) Am not directly financially responsible for the declarant's medical care; and
(E) Have no present claim against any portion of the estate of the declarant;

(4) Declarant has signed this document in my presence as above-instructed, on the date above first shown.

Witness...................................

Address...................................

Witness...................................

Address...................................

Additional witness required when living will is signed in a hospital or skilled nursing facility.

I hereby witness this living will and attest that I believe the declarant to be of sound mind and to have made this living will willingly and voluntarily.

Witness:..
Medical director of skilled nursing facility or staff physician not participating in care of the patient or chief of the hospital medical staff or staff physician not participating in care of the patient."

STATE OF HAWAII

DECLARATION

A. Statement of Declarant

Declaration made this .... day of ....(month, year). I, ...(name), being of sound mind, wilfully and voluntarily make known my desire that my dying shall not be artificially prolonged under the circumstances set forth below, and do hereby declare:

If at any time I should have an incurable or irreversible condition certified to be terminal by two physicians who have personally examined me, one of whom shall be my attending physician, and the physicians have determined that I am unable to make decisions concerning my medical treatment, and that without administration of life-sustaining treatment my death will occur in a relatively short time, and where the application of life-sustaining procedures would serve only to prolong artificially the dying process, I direct that such procedures be withheld or withdrawn, and that I be permitted to die naturally with only the administration of medication, nourishment, or fluids or the performance of any medical procedure deemed necessary to provide me with comfort care or to alleviate pain.

In the absence of my ability to give directions regarding the use of such life-sustaining procedures, it is my intention that this declaration shall be honored by my family and physician(s) as the final expressions of my legal right to refuse medical or surgical treatment and accept the consequences from such refusal.

I understand the full import of this declaration and I am emotionally and mentally competent to make this declaration.

Signed..................................
Address.................................

B. Statement of Witnesses

I am at least 18 years of age and

-not related to the declarant by blood, marriage, or adoption; and
-not the attending physician, an employee of the attending physician, or
an employee of the medical care facility in which the declarant is a patient.

The declarant is personally known to me and I believe the declarant to be of sound mind.

Witness................................
Address................................

Witness................................
Address................................

C. Notarization

Subscribed, sworn to and acknowledged before me by............................., the declarant, and subscribed and sworn to before me by ....and ...., witnesses, this .... day of................., 19......

(SEAL) Signed......................................
....
(official capacity of officer)

STATE OF IDAHO

A LIVING WILL

A Directive to Withhold or to Provide Treatment

To my family, my relatives, my friends, my physicians, my employers, and all others whom it may concern.

Directive made this........day of.............................., 19............ .I,..................................(name), being of sound mind, willfully, and voluntarily make known my desire that my life shall not be prolonged artificially under the circumstances set forth below, do hereby declare:

1. If at any time I should have an incurable injury, disease, illness or condition certified to be terminal by two medical doctors who have examined me, and where the application of life-sustaining procedures of any kind would serve only to prolong artificially the moment of my death, and where a medical doctor determines that my death is imminent, whether or not life-sustaining procedures are utilized, or I have been diagnosed as being in a persistent vegetative state, I direct that the following marked expression of my intent be followed and that I be permitted to die naturally, and that I receive medical treatment or care that may be required to keep me free of pain or distress.
"Check One Box"
❑ If at any time I should become unable to communicate my instructions, then I direct that all medical treatment, care, and nutrition and hydration necessary to restore my health, sustain my life, and to abolish or alleviate pain or distress be provided to me. Nutrition and hydration shall not be withheld or withdrawn from me if I would die from malnutrition or dehydration rather than from my injury, disease, illness or condition.
❑ If at any time I should become unable to communicate my instructions and where the application of artificial life-sustaining procedures shall serve only to prolong artificially the moment of my death, I direct such procedures be withheld or withdrawn except for the administration of nutrition and hydration.
❑ If at any time I should become unable to communicate my instructions and where the application of artificial life-sustaining procedures shall serve only to prolong artificially the moment of my death, I direct such procedures be withheld or withdrawn including withdrawal of the administration of nutrition and hydration.
2. In the absence of my ability to give directions regarding the use of life-sustaining procedures, I hereby appoint..........................(name) currently residing at.., as my attorney-in-fact/proxy for the making of decisions relating to my health care in my place; and it is my intention that this appointment shall be honored by him/her, by my family, relatives, friends, physicians and lawyer as the final expression of my legal right to refuse medical or surgical treatment; and I accept the consequences of such a decision. I have duly executed a Durable Power of Attorney for health care decisions on this date.
3. In the absence of my ability to give further directions regarding my treatment, including life-sustaining procedures, it is my intention that this directive shall be honored by my family and physicians as the final expression of my legal right to refuse or accept medical and surgical treatment, and I accept the consequences of such refusal.
4. If I have been diagnosed as pregnant and that diagnosis is known to any interested person, this directive shall have no force during the course of my pregnancy.
5. I understand the full importance of this directive and am emotionally and mentally competent to make this directive. No participant in the making of this directive or in its being carried into effect, whether it be a medical doctor, my spouse, a relative, friend or any other person shall be held responsible in any way, legally, professionally or socially, for complying with my directions.

Signed..
City, county and state of residence..

The declarant has been known to me personally and I believe him/her to be of sound mind.

Witness.......................................Witness...

Address.......................................Address...

[See Durable Power of Attorney for Health Care for the State of Idaho, in Appendix C]

STATE OF ILLINOIS

DECLARATION

This declaration is made this........day of........................(month, year).
I, ...(name), being of sound mind, willfully and voluntarily make known my desires that my moment of death shall not be artificially postponed.

If at any time I should have an incurable and irreversible injury, disease, or illness judged to be a terminal condition by my attending physician who has personally examined me and has determined that my death is imminent except for death delaying procedures, I direct that such procedures which would only prolong the dying process be withheld or withdrawn, and that I be permitted to die naturally with only the administration of medication, sustenance, or the performance of any medical procedure deemed necessary by my attending physician to provide me with comfort care.

In the absence of my ability to give directions regarding the use of such death delaying procedures, it is my intention that this declaration shall be honored by my family and physician as the final expression of my legal right to refuse medical or surgical treatment and accept the consequences from such refusal.

Signed................................

City, County and State of Residence..

The declarant is personally known to me and I believe him or her to be of sound mind. I saw the declarant sign the declaration in my presence (or the declarant acknowledged in my presence that he or she had signed the declaration) and I signed the declaration as a witness in the presence of the declarant. I did not sign the declarant's signature above for or at the direction of the declarant. At the date of this instrument, I am not entitled to any portion of the estate of the declarant according to the laws of intestate succession or, to the best of my knowledge and belief, under any will of declarant or other instrument taking effect at declarant's death, or directly financially responsible for declarant's medical care.

Witness..
Witness..

STATE OF INDIANA

LIVING WILL DECLARATION

Declaration made this........day of........................(month, year).
I, ...(name), being at least eighteen (18) years old and of sound mind, willfully and voluntarily make known my desires that my dying shall not be artificially prolonged under the circumstances set forth below, and I declare:

If at any time I have an incurable injury, disease, or illness certified in writing to be a terminal condition by my attending physician, and my attending physician has determined that my death will occur within a short period of time, and the use of life-prolonging procedures would serve only to artificially prolong the dying process, I direct that such procedures be withheld or withdrawn, and that I be permitted to die naturally with only the provision of appropriate nutrition and hydration and the administration of medication and the performance of any medical procedure necessary to provide me with comfort care or to alleviate pain.

In the absence of my ability to give directions regarding the use of life-prolonging procedures, it is my intention that this declaration be honored by my family and physician as the final expression of my legal right to refuse medical or surgical treatment and accept the consequences of the refusal.

I understand the full import of this declaration.

Signed...

City, County, and State of Residence..

The declarant has been personally known to me, and I believe (him/her) to be of sound mind. I did not sign the declarant's signature above for or at the direction of the declarant. I am not a parent, spouse, or child of the declarant. I am not entitled to any part of the declarant's estate or directly financially responsible for the declarant's medical care. I am competent and at least eighteen (18) years old.

Witness............................Date.........................

Witness............................Date.........................

****

INDIANA LIFE-PROLONGING PROCEDURES DECLARATION

Declaration made this........day of........................(month, year).
I, ...(name), being at least eighteen (18) years old and of sound mind, willfully and voluntarily make known my desire that if at any time I have an incurable injury, disease, or illness determined to be a terminal condition I request the use of life-prolonging procedures that would extend my life. This includes appropriate nutrition and hydration, the administration of medication, and the performance of all other medical procedures necessary to extend my life, to provide comfort care, or to alleviate pain.

In the absence of my ability to give directions regarding the use of life-prolonging procedures, it is my intention that this declaration be honored by my family and physician as the final expression of my legal right to request medical or surgical treatment and accept the consequences of the request.

I understand the full import of this declaration.

Signed..

City, County, and State of Residence..

The declarant has been personally known to me, and I believe (him/her) to be of sound mind. I am competent and at least eighteen (18) years old.

Witness....................................Date...........................

Witness....................................Date...........................

STATE OF IOWA

DECLARATION

If I should have an incurable or irreversible condition that will cause my death within a relatively short time, it is my desire that my life not be prolonged by administration of life-sustaining procedures. If my condition is terminal and I am unable to participate in decisions regarding my medical treatment, I direct my attending physician to withhold or withdraw procedures that merely prolong the dying process and are not necessary to my comfort or freedom from pain.

Signed this........day of.................., ...(month, year).

Signature..

City, County, and State of Residence...

The declarant is known to me and voluntarily signed this document in my presence.

Witness..

Address..

Witness..

Address..

STATE OF KANSAS

DECLARATION

Declaration made this........day of........................(month, year).
I, ...(name), being of sound mind, willfully and voluntarily make known my desire that my dying shall not be artificially prolonged under the circumstances set forth below, do hereby declare:

If at any time I should have an incurable injury, disease, or illness certified to be a terminal condition by two physicians who have personally examined me, one of whom shall be my attending physician, and the physicians have determined that my death will occur whether or not life-sustaining procedures are utilized and where the application of life-sustaining procedures would serve only to artificially prolong the dying process, I direct that such procedures be withheld or withdrawn, and that I be permitted to die naturally with only the administration of medication or the performance of any medical procedure deemed necessary to provide me with comfort care.

In the absence of my ability to give directions regarding the use of such life-sustaining procedures, it is my intention that this declaration shall be honored by my family and physician(s) as the final expression of my legal right to refuse medical or surgical treatment and accept the consequences from such refusal.

I understand the full import of this declaration and I am emotionally and mentally competent to make this declaration.

Signed...

City, County, and State of Residence...

The declarant has been personally known to me and I believe him or her to be of sound mind. I did not sign the declarant's signature above for or at the direction of the declarant. I am not related to the declarant by blood or marriage, entitled to any portion of the estate of the declarant according to the laws of intestate succession or under any will of declarant or codicil thereto, or directly financially responsible for declarant's medical care.

Witness..

Witness..

STATE OF KENTUCKY

DECLARATION

Declaration made this ...... day of ...., ... (month, year). I, ...willfully and voluntarily make known my desire that my dying shall not be artificially prolonged under the circumstances set forth below, and do hereby declare:

If at any time I should have a terminal condition and my attending and one (1) other physician in their discretion, have determined such condition is incurable and irreversible and will result in death within a relatively short time, and where the application of life-prolonging treatment would serve only to artificially prolong the dying process, I direct that such treatment be withheld or withdrawn, and that I be permitted to die naturally with only the administration of medication or the performance of any medical treatment deemed necessary to alleviate pain or for nutrition or hydration.

In the absence of my ability to give directions regarding the use of such life-prolonging treatment, it is my intention that this declaration shall be honored by my attending physician and my family as the final expression of my legal right to refuse medical or surgical treatment and I accept the consequences of such refusal.

If I have been diagnosed as pregnant and that diagnosis is known to my attending physician, this directive shall have no force or effect during the course of my pregnancy.

I understand the full import of this declaration and I am emotionally and mentally competent to make this declaration.

STATE OF KENTUCKY)
) Sct.
COUNTY OF......................)

Before me, the undersigned authority, on this day personally appeared ...., Living Will Declarant, and .... and ...., known to me to be witnesses whose names are each signed to the foregoing instrument, and all these persons being first duly sworn, ..., Living Will Declarant, declared to me and to the witnesses in my presence that the instrument is the Living Will Declaration of the declarant and that the declarant has willingly signed and that such declarant executed it as a free and voluntary act for the purposes therein expressed; and each of the witnesses stated to me, in the presence and hearing of the Living Will Declarant, that the declarant signed the declaration as witness and to the best of such witness's knowledge, the Living Will Declarant was eighteen (18) years of age or older, of sound mind and under no constraint or undue influence.

....
Living Will Declarant

....
Witness

....
Address

....
Witness

....
Address

Subscribed, sworn to and acknowledged before me by ...., Living Will Declarant, and subscribed and sworn before me by .... and ...., witnesses, on this the .... day of ....(year).

....
Notary Public State at Large

....
Date my commission expires

STATE OF LOUISIANA

DECLARATION

Declaration made this........day of........................(month, year).

I, ...(name), being of sound mind, willfully and voluntarily make known my desire that my dying shall not be artificially prolonged under the circumstances set forth below and do hereby declare:

If at any time I should have an incurable injury, disease, or illness certified to be a terminal and irreversible condition by two physicians who have personally examined me, one of whom shall be my attending physician, and the physicians have determined that my death will occur whether or not life-sustaining procedures are utilized and where the application of life-sustaining procedures would serve only to prolong artificially the dying process, I direct that such procedures be withheld or withdrawn and that I be permitted to die naturally with only the administration of medication or the performance of any medical procedure deemed necessary to provide me with comfort care.

In the absence of my ability to give directions regarding the use of such life-sustaining procedures, it is my intention that this declaration shall be honored by my family and physician(s) as the final expression of my legal right to refuse medical or surgical treatment and accept the consequences from such refusal.

I understand the full import of this declaration and I am emotionally and mentally competent to make this declaration.

Signed..

City, Parish and State of Residence...

The declarant has been personally known to me and I believe him or her to be of sound mind.

Witness..

Witness..

STATE OF MAINE

DECLARATION

If I should have an incurable or irreversible condition that will cause my death within a short time, and if I am unable to participate in decisions regarding my medical treatment, I direct my attending physician to withhold or withdraw procedures that merely prolong the dying process and are not necessary to my comfort or freedom from pain.

Signed this........day of.......................................(Month, year).

Signature..

City, County, and
State of Residence..

The declarant is known to me and voluntarily signed this document in my presence.

Witness...

Address...

....

Witness...

Address...

....

STATE OF MARYLAND

"DECLARATION

On this ......day of ....(month, year), I, ...(name), being of sound mind, willfully and voluntarily direct that my dying shall not be artificially prolonged under the circumstances set forth in this declaration.

If at any time I should have an incurable injury, disease, or illness certified to be a terminal condition by two (2) physicians who have personally examined me, one (1) of whom shall be my attending physician, and the physicians have determined that my death is imminent and will occur whether or not life-sustaining procedures are utilized and where the application of such procedures would serve only to artificially prolong the dying process, I direct that such procedures be withheld or withdrawn, and that I be permitted to die naturally with only the administration of medication, the administration of food and water, and the performance of any medical procedure that is necessary to provide comfort care or alleviate pain. In the absence of my ability to give directions regarding the use of such life-sustaining procedures, it is my intention that this declaration shall be honored by my family and physician(s) as the final expression of my right to control my medical care and treatment.

I am legally competent to make this declaration, and I understand its full import.

Signed..

Address...

....

Under penalty of perjury, we state that this declaration was signed by................................ in the presence of the undersigned who, at....................... request, in ....presence, and in the presence of each other, have hereunto signed our names as witnesses this........day of...................... 19..... Further, each of us individually, states that: The declarant is known to me, and I believe the declarant to be of sound mind. I did not sign the declarant's signature to this declaration. Based upon information and belief, I am not related to the declarant by blood or marriage, a creditor of the declarant, entitled to any portion of the estate of the declarant under any existing testamentary instrument of the declarant, entitled to any financial benefit by reason of the death of the declarant, financially or otherwise responsible for the declarant's medical care, nor an employee of any such person or institution.

....   Address.......................................

....

....   Address.......................................

...."

STATE OF MINNESOTA

"HEALTH CARE DECLARATION

Notice:
This is an important legal document. Before signing this document, you should know these important facts:

(a) This document gives your health care providers or your designated proxy the power and guidance to make health care decisions according to your wishes when you are in a terminal condition and cannot do so. This document may include what kind of treatment you want or do not want and under what circumstances you want these decisions to be made. You may state where you want or do not want to receive any treatment.
(b) If you name a proxy in this document and that person agrees to serve as your proxy, that person has a duty to act consistently with your wishes. If the proxy does not know your wishes, the proxy has the duty to act in your best interests. If you do not name a proxy, your health care providers have a duty to act consistently with your instructions or tell you that they are unwilling to do so.
(c) This document will remain valid and in effect until and unless you amend or revoke it. Review this document periodically to make sure it continues to reflect your preferences. You may amend or revoke the declaration at any time by notifying your health care providers.
(d) Your named proxy has the same right as you have to examine your medical records and to consent to their disclosure for purposes related to your health care or insurance unless you limit this right in this document.
(e) If there is anything in this document that you do not understand, you should ask for professional help to have it explained to you.
TO MY FAMILY, DOCTORS, AND ALL THOSE CONCERNED WITH MY CARE:
I, ..., being an adult of sound mind, willfully and voluntarily make this statement as a directive to be followed if I am in a terminal condition and become unable to participate in decisions regarding my health care. I understand that my health care providers are legally bound to act consistently with my wishes, within the limits of reasonable medical practice and other applicable law. I also understand that I have the right to make medical and health care decisions for myself as long as I am able to do so and to revoke this declaration at any time.

(1) The following are my feelings and wishes regarding my health care (you may state the circumstances under which this declaration applies):
....
....
....
....
(2) I particularly want to have all appropriate health care that will help in the following ways (you may give instructions for care you do want):
....
....
....
....
(3) I particularly do not want the following (you may list specific treatment you do not want in certain circumstances):
....
....
(4) I particularly want to have the following kinds of life-sustaining treatment if I am diagnosed to have a terminal condition (you may list the specific types of life-sustaining treatment that you do want if you have a terminal condition):

....
....
....
....

(5) I particularly do not want the following kinds of life-sustaining treatment if I am diagnosed to have a terminal condition (you may list the specific types of life-sustaining treatment that you do not want if you have a terminal condition):

....
....
....
....

(6) I recognize that if I reject artificially administered sustenance, then I may die of dehydration or malnutrition rather than from my illness or injury. The following are my feelings and wishes regarding artificially administered sustenance should I have a terminal condition (you may indicate whether you wish to receive food and fluids given to you in some other way than by mouth if you have a terminal condition):

....
....
....
....

(7) Thoughts I feel are relevant to my instructions. (You may, but need not, give your religious beliefs, philosophy, or other personal values that you feel are important. You may also state preferences concerning the location of your care.)

....
....
....
....

(8) Proxy designation. (If you wish, you may name someone to see that your wishes are carried out, but you do not have to do this. You may also name a proxy without including specific instructions regarding your care. If you name a proxy, you should discuss your wishes with that person.)

If I become unable to communicate my instructions, I designate the following person(s) to act on my behalf consistently with my instructions, if any, as stated in this document. Unless I write instructions that limit my proxy's authority, my proxy has full power and authority to make health care decisions for me. If a guardian or conservator of the person is to be appointed for me, I nominate my proxy named in this document to act as guardian or conservator of my person.

Name:..
Address:..
Phone Number:..
Relationship: (If any) ....

If the person I have named above refuses or is unable or unavailable to act on my behalf, or if I revoke that person's authority to act as my proxy, I authorize the following person to do so:

Name:..
Address:..
Phone Number:..
Relationship: (if any) ....

I understand that I have the right to revoke the appointment of the persons named above to act on my behalf at any time by communicating that decision to the proxy or my health care provider.

DATE:..
SIGNED:..
STATE OF: ....

COUNTY OF:...

Subscribed, sworn to, and acknowledged before me by .... on this ....day of ...., 19.....

....

NOTARY PUBLIC

OR

(Sign and date here in the presence of two adult witnesses, neither of whom is entitled to any part of your estate under a will or by application of law, and neither of whom is your proxy.)
I certify that the declarant voluntarily signed this declaration in my presence and that the declarant is personally known to me. I am not named as a proxy by the declaration, and to the best of my knowledge, I am not entitled to any part of the estate of the declarant under a will or by operation of law.

Witness............................Address...................................

Witness............................Address...................................

STATE OF MISSISSIPPI

DECLARATION OF INTENT

DECLARATION made on................(date) by....................................(person's name) of ....(address),..........................(Social Security Number).

I, ..., being of sound mind, declare that if at any time I should suffer a terminal physical condition which causes me severe distress or unconsciousness, and my physician, with the concurrence of two (2) other physicians, believes that there is no expectation of my regaining consciousness or a state of health that is meaningful to me and but for the use of life-sustaining mechanisms my death would be imminent, I desire that the mechanisms be withdrawn so that I may die naturally. However, if I have been diagnosed as pregnant and that diagnosis is known to my physician, this declaration shall have no force or effect during the course of my pregnancy. I further declare that this declaration shall be honored by my family and my physician as the final expression of my desires concerning the manner in which I die.

SIGNED...

I hereby witness this declaration and attest that:
(1) I personally know the Declarant and believe the Declarant to be of sound mind.
(2) To the best of my knowledge, at the time of the execution of this declaration, I:
(a) Am not related to the Declarant by blood or marriage,
(b) Do not have any claim on the estate of the Declarant,
(c) Am not entitled to any portion of the Declarant's estate by any will or by operation of law, and
(d) Am not a physician attending the Declarant or a person employed by a physician attending the Declarant.

WITNESS..

ADDRESS..

SOCIAL SECURITY NUMBER..................................

WITNESS..

ADDRESS..

SOCIAL SECURITY NUMBER..................................

[This declaration shall be filed with the bureau of vital statistics of the state board of health.]

STATE OF MISSISSIPPI

REVOCATION OF DECLARATION

On.................(date), I, ..., (person's name), of .... (address), ... (Social Security Number), being of sound mind, revoke the declaration made on................................(date declaration made) regarding the manner in which I die.

SIGNED..

I hereby witness this revocation and attest that:
(1) I personally know the maker of this revocation and believe the maker of this revocation to be of sound mind.
(2) To the best of my knowledge, at the time of the execution of this revocation, I:
(a) Am not related to the maker of this revocation by blood or marriage,
(b) Do not have any claim on the estate of the maker of this revocation,
(c) Am not entitled to any portion of the estate of the maker of this revocation by any will or by operation of law, and
(d) Am not a physician attending the maker of the revocation or a person employed by a physician attending the maker of this revocation.

WITNESS....................................

ADDRESS....................................

SOCIAL SECURITY NUMBER................................

WITNESS....................................

ADDRESS....................................

SOCIAL SECURITY NUMBER................................

[This revocation shall be filed with the bureau of vital statistics of the state board of health.]

STATE OF MISSOURI

DECLARATION

I have the primary right to make my own decisions concerning treatment that might unduly prolong the dying process. By this declaration I express to my physician, family and friends my intent. If I should have a terminal condition it is my desire that my dying not be prolonged by administration of death-prolonging procedures. If my condition is terminal and I am unable to participate in decisions regarding my medical treatment, I direct my attending physician to withhold or withdraw medical procedures that merely prolong the dying process and are not necessary to my comfort or to alleviate pain. It is not my intent to authorize affirmative or deliberate acts or omissions to shorten my life rather only to permit the natural process of dying.

Signed this........day of......................................

Signature..

City, County, and State of Residence...

The declarant is known to me, is eighteen years of age or older, of sound mind and voluntarily signed this document in my presence.

Witness..

Address..

Witness..

Address..

REVOCATION PROVISION

I hereby revoke the above declaration,

Signed......................................
(Signature of Declarant)

Date...

STATE OF MONTANA

DECLARATION

If I should have an incurable or irreversible condition that will cause my death within a relatively short time, it is my desire that my life not be prolonged by administration of life-sustaining procedures. If my condition is terminal and I am unable to participate in decisions regarding my medical treatment, I direct my attending physician to withhold or withdraw procedures that merely prolong the dying process and are not necessary to my comfort or freedom from pain. It is my intention that this declaration shall be valid until revoked by me.

Signed this........day of...................., ...

Signature...

City, County, and State of Residence......................................

The declarant is known to me and voluntarily signed this document in my presence.

Witness...

Address...

Witness...

Address...

STATE OF NEVADA

DIRECTIVE TO PHYSICIANS

Date..

I, ...(name), being of sound mind, intentionally and voluntarily declare:

1. If at any time I am in a terminal condition and become comatose or am otherwise rendered incapable of communicating with my attending physician, and my death is imminent because of an incurable disease, illness or injury, I direct that life-sustaining procedures be withheld or withdrawn, and that I be permitted to die naturally.

2. It is my intention that this directive be honored by my family and attending physician as the final expression of my legal right to refuse medical or surgical treatment and to accept the consequences of my refusal.

3. If I have been found to be pregnant, and that fact is known to my physician, this directive is void during the course of my pregnancy. I understand the full import of this directive, and I am emotionally and mentally competent to execute it.

Signed.......................................

City, County, and State of Residence...

The declarant has been personally known to me and I believe
.... to be of sound mind.

Witness......................................

Witness......................................

[Section 3 of the declaration form should be omitted for male declarants.]

STATE OF NEW HAMPSHIRE

DECLARATION

Declaration made this........day of.............(month, year).
I, ...(name), being of sound mind, willfully and voluntarily make known my desire that my dying shall not be artificially prolonged under the circumstances set forth below, do hereby declare:
If at any time I should have an incurable injury, disease, or illness certified to be a terminal condition by 2 physicians who have personally examined me, one of whom shall be my attending physician, and the physicians have determined that my death will occur whether or not life-sustaining procedures are utilized and where the application of life-sustaining procedures would serve only to artificially prolong the dying process, I direct that such procedures be withheld or withdrawn, and that I be permitted to die naturally with only the administration of medication, sustenance, or the performance of any medical procedure deemed necessary to provide me with comfort care.
In the absence of my ability to give directions regarding the use of such life-sustaining procedures, it is my intention that this declaration shall be honored by my family and physicians as the final expression of my right to refuse medical or surgical treatment and accept the consequences of such refusal.
I understand the full import of this declaration, and I am emotionally and mentally competent to make this declaration.

Signed...

State of..................................
...........................County

We, the declarant and witnesses, being duly sworn each declare to the notary public or justice of the peace or other official signing below as follows:
1. The declarant signed the instrument as a free and voluntary act for the purposes expressed, or expressly directed another to sign for him.
2. Each witness signed at the request of the declarant, in his presence, and in the presence of the other witness.
3. To the best of my knowledge, at the time of the signing the declarant was at least 18 years of age, and was of sane mind and under no constraint or undue influence.

.................................Declarant
...................................Witness
...................................Witness

The affidavit shall be made before a notary public or justice of the peace or other official authorized to administer oaths in the place of execution, who shall not also serve as a witness, and who shall complete and sign a certificate in content and form substantially as follows:

Sworn to me and signed before me by ...., declarant
.... and ...., witnesses
on.......................................
....
Signature
....
Official Capacity

STATE OF NORTH CAROLINA

"DECLARATION OF A DESIRE FOR A NATURAL DEATH"

"I, ...(name), being of sound mind, desire that my life not be prolonged by extraordinary means if my condition is determined to be terminal and incurable. I am aware and understand that this writing authorizes a physician to withhold or discontinue extraordinary means.
"This the........day of....................................
Signature..

"I hereby state that the declarant, ..., being of sound mind signed the above declaration in my presence and that I am not related to the declarant by blood or marriage and that I do not know or have a reasonable expectation that I would be entitled to any portion of the estate of the declarant under any existing will or codicil of the declarant or as an heir under the Intestate Succession Act if the declarant died on this date without a will. I also state that I am not the declarant's attending physician or an employee of the declarant's attending physician, or an employee of a health facility in which the declarant is a patient or an employee of a nursing home or any group-care home where the declarant resides. I further state that I do not now have any claim against the declarant.
Witness...
Witness.."

The clerk or the assistant clerk, or a notary public may, upon proper proof, certify the declaration as follows:

"CERTIFICATE"
"I, ..., Clerk (Assistant Clerk) of Superior Court or Notary Public (circle one as appropriate) for .... County hereby certify that ...., the declarant, appeared before me and swore to me and to the witnesses in my presence that this instrument is his Declaration Of A Desire For A Natural Death, and that he had willingly and voluntarily made and executed it as his free act and deed for the purposes expressed in it.
"I further certify that ....and ...., witnesses, appeared before me and swore that they witnessed ...., declarant, sign the attached declaration, believing him to be of sound mind; and also swore that at the time they witnessed the declaration (i) they were not related within the third degree to the declarant or to the declarant's spouse, and (ii) they did not know or have a reasonable expectation that they would be entitled to any portion of the estate of the declarant upon the declarant's death under any will of the declarant or codicil thereto then existing or under the Intestate Succession Act as it provides at that time, and (iii) they were not a physician attending the declarant or an employee of an attending physician or an employee of a health facility in which the declarant was a patient or an employee of a nursing home or any group-care home in which the declarant resided, and (iv) they did not have a claim against the declarant. I further certify that I am satisfied as to the genuineness and due execution of the declaration.
"This the ....day of ....
Clerk (Assistant Clerk) of Superior Court or
Notary Public (circle one as appropriate)
for the County of ...."

The above declaration may be proved by the clerk or the assistant clerk, or a notary public in the following manner:
(1) Upon the testimony of the two witnesses; or
(2) If the testimony of only one witness is available, then
a. Upon the testimony of such witness, and

b. Upon proof of the handwriting of the witness who is dead or whose testimony is otherwise unavailable, and

c. Upon proof of the handwriting of the declarant, unless he signed by his mark; or upon proof of such other circumstances as will satisfy the clerk or assistant clerk of the superior court, or a notary public as to the genuineness and due execution of the declaration.

(3) If the testimony of none of the witnesses is available, such declaration may be proved by the clerk or assistant clerk, or a notary public

a. Upon proof of the handwriting of the two witnesses whose testimony is unavailable, and

b. Upon compliance with paragraph c of subdivision (2) above.

Due execution may be established, where the evidence required above is unavoidably lacking or inadequate, by testimony of other competent witnesses as to the requisite facts.

The testimony of a witness is unavailable within the meaning of this subsection when the witness is dead, out of the State, not to be found within the State, insane or otherwise incompetent, physically unable to testify or refuses to testify.

If the testimony of one or both of the witnesses is not available the clerk or the assistant clerk, or a notary public or superior court may, upon proper proof, certify the declaration as follows:

"CERTIFICATE"

"I, ..., Clerk (Assistant Clerk) of Court for the Superior Court or Notary Public (circle one as appropriate) of .... County hereby certify that based upon the evidence before me I am satisfied as to the genuineness and due execution of the attached declaration by ...., declarant, and that the declarant's signature was witnessed by .... and ...., who at the time of the declaration met the qualifications of G.S.90-321(c)(3).

"This the........day of......................., ...

....

Clerk (Assistant Clerk) of Superior Court or
Notary Public (circle one as appropriate) for
..........................County."

STATE OF NORTH DAKOTA

DECLARATION TO WITHDRAW OR WITHHOLD LIFE-PROLONGING TREATMENT

Declaration made this ....day of .... (month, year).
I, ...(name), being at least eighteen years of age and of sound mind, willfully and voluntarily make known my desire that my life must not be artificially prolonged under the circumstances set forth below, and do hereby declare:
1. If at any time I should have an incurable condition caused by injury, disease, or illness certified to be a terminal condition by two physicians, and where the application of life-prolonging treatment would serve only to artificially prolong the process of my dying and my attending physician determines that my death is imminent whether or not life-prolonging treatment is utilized, I direct that such treatment be withheld or withdrawn, and that I be permitted to die naturally.
2. In the absence of my ability to give directions regarding the use of such life-prolonging treatment, it is my intention that this declaration be honored by my family and physicians as the final expression of my legal right to refuse medical or surgical treatment and accept the consequences of that refusal, which is death.
3. If I have been diagnosed as pregnant and that diagnosis is known to my physician, this declaration is not effective during the course of my pregnancy.
4. I understand the full import of this declaration and I am emotionally and mentally competent to make this declaration.
5. I understand that I may revoke this declaration at any time.

Signed..

City, County, and State of Residence...

The declarant has been personally known to me and I believe the declarant to be of sound mind. I am not related to the declarant by blood or marriage, nor would I be entitled to any portion of the declarant's estate upon the declarant's death. I am not the declarant's attending physician, a person who has a claim against any portion of the declarant's estate upon the declarant's death, or a person directly financially responsible for the declarant's medical care.

Witness..

Witness..

STATE OF NORTH DAKOTA

DECLARATION TO DIRECT THE USE OF LIFE-PROLONGING TREATMENT

Declaration made this ....day of .... (month, year).

I, ...(name), being at least eighteen years of age and of sound mind, willfully and voluntarily make known my desire to extend my life under the circumstances set forth below, and do hereby declare:

1. If at any time I should have an incurable condition caused by injury, disease, or illness certified to be a terminal condition by two physicians, I direct the use of life-prolonging treatment that could extend my life.

2. In the absence of my ability to give directions regarding the use of such life-prolonging treatment, it is my intention that this declaration be honored by my family and physicians as the final expression of my legal right to direct medical or surgical treatment and accept the consequences of that directive.

3. I understand the full import of this declaration and I am emotionally and mentally competent to make this declaration.

4. I understand that I may revoke this declaration at any time.

Signed...

City, County, and State of Residence..

The declarant has been personally known to me and I believe the declarant to be of sound mind. I am not related to the declarant by blood or marriage, nor would I be entitled to any portion of the declarant's estate upon the declarant's death. I am not the declarant's attending physician, a person who has a claim against any portion of the declarant's estate upon the declarant's death, or a person directly financially responsible for the declarant's medical care.

Witness......................................

Witness......................................

STATE OF OKLAHOMA

DIRECTIVE TO PHYSICIANS

Directive made this........day of................(month, year).
I, ...(name), being of sound mind and twenty-one (21) years of age or older, willfully and voluntarily make known my desire that my life shall not be artificially prolonged under the circumstances set forth below, and do hereby declare:

1. If at any time I should have an incurable irreversible condition caused by injury, disease, or illness certified to be a terminal condition by two physicians, I direct that life-sustaining procedures be withheld or withdrawn and that I be permitted to die naturally, if the application of life-sustaining procedures would serve only to artificially prolong the moment of my death and my attending physician determines that my death is imminent whether or not life-sustaining procedures are utilized;

2. In the absence of my ability to give directions regarding the use of such life-sustaining procedures, it is my intention that this directive shall be honored by my family and physicians as the final expression of my legal right to refuse medical or surgical treatment and accept the consequences of such refusal;

3. If I have been diagnosed as pregnant and that diagnosis is known to my physician, this directive shall have no force or effect during the course of my pregnancy;

4. I have been diagnosed and notified as having a terminal condition by ...., M.D. or D.O., whose address is ...., and whose telephone number is .... I understand that if I have not filled in the name and address of the physician, it shall be presumed that I did not have a terminal condition when I made out this directive;

5. This directive shall be in effect until it is revoked;

6. I understand the full import of this directive and I am emotionally and mentally competent to make this directive;

7. I understand that I may revoke this directive at any time.

Signed..................................

City, County, and State of Residence..

The declarant has been personally known to me and I believe said declarant to be of sound mind. I am twenty-one (21) years of age or older, I am not related to the declarant by blood or marriage, nor would I be entitled to any portion of the estate of the declarant upon the death of said declarant, nor am I the attending physician of the declarant or an employee of the attending physician or a health care facility in which the declarant is a patient, or a patient in the health care facility in which the declarant is a patient, nor am I financially responsible for the medical care of the declarant, or any person who has a claim against any portion of the estate of the declarant upon the death of the declarant.

Witness..

Witness..

State of Oklahoma
County of.................................
Before me, the undersigned authority, on this day personally appeared...................................... (declarant), ... (witness) and............................ (witness) whose names are subscribed to the foregoing instrument in their respective capacities, and, all of said persons being by me duly sworn, the declarant declared to me and to the said witnesses in my presence that said instrument is his or her "Directive to Physicians," and that the declarant had willingly and voluntarily made and executed it as the free act and deed of the declarant for the purposes therein expressed.

The foregoing instrument was acknowledged before me this........day of ...., 19......

Signed................................
Notary Public in and for
.... County, Oklahoma

My Commission Expires ....day of....................., 19.......

STATE OF OREGON

DIRECTIVE TO PHYSICIANS

Directive made this........day of ....(month, year).
I, ...(name), being of sound mind, wilfully and voluntarily make known my desire that my life shall not be artificially prolonged under the circumstances set forth below and do hereby declare:

1. If at any time I should have an incurable injury, disease or illness certified to be a terminal condition by two physicians, one of whom is the attending physician, and where the application of life-sustaining procedures would serve only to artificially prolong the moment of my death and where my physician determines that my death is imminent whether or not life-sustaining procedures are utilized, I direct that such procedures be withheld or withdrawn, and that I be permitted to die naturally.

2. In the absence of my ability to give directions regarding the use of such life-sustaining procedures, it is my intention that this directive shall be honored by my family and physician(s) as the final expression of my legal right to refuse medical or surgical treatment and accept the consequences from such refusal.

3. I understand the full import of this directive and I am emotionally and mentally competent to make this directive.

Signed.....................................

City, County, and State of Residence...

I hereby witness this directive and attest that:

(1) I personally know the Declarant and believe the Declarant to be of sound mind.

(2) To the best of my knowledge, at the time of the execution of this directive, I:
(a) Am not related to the Declarant by blood or marriage,
(b) Do not have any claim on the estate of the Declarant,
(c) Am not entitled to any portion of the Declarant's estate by any will or by operation of law, and
(d) Am not a physician attending the Declarant, a person employed by a physician attending the Declarant or a person employed by a health facility in which the Declarant is a patient.

(3) I understand that if I have not witnessed this directive in good faith I may be responsible for any damages that arise out of giving this directive its intended effect.

Witness.......................................

Witness.......................................

STATE OF SOUTH CAROLINA

DECLARATION OF A DESIRE FOR A NATURAL DEATH

COUNTY OF ....
I, ...(name), being at least eighteen years of age and a resident of and domiciled in the City of ...., County of ....,
State of South Carolina, make this Declaration this........day of ...., 19......
I wilfully and voluntarily make known my desire that no life-sustaining procedures be used to prolong my dying if my condition is terminal, and I do hereby declare:
If at any time I have a condition certified to be a terminal condition by two physicians who have personally examined me, one of whom is my attending physician, and the physicians have determined that my death will occur within a relatively short period of time without the use of life-sustaining procedures and where the application of life-sustaining procedures would serve only to prolong the dying process, I direct that the procedures be withheld or withdrawn, and that I be permitted to die naturally with only the administration of medication or the performance of any medical procedure necessary to provide me with comfort care.
In the absence of my ability to give directions regarding the use of such life-sustaining procedures, it is my intention that this Declaration be honored by my family and physicians and any health facility in which I may be a patient as the final expression of my legal right to refuse medical or surgical treatment, and I accept the consequences from such refusal.
I am aware that this Declaration authorizes a physician to withhold or withdraw life-sustaining procedures.
I am emotionally and mentally competent to make this Declaration.
THIS DECLARATION MAY BE REVOKED:
(1) BY BEING DEFACED, TORN, OBLITERATED, OR OTHERWISE DESTROYED, IN EXPRESSION OF THE DECLARANT'S INTENT TO REVOKE, BY THE DECLARANT OR BY SOME PERSON IN THE PRESENCE OF AND BY THE DIRECTION OF THE DECLARANT. REVOCATION BY DESTRUCTION OF ONE OR MORE OF MULTIPLE ORIGINAL DECLARATIONS REVOKES ALL OF THE ORIGINAL DECLARATIONS. THE REVOCATION OF THE ORIGINAL DECLARATIONS ACTUALLY NOT DESTROYED BECOMES EFFECTIVE ONLY UPON COMMUNICATION TO THE ATTENDING PHYSICIAN. THE ATTENDING PHYSICIAN SHALL RECORD IN THE DECLARANT'S MEDICAL RECORD THE TIME AND DATE WHEN THE PHYSICIAN RECEIVED NOTIFICATION OF THE REVOCATION;
(2) BY A WRITTEN REVOCATION SIGNED AND DATED BY THE DECLARANT EXPRESSING HIS OR HER INTENT TO REVOKE. THE REVOCATION BECOMES EFFECTIVE ONLY UPON COMMUNICATION TO THE ATTENDING PHYSICIAN. THE ATTENDING PHYSICIAN SHALL RECORD IN THE DECLARANT'S MEDICAL RECORD THE TIME AND DATE WHEN THE PHYSICIAN RECEIVED NOTIFICATION OF THE WRITTEN REVOCATION.
(3) BY AN ORAL EXPRESSION BY THE DECLARANT OF HIS INTENT TO REVOKE THE DECLARATION. THE REVOCATION BECOMES EFFECTIVE ONLY UPON COMMUNICATION TO THE ATTENDING PHYSICIAN BY THE DECLARANT. HOWEVER, AN ORAL REVOCATION MADE BY THE DECLARANT BECOMES EFFECTIVE UPON COMMUNICATION TO THE ATTENDING PHYSICIAN BY A PERSON OTHER THAN THE DECLARANT IF:
(a) THE PERSON WAS PRESENT WHEN THE ORAL REVOCATION WAS MADE;
(b) THE REVOCATION WAS COMMUNICATED TO THE PHYSICIAN WITHIN A REASONABLE TIME;
(c) THE PHYSICAL OR MENTAL CONDITION OF THE DECLARANT MAKES IT IMPOSSIBLE FOR THE PHYSICIAN TO CONFIRM THROUGH SUBSEQUENT CONVERSATION WITH THE DECLARANT THAT THE REVOCATION HAS OCCURRED.
THE ATTENDING PHYSICIAN SHALL RECORD IN THE PATIENT'S MEDICAL RECORD THE TIME, DATE, AND PLACE OF THE REVOCATION AND THE TIME, DATE, AND PLACE, IF DIF-

FERENT, OF WHEN HE RECEIVED NOTIFICATION OF THE REVOCATION. TO BE EFFECTIVE AS A REVOCATION, THE ORAL EXPRESSION CLEARLY MUST INDICATE A DESIRE THAT THE DECLARATION NOT BE GIVEN EFFECT OR THAT LIFE-SUSTAINING PROCEDURES BE ADMINISTERED.

(4) BY A WRITTEN, SIGNED, AND DATED REVOCATION OR AN ORAL REVOCATION BY A PERSON DESIGNATED BY THE DECLARANT IN THE DECLARATION, EXPRESSING THE DESIGNEE'S INTENT PERMANENTLY OR TEMPORARILY TO REVOKE THE DECLARATION, THE REVOCATION BECOMES EFFECTIVE ONLY UPON COMMUNICATION TO THE ATTENDING PHYSICIAN BY THE DESIGNEE. THE ATTENDING PHYSICIAN SHALL RECORD IN THE DECLARANT'S MEDICAL RECORD THE TIME, DATE, AND PLACE OF THE REVOCATION AND THE TIME, DATE, AND PLACE, IF DIFFERENT, OF WHEN THE PHYSICIAN RECEIVED NOTIFICATION OF THE REVOCATION. A DESIGNEE MAY REVOKE ONLY IF THE DECLARANT IS INCOMPETENT TO DO SO. IF THE DECLARANT WISHES TO DESIGNATE A PERSON WITH AUTHORITY TO REVOKE THE DECLARATION ON HIS BEHALF, THE NAME AND ADDRESS OF THAT PERSON MUST BE ENTERED BELOW:

.... ADDRESS...

NAME OF DESIGNEE

....

Declarant

STATE OF .... **AFFIDAVIT**

COUNTY OF ....

We, ... and.................................., the undersigned witnesses to the foregoing Declaration, dated the........day of ...., 19...., being first duly sworn, declare to the undersigned authority, on the basis of our best information and belief, that the Declaration was on that date signed by the declarant as and for his **DECLARATION OF A DESIRE FOR A NATURAL DEATH** in our presence and we, at his request and in his presence, and in the presence of each other, subscribe our names as witnesses on that date. The declarant is personally known to us, and we believe him to be of sound mind. Each of us affirms that he is qualified as a witness to this Declaration under the provisions of the South Carolina Death With Dignity Act in that he is not related to the declarant by blood or marriage, either as a spouse, lineal ancestor, descendant of the parents of the declarant, or spouse of any of them; nor directly financially responsible for the declarant's medical care; nor entitled to any portion of the declarant's estate upon his decease, whether under any will or as an heir by intestate succession; nor the beneficiary of a life insurance policy of the declarant; nor the declarant's attending physician; nor an employee of the attending physician; nor a person who has a claim against the declarant's decedent's estate as of this time. No more than one of us is an employee of a health facility in which the declarant is a patient. If the declarant is a patient in a hospital or skilled or intermediate care nursing facility at the date of execution of this Declaration at least one of us is an ombudsman designated by the State Ombudsman, Office of the Governor.

....

Witness

....

Witness

Subscribed before me by ....,

the declarant, and subscribed and sworn to before me by .... and ....,

the witnesses, this........day of ...., 19.....

Notary Public for ....

My commission expires: ....

SEAL

STATE OF TENNESSEE

LIVING WILL

I, ...(name), willfully and voluntarily make known my desire that my dying shall not be artificially prolonged under the circumstances set forth below, and do hereby declare:

If at any time I should have a terminal condition and my attending physician has determined that there can be no recovery from such condition and my death is imminent, where the application of life-prolonging procedures would serve only to artificially prolong the dying process, I direct that such procedures be withheld or withdrawn, and that I be permitted to die naturally with only the administration of medications or the performance of any medical procedure deemed necessary to provide me with comfortable care or to alleviate pain.
In the absence of my ability to give directions regarding the use of such life-prolonging procedures, it is my intention that this declaration shall be honored by my family and physician as the final expression of my legal right to refuse medical or surgical treatment and accept the consequences of such refusal.

I understand the full import of this declaration, and I am emotionally and mentally competent to make this declaration. In acknowledgment whereof, I do hereinafter affix my signature on this the........day of ...., 19....

....
Declarant

We, the subscribing witnesses hereto, are personally acquainted with and subscribe our names hereto at the request of the declarant, an adult, whom we believe to be of sound mind, fully aware of the action taken herein and its possible consequence.

We, the undersigned witnesses, further declare that we are not related to the declarant by blood or marriage; that we are not entitled to any portion of the estate of the declarant upon his decease under any will or codicil thereto presently existing or by operation of law then existing; that we are not the attending physician, an employee of the attending physician or a health facility in which the declarant is a patient; and that we are not a person who, at the present time, has a claim against any portion of the estate of the declarant upon his death.

....
Witness

....
Witness

Subscribed, sworn to and acknowledged before me by................................, the declarant, and subscribed and sworn to before me by................................
and ...., witnesses, this........day of ...., 19......

....
Notary Public

STATE OF TEXAS

"DIRECTIVE TO PHYSICIANS

"Directive made this.......day of............................(month, year).
"I ...., being of sound mind, willfully and voluntarily make known my desire that my life shall not be artificially prolonged under the circumstances set forth in this directive.
"1. If at any time I should have an incurable condition caused by injury, disease, or illness certified to be a terminal condition by two physicians, and if the application of life-sustaining procedures would serve only to artificially postpone the moment of my death, and if my attending physician determines that my death is imminent whether or not life-sustaining procedures are used, I direct that those procedures be withheld or withdrawn, and that I be permitted to die naturally.
"2. In the absence of my ability to give directions regarding the use of those life-sustaining procedures, it is my intention that this directive be honored by my family and physicians as the final expression of my legal right to refuse medical or surgical treatment and accept the consequences from such refusal.
"3. If I have been diagnosed as pregnant and that diagnosis is known to my physician, this directive has no effect during my pregnancy.
"4. This directive is in effect until it is revoked.
"5. I understand the full import of this directive and I am emotionally and mentally competent to make this directive.
"6. I understand that I may revoke this directive at any time.

"Signed..

City, County, and State of Residence...

The declarant has been personally known to me and I believe the declarant to be of sound mind. I am not related to the declarant by blood or marriage. I would not be entitled to any portion of the declarant's estate on the declarant's death. I am not the attending physician of the declarant or an employee of the attending physician or a health facility in which the declarant is a patient. I am not a patient in the health care facility in which the declarant is a patient. I have no claim against any portion of the declarant's estate on the declarant's death.

"Witness..
"Witness.."

STATE OF UTAH

DIRECTIVE TO PHYSICIANS AND PROVIDERS OF MEDICAL SERVICES
(Pursuant to Section 75-2-1104, UCA)

This directive is made this........day of ...., ...

1. I, ...(name), being of sound mind, willfully and voluntarily make known my desire that my life not be artificially prolonged by life-sustaining procedures except as I may otherwise provide in this directive.

2. I declare that if at any time I should have an injury, disease, or illness, which is certified in writing to be a terminal condition by two physicians who have personally examined me, and in the opinion of those physicians the application of life-sustaining procedures would serve only to unnaturally prolong the moment of my death and to unnaturally postpone or prolong the dying process, I direct that these procedures be withheld or withdrawn and my death be permitted to occur naturally.

3. I expressly intend this directive to be a final expression of my legal right to refuse medical or surgical treatment and to accept the consequences from this refusal which shall remain in effect notwithstanding my future inability to give current medical directions to treating physicians and other providers of medical services.

4. I understand that the term "life-sustaining procedure" does not include the administration of medication or sustenance, or the performance of any medical procedure deemed necessary to provide comfort care, or to alleviate pain, except to the extent I specify below that any of these procedures be considered life-sustaining.

5. I reserve the right to give current medical directions to physicians and other providers of medical services so long as I am able, even though these directions may conflict with the above written directive that life-sustaining procedures be withheld or withdrawn.

6. I understand the full import of this directive and declare that I am emotionally and mentally competent to make this directive.

....Declarant's signature

....City, County, and State of Residence

We witnesses certify that each of us is 18 years of age or older and each personally witnessed the declarant sign or direct the signing of this directive; that we are acquainted with the declarant and believe him to be of sound mind; that the declarant's desires are as expressed above; that neither of us is a person who signed the above directive on behalf of the declarant; that we are not related to the declarant by blood or marriage nor are we entitled to any portion of declarant's estate according to the laws of intestate succession of this state or under any will or codicil of declarant; that we are not directly financially responsible for declarant's medical care; and that we are not agents of any health care facility in which the declarant may be a patient at the time of signing this directive.

....	....
Signature of Witness	Signature of Witness
....	....
Address of Witness	Address of Witness

STATE OF UTAH

DIRECTIVE TO PHYSICIANS AND PROVIDERS OF MEDICAL SERVICES AFTER INJURY OR ILLNESS IS INCURRED
(Pursuant to Section 75-2-1105, UCA)

I, ..., certify that I am serving as the attending physician for .... of ....,who has been under my care since the........day of ...., ...
1. This declarant ...., is currently suffering from the following injury, disease, or illness:
2. I certify that I have explained to the declarant to the extent he is able to understand, and to the available persons acting as proxy, the reasonable available alternatives for his care and treatment.
3. I certify that the care and treatment alternatives directed below are:
.... (a) directed by the declarant; or
.... (b) that the declarant has a physical or medical condition which renders him unable to give personal directions for care and treatment and that the care and treatment alternatives directed below are in my opinion, and in the opinion of the declarant's proxy, what the declarant would probably decide if able to give current directions concerning his care and treatment.

Date:....................................... ....Signature of attending physician

The following care and treatment or withholding of treatment is directed with respect to the declarant:
....
....

....
Relationship to declarant of person signing on declarant's behalf, if applicable

....
Signature of declarant or person authorized by law to sign directive as a proxy on behalf of declarant

....
Address of Signer

....
City, County, and State of residence of Signer

We witnesses certify that each of us is 18 years of age or older; that we personally witnessed the declarant or a proxy sign this directive; that we are acquainted with the declarant and, if the foregoing was signed by a proxy, also the proxy; that we believe that care and treatment alternatives directed above are in the interest of declarant and what declarant has decided or would probably decide for himself if able to give current directions concerning his care and treatment; that neither of us signed the above directive for or on behalf of declarant; that we are not related to the declarant by blood or marriage nor are we entitled to any portion of declarant's estate according to the laws of intestate succession of this state or under any will or codicil of the declarant; that we are not directly financially responsible for declarant's medical care; and that we are not agents of any health care facility in which declarant may be a patient at the time of signing this directive.

....
Signature of Witness

....
Signature of Witness

....
Address of Witness

....
Address of Witness

STATE OF VERMONT

TERMINAL CARE DOCUMENT

"To my family, my physician, my lawyer, my clergyman. To any medical facility in whose care I happen to be. To any individual who may become responsible for my health, welfare or affairs.

"Death is as much a reality as birth, growth, maturity and old age—it is the one certainty of life. If the time comes when I, ..., can no longer take part in decisions of my own future, let this statement stand as an expression of my wishes, while I am still of sound mind.

"If the situation should arise in which I am in a terminal state and there is no reasonable expectation of my recovery, I direct that I be allowed to die a natural death and that my life not be prolonged by extraordinary measures. I do, however, ask that medication be mercifully administered to me to alleviate suffering even though this may shorten my remaining life.

"This statement is made after careful consideration and is in accordance with my strong convictions and beliefs. I want the wishes and directions here expressed carried out to the extent permitted by law. Insofar as they are not legally enforceable, I hope that those to whom this will is addressed will regard themselves as morally bound by these provisions.

Signed:..

Date:...

Witness:...

Witness:...

Copies of this request have been given to:

....

....

...."

STATE OF VIRGINIA

DECLARATION

Declaration made this........day of......................... (month,year).

I, ...(name), willfully and voluntarily make known my desire that my dying shall not be artificially prolonged under the circumstances set forth below, and do hereby declare:

CHOOSE ONLY ONE OF THE NEXT TWO PARAGRAPHS AND CROSS THROUGH THE OTHER

If at any time I should have a terminal condition and my attending physician has determined that there can be no recovery from such condition, my death is imminent, and I am comatose, incompetent or otherwise mentally or physically incapable of communication, I designate .... to make a decision on my behalf as to whether life-prolonging procedures shall be withheld or withdrawn. In the event that my designee decides that such procedures shall be withheld or withdrawn, I wish to be permitted to die naturally with only the administration of medication or the performance of any medical procedure deemed necessary to provide me with comfort care or to alleviate pain.

OR

If at any time I should have a terminal condition and my attending physician has determined that there can be no recovery from such condition and my death is imminent, where the application of life-prolonging procedures would serve only to artificially prolong the dying process, I direct that such procedures be withheld or withdrawn, and that I be permitted to die naturally with only the administration of medication or the performance of any medical procedure deemed necessary to provide me with comfort care or to alleviate pain.

In the absence of my ability to give directions regarding the use of such life-prolonging procedures, it is my intention that this declaration shall be honored by my family and physician as the final expression of my legal right to refuse medical or surgical treatment and accept the consequences of such refusal.

I understand the full import of this declaration and I am emotionally and mentally competent to make this declaration.

....
(Signed)

The declarant is known to me and I believe him or her to be of sound mind.

....
Witness

....
Witness

STATE OF WASHINGTON

DIRECTIVE TO PHYSICIANS

Directive made this........day of ....(month, year).

I, ...(name), being of sound mind, wilfully and voluntarily make known my desire that my life shall not be artificially prolonged under the circumstances set forth below, and do hereby declare that:

(a) If at any time I should have an incurable injury, disease, or illness certified to be a terminal condition by two physicians, and where the application of life-sustaining procedures would serve only to artificially prolong the moment of my death and where my physician determines that my death is imminent whether or not life-sustaining procedures are utilized, I direct that such procedures be withheld or withdrawn, and that I be permitted to die naturally.

(b) In the absence of my ability to give directions regarding the use of such life-sustaining procedures, it is my intention that this directive shall be honored by my family and physician(s) as the final expression of my legal right to refuse medical or surgical treatment and I accept the consequences from such refusal.

(c) If I have been diagnosed as pregnant and that diagnosis is known to my physician, this directive shall have no force or effect during the course of my pregnancy.

(d) I understand the full import of this directive and I am emotionally and mentally competent to make this directive.

Signed..

City, County, and State of Residence...

The declarer has been personally known to me and I believe him or her to be of sound mind.

Witness..

Witness..

[Prior to effectuating a directive the diagnosis of a terminal condition by two physicians shall be verified in writing, attached to the directive, and made a permanent part of the patient's medical records.]

STATE OF WEST VIRGINIA

"DECLARATION

"Declaration made this........day of ....(month, year).
I, ...(name), being of sound mind, willfully and voluntarily make known my desires that my dying shall not be artificially prolonged under the circumstances set forth below, do declare:

"If at any time I should have an incurable injury, disease or illness certified to be a terminal condition by two physicians who have personally examined me, one of whom is my attending physician, and the physicians have determined that my death will occur whether or not life-sustaining procedures are utilized and where the application of life-sustaining procedures would serve only to artificially prolong the dying process, I direct that such procedures be withheld or withdrawn, and that I be permitted to die naturally with only the administration of nutrition, medication or the performance of any medical procedure deemed necessary to provide me with comfort, care or to alleviate pain.

"In the absence of my ability to give directions regarding the use of such life-sustaining procedures, it is my intention that this declaration be honored by my family and physician(s) as the final expression of my legal right to refuse medical or surgical treatment and accept the consequences resulting from such refusal.

"I understand the full import of this declaration and I am emotionally and mentally competent to make this declaration.

"Signed...
"Address.......................................
....

"I did not sign the declarant's signature above for or at the direction of the declarant. I am at least eighteen years of age and am not related to the declarant by blood or marriage, entitled to any portion of the estate of the declarant according to the laws of intestate succession of the State of West Virginia or to the best of my knowledge under any will of declarant or codicil thereto, or directly financially responsible for declarant's medical care. I am not the declarant's attending physician, an employee of the attending physician, nor an employee of the health facility in which the declarant is a patient.

"Witness..

"Witness..

"STATE OF ...., "COUNTY OF ...., to-wit:
"This day personally appeared before me, the undersigned authority, a Notary Public in and for .... County, ... (State), ... (witness) and .... (witness) who, being first duly sworn, say that they are the subscribing witnesses to the declaration of .... (declarant), which declaration is dated the.......day of ...., 19, ...; and that on the said date the said .... (declarant), the declarant, signed, sealed, published and declared the same as and for his declaration, in the presence of both these affiants; and that these affiants, at the request of said declarant, in the presence of each other, and in the presence of said declarant, all present at the same time, signed their names as attesting witnesses to said declaration.

"Affiants further say that this affidavit is made at the request of...... .... (declarant), declarant, and in his presence, and that .... (declarant), at the time the declaration was executed, was in the opinion of affiants, of sound mind and memory, and over the age of eighteen years.

....

"Taken, subscribed, and sworn to before me by .... (witness) and .... (witness) this........day of ...., 19.......

"My commission expires:

"..

Notary Public."

STATE OF WISCONSIN

DECLARATION TO PHYSICIANS

Declaration made this........day of ....(month),........(year).

1. I, ..., being of sound mind, wilfully and voluntarily state my desire that my dying may not be artificially prolonged if I have an incurable injury or illness certified to be a terminal condition by 2 physicians who have personally examined me, one of whom is my attending physician, and if the physicians have determined that my death is imminent, so that the application of life-sustaining procedures would serve only to prolong artificially the dying process. Under these circumstances, I direct that life-sustaining procedures be withheld or withdrawn and that I be permitted to die naturally, with only:
a. The continuation of nutritional support and fluid maintenance; and
b. The alleviation of pain by administering medication or other medical procedure.

2. If I am unable to give directions regarding the use of life-sustaining procedures, I intend that my family and physician honor this declaration as the final expression of my legal right to refuse medical or surgical treatment and to accept the consequences from this refusal.

3. If I have been diagnosed as pregnant and my physician knows of this diagnosis, this declaration has no effect during the course of my pregnancy.

4. This declaration takes effect immediately.

I understand this declaration and I am emotionally and mentally competent to make this declaration.

Signed...

Address...

I know the declarant personally and I believe him or her to be of sound mind. I am not related to the declarant by blood or marriage, and am not entitled to any portion of the declarant's estate under any will of the declarant. I am neither the declarant's attending physician, the attending nurse, the attending medical staff nor an employe of the attending physician or of the inpatient health care facility in which the declarant may be a patient and I have no claim against the declarant's estate at this time, except that, if I am not a health care provider who is involved in the medical care of the declarant, I may be an employe of the inpatient health care facility regardless of whether or not the facility may have a claim against the estate of the declarant.

Witness...

Witness...

[This declaration is executed as provided in chapter 154, Wisconsin Statutes.]

STATE OF WYOMING

DECLARATION

Declaration made this........day of ....(month, year).
I, ...(name), being of sound mind, willfully and voluntarily make known my desire that my dying shall not be artificially prolonged under the circumstances set forth below, do hereby declare:

If at any time I should have an incurable injury, disease or other illness certified to be a terminal condition by two (2) physicians who have personally examined me, one (1) of whom shall be my attending physician, and the physicians have determined that my death will occur whether or not life-sustaining procedures are utilized and where the application of life-sustaining procedures would serve only to artificially prolong the dying process, I direct that such procedures be withheld or withdrawn, and that I be permitted to die naturally with only the administration of medication or the performance of any medical procedure deemed necessary to provide me with comfort care.

If, in spite of this declaration, I am comatose or otherwise unable to make treatment decisions for myself, I HEREBY designate ....
to make treatment decisions for me.

In the absence of my ability to give directions regarding the use of life-sustaining procedures, it is my intention that this declaration shall be honored by my family and physician(s) and agent as the final expression of my legal right to refuse medical or surgical treatment and accept the consequences from this refusal. I understand the full import of this declaration and I am emotionally and mentally competent to make this declaration.

Signed..

City, County, and State of Residence.............................

The declarant has been personally known to me and I believe him or her to be of sound mind. I did not sign the declarant's signature above for or at the direction of the declarant. I am not related to the declarant by blood or marriage, entitled to any portion of the estate of the declarant according to the laws of intestate succession or under any will of the declarant or codicil thereto, or directly financially responsible for declarant's medical care.

Witness..

Witness..

Appendix B

Instructions and Form to Execute a Living Will in States Without Specific Natural Death Laws*

(*Or for use in states with such legislation that have not specified a model form in their statutes)

(a) Fill in the day of the month, the month, and the year in paragraph 2.
(b) Print your name in the third paragraph in the space provided.
(c) Check one of the boxes, indicating the degree of life support you wish to have in the event of a terminal condition.
(d) Under "Additional specific instructions," add any personalized instructions you desire. For example: "I freely give my permission for donations of any of my tissues or organs which would be of value as transplants." "Measures of artificial life-support in the face of imminent death which I specifically refuse are: (1) Nasogastric or gastronomy tube feeding or intraveneous feeding when I am paralyzed or unable to take nourishment by mouth; (2) amputation of any of my limbs; (3) blood transfusions or dialysis; (4) mechanical respiration when I am no longer able to breath on my own; (5) cardio-pulmonary resuscitation by any means when my heart has stopped beating; (6) radiation treatments; (7) organ transplants; or ______________________." "I wish to live out my last days at home rather than in a hospital if it does not jeopardize the chance of my recovery to a meaningful and sentient life and does not impose an undue burden on my family." You may add additional sheets of paper as necessary. Be sure to date and sign each additional sheet.
(e) If you wish to designate someone else to make medical treatment decisions on your behalf in the event you become incompetent or otherwise incapacitated, fill in the Durable Power of Attorney section. Indicate the name of the individual and his or her address and telephone number you designate as your proxy in the space provided (after first discussing the matter with the person in question). In addition to filling in the Durable Power of Attorney part of the Living Will, it is recommended that you fill out a separate Durable Power of Attorney for Health Care form (see Appendices C and D). This is repetitious, but the DPA/HC form itself in most cases provides additional space to go into greater detail about your wishes in this respect, to appoint alternate proxies, and to place any limitations you wish on your agent's authority.
(f) Sign the Living Will and include your address in the spaces on the second page.
(g) Have two witnesses meeting the criteria outlined in the footnote witness your declaration and sign it, with their addresses, in the spaces provided.
(h) In addition, notarization is highly recommended as well, whenever possible. Space is provided at the bottom of the second page for notarization.

LIVING WILL

To my Family, my Physician, my Lawyer, my Clergy. To any Medical Facility in whose care I happen to be. To any individual who may become responsible for my health, welfare, or affairs:

Directive made this ....day of ...., 19......

I, ...(NAME), being an adult of sound mind, willfully and voluntarily make this directive as an expression of my wishes to be followed in the event I become incapacitated and unable to participate in decisions regarding my medical care.

If at any time a situation should arise when I am in an irreversible or incurable terminal condition from which there is no reasonable expectation of my recovery, as certified by two physicians, one of whom is my attending physician, or when the use of life-sustaining treatment would only prolong artificially the moment of my death, I direct that this expression of my wishes be followed and that I be allowed to die and not be kept alive by medications, artificial means, or "heroic" or extraordinary measures. I do, however, request that medication be mercifully administered to me to alleviate suffering even though this may shorten my remaining life.

This statement is made after careful consideration and is in accordance with my strong convictions and beliefs. I want the wishes and directions here expressed carried out to the extent permitted by law. To the extent that the provisions of this Living Will are not legally enforceable, I hope that those to whom this Will is addressed will regard themselves as morally bound by them.

Check one box:

❑ If at any time I should become unable to communicate my instructions, then I direct that all medical treatment, care, and nutrition and hydration necessary to restore my health, sustain my life, and to abolish or alleviate pain or distress be provided to me. Nutrition and hydration shall not be withheld or withdrawn from me if I would die from malnutrition or dehydration rather than from my injury, disease, illness or condition.
❑ If at any time I should become unable to communicate my instructions and where the application of artificial life-sustaining procedures shall serve only to prolong artificially the moment of my death, I direct such procedures be withheld or withdrawn except for the administration of nutrition and hydration.
❑ If at any time I should become unable to communicate my instructions and where the application of artificial life-sustaining procedures shall serve only to prolong artificially the moment of my death, I direct such procedures be withheld or withdrawn, including withdrawal of the administration of nutrition and hydration.

Additional specific instructions (optional):..
....
....

I appoint...(NAME), whose address and telephone number is
....,
to serve as my health care agent, to make medical treatment decisions on my behalf, consistent with this directive and with my wishes which may be communicated in other ways as well.
If I am female and have been diagnosed as pregnant and that diagnosis is known to my attending physician, this directive shall have no force or effect during the course of my pregnancy.*

[*You may cross out this provision if you choose to do so, bearing in mind that this provision may be legally enforceable in your state under certain circumstances.]

....
Signature

....
Address

WITNESSES**

The declarant is personally known to me and I believe the declarant to be an adult and of sound mind.

....
Witness

....
Address

....
Witness

....
Address

NOTARIZATION***

State of ....)
) ss.
County of ....)

Subscribed and sworn to before me by ...., Declarant, and .... and ...., Witnesses, as the voluntary act and deed of the declarant this .... day of ...., 19.......

My commission expires:

....
Notary Public

[It is recommended that the declarant select witnesses who are: *not* related to the declarant by blood, marriage, or adoption; *not* entitled to any portion of the estate of the declarant by will or codicil, or according to the laws of intestate succession; *not* directly financially responsible for the declarant's medical care; *not* the declarant's physician or an employee of that physician; *not* an employee of a hospital where the declarant is a patient; *not* an employee of a nursing home or any group-care home in which the declarant resides; *not* a patient in a health care facility in which the declarant is a patient. The majority of states with Living Will legislation disqualify some or all of these individuals from serving as witnesses to the Directive.]**

[*The majority of states with Living Will legislation require the signatures of two witnesses. Some states give a choice of either witnesses or notarization. Other states require both. Ideally, both witnesses <u>and</u> notarization should be used.]**

Appendix C

State-Mandated Durable Powers of Attorney for Health Care and Related Forms*

(*The Kentucky Designation of Health Care Surrogate, the New York Health Care Proxy, and the Utah Power of Attorney excerpted from the Utah Living Will statute)

STATE OF CALIFORNIA

STATUTORY FORM DURABLE POWER OF ATTORNEY FOR HEALTH CARE
(California Civil Code Section 2500)

WARNING TO PERSON EXECUTING THIS DOCUMENT

THIS IS AN IMPORTANT LEGAL DOCUMENT WHICH IS AUTHORIZED BY THE KEENE HEALTH CARE AGENT ACT. BEFORE EXECUTING THIS DOCUMENT, YOU SHOULD KNOW THESE IMPORTANT FACTS:

THIS DOCUMENT GIVES THE PERSON YOU DESIGNATE AS YOUR AGENT (THE ATTORNEY IN FACT) THE POWER TO MAKE HEALTH CARE DECISIONS FOR YOU. YOUR AGENT MUST ACT CONSISTENTLY WITH YOUR DESIRES AS STATED IN THIS DOCUMENT OR OTHERWISE MADE KNOWN.

EXCEPT AS YOU OTHERWISE SPECIFY IN THIS DOCUMENT, THIS DOCUMENT GIVES YOUR AGENT THE POWER TO CONSENT TO YOUR DOCTOR NOT GIVING TREATMENT OR STOPPING TREATMENT NECESSARY TO KEEP YOU ALIVE.

NOTWITHSTANDING THIS DOCUMENT, YOU HAVE THE RIGHT TO MAKE MEDICAL AND OTHER HEALTH CARE DECISIONS FOR YOURSELF SO LONG AS YOU CAN GIVE INFORMED CONSENT WITH RESPECT TO THE PARTICULAR DECISION. IN ADDITION, NO TREATMENT MAY BE GIVEN TO YOU OVER YOUR OBJECTION AT THE TIME, AND HEALTH CARE NECESSARY TO KEEP YOU ALIVE MAY NOT BE STOPPED OR WITHHELD IF YOU OBJECT AT THE TIME.

THIS DOCUMENT GIVES YOUR AGENT AUTHORITY TO CONSENT, TO REFUSE TO CONSENT, OR TO WITHDRAW CONSENT TO ANY CARE, TREATMENT, SERVICE, OR PROCEDURE TO MAINTAIN, DIAGNOSE, OR TREAT A PHYSICAL OR MENTAL CONDITION. THIS POWER IS SUBJECT TO ANY STATEMENT OF YOUR DESIRES AND ANY LIMITATIONS THAT YOU INCLUDE IN THIS DOCUMENT. YOU MAY STATE IN THIS DOCUMENT ANY TYPES OF TREATMENT THAT YOU DO NOT DESIRE. IN ADDITION, A COURT CAN TAKE AWAY THE POWER OF YOUR AGENT TO MAKE HEALTH CARE DECISIONS FOR YOU IF YOUR AGENT (1) AUTHORIZES ANYTHING THAT IS ILLEGAL, (2) ACTS CONTRARY TO YOUR KNOWN DESIRES, OR (3) WHERE YOUR DESIRES ARE NOT KNOWN, DOES ANYTHING THAT IS CLEARLY CONTRARY TO YOUR BEST INTERESTS.

UNLESS YOU SPECIFY A SHORTER PERIOD IN THIS DOCUMENT, THIS POWER WILL EXIST FOR SEVEN YEARS FROM THE DATE YOU EXECUTE THIS DOCUMENT AND, IF YOU ARE UNABLE TO MAKE HEALTH CARE DECISIONS FOR YOURSELF AT THE TIME WHEN THIS SEVEN-YEAR PERIOD ENDS, THIS POWER WILL CONTINUE TO EXIST UNTIL THE TIME WHEN YOU BECOME ABLE TO MAKE HEALTH CARE DECISIONS FOR YOURSELF.

YOU HAVE THE RIGHT TO REVOKE THE AUTHORITY OF YOUR AGENT BY NOTIFYING YOUR AGENT OR YOUR TREATING DOCTOR, HOSPITAL, OR OTHER HEALTH CARE PROVIDER ORALLY OR IN WRITING OF THE REVOCATION.

YOUR AGENT HAS THE RIGHT TO EXAMINE YOUR MEDICAL RECORDS AND TO CONSENT TO THEIR DISCLOSURE UNLESS YOU LIMIT THIS RIGHT IN THIS DOCUMENT.

UNLESS YOU OTHERWISE SPECIFY IN THIS DOCUMENT, THIS DOCUMENT GIVES YOUR AGENT THE POWER AFTER YOU DIE TO (1) AUTHORIZE AN AUTOPSY, (2) DONATE YOUR BODY OR PARTS THEREOF FOR TRANSPLANT OR THERAPEUTIC OR EDUCATIONAL OR SCIENTIFIC PURPOSES, AND (3) DIRECT THE DISPOSITION OF YOUR REMAINS.

THIS DOCUMENT REVOKES ANY PRIOR DURABLE POWER OF ATTORNEY FOR HEALTH CARE.

YOU SHOULD CAREFULLY READ AND FOLLOW THE WITNESSING PROCEDURE DESCRIBED AT THE END OF THIS FORM. THIS DOCUMENT WILL NOT BE VALID UNLESS YOU COMPLY WITH THE WITNESSING PROCEDURE.

IF THERE IS ANYTHING IN THIS DOCUMENT THAT YOU DO NOT UNDERSTAND, YOU SHOULD ASK A LAWYER TO EXPLAIN IT TO YOU.

YOUR AGENT MAY NEED THIS DOCUMENT IMMEDIATELY IN CASE OF AN EMERGENCY THAT REQUIRES A DECISION CONCERNING YOUR HEALTH CARE. EITHER KEEP THIS DOCUMENT WHERE IT IS IMMEDIATELY AVAILABLE TO YOUR AGENT AND ALTERNATE AGENTS OR GIVE EACH OF THEM AN EXECUTED COPY OF THIS DOCUMENT. YOU MAY ALSO WANT TO GIVE YOUR DOCTOR AN EXECUTED COPY OF THIS DOCUMENT.

DO NOT USE THIS FORM IF YOU ARE A CONSERVATEE UNDER THE LANTERMAN-PETRIS-SHORT ACT AND YOU WANT TO APPOINT YOUR CONSERVATOR AS YOUR AGENT. YOU CAN DO THAT ONLY IF THE APPOINTMENT DOCUMENT INCLUDES A CERTIFICATE OF ATTORNEY.

1. DESIGNATION OF HEALTH CARE AGENT. I,................ ....

(Insert your name and address)

do hereby designate and appoint....................... ....

(Insert name, address, and telephone number of one individual only as your agent to make health care decisions for you. None of the following may be designated as your agent: (1) your treating health care provider, (2) a nonrelative employee of your treating health care provider, (3) an operator of a community care facility, or (4) a nonrelative employee of an operator of a community care facility.)

as my attorney in fact (agent) to make health care decisions for me as authorized in this document. For the purposes of this document, "health care decision" means consent, refusal of consent, or withdrawal of consent to any care, treatment, service, or procedure to maintain, diagnose, or treat an individual's physical or mental condition.

2. CREATION OF DURABLE POWER OF ATTORNEY FOR HEALTH CARE. By this document I intend to create a durable power of attorney for health care under Sections 2430 to 2443, inclusive, of the California Civil Code. This power of attorney is authorized by the Keene Health Care Agent Act and shall be construed in accordance with the provisions of Sections 2500 to 2506, inclusive, of the California Civil Code. This power of attorney shall not be affected by my subsequent incapacity.

3. GENERAL STATEMENT OF AUTHORITY GRANTED. Subject to any limitations in this document, I hereby grant to my agent full power and authority to make health care decisions for me to the same extent that I could make such decisions for myself if I had the capacity to do so. In exercising this authority, my agent shall make health care decisions that are consistent with my desires as stated in this document or otherwise made known to my agent, including, but not limited to, my desires concerning obtaining or refusing or withdrawing life-prolonging care, treatment, services, and procedures.

(If you want to limit the authority of your agent to make health care decisions for you, you can state the limitations in paragraph 4 ("Statement of Desires, Special Provisions, and Limitations") below. You can indicate your desires by including a statement of your desires in the same paragraph.)

4. STATEMENT OF DESIRES, SPECIAL PROVISIONS, AND LIMITATIONS.

(Your agent must make health care decisions that are consistent with your known desires. You can, but are not required to, state your desires in the space provided below. You should consider whether you want to include a statement of your desires concerning life-prolonging care, treatment, services, and procedures. You can also include a statement of your desires concerning other matters relating to your health care. You can also make your desires known to your agent by discussing your desires with your agent or by some other means. If there are any types of treatment that you do not want to be used, you should state them in the space below. If you want to limit in any other way the authority given your agent by this document, you should state the limits in the space below. If you do not state any limits, your agent will have broad powers to make health care decisions for you, except to the extent that there are limits provided by law.)

In exercising the authority under this durable power of attorney for health care, my agent shall act consistently with my desires as stated below and is subject to the special provisions and limitations stated below:
(a) Statement of desires concerning life-prolonging care, treatment, services, and procedures:

....

....

....

....

....

....

....

....

(b) Additional statement of desires, special provisions, and limitations:

....

....

....

....

....

....

....

....

(You may attach additional pages if you need more space to complete your statement. If you attach additional pages, you must date and sign EACH of the additional pages at the same time you date and sign this document.)

5. INSPECTION AND DISCLOSURE OF INFORMATION RELATING TO MY PHYSICAL OR MENTAL HEALTH. Subject to any limitations in this document, my agent has the power and authority to do all of the following:
(a) Request, review, and receive any information, verbal or written, regarding my physical or mental health, including, but not limited to, medical and hospital records.
(b) Execute on my behalf any releases or other documents that may be required in order to obtain this information.
(c) Consent to the disclosure of this information.
(If you want to limit the authority of your agent to receive and disclose information relating to your health, you must state the limitations in paragraph 4 ("Statement of Desires, Special Provisions, and Limitations") above.)

6. SIGNING DOCUMENTS, WAIVERS, AND RELEASES. Where necessary to implement the health care decisions that my agent is authorized by this document to make, my agent has the power and authority to execute on my behalf all of the following:
(a) Documents titled or purporting to be a "Refusal to Permit Treatment" and "Leaving Hospital Against Medical Advice."
(b) Any necessary waiver or release from liability required by a hospital or physician.

7. AUTOPSY; ANATOMICAL GIFTS; DISPOSITION OF REMAINS. Subject to any limitations in this document, my agent has the power and authority to do all of the following:
(a) Authorize an autopsy under Section 7113 of the Health and Safety Code.
(b) Make a disposition of a part or parts of my body under the Uniform Anatomical Gift Act (Chapter 3.5 (commencing with Section 76150) of Part I of Division 7 of the Health and Safety Code).
(c) Direct the disposition of my remains under Section 7100 of the Health and Safety Code.
(If you want to limit the authority of your agent to consent to an autopsy, make an anatomical gift, or direct the disposition of your remains, you must state the limitations in paragraph 4 ("Statement of Desires, Special Provisions, and Limitations") above.)

8. DURATION.
(Unless you specify a shorter period in the space below, this power of attorney will exist for seven years from the date you execute this document and, if you are unable to make health care decisions for yourself at the time when this seven-year period ends, the power will continue to exist until the time when you become able to make health care decisions for yourself.)
This durable power of attorney for health care expires on...
(Fill in this space ONLY if you want the authority of your agent to end EARLIER than the seven-year period described above.)
9. DESIGNATION OF ALTERNATE AGENTS.
(You are not required to designate any alternate agents but you may do so. Any alternate agent you designate will be able to make the same health care decisions as the agent you designated in paragraph 1, above, in the event that agent is unable or ineligible to act as your agent. If the agent you designated is your spouse, he or she becomes ineligible to act as your agent if your marriage is dissolved.)
If the person designated as my agent in paragraph 1 is not available or becomes ineligible to act as my agent to make a health care decision for me or loses the mental capacity to make health care decisions for me, or if I revoke that person's appointment or authority to act as my agent to make health care decisions for me, then I designate and appoint the following persons to serve as my agent to make health care decisions for me as authorized in this document, such persons to serve in the order listed below:
A. First Alternate Agent.......................................

....
(Insert name, address, and telephone number of first alternate agent)
B. Second Alternate Agent.......................................

....
(Insert name, address, and telephone number of second alternate agent)
10. NOMINATION OF CONSERVATOR OF PERSON.
(A conservator of the person may be appointed for you if a court decides that one should be appointed. The conservator is responsible for your physical care, which under some circumstances includes making health care decisions for you. You are not required to nominate a conservator but you may do so. The court will appoint the person you nominate unless that would be contrary to your best interests. You may, but are not required to, nominate as your conservator the same person you named in paragraph 1 as your health care agent. You can nominate an individual as your conservator by completing the space below.)
If a conservator of the person is to be appointed for me, I nominate the following individual to serve as conservator of the person..

....
(Insert name and address of person nominated as conservator of the person)
11. PRIOR DESIGNATIONS REVOKED. I revoke any prior durable power of attorney for health care.

DATE AND SIGNATURE OF PRINCIPAL (YOU MUST DATE AND SIGN THIS POWER OF ATTORNEY)

I sign my name to this Statutory Form Durable Power of Attorney for Health Care on ....(Date) at ....(City),...................(State).

....
(You sign here)

(THIS POWER OF ATTORNEY WILL NOT BE VALID UNLESS IT IS SIGNED BY TWO QUALIFIED WITNESSES WHO ARE PRESENT WHEN YOU SIGN OR ACKNOWLEDGE YOUR SIGNATURE. IF YOU HAVE ATTACHED ANY ADDITIONAL PAGES TO THIS FORM, YOU MUST DATE AND

SIGN EACH OF THE ADDITIONAL PAGES AT THE SAME TIME YOU DATE AND SIGN THIS POWER OF ATTORNEY.)

DATE AND SIGNATURE OF PRINCIPAL
(YOU MUST DATE AND SIGN THIS POWER OF ATTORNEY)

STATEMENT OF WITNESSES
(This document must be witnessed by two qualified adult witnesses. None of the following may be used as a witness: (1) a person you designate as your agent or alternate agent, (2) a health care provider, (3) an employee of a health care provider, (4) the operator of a community care facility, (5) an employee of an operator of a community care facility. At least one of the witnesses must make the additional declaration set out following the place where the witnesses sign.)
(READ CAREFULLY BEFORE SIGNING. You can sign as a witness only if you personally know the principal or the identity of the principal is proved to you by convincing evidence.)
(To have convincing evidence of the identity of the principal, you must be presented with and reasonably rely on any one or more of the following:
(1) An identification card or driver's license issued by the California Department of Motor Vehicles that is current or has been issued within five years.
(2) A passport issued by the Department of State of the United States that is current or has been issued within five years.
(3) Any of the following documents if the document is current or has been issued within five years and contains a photograph and description of the person named on it, it is signed by the person, and bears a serial or other identifying number:
(a) A passport issued by a foreign government that has been stamped by the United States Immigration and Naturalization Service.
(b) A driver's license issued by a state other than California or by a Canadian or Mexican public agency authorized to issue drivers' licenses.
(c) An identification card issued by a state other than California.
(d) An identification card issued by any branch of the armed forces of the United States.)
(Other kinds of proof of identity are not allowed.)
I declare under penalty of perjury under the laws of California that the person who signed or acknowledged this document is personally known to me (or proved to me on the basis of convincing evidence) to be the principal, that the principal signed or acknowledged this durable power of attorney in my presence, that the principal appears to be of sound mind and under no duress, fraud, or undue influence, that I am not the person appointed as attorney in fact by this document, and that I am not a health care provider, an employee of a health care provider, the operator of a community care facility, nor an employee of an operator of a community care facility.
Signature:.............................Residence Address...
PrintName:...
Date:.................................
Signature:......................................Residence Address...
PrintName:..
Date:................................
(AT LEAST ONE OF THE ABOVE WITNESSES MUST ALSO SIGN THE FOLLOWING DECLARATION.)
I further declare under penalty of perjury under the laws of California that I am not related to the principal by blood, marriage, or adoption, and, to the best of my knowledge, I am not entitled to any part of the estate of the principal upon the death of the principal under a will now existing or by operation of law.
Signature:.....................................
Signature:.....................................

STATEMENT OF PATIENT ADVOCATE OR OMBUDSMAN

(If you are a patient in a skilled nursing facility, one of the witnesses must be a patient advocate or ombudsman. The following statement is required only if you are a patient in a skilled nursing facility—a health care facility that provides the following basic services: skilled nursing care and supportive care to patients whose primary need is for availability of skilled nursing care on an extended basis. The patient advocate or ombudsman must sign both parts of the "Statement of Witnesses" above AND must also sign the following statement.)

I further declare under penalty of perjury under the laws of California that I am a patient advocate or ombudsman as designated by the State Department of Aging and that I am serving as a witness as required by subdivision (f) of Section 2432 of the Civil Code.

Signature:..

DISTRICT OF COLUMBIA

DURABLE POWER OF ATTORNEY FOR HEALTH CARE

"INFORMATION ABOUT THIS DOCUMENT

"THIS IS AN IMPORTANT LEGAL DOCUMENT. BEFORE SIGNING THIS DOCUMENT, IT IS VITAL FOR YOU TO KNOW AND UNDERSTAND THESE FACTS:

"THIS DOCUMENT GIVES THE PERSON YOU NAME AS YOUR ATTORNEY IN FACT THE POWER TO MAKE HEALTH-CARE DECISIONS FOR YOU IF YOU CANNOT MAKE THE DECISIONS FOR YOURSELF.

"AFTER YOU HAVE SIGNED THIS DOCUMENT, YOU HAVE THE RIGHT TO MAKE HEALTH-CARE DECISIONS FOR YOURSELF IF YOU ARE MENTALLY COMPETENT TO DO SO. IN ADDITION, AFTER YOU HAVE SIGNED THIS DOCUMENT, NO TREATMENT MAY BE GIVEN TO YOU OR STOPPED OVER YOUR OBJECTION IF YOU ARE MENTALLY COMPETENT TO MAKE THAT DECISION.

"YOU MAY STATE IN THIS DOCUMENT ANY TYPE OF TREATMENT THAT YOU DO NOT DESIRE AND ANY THAT YOU WANT TO MAKE SURE YOU RECEIVE.

"YOU HAVE THE RIGHT TO TAKE AWAY THE AUTHORITY OF YOUR ATTORNEY IN FACT, UNLESS YOU HAVE BEEN ADJUDICATED INCOMPETENT, BY NOTIFYING YOUR ATTORNEY IN FACT OR HEALTH-CARE PROVIDER EITHER ORALLY OR IN WRITING. SHOULD YOU REVOKE THE AUTHORITY OF YOUR ATTORNEY IN FACT, IT IS ADVISABLE TO REVOKE IN WRITING AND TO PLACE COPIES OF THE REVOCATION WHEREVER THIS DOCUMENT IS LOCATED.

"IF THERE IS ANYTHING IN THIS DOCUMENT THAT YOU DO NOT UNDERSTAND, YOU SHOULD ASK A SOCIAL WORKER, LAWYER, OR OTHER PERSON TO EXPLAIN IT TO YOU.

*****

"YOU SHOULD KEEP A COPY OF THIS DOCUMENT AFTER YOU HAVE SIGNED IT. GIVE A COPY TO THE PERSON YOU NAME AS YOUR ATTORNEY IN FACT. IF YOU ARE IN A HEALTH-CARE FACILITY, A COPY OF THIS DOCUMENT SHOULD BE INCLUDED IN YOUR MEDICAL RECORD.

"POWER OF ATTORNEY FOR HEALTH CARE

"I, ..., hereby appoint:

....	....
name	home address
....	....
home telephone number	
....	....
work telephone number	

as my attorney in fact to make health-care decisions for me if I become unable to make my own health-care decisions. This gives my attorney in fact the power to grant, refuse, or withdraw consent on my behalf for any health-care service, treatment or procedure. My attorney in fact also has the authority to talk to health-care personnel, get information and sign forms necessary to carry out these decisions.

"If the person named as my attorney in fact is not available or is unable to act as my attorney in fact, I appoint the following person to serve in the order listed below:

1.

....

name home address

....

home telephone number

....

work telephone number

2.

....

name home address

....

home telephone number

....

work telephone number

"With this document, I intend to create a power of attorney for health care, which shall take effect if I become incapable of making my own health-care decisions and shall continue during that incapacity.
"My attorney in fact shall make health-care decisions as I direct below or as I make known to my attorney in fact in some other way.
"(a) STATEMENT OF DIRECTIVES CONCERNING LIFE-PROLONGING CARE, TREATMENT, SERVICES, AND PROCEDURES:

....
....
....
....
....
....
....

"(b) SPECIAL PROVISIONS AND LIMITATIONS:

....
....
....
....
....
....

"BY MY SIGNATURE I INDICATE THAT I UNDERSTAND THE PURPOSE AND EFFECT OF THIS DOCUMENT.
"I sign my name to this form on .... (date) at: .... (address).

....
Signature

"WITNESSES

"I declare that the person who signed or acknowledged this document is personally known to me, that the person signed or acknowledged this durable power of attorney for health care in my presence, and that the person appears to be of sound mind and under no duress, fraud, or undue influence. I am not the person appointed as the attorney in fact by this document, nor am I the health-care provider of the principal or an employee of the health-care provider of the principal:

First Witness
Signature:..
Home Address: ....
Print Name: ....
Date:...

Second Witness
Signature:..
Home Address: ....
Print Name: ....
Date:..

(AT LEAST 1 OF THE WITNESSES LISTED ABOVE SHALL ALSO SIGN THE FOLLOWING DECLARATION.)

"I further declare that I am not related to the principal by blood, marriage or adoption, and, to the best of my knowledge, I am not entitled to any part of the estate of the principal under a currently existing will or by operation of law.

Signature:...
Signature:..".

STATE OF GEORGIA

"GEORGIA STATUTORY SHORT FORM

DURABLE POWER OF ATTORNEY FOR HEALTH CARE

NOTICE: THE PURPOSE OF THIS POWER OF ATTORNEY IS TO GIVE THE PERSON YOU DESIGNATE (YOUR AGENT) BROAD POWERS TO MAKE HEALTH CARE DECISIONS FOR YOU, INCLUDING POWER TO REQUIRE, CONSENT TO, OR WITHDRAW ANY TYPE OF PERSONAL CARE OR MEDICAL TREATMENT FOR ANY PHYSICAL OR MENTAL CONDITION AND TO ADMIT YOU TO OR DISCHARGE YOU FROM ANY HOSPITAL, HOME, OR OTHER INSTITUTION; BUT NOT INCLUDING PSYCHOSURGERY, STERILIZATION, OR INVOLUNTARY HOSPITALIZATION OR TREATMENT COVERED BY TITLE 37 OF THE OFFICIAL CODE OF GEORGIA ANNOTATED. THIS FORM DOES NOT IMPOSE A DUTY ON YOUR AGENT TO EXERCISE GRANTED POWERS; BUT, WHEN A POWER IS EXERCISED, YOUR AGENT WILL HAVE TO USE DUE CARE TO ACT FOR YOUR BENEFIT AND IN ACCORDANCE WITH THIS FORM. A COURT CAN TAKE AWAY THE POWERS OF YOUR AGENT IF IT FINDS THE AGENT IS NOT ACTING PROPERLY. YOU MAY NAME COAGENTS AND SUCCESSOR AGENTS UNDER THIS FORM, BUT YOU MAY NOT NAME A HEALTH CARE PROVIDER WHO MAY BE DIRECTLY OR INDIRECTLY INVOLVED IN RENDERING HEALTH CARE TO YOU UNDER THIS POWER. UNLESS YOU EXPRESSLY LIMIT THE DURATION OF THIS POWER IN THE MANNER PROVIDED BELOW OR UNTIL YOU REVOKE THIS POWER OR A COURT ACTING ON YOUR BEHALF TERMINATES IT, YOUR AGENT MAY EXERCISE THE POWERS GIVEN IN THIS POWER THROUGHOUT YOUR LIFETIME, EVEN AFTER YOU BECOME DISABLED, INCAPACITATED, OR INCOMPETENT. THE POWERS YOU GIVE YOUR AGENT, YOUR RIGHT TO REVOKE THOSE POWERS, AND THE PENALTIES FOR VIOLATING THE LAW ARE EXPLAINED MORE FULLY IN CODE SECTIONS 31-36-6, 31-36-9, AND 31-36-10 OF THE GEORGIA 'DURABLE POWER OF ATTORNEY FOR HEALTH CARE ACT' OF WHICH THIS FORM IS A PART. THAT ACT EXPRESSLY PERMITS THE USE OF ANY DIFFERENT FORM OF POWER OF ATTORNEY YOU MAY DESIRE. IF THERE IS ANYTHING ABOUT THIS FORM THAT YOU DO NOT UNDERSTAND, YOU SHOULD ASK A LAWYER TO EXPLAIN IT TO YOU.

DURABLE POWER OF ATTORNEY made this .... day of ...., 19 .....
1. I, ...
(insert name and address of principal)
hereby appoint ....
(insert name and address of agent)
as my attorney in fact (my agent) to act for me and in my name in any way I could act in person to make any and all decisions for me concerning my personal care, medical treatment, hospitalization, and health care and to require, withhold, or withdraw any type of medical treatment or procedure, even though my death may ensue. My agent shall have the same access to my medical records that I have, including the right to disclose the contents to others. My agent shall also have full power to make a disposition of any part or all of my body for medical purposes, authorize an autopsy of my body, and direct the disposition of my remains.

THE ABOVE GRANT OF POWER IS INTENDED TO BE AS BROAD AS POSSIBLE SO THAT YOUR AGENT WILL HAVE AUTHORITY TO MAKE ANY DECISION YOU COULD MAKE TO OBTAIN OR TERMINATE ANY TYPE OF HEALTH CARE, INCLUDING WITHDRAWAL OF NOURISHMENT AND FLUIDS AND OTHER LIFE-SUSTAINING OR DEATH-DELAYING MEASURES, IF YOUR AGENT BELIEVES SUCH ACTION WOULD BE CONSISTENT WITH YOUR INTENT AND DESIRES. IF YOU WISH TO LIMIT THE SCOPE OF YOUR AGENT'S POWERS OR PRESCRIBE SPE-

CIAL RULES TO LIMIT THE POWER TO MAKE AN ANATOMICAL GIFT, AUTHORIZE AUTOPSY, OR DISPOSE OF REMAINS, YOU MAY DO SO IN THE FOLLOWING PARAGRAPHS.

2. The powers granted above shall not include the following powers or shall be subject to the following rules or limitations (here you may include any specific limitations you deem appropriate, such as your own definition of when life-sustaining or death-delaying measures should be withheld; a direction to continue nourishment and fluids or other life-sustaining or death-delaying treatment in all events; or instructions to refuse any specific types of treatment that are inconsistent with your religious beliefs or unacceptable to you for any other reason, such as blood transfusion, electroconvulsive therapy, or amputation):

....

....

....

THE SUBJECT OF LIFE-SUSTAINING OR DEATH-DELAYING TREATMENT IS OF PARTICULAR IMPORTANCE. FOR YOUR CONVENIENCE IN DEALING WITH THAT SUBJECT, SOME GENERAL STATEMENTS CONCERNING THE WITHHOLDING OR REMOVAL OF LIFE-SUSTAINING OR DEATH-DELAYING TREATMENT ARE SET FORTH BELOW. IF YOU AGREE WITH ONE OF THESE STATEMENTS, YOU MAY INITIAL THAT STATEMENT, BUT DO NOT INITIAL MORE THAN ONE.

I do not want my life to be prolonged nor do I want life- sustaining or death-delaying treatment to be provided or continued if my agent believes the burdens of the treatment outweigh the expected benefits. I want my agent to consider the relief of suffering, the expense involved, and the quality as well as the possible extension of my life in making decisions concerning life-sustaining or death-delaying treatment.

Initialed...................

I want my life to be prolonged and I want life-sustaining or death-delaying treatment to be provided or continued unless I am in a coma, including a persistent vegetative state, which my attending physician believes to be irreversible, in accordance with reasonable medical standards at the time of reference. If and when I have suffered such an irreversible coma, I want life-sustaining or death-delaying treatment to be withheld or discontinued.

Initialed....................

I want my life to be prolonged to the greatest extent possible without regard to my condition, the chances I have for recovery, or the cost of the procedures.

Initialed....................

THIS POWER OF ATTORNEY MAY BE AMENDED OR REVOKED BY YOU AT ANY TIME AND IN ANY MANNER WHILE YOU ARE ABLE TO DO SO. IN THE ABSENCE OF AN AMENDMENT OR REVOCATION, THE AUTHORITY GRANTED IN THIS POWER OF ATTORNEY WILL BECOME EFFECTIVE AT THE TIME THIS POWER IS SIGNED AND WILL CONTINUE UNTIL YOUR DEATH AND WILL CONTINUE BEYOND YOUR DEATH IF ANATOMICAL GIFT, AUTOPSY, OR DISPOSITION OF REMAINS IS AUTHORIZED, UNLESS A LIMITATION ON THE BEGINNING DATE OR DURATION IS MADE BY INITIALING AND COMPLETING EITHER OR BOTH OF THE FOLLOWING:

3. ( ) This power of attorney shall become effective on .... (insert a future date or event during your lifetime, such as court determination of your disability, incapacity, or incompetency, when you want this power to take effect).

4. ( ) This power of attorney shall terminate on .... (insert a future date or event, such as court determination of your disability, incapacity, or incompetency, when you want this power to terminate prior to your death).

IF YOU WISH TO NAME SUCCESSOR AGENTS, INSERT THE NAMES AND ADDRESSES OF SUCH SUCCESSORS IN THE FOLLOWING PARAGRAPH:

5. If any agent named by me shall die, become legally disabled, incapacitated, or incompetent, or resign, refuse to act, or be unavailable, I name the following (each to act successively in the order named) as successors to such agent:

....

....

IF YOU WISH TO NAME A GUARDIAN OF YOUR PERSON IN THE EVENT A COURT DECIDES THAT ONE SHOULD BE APPOINTED, YOU MAY, BUT ARE NOT REQUIRED TO, DO SO BY INSERTING THE NAME OF SUCH GUARDIAN IN THE FOLLOWING PARAGRAPH. THE COURT WILL APPOINT THE PERSON NOMINATED BY YOU IF THE COURT FINDS THAT SUCH APPOINTMENT WILL SERVE YOUR BEST INTERESTS AND WELFARE. YOU MAY, BUT ARE NOT REQUIRED TO, NOMINATE AS YOUR GUARDIAN THE SAME PERSON NAMED IN THIS FORM AS YOUR AGENT.

6. If a guardian of my person is to be appointed, I nominate the following to serve as such guardian:

....

(insert name and address of nominated guardian of the person)

7. I am fully informed as to all the contents of this form and understand the full import of this grant of powers to my agent.

Signed....................................

(Principal)

The principal has had an opportunity to read the above form and has signed the above form in our presence. We, the undersigned, each being over 18 years of age, witness the principal's signature at the request and in the presence of the principal, and in the presence of each other, on the date and year above set out.

Witnesses	Addresses:
....	....
	....
....	....
	....

Additional witness required when health care agency is signed in a hospital or skilled nursing facility.

I hereby witness this health care agency and attest that I believe the principal to be of sound mind and to have made this health care agency willingly and voluntarily.

Witness:...

Attending Physician

Address:...

....

YOU MAY, BUT ARE NOT REQUIRED TO, REQUEST YOUR AGENT AND SUCCESSOR AGENTS TO PROVIDE SPECIMEN SIGNATURES BELOW. IF YOU INCLUDE SPECIMEN SIGNATURES IN THIS POWER OF ATTORNEY, YOU MUST COMPLETE THE CERTIFICATION OPPOSITE THE SIGNATURES OF THE AGENTS.

Specimen signatures of agent and successor(s)	I certify that the signature of my agent and successor(s) is correct.
.... (Agent)	.... (Principal)
.... (Successor agent)	.... (Principal)
.... (Successor agent)	.... (Principal)

STATE OF IDAHO

A DURABLE POWER OF ATTORNEY FOR HEALTH CARE

1. DESIGNATION OF HEALTH CARE AGENT.
I,..
(insert your name and address)

do hereby designate and appoint ....
(Insert name, address, and telephone number of one individual only as your agent to make health care decisions for you. None of the following may be designated as your agent: (1) your treating health care provider, (2) a nonrelative employee of your treating health care provider, (3) an operator of a community care facility, or (4) a nonrelative employee of an operator of a community care facility).

as my attorney in fact (agent) to make health care decisions for me as authorized in this document. For the purposes of this document, "health care decision" means consent, refusal of consent, or withdrawal of consent to any care, treatment, or procedure to maintain, diagnose, or treat an individual's physical condition.
2. CREATION OF DURABLE POWER OF ATTORNEY FOR HEALTH CARE. By this document I intent to create a durable power of attorney for health care. This power of attorney shall not be affected by my subsequent incapacity.
3. GENERAL STATEMENT OF AUTHORITY GRANTED. Subject to any limitations in this document, I hereby grant to my agent full power and authority to make health care decisions for me to the same extent that I could make such decisions for myself if I had the capacity to do so. In exercising this authority, my agent shall make health care decisions that are consistent with my desires as stated in this document or otherwise made known to my agent, including, but not limited to, my desires concerning obtaining or refusing or withdrawing life-prolonging care, treatment, services, and procedures. (If you want to limit the authority of your agent to make health care decisions for you, you can state the limitations in paragraph 4 ("Statement of Desires, Special Provisions, and Limitations") below. You can indicate your desires by including a statement of your desires in the same paragraph.)
4. STATEMENT OF DESIRES, SPECIAL PROVISIONS, AND LIMITATIONS. (Your agent must make health care decisions that are consistent with your known desires. You can, but are not required to, state your desires in the space provided below. You should consider whether you want to include a statement of your desires concerning life-prolonging care, treatment, services, and procedures. You can also include a statement of your desires concerning other matters relating to your health care. You can also make your desires known to your agent by discussing your desires with your agent or by some other means. If there are any types of treatment that you do not want to be used, you should state them in the space below. If you want to limit in any other way the authority given your agent by this document, you should state the limits in the space below. If you do not state any limits, your agent will have broad powers to make health care decisions for you, except to the extent that there are limits provided by law.)
In exercising the authority under this durable power of attorney for health care, my agent shall act consistently with my desires as stated below and is subject to the special provisions and limitations stated in the living will. Additional statement of desires, special provisions, and limitations:
....
....
(You may attach additional pages if you need more space to complete your statement. If you attach additional pages, you must date and sign each of the additional pages at the same time you date and sign this document.)
5. INSPECTION AND DISCLOSURE OF INFORMATION RELATING TO MY PHYSICAL OR MENTAL HEALTH. Subject to any limitations in this document, my agent has the power and authority to do all of the following:

(a) Request, review, and receive any information, verbal or written, regarding my physical or mental health, including, but not limited to, medical and hospital records.
(b) Execute on my behalf any releases or other documents that may be required in order to obtain this information.
(c) Consent to the disclosure of this information.
(d) Consent to the donation of any of my organs for medical purposes. (If you want to limit the authority of your agent to receive and disclose information relating to your health, you must state the limitations in paragraph 4 ("Statement of Desires, Special Provisions, and Limitations") above.)
6. SIGNING DOCUMENTS, WAIVERS, AND RELEASES. Where necessary to implement the health care decisions that my agent is authorized by this document to make, my agent has the power and authority to execute on my behalf all of the following:
(a) Documents titled or purporting to be a "Refusal to Permit Treatment" and "Leaving Hospital Against Medical Advice."
(b) Any necessary waiver or release from liability required by a hospital or physician.
7. DESIGNATION OF ALTERNATE AGENTS.
(You are not required to designate any alternate agents but you may do so. Any alternate agent you designate will be able to make the same health care decisions as the agent you designated in paragraph 1, above, in the event that agent is unable or ineligible to act as your agent. If the agent you designated is your spouse, he or she becomes ineligible to act as your agent if your marriage is dissolved.)
If the person designated as my agent in paragraph 1 is not available or becomes ineligible to act as my agent to make a health care decision for me or loses the mental capacity to make health care decisions for me, or if I revoke that person's appointment or authority to act as my agent to make health care decisions for me, then I designate and appoint the following persons to serve as my agent to make health care decisions for me as authorized in this document, such persons to serve in the order listed below:
A. First Alternate Agent

....

(Insert name, address, and telephone number of first alternate agent)
B. Second Alternate Agent

....

(Insert name, address, and telephone number of second alternate agent)

8. PRIOR DESIGNATIONS REVOKED. I revoke any prior durable power of attorney for health care.

DATE AND SIGNATURE OF PRINCIPAL
(You Must Date and Sign This Power of Attorney)

I sign my name to this Statutory Form Durable Power of Attorney for Health Care on ....(Date) at .... (City), ...(State).

....

(You sign here)
(This Power of Attorney will not be valid unless it is signed by two qualified witnesses who are present when you sign or acknowledge your signature. If you have attached any additional pages to this form, you must date and sign each of the additional pages at the same time you date and sign this Power of Attorney.)

STATEMENT OF WITNESSES

(This document must be witnessed by two qualified adult witnesses. None of the following may be used as a witness: (1) a person you designate as your agent or alternate agent, (2) a health care provider, (3) an employee of a health care provider, (4) the operator of a community care facility, (5) an employee of an operator of a community care facility. At least one of the witnesses must make the additional declaration set out following the place where the witnesses sign.)

I declare under penalty of perjury under the laws of Idaho that the person who signed or acknowledged this document is personally known to me (or proved to me on the basis of convincing evidence) to be the principal, that the principal signed or acknowledged this durable power of attorney in my presence, that the principal appears to be of sound mind and under no duress, fraud, or undue influence, that I am not the person appointed as attorney in fact by this document, and that I am not a health care provider, an employee of a health care provider, the operator of a community care facility, nor an employee of an operator of a community care facility.

Signature:..

Print name: ....

Date: .... Residence address: ....

Signature:..

Print name: ....

Date: .... Residence address: ....

(At least one of the above witnesses must also sign)

I further declare under penalty of perjury under the laws of Idaho that I am not related to the principal by blood, marriage, or adoption, and, to the best of my knowledge, I am not entitled to any part of the estate of the principal upon the death of the principal under a will now existing or by operation of law.

Signature:..

Signature:..

NOTARY

(Signer of instrument may either have it witnessed as above or have his/her signature notarized as below, to legalize this instrument.)

State of Idaho

County of .... ss.

On this ....day of .... 19 ....

before me personally appeared ....

(full name of signer of instrument)

to me known (or proved to me on basis of satisfactory evidence) to be the person whose name is subscribed to this instrument, and acknowledged that he/she executed it. I declare under penalty of perjury that the person whose name is subscribed to this instrument appears to be of sound mind and under no duress, fraud or undue influence.

....

(Signature of Notary)

STATE OF ILLINOIS

ILLINOIS STATUTORY SHORT FORM POWER OF ATTORNEY FOR HEALTH CARE

(NOTICE: THE PURPOSE OF THIS POWER OF ATTORNEY IS TO GIVE THE PERSON YOU DESIGNATE (YOUR "AGENT") BROAD POWERS TO MAKE HEALTH CARE DECISIONS FOR YOU, INCLUDING POWER TO REQUIRE, CONSENT TO OR WITHDRAW ANY TYPE OF PERSONAL CARE OR MEDICAL TREATMENT FOR ANY PHYSICAL OR MENTAL CONDITION AND TO ADMIT YOU TO OR DISCHARGE YOU FROM ANY HOSPITAL, HOME OR OTHER INSTITUTION. THIS FORM DOES NOT IMPOSE A DUTY ON YOUR AGENT TO EXERCISE GRANTED POWERS; BUT WHEN POWERS ARE EXERCISED, YOUR AGENT WILL HAVE TO USE DUE CARE TO ACT FOR YOUR BENEFIT AND IN ACCORDANCE WITH THIS FORM AND KEEP A RECORD OF RECEIPTS, DISBURSEMENTS AND SIGNIFICANT ACTIONS TAKEN AS AGENT. A COURT CAN TAKE AWAY THE POWERS OF YOUR AGENT IF IT FINDS THE AGENT IS NOT ACTING PROPERLY. YOU MAY NAME SUCCESSOR AGENTS UNDER THIS FORM BUT NOT CO-AGENTS, AND NO HEALTH CARE PROVIDER MAY BE NAMED. UNLESS YOU EXPRESSLY LIMIT THE DURATION OF THIS POWER IN THE MANNER PROVIDED BELOW, UNTIL YOU REVOKE THIS POWER OR A COURT ACTING ON YOUR BEHALF TERMINATES IT, YOUR AGENT MAY EXERCISE THE POWERS GIVEN HERE THROUGHOUT YOUR LIFETIME, EVEN AFTER YOU BECOME DISABLED. THE POWERS YOU GIVE YOUR AGENT, YOUR RIGHT TO REVOKE THOSE POWERS AND THE PENALTIES FOR VIOLATING THE LAW ARE EXPLAINED MORE FULLY IN SECTIONS 4-5, 4-6,4-9 AND 4-10(b) OF THE ILLINOIS "POWERS OF ATTORNEY FOR HEALTH CARE LAW" OF WHICH THIS FORM IS A PART. THAT LAW EXPRESSLY PERMITS THE USE OF ANY DIFFERENT FORM OF POWER OF ATTORNEY YOU MAY DESIRE. IF THERE IS ANYTHING ABOUT THIS FORM THAT YOU DO NOT UNDERSTAND, YOU SHOULD ASK A LAWYER TO EXPLAIN IT TO YOU.)

POWER OF ATTORNEY made this ....day of .... (month, year).

1.I,..

(insert name and address of principal)

hereby appoint:

....

(insert name and address of agent)

as my attorney-in-fact (my "agent") to act for me and in my name (in any way I could act in person) to make any and all decisions for me concerning my personal care, medical treatment, hospitalization and health care and to require, withhold or withdraw any type of medical treatment or procedure, even though my death may ensue. My agent shall have the same access to my medical records that I have, including the right to disclose the contents to others. My agent shall also have full power to make a disposition of any part or all of my body for medical purposes, authorize an autopsy and direct the disposition of my remains.

(THE ABOVE GRANT OF POWER IS INTENDED TO BE AS BROAD AS POSSIBLE SO THAT YOUR AGENT WILL HAVE AUTHORITY TO MAKE ANY DECISION YOU COULD MAKE TO OBTAIN OR TERMINATE ANY TYPE OF HEALTH CARE, INCLUDING WITHDRAWAL OF FOOD AND WATER AND OTHER LIFE-SUSTAINING MEASURES, IF YOUR AGENT BELIEVES SUCH ACTION WOULD BE CONSISTENT WITH YOUR INTENT AND DESIRES. IF YOU WISH TO LIMIT THE SCOPE OF YOUR AGENT'S POWERS OR PRESCRIBE SPECIAL RULES OR LIMIT THE POWER TO MAKE AN ANATOMICAL GIFT, AUTHORIZE AUTOPSY OR DISPOSE OF REMAINS, YOU MAY DO SO IN THE FOLLOWING PARAGRAPHS.)

2. The powers granted above shall not include the following powers or shall be subject to the following rules or limitations (here you may include any specific limitations you deem appropriate, such as: your own definition of when life-sustaining measures should be withheld; a direction to continue food and fluids or life-sustaining treatment in all events; or instructions to refuse any specific types of treatment that are inconsistent with your religious beliefs or unacceptable to you for any other reason, such as blood transfusion, electro-convulsive therapy, amputation, psychosurgery, voluntary admission to a mental institution, etc.):

....

....

....

....

....

(THE SUBJECT OF LIFE-SUSTAINING TREATMENT IS OF PARTICULAR IMPORTANCE. FOR YOUR CONVENIENCE IN DEALING WITH THAT SUBJECT, SOME GENERAL STATEMENTS CONCERNING THE WITHHOLDING OR REMOVAL OF LIFE-SUSTAINING TREATMENT ARE SET FORTH BELOW. IF YOU AGREE WITH ONE OF THESE STATEMENTS, YOU MAY INITIAL THAT STATEMENT; BUT DO NOT INITIAL MORE THAN ONE):

I do not want my life to be prolonged nor do I wanted life-sustaining treatment to be provided or continued if my agent believes the burdens of treatment outweigh the expected benefits. I want my agent to consider the relief of suffering, the expense involved and the quality as well as the possible extension of my life in making decisions concerning life-sustaining treatment.

Initialed...

I want my life to be prolonged and I wanted life-sustaining treatment to be provided or continued unless I am in a coma which my attending physician believes to be irreversible, in accordance with reasonable medical standards at the time of reference. If and when I have suffered irreversible coma, I want life-sustaining treatment to be withheld or discontinued.

Initialed...

I want my life to be prolonged to the greatest extent possible without regard to my condition, the chances I have for recovery or the cost of the procedures.

Initialed...

(THIS POWER OF ATTORNEY MAY BE AMENDED OR REVOKED BY YOU IN THE MANNER PROVIDED IN SECTION 4-6 OF THE ILLINOIS "POWERS OF ATTORNEY FOR HEALTH CARE LAW." ABSENT AMENDMENT OR REVOCATION, THE AUTHORITY GRANTED IN THIS POWER OF ATTORNEY WILL BECOME EFFECTIVE AT THE TIME THIS POWER IS SIGNED AND WILL CONTINUE UNTIL YOUR DEATH, AND BEYOND IF ANATOMICAL GIFT, AUTOPSY OR DISPOSITION OF REMAINS IS AUTHORIZED, UNLESS A LIMITATION ON THE BEGINNING DATE OR DURATION IS MADE BY INITIALING AND COMPLETING EITHER OR BOTH OF THE FOLLOWING):

3. ( ) This power of attorney shall become effective on ....
(insert a future date or event during your lifetime, such as court determination of your disability, when you want this power to first take effect)

4. ( ) This power of attorney shall terminate on ....
(insert a future date or event, such as court determination of your disability, when you want this power to terminate prior to your death)

(IF YOU WISH TO NAME SUCCESSOR AGENTS, INSERT THE NAMES AND ADDRESSES OF SUCH SUCCESSORS IN THE FOLLOWING PARAGRAPH.)

5. If any agent named by me shall die, become incompetent, resign, refuse to accept the office of agent or be unavailable, I name the following (each to act alone and successively, in the order named) as successors to such agent:

....

....

For purposes of this paragraph 5, a person shall be considered to be incompetent if and while the person is a minor or an adjudicated incompetent or disabled person or the person is unable to give prompt and intelligent consideration to health care matters, as certified by a licensed physician.

(IF YOU WISH TO NAME YOUR AGENT AS GUARDIAN OF YOUR PERSON, IN THE EVENT A COURT DECIDES THAT ONE SHOULD BE APPOINTED, YOU MAY, BUT ARE NOT REQUIRED TO, DO SO BY RETAINING THE FOLLOWING PARAGRAPH. THE COURT WILL APPOINT YOUR AGENT IF THE COURT FINDS THAT SUCH APPOINTMENT WILL SERVE YOUR BEST INTERESTS AND WELFARE. STRIKE OUT PARAGRAPH 6 IF YOU DO NOT WANT YOUR AGENT TO ACT AS GUARDIAN.)

6. If a guardian of my person is to be appointed, I nominate the agent acting under this power of attorney as such guardian, to serve without bond or security (insert name and address of nominated guardian of the person)

7. I am fully informed as to all the contents of this form and understand the full import of this grant of powers to my agent.

Signed...

principal)

The principal has had an opportunity to read the above form and has signed the form or acknowledged his or her signature or mark on the form in my presence.

.... Residing at..

(witness)

(YOU MAY, BUT ARE NOT REQUIRED TO, REQUEST YOUR AGENT AND SUCCESSOR AGENTS TO PROVIDE SPECIMEN SIGNATURES BELOW. IF YOU INCLUDE SPECIMEN SIGNATURES IN THIS POWER OF ATTORNEY, YOU MUST COMPLETE THE CERTIFICATION OPPOSITE THE SIGNATURES OF THE AGENTS.

Specimen signatures of agent (and successors)	I certify that the signatures of my agent (and successors) are correct
.... (agent)	.... (principal)
.... (successor agent)	.... (principal)
.... (successor agent)	.... (principal)

STATE OF KANSAS

DURABLE POWER OF ATTORNEY FOR HEALTH CARE DECISIONS GENERAL STATEMENT OF AUTHORITY GRANTED

I,.., designate and appoint:

Name:..

Address:..

Telephone Number:..

to be my agent for health care decisions and pursuant to the language stated below, on my behalf to:
(1) Consent, refuse consent, or withdraw consent to any care, treatment, service or procedure to maintain, diagnose or treat a physical or mental condition, and to make decisions about organ donation, autopsy and disposition of the body.
(2) make all necessary arrangements at any hospital, psychiatric hospital or psychiatric treatment facility, hospice, nursing home or similar institution; to employ or discharge health care personnel to include physicians, psychiatrists, psychologists, dentists, nurses, therapists or any other person who is licensed, certified or otherwise authorized or permitted by the laws of this state to administer health care as the agent shall deem necessary for my physical, mental and emotional well being; and
(3) request, receive and review any information, verbal or written, regarding my personal affairs or physical or mental health including medical and hospital records and to execute any releases of other documents that may be required in order to obtain such information.
In exercising the grant of authority set forth above my agent for health care decisions shall:

....

....

....

....

(Here may be inserted any special instructions or statement of the principal's desire to be followed by the agent in exercising the authority granted).

LIMITATIONS OF AUTHORITY

(1) The powers of the agent herein shall be limited to the extent set out in writing in this durable power of attorney for health care decisions, and shall not include the power to revoke or invalidate any previously existing declaration made in accordance with the natural death act.
(2) The agent shall be prohibited from authorizing consent for the following items:

....

....

(3) The durable power of attorney for health care decisions shall be subject to the additional following limitations:

....

....

EFFECTIVE TIME

This power of attorney for health care decisions shall become effective (*immediately and shall not be affected by my subsequent disability or incapacity or upon the occurrence of my disability or incapacity).*

REVOCATION

Any durable power of attorney for health care decisions I have previous made is hereby revoked.
(This durable power of attorney for health care decisions shall be revoked *by an instrument in writing executed and witnessed or acknowledged in the same manner as required herein or set out another manner of revocation, if desired).*

EXECUTION

Executed this ...., at ...., Kansas.

....
Principal

This document must be: (1) Witnessed by two individuals of lawful age who are not the agent, nor related to the principal by blood, marriage or adoption, not entitled to any portion of principal's estate and not financially responsible for principal's health care: OR (2) acknowledged by a notary public.

.... Witness	.... Witness
.... Address	.... Address

(OR)

STATE OF ....)
COUNTY OF ....) SS.
This instrument was acknowledged before me .... (date) by .... (name of person)

....
(Signature of notary public)

(Seal, if any)

My appointment expires: ....

Copies

STATE OF KENTUCKY

DESIGNATION OF HEALTH CARE SURROGATE

I designate .... as my health care surrogate(s)* to make any health care decisions for me when I no longer have decisional capacity. If .... refuses or is not able to act for me, I designate .... as my health care surrogate(s).*
Any prior designation is revoked.
Signed this .... day of ...., 19 ....

....
Signature of grantor
....
....
Address of grantor

In our joint presence, the grantor, who is of sound mind and eighteen years of age, or older, voluntarily dated and signed this writing or directed it to be dated and signed for the grantor.

....
Signature of witness
....
....
Address of witness

....
Signature of witness
....
....
Address of witness

OR

STATE OF KENTUCKY)
.... County)
Before me, the undersigned authority, came the grantor who is of sound mind and eighteen (18) years of age, or older, and acknowledged that he voluntarily dated and signed this writing or directed it to be signed and dated as above.
Done this .... day of ...., 19 ......

....
Signature of Notary Public or other officer

Date commission expires: ....

[*A grantor may designate one (1) or more adults as a surrogate or successor surrogate to make any health care decision on behalf of the grantor. During any period in which two (2) or more surrogates are serving, all decisions shall be by unanimous consent of all then acting surrogates unless the designation provides otherwise.]

STATE OF NEVADA

DURABLE POWER OF ATTORNEY FOR HEALTH CARE DECISIONS

WARNING TO PERSON EXECUTING THIS DOCUMENT

THIS IS AN IMPORTANT LEGAL DOCUMENT. IT CREATES A DURABLE POWER OF ATTORNEY FOR HEALTH CARE. BEFORE EXECUTING THIS DOCUMENT, YOU SHOULD KNOW THESE IMPORTANT FACTS:

1. THIS DOCUMENT GIVES THE PERSON YOU DESIGNATE AS YOUR ATTORNEY-IN-FACT THE POWER TO MAKE HEALTH CARE DECISIONS FOR YOU. THIS POWER IS SUBJECT TO ANY LIMITATIONS OR STATEMENT OF YOUR DESIRES THAT YOU INCLUDE IN THIS DOCUMENT. THE POWER TO MAKE HEALTH CARE DECISIONS FOR YOU MAY INCLUDE CONSENT, REFUSAL OF CONSENT, OR WITHDRAWAL OF CONSENT TO ANY CARE, TREATMENT, SERVICE, OR PROCEDURE TO MAINTAIN, DIAGNOSE, OR TREAT A PHYSICAL OR MENTAL CONDITION. YOU MAY STATE IN THIS DOCUMENT ANY TYPES OF TREATMENT OR PLACEMENTS THAT YOU DO NOT DESIRE.
2. THE PERSON YOU DESIGNATE IN THIS DOCUMENT HAS A DUTY TO ACT CONSISTENT WITH YOUR DESIRES AS STATED IN THIS DOCUMENT OR OTHERWISE MADE KNOWN OR, IF YOUR DESIRES ARE UNKNOWN, TO ACT IN YOUR BEST INTERESTS.
3. EXCEPT AS YOU OTHERWISE SPECIFY IN THIS DOCUMENT, THE POWER OF THE PERSON YOU DESIGNATE TO MAKE HEALTH CARE DECISIONS FOR YOU MAY INCLUDE THE POWER TO CONSENT TO YOUR DOCTOR NOT GIVING TREATMENT OR STOPPING TREATMENT WHICH WOULD KEEP YOU ALIVE.
4. UNLESS YOU SPECIFY A SHORTER PERIOD IN THIS DOCUMENT, THIS POWER WILL EXIST INDEFINITELY FROM THE DATE YOU EXECUTE THIS DOCUMENT AND, IF YOU ARE UNABLE TO MAKE HEALTH CARE DECISIONS FOR YOURSELF, THIS POWER WILL CONTINUE TO EXIST UNTIL THE TIME WHEN YOU BECOME ABLE TO MAKE HEALTH CARE DECISIONS FOR YOURSELF.
5. NOTWITHSTANDING THIS DOCUMENT, YOU HAVE THE RIGHT TO MAKE MEDICAL AND OTHER HEALTH CARE DECISIONS FOR YOURSELF SO LONG AS YOU CAN GIVE INFORMED CONSENT WITH RESPECT TO THE PARTICULAR DECISION. IN ADDITION, NO TREATMENT MAY BE GIVEN TO YOU OVER YOUR OBJECTION, AND HEALTH CARE NECESSARY TO KEEP YOU ALIVE MAY NOT BE STOPPED IF YOU OBJECT.
6. YOU HAVE THE RIGHT TO REVOKE THE APPOINTMENT OF THE PERSON DESIGNATED IN THIS DOCUMENT TO MAKE HEALTH CARE DECISIONS FOR YOU BY NOTIFYING THAT PERSON OF THE REVOCATION ORALLY OR IN WRITING.
7. YOU HAVE THE RIGHT TO REVOKE THE AUTHORITY GRANTED TO THE PERSON DESIGNATED IN THIS DOCUMENT TO MAKE HEALTH CARE DECISIONS FOR YOU BY NOTIFYING THE TREATING PHYSICIAN, HOSPITAL, OR OTHER PROVIDER OF HEALTH CARE ORALLY OR IN WRITING.
8. THE PERSON DESIGNATED IN THIS DOCUMENT TO MAKE HEALTH CARE DECISIONS FOR YOU HAS THE RIGHT TO EXAMINE YOUR MEDICAL RECORDS AND TO CONSENT TO THEIR DISCLOSURE UNLESS YOU LIMIT THIS RIGHT IN THIS DOCUMENT.
9. THIS DOCUMENT REVOKES ANY PRIOR DURABLE POWER OF ATTORNEY FOR HEALTH CARE.
10. IF THERE IS ANYTHING IN THIS DOCUMENT THAT YOU DO NOT UNDERSTAND, YOU SHOULD ASK A LAWYER TO EXPLAIN IT TO YOU.

1.DESIGNATION OF HEALTH
CARE AGENT.

I,...(your name)
do hereby designate and appoint: Name :...
Address:..
Telephone Number:..
as my attorney-in-fact to make health care decisions for me as authorized in this document.

(Insert the name and address of the person you wish to designate as your attorney-in-fact to make health care decisions for you. None of the following may be designated as your attorney-in-fact: (1) your treating provider of health care, (2) an employee of your treating provider of health care, (3) an operator of a health care facility, or (4) an employee of an operator of a health care facility.)

2. CREATION OF DURABLE POWER OF ATTORNEY FOR HEALTH CARE.

By this document I intend to create a durable power of attorney by appointing the person designated above to make health care decisions for me. This power of attorney shall not be affected by my subsequent incapacity.

3. GENERAL STATEMENT OF AUTHORITY GRANTED.

In the event that I am incapable of giving informed consent with respect to health care decisions, I hereby grant to the attorney-in-fact named above full power and authority to make health care decisions for me before, or after my death, including: consent, refusal of consent, or withdrawal of consent to any care, treatment, service, or procedure to maintain, diagnose, or treat a physical or mental condition, subject only to the limitations and special provisions, if any, set forth in paragraph 4 or 6.

4. SPECIAL PROVISIONS AND LIMITATIONS.

(You attorney-in-fact is not permitted to consent to any of the following: commitment to or placement in a mental health treatment facility, convulsive treatment, psychosurgery, sterilization, or abortion. If there are any other types of treatment or placement that you do not want your attorney-in-fact's authority to give consent for or other restrictions you wish to place on his or her attorney-in-fact's authority, you should list them in the space below. If you do not write any limitations, your attorney-in-fact will have the broad powers to make health care decisions on your behalf which are set forth in paragraph 3, except to the extent that there are limits provided by law.)

In exercising the authority under this durable power of attorney for health care, the authority of my attorney-in-fact is subject to the following special provisions and limitations:

....

....

....

5. DURATION.

I understand that this power of attorney will exist indefinitely from the date I execute this document unless I establish a shorter time. If I am unable to make health care decisions for myself when this power of attorney expires, the authority I have granted my attorney-in-fact will continue to exist until the time when I become able to make health care decisions for myself.

(IF APPLICABLE)

I wish to have this power of attorney end on the following date:..........................

6. STATEMENT OF DESIRES.

(With respect to decisions to withhold or withdraw life-sustaining treatment, your attorney-in-fact must make health care decisions that are consistent with your known desires. You can, but are not required to, indicate your desires below. If your desires are unknown, your attorney-in-fact has the duty to act in your best interests; and, under some circumstances, a judicial proceeding may be necessary so that a court can determine the health care decision that is in your best interests. If you wish to indicate your desires, you may INITIAL the statement or statements that reflect your desires and/or write your own statements in the space below.)

(If the statement reflects your desires, initial the box next to the statement.)

1. I desire that my life be prolonged to the greatest extent possible, without regard to my condition, the chances I have for recovery or long term survival, or the cost of the procedures [...............]

2. If I am in a coma which my doctors have reasonably concluded is irreversible, I desire that life-sustaining or prolonging treatments not be used. (Also should utilize provisions of Nevada Revised Statutes 449.610 et seq. if this subparagraph is initialed.) [..............]

3. If I have an incurable or terminal condition or illness and no reasonable hope of long term recovery or survival, I desire that life-sustaining or prolonging treatments not be used. (Also should utilize provisions of Nevada Revised Statutes 449.610 et seq. if this subparagraph is initialed.) [..............]

4. I do not desire treatment to be provided and/or continued if the burdens of the treatment outweigh the expected benefits. My attorney-in-fact is to consider the relief of suffering, the preservation or restoration of functioning, and the quality as well as the extent of the possible extension of my life [..............]

(If you wish to change your answer, you may do so by drawing an "X" through the answer you do not want, and circling the answer you prefer.)

Other or Additional Statements of Desires: ....

....

....

....

....

....

7. DESIGNATION OF ALTERNATE ATTORNEY-IN-FACT.

(You are not required to designate any alternate attorney-in-fact but you may do so. Any alternate attorney-in-fact you designate will be able to make the same health care decisions as the attorney-in-fact designated in paragraph 1, page 2, in the event that he or she is unable or unwilling to act as your attorney-in-fact. Also, if the attorney-in-fact designated in paragraph 1 is your spouse, his or her designation as your attorney-in-fact is automatically revoked by law if your marriage is dissolved.)

If the person designated in paragraph 1 as my attorney-in-fact is unable to make health care decisions for me, then I designate the following persons to serve as my attorney-in-fact to make health care decisions for me as authorized in this document, such persons to serve in the order listed below:

A. First Alternate Attorney-in-fact

Name:..
Address:...
Telephone Number: ....

B. Second Alternate Attorney-in-fact

Name:..
Address:...
Telephone Number: ....

8. PRIOR DESIGNATIONS REVOKED. I revoke any prior durable power of attorney for health care.

(YOU MUST DATE AND SIGN THIS POWER OF ATTORNEY)

I sign my name to this Durable Power of Attorney for Health Care on .... (date) at ....(city).......................................(state)

....
(Signature)

(THIS POWER OF ATTORNEY WILL NOT BE VALID FOR MAKING HEALTH CARE DECISIONS UNLESS IT IS EITHER (1) SIGNED BY AT LEAST TWO QUALIFIED WITNESSES WHO ARE PERSONALLY KNOWN TO YOU AND WHO ARE PRESENT WHEN YOU SIGN OR ACKNOWLEDGE YOUR SIGNATURE OR (2) ACKNOWLEDGED BEFORE A NOTARY PUBLIC.)

CERTIFICATE OF ACKNOWLEDGEMENT OF NOTARY PUBLIC
(You may use acknowledgement before a notary public instead of the statement of witnesses.)

State of Nevada)
) ss.
County of....................)

On this ....day of ....in the year ...., before me, ... (here insert name of notary public) personally appeared ....(here insert name of principal) personally known to me (or proved to me on the basis of satisfactory evidence) to be the person whose name is subscribed to this instrument, and acknowledged that he or she executed it. I declare under penalty of perjury that the person whose name is ascribed to this instrument appears to be of sound mind and under no duress, fraud, or undue influence.

NOTARY SEAL ....
(Signature of Notary Public)

STATEMENT OF WITNESSES
(You should carefully read and follow this witnessing procedure. This document will not be valid unless you comply with the witnessing procedure. If you elect to use witnesses instead of having this document notarized you must use two qualified adult witnesses. None of the following may be used as a witness: (1) a person you designate as the attorney-in-fact, (2) a provider of health care, (3) an employee of a provider of health care, (4) the operator of a health care facility, (5) an employee of an operator of a health care facility. At least one of the witnesses must make the additional declaration set out following the place where the witnesses sign.)

I declare under penalty of perjury that the principal is personally known to me, that the principal signed or acknowledged this durable power of attorney in my presence, that the principal appears to be of sound mind and under no duress, fraud, or undue influence, that I am not the person appointed as attorney-in-fact by this document, and that I am not a provider of health care, an employee of a provider of health care, the operator of a community care facility, nor an employee of an operator of a health care facility.

Signature:......................... Residence Address:...
Print Name:...
Date:..
Signature:......................... Residence Address:...
Print Name:...
Date:..

(AT LEAST ONE OF THE ABOVE WITNESSES MUST ALSO SIGN THE FOLLOWING DECLARATION.)

I declare under penalty of perjury that I am not related to the principal by blood, marriage, or adoption, and to the best of my knowledge I am not entitled to any part of the estate of the principal upon the death of the principal under a will now existing or by operation of law.
Signature:...
Signature:...

Name:.............................. Address...
Print Name:...
Date:...

COPIES: You should retain an executed copy of this document and give one to your attorney-in-fact. The power of attorney should be available so a copy may be given to your providers of health care.

STATE OF NEW YORK

Health Care Proxy

I...(name of principal) hereby appoint ....(name, home address and telephone number of agent) as my health care agent* to make any and all health care decisions for me, except to the extent I state otherwise.

This health care proxy shall take effect in the event I become unable to make my own health care decisions.

NOTE: Although not necessary, and neither encouraged nor discouraged, you may wish to state instructions or wishes, and limit your agent's authority. Unless your agent knows your wishes about artificial nutrition and hydration, your agent will not have authority to decide about artificial nutrition and hydration. If you choose to state instructions, wishes, or limits, please do so below:

....

....

....

I direct my agent to make health care decisions in accordance with my wishes and instructions as stated above or as otherwise known to him or her. I also direct my agent to abide by any limitations on his or her authority as stated above or as otherwise known to him or her.

In the event the person I appoint above is unable, unwilling or unavailable to act as my health care agent, I hereby appoint...(name, home address and telephone number of alternate agent) as my health care agent.

I understand that, unless I revoke it, this proxy will remain in effect indefinitely or until the date or occurrence of the condition I have stated below:

(Please complete the following if you do NOT want this health care proxy to be in effect indefinitely):

This proxy shall expire:...(Specify date or condition)

Signature:...

Address:...

Date:...

I declare that the person who signed or asked another to sign this document is personally known to me and appears to be of sound mind and acting willingly and free from duress. He or she signed (or asked another to sign for him or her) this document in my presence and that person signed in my presence. I am not the person appointed as agent by this document.

**Witness:...

Address:...

**Witness:...

Address:...

[*Restrictions on who may be a health care agent: (1) A nonrelative operator, administrator, or employee of a hospital in which the principal is a patient may not serve as a health care agent. (2) If a physician is appointed agent, the physician shall not act as the patient's attending physician after the authority under the health care proxy commences, unless the physician declines the appointment as agent at or before such time. (3) No physician affiliated with a mental hygiene facility or a psychiatric unit of a general hospital may serve as agent for a principal residing in or being treated by such facility or unit unless the physician is related to the principal by blood, marriage or adoption. (4) No person who is not the spouse, child, parent, brother, sister or grandparent of the principal, or is the issue of, or married to, such person, shall be appointed as a health care agent if, at the time of appointment, he or she is presently appointed health care agent for ten principals.]

[Restrictions on witnesses: (1) For persons who reside in a mental hygiene facility operated or licensed by the office of mental health, at least one witness shall be an individual who is not affiliated with the facility and at least one witness shall be a physician certified by the American Board of Psychiatry and Neurology. (2) For persons who reside in a mental hygiene facility operated or licensed by the office of mental retardation and developmental disabilities, at least one witness shall be an individual who is not affiliated with the facility and at least one witness shall be a physician or clinical psychologist who either is employed by a school named in section 13.17 of the mental hygiene law or who has been employed for a minimum of two years to render care and service in a facility operated or licensed by the office of mental retardation and developmental disabilities in accordance with regulations approved by the commissioner. Such regulations shall require that a physician or clinical psychologist possess specialized training or three years experience in treating developmental disabilities.]**

STATE OF OHIO

DURABLE POWER OF ATTORNEY FOR HEALTH CARE

"Notice to Person Executing This Document

This is an important legal document. Before executing this document, you should know these facts:

This document gives the person you designate (the attorney in fact) the power to make **MOST** health care decisions for you if you lose the capacity to make informed health care decisions for yourself. This power is effective only when you lose the capacity to make informed health care decisions for yourself and, notwithstanding this document, as long as you have the capacity to make informed health care decisions for yourself, you retain the right to make all medical and other health care decisions for yourself.

You may include specific limitations in this document on the authority of the attorney in fact to make health care decisions for you.

Subject to any specific limitations you include in this document, if you do lose the capacity to make an informed decision on a health care matter, the attorney in fact **GENERALLY** will be authorized by this document to make health care decisions for you to the same extent as you could make those decisions for yourself, if you had the capacity to do so. The authority of the attorney in fact to make health care decisions for you **GENERALLY** will include the authority to give informed consent, or to withdraw informed consent to any care, treatment, service, or procedure to maintain, diagnose, or treat a physical or mental condition.

HOWEVER, even if the attorney in fact has general authority to make health care decisions for you under this document, the attorney in fact **NEVER** will be authorized to do any of the following:

(1) Refuse or withdraw informed consent to health care necessary to maintain your life (unless you are suffering from an illness or injury that is likely to result in imminent death, regardless of the type, nature, and amount of health care provided);

(2) Refuse or withdraw informed consent to health care necessary to provide you with comfort care (except that, if he is not prohibited from doing so under (4) below, the attorney in fact could refuse or withdraw informed consent to the provision of nutrition or hydration to you);

(3) Refuse or withdraw informed consent to health care for you if you are pregnant and if the refusal or withdrawal would terminate the pregnancy (unless the pregnancy or health care would pose a substantial risk to your life, or unless your attending physician and at least one other physician determine, to a reasonable degree of medical certainty, that the fetus would not be born alive);

(4) Refuse or withdraw informed consent to the provision of nutrition or hydration to you, unless, prior to the refusal or withdrawal of that informed consent, your attending physician and at least one other physician record their opinions that the provision of nutrition or hydration would not provide comfort to you, and additionally that either of the following situations exists: your death is imminent whether or not nutrition or hydration is provided to you, and the nonprovision of nutrition or hydration to you is not likely to result in your death by malnutrition or dehydration; **OR** if nutrition or hydration were provided to you, it could not be assimilated or would shorten your life.

(5) Withdraw informed consent to any health care to which you previously consented, unless a change in your physical condition has significantly decreased the benefit of that health care to you, or unless the health care is not, or is no longer, significantly effective in achieving the purposes for which you consented to its use.

Additionally, when exercising his authority to make health care decisions for you, the attorney in fact will have to act consistently with your desires or, if your desires are unknown, to act in your best interest. You may express your desires to the attorney in fact by including them in this document or by making them known to him in another manner.

When acting pursuant to this document, the attorney in fact **GENERALLY** will have the same rights that you have to receive information about proposed health care, to review health care records, and to consent to the disclosure of health care records. You can limit that right in this document if you so choose.

Generally, you may designate any competent adult as the attorney in fact under this document. However, you **CANNOT** designate a physician who is treating you, or an employee or agent of a physician who is treating you, or an employee or agent of a health care facility at which you are being treated as the attorney in fact under it.

Unless you specify a shorter period in this document, the document and the power it grants to the attorney in fact will be in effect for seven years from the date of its execution. However, if you lack the capacity to make informed health care decisions on the date that the document and the power it grants to the attorney in fact otherwise would expire, the document and the power it grants will continue in effect until you regain the capacity to make informed health care decisions for yourself.

You have the right to revoke the designation of the attorney in fact by giving him oral or written notice of the revocation. You have the right to revoke the authority of the attorney in fact to make health care decisions for you by giving oral or written notice of the revocation to your physician or another physician who is providing you with health care. You have the right to revoke this document and the authority granted to the attorney in fact under this document by canceling, obliterating, or destroying it with the intent to revoke it, or by doing anything else that clearly communicates your intent to revoke the document.

If you execute this document and create a valid durable power of attorney for health care with it, it will revoke any prior, valid durable power of attorney for health care that you created, unless you indicate otherwise in this document.

This document is not valid as a durable power of attorney for health care unless it either is acknowledged before a notary public or it is attested and signed by at least two adult witnesses who personally know you and who are present when you sign or acknowledge your signature. No person who is related to you by blood, marriage, or adoption, and no person who is entitled to benefit in any way from your death may be a witness. The attorney in fact, physicians, and employees or agents of a physician or a health care facility are ineligible to be witnesses.

If there is anything in this document that you do not understand, you should ask your lawyer to explain it to you."

1. DESIGNATION OF HEALTH CARE AGENT. I,..(insert your name) do hereby designate and appoint: Name:...

Address:...

Telephone Number:...

as my attorney-in-fact to make health care decisions for me as authorized in this document.

(Insert the name and address of the person you wish to designate as your attorney-in-fact to make health care decisions for you. None of the following may be designated as your attorney-in-fact: (1) a physician who is treating you, (2) an employee of a physician who is treating you, or (3) an employee or agent of a health care facility at which you are being treated.)

2. CREATION OF DURABLE POWER OF ATTORNEY FOR HEALTH CARE.

By this document I intend to create a durable power of attorney by appointing the person designated above to make health care decisions for me. This power of attorney shall not be affected by my subsequent incapacity.

3. GENERAL STATEMENT OF AUTHORITY GRANTED.

In the event that I am incapable of giving informed consent with respect to health care decisions, I hereby grant to the attorney-in-fact named above full power and authority to make health care decisions for me before, or after my death, including: consent, refusal of consent, or withdrawal of consent to any care, treatment, service, or procedure to maintain, diagnose, or treat a physical or mental condition, subject only to the limitations and special provisions, if any, set forth in paragraph 4 or 6.

4. SPECIAL PROVISIONS AND LIMITATIONS.

(You attorney-in-fact is not permitted to consent to any of the following: (A) Refuse or withdraw informed consent to health care necessary to maintain your life (unless you are suffering from an illness or injury that is likely to result in imminent death, regardless of the type, nature, and amount of health care provided);
(B) Refuse or withdraw informed consent to health care necessary to provide you with comfort care (except that, if he is not prohibited from doing so under (D) below, the attorney in fact could refuse or withdraw informed consent to the provision of nutrition or hydration to you);
(C) Refuse or withdraw informed consent to health care for you if you are pregnant and if the refusal or withdrawal would terminate the pregnancy (unless the pregnancy or health care would pose a substantial risk to your life, or unless your attending physician and at least one other physician determine, to a reasonable degree of medical certainty, that the fetus would not be born alive);
(D) Refuse or withdraw informed consent to the provision of nutrition or hydration to you, unless, prior to the refusal or withdrawal of that informed consent, your attending physician and at least one other physician record their opinions that the provision of nutrition or hydration would not provide comfort to you, and additionally that either of the following situations exists: your death is imminent whether or not nutrition or hydration is provided to you, and the nonprovision of nutrition or hydration to you is not likely to result in your death by malnutrition or dehydration; **OR** if nutrition or hydration were provided to you, it could not be assimilated or would shorten your life.
(E) Withdraw informed consent to any health care to which you previously consented, unless a change in your physical condition has significantly decreased the benefit of that health care to you, or unless the health care is not, or is no longer, significantly effective in achieving the purposes for which you consented to its use.

If there are any other types of treatment or placement that you do not want your attorney-in-fact's authority to give consent for or other restrictions you wish to place on his or her attorney-in-fact's authority, you should list them in the space below. If you do not write any limitations, your attorney-in-fact will have the broad powers to make health care decisions on your behalf which are set forth in paragraph 3, except to the extent that there are limits provided by law.)
In exercising the authority under this durable power of attorney for health care, the authority of my attorney-in-fact is subject to the following special provisions and limitations:

....

....

....

5. DURATION.

I understand that this power of attorney will exist for seven years from the date I execute this document unless I establish a shorter time. If I am unable to make health care decisions for myself when this power of attorney expires, the authority I have granted my attorney-in-fact will continue to exist until the time when I become able to make health care decisions for myself.
This durable power of attorney for health care expires on..
(Fill in this space ONLY if you want the authority of your agent to end EARLIER than the seven-year period described above.)

6. STATEMENT OF DESIRES.

(With respect to decisions to withhold or withdraw life-sustaining treatment, your attorney-in-fact must make health care decisions that are consistent with your known desires. You can, but are not required to, indicate your desires below (or you may make them known to your attorney-in-fact in another manner). If your desires are unknown, your attorney-in-fact has the duty to act in your best interests; and, under some circumstances, a judicial proceeding may be necessary so that a court can determine the health care decision that is in your best interests.
(A) Statement of your desires concerning life-prolonging care, treatment, services, and procedures:

....

....
....
....
....
....
....
....

(B) Additional statement of desires, special provisions, and limitations:

....
....
....
....
....
....
....
....

(You may attach additional pages if you need more space to complete your statement. If you attach additional pages, you must date and sign EACH of the additional pages at the same time you date and sign this document.)

7. PRIOR DESIGNATIONS REVOKED. I revoke any prior durable power of attorney for health care.

(YOU MUST DATE AND SIGN THIS POWER OF ATTORNEY)

I sign my name to this Durable Power of Attorney for Health Care on .... (date) at ....(city)................................(state)

....
(Signature)

(THIS POWER OF ATTORNEY WILL NOT BE VALID FOR MAKING HEALTH CARE DECISIONS UNLESS IT IS EITHER (1) SIGNED BY AT LEAST TWO QUALIFIED WITNESSES WHO ARE PERSONALLY KNOWN TO YOU AND WHO ARE PRESENT WHEN YOU SIGN OR ACKNOWLEDGE YOUR SIGNATURE OR (2) ACKNOWLEDGED BEFORE A NOTARY PUBLIC.)

CERTIFICATE OF ACKNOWLEDGEMENT OF NOTARY PUBLIC
(You may use acknowledgement before a notary public instead of the statement of witnesses.)

State of Ohio)
) ss.
Countyof..............................)

On this ....day of ...., in the year ...., before me, ... (here insert name of notary public) personally appeared ....(here insert name of principal) personally known to me (or proved to me on the basis of satisfactory evidence) to be the person whose name is subscribed to this instrument, and acknowledged that he or she executed it. I declare under penalty of perjury that the person whose name is ascribed to this instrument appears to be of sound mind and under no duress, fraud, or undue influence.

NOTARY SEAL

....
(Signature of Notary Public)

STATEMENT OF WITNESSES

(You should carefully read and follow this witnessing procedure. This document will not be valid unless you comply with the witnessing procedure. If you elect to use witnesses instead of having this document notarized you must use two qualified adult witnesses. None of the following may be used as a witness: (1) a person you designate as the attorney-in-fact, (2) a physician, (3) an employee or agent of a physician or of a health care facility. In addition, no person who is related to you by blood, marriage, or adoption, and no person who is entitled to benefit in any way from your death may serve as a witness to this document.)

I declare under penalty of perjury that the principal is personally known to me, that the principal signed or acknowledged this durable power of attorney in my presence, that the principal appears to be of sound mind and under no duress, fraud, or undue influence, that I am not the person appointed as attorney-in-fact by this document, and that I am not a physician, an employee or agent of a physician, or an employee or agent of a health care facility.

I also declare, under penalty of perjury, that I am not related to the principal by blood, marriage, or adoption, and that I am not entitled to benefit in any way from the death of the principal.

Signature:.. Residence Address: ....
Print Name:..
Date:..
Signature:.. Residence Address: ....
Print Name:..
Date:..

COPIES: You should retain an executed copy of this document and give one to your attorney-in-fact. The power of attorney should be available so a copy may be given to your physician as well.

STATE OF OREGON

POWER OF ATTORNEY FOR HEALTH CARE

I appoint ...., whose address is ...., and whose telephone number is ...., as my attorney-in-fact for health care decisions. I appoint ...., whose address is ...., and whose telephone number is ...., as my alternative attorney-in-fact for health care decisions. I authorize my attorney-in-fact appointed by this document to make health care decisions for me when I am incapable of making my own health care decisions. I have read the warning below and understand the consequences of appointing a power of attorney for health care.

I direct that my attorney-in-fact comply with the following instructions or limitations: ....

....

In addition, I direct that my attorney-in-fact have authority to make decisions regarding the following:

.........Withholding or withdrawal of life-sustaining procedures with the understanding that death may result.

.........Withholding or withdrawal of artificially administered hydration or nutrition or both with the understanding that dehydration, malnutrition and death may result.

....

(Signature of person making appointment/Date)

DECLARATION OF WITNESSES

We declare that the principal is personally known to us, that the principal signed or acknowledged the principal's signature on this power of attorney for health care in our presence, that the principal appears to be of sound mind and not under duress, fraud or undue influence, that neither of us is the person appointed as attorney-in-fact by this document or the principal's attending physician. Witnessed by:

....	....
(Signature of Witness/Date)	(Printed Name of Witness)
....	....
(Signature of Witness/Date)	Printed Name of Witness)

ACCEPTANCE OF APPOINTMENT OF POWER OF ATTORNEY

I accept this appointment and agree to serve as attorney-in-fact for health care decisions. I understand I have a duty to act consistently with the desires of the principal as expressed in this appointment. I understand that this document gives me authority over health care decisions for the principal only if the principal becomes incapable. I understand that I must act in good faith in exercising my authority under this power of attorney. I understand that the principal may revoke this power of attorney at any time in any manner, and that I have a duty to inform the principal's attending physician promptly upon any revocation.

....

(Signature of Attorney-in-fact/Date)

....

(Printed name)

....

(Signature of Alternate Attorney-in-fact/Date)

....

(Printed name)

WARNING TO PERSON APPOINTING A POWER OF ATTORNEY FOR HEALTH CARE

This is an important legal document. It creates a power of attorney for health care. Before signing this document, you should know these important facts.

This document gives the person you designate as your attorney-in-fact the power to make health care decisions for you, subject to any limitations, specifications or statement of your desires that you include in this document.

For this document to be effective, your attorney-in-fact must accept the appointment in writing.

The person you designate in this document has a duty to act consistently with your desires as stated in this document or otherwise made known or, if your desires are unknown, to act in a manner consistent with what the person in good faith believes to be in your best interest. The person you designate in this document does, however, have the right to withdraw from this duty at any time.

This power will continue in effect for a period of seven years unless you become unable to participate in health care decisions for yourself during that period. If this occurs, the power will continue in effect until you are able to participate in those decisions again.

You have the right to revoke the appointment of the person designated in this document at any time by notifying that person or your health care provider of the revocation orally or in writing.

Despite this document, you have the right to make medical and other health care decisions for yourself as long as you are able to participate knowledgeably in those decisions.

If there is anything in this document that you do not understand, you should ask a lawyer to explain it to you.

This power of attorney will not be valid for making health care decisions unless it is signed by two qualified witnesses who are personally known to you and who are present when you sign or acknowledge your signature.

STATE OF RHODE ISLAND

STATUTORY FORM DURABLE POWER OF ATTORNEY FOR HEALTH CARE

WARNING TO PERSON EXECUTING THIS DOCUMENT

This is an important legal document which is authorized by the general laws of this state. Before executing this document, you should know these important facts:

You must be at least eighteen (18) years of age and a resident of the state of Rhode Island for this document to be legally valid and binding.

This document gives the person you designate as your agent (the attorney in fact) the power to make health care decisions for you. Your agent must act consistently with your desires as stated in this document or otherwise made known.

Except as you otherwise specify in this document, this document gives your agent the power to consent to your doctor not giving treatment or stopping treatment necessary to keep you alive.

Notwithstanding this document, you have the right to make medical and other health care decisions for yourself so long as you can give informed consent with respect to the particular decision. In addition, no treatment may be given to you over your objection at the time, and health care necessary to keep you alive may not be stopped or withheld if you object at the time.

This document gives your agent authority to consent, to refuse to consent, or to withdraw consent to any care, treatment, service, or procedure to maintain, diagnose, or treat a physical or mental condition. This power is subject to any statement of your desires and any limitation that you include in this document. You may state in this document any types of treatment that you do not desire. In addition, a court can take away the power of your agent to make health care decisions for you if your agent:

(1) Authorizes anything that is illegal,

(2) Acts contrary to your known desires, or

(3) Where your desires are not known, does anything that is clearly contrary to your best interests.

Unless you specify a specific period, this power will exist until you revoke it. Your agent's power and authority ceases upon your death.

You have the right to revoke the authority of your agent by notifying your agent or your treating doctor, hospital, or other health care provider orally or in writing of the revocation.

Your agent has the right to examine your medical records and to consent to their disclosure unless you limit this right in this document.

This document revokes any prior durable power of attorney for health care.

You should carefully read and follow the witnessing procedure described at the end of this form. This document will not be valid unless you comply with the witnessing procedure.

If there is anything in this document that you do not understand, you should ask a lawyer to explain it to you.

Your agent may need this document immediately in case of an emergency that requires a decision concerning your health care. Either keep this document where it is immediately available to your agent and alternate agents or give each of them an executed copy of this document. You may also want to give your doctor an executed copy of this document.

(1) DESIGNATION OF HEALTH CARE AGENT. I, ...
....(insert your name and address)
do hereby designate and appoint: ....
(insert name, address, and telephone number of one individual only as your agent to make health care decisions for you. None of the following may be designated as your agent: (1) your treating health care provider, (2) a nonrelative employee of your treating health care provider, (3) an operator of a community care facility, or (4) a nonrelative employee of an operator of a community care facility.) as my attorney in fact (agent) to make health care decisions for me as authorized in this document. For the purposes of this document, "health

care decision" means consent, refusal of consent, or withdrawal of consent to any care, treatment, service, or procedure to maintain, diagnose, or treat an individual's physical or mental condition.

(2) CREATION OF DURABLE POWER OF ATTORNEY FOR HEALTH CARE. By this document I intend to create a durable power of attorney for health care.

(3) GENERAL STATEMENT OF AUTHORITY GRANTED. Subject to any limitations in this document, I hereby grant to my agent full power and authority to make health care decisions for me to the same extent that I could make such decisions for myself if I had the capacity to do so. In exercising this authority, my agent shall make health care decisions that are consistent with my desires as stated in this document or otherwise made known to my agent, including, but not limited to, my desires concerning obtaining or refusing or withdrawing life-prolonging care, treatment, services, and procedures.

(If you want to limit the authority of your agent to make health care decisions for you, you can state the limitations in paragraph 4 ("Statement of Desires, Special Provisions, and Limitations") below. You can indicate your desires by including a statement of your desires in the same paragraph.)

(4) STATEMENT OF DESIRES, SPECIAL PROVISIONS, AND LIMITATIONS. (Your agent must make health care decisions that are consistent with your known desires. You can, but are not required to, state your desires in the space provided below. You should consider whether you want to include a statement of your desires concerning life-prolonging care, treatment, services, and procedures. You can also include a statement of your desires concerning other matters relating to your health care. You can also make your desires known to your agent by discussing your desires with your agent or by some other means. If there are any types of treatment that you do not want to be used, you should state them in the space below. If you want to limit in any other way the authority given your agent by this document, you should state the limits in the space below. If you do not state any limits, your agent will have broad powers to make health care decisions for you, except to the extent that there are limits provided by law.)

In exercising the authority under this durable power of attorney for health care, my agent shall act consistently with my desires as stated below and is subject to the special provisions and limitations stated below:

(a) Statement of desires concerning life-prolonging care, treatment, services, and procedures:

....

....

....

....

....

....

....

....

(b) Additional statement of desires, special provisions, and limitations regarding health care decisions:

....

....

....

....

....

....

....

....

(You may attach additional pages if you need more space to complete your statement. If you attach additional pages, you must date and sign EACH of the additional pages at the same time you date and sign this document.) If you wish to make a gift of any bodily organ you may do so pursuant to the Uniform Anatomical Gift Act.

(5) INSPECTION AND DISCLOSURE OF INFORMATION RELATING TO MY PHYSICAL OR MENTAL HEALTH. Subject to any limitations in this document, my agent has the power and authority to do all of the following:

(a) Request, review, and receive any information, verbal or written, regarding my physical or mental health, including, but not limited to, medical and hospital records.
(b) Execute on my behalf any releases or other documents that may be required in order to obtain this information.
(c) Consent to the disclosure of this information.
(If you want to limit the authority of your agent to receive and disclose information relating to your health, you must state the limitations in paragraph 4 ("Statement of desires, special provisions, and limitations") above.)
(6) SIGNING DOCUMENTS, WAIVERS, AND RELEASES. Where necessary to implement the health care decisions that my agent is authorized by this document to make, my agent has the power and authority to execute on my behalf all of the following:
(a) Documents titled or purporting to be a "Refusal to Permit Treatment" and "Leaving Hospital Against Medical Advice."
(b) Any necessary waiver or release from liability required by a hospital or physician.
(7) DURATION. (Unless you specify a shorter period in the space below, this power of attorney will exist until revoked.)
This durable power of attorney for health care expires on..
(Fill in this space ONLY if you want the authority of your agent to end on a specific date.)
(8) DESIGNATION OF ALTERNATE AGENTS.
(You are not required to designate any alternate agents but you may do so. Any alternate agent you designate will be able to make the same health care decisions as the agent you designated in paragraph 1 above, in the event that agent is unable or ineligible to act as your agent. If the agent you designated is your spouse, he or she becomes ineligible to act as your agent if your marriage is dissolved.)
If the person designated as my agent in paragraph 1 is not available or becomes ineligible to act as my agent to make a health care decision for me or loses the mental capacity to make health care decisions for me, or if I revoke that person's appointment or authority to act as my agent to make health care decisions for me, then I designate and appoint the following persons to serve as my agent to make health care decisions for me as authorized in this document, such persons to serve in the order listed below:
(A) First Alternate Agent: ....
....
(Insert name, address, and telephone number of first alternate agent.)
(B) Second Alternate Agent: ....
....
(Insert name, address, and telephone number of second alternate agent.)
(9) PRIOR DESIGNATIONS REVOKED. I revoke any prior durable power of attorney for health care.

DATE AND SIGNATURE OF PRINCIPAL
(YOU MUST DATE AND SIGN THIS POWER OF ATTORNEY)

I sign my name to this Statutory Form Durable Power of Attorney for Health Care on .... (Date) at ....(City),..(State)

....
(You sign here)

(THIS POWER OF ATTORNEY WILL NOT BE VALID UNLESS IT IS SIGNED BY TWO (2) QUALIFIED WITNESSES WHO ARE PRESENT WHEN YOU SIGN OR ACKNOWLEDGE YOUR SIGNATURE. IF YOU HAVE ATTACHED ANY ADDITIONAL PAGES TO THIS FORM, YOU MUST DATE AND SIGN EACH OF THE ADDITIONAL PAGES AT THE SAME TIME YOU DATE AND SIGN THIS POWER OF ATTORNEY.)

STATEMENT OF WITNESSES

(This document must be witnessed by two (2) qualified adult witnesses. None of the following may be used as a witness:
(1) A person you designate as your agent or alternate agent,
(2) A health care provider,
(3) An employee of a health care provider,
(4) The operator of a community care facility,
(5) An employee of an operator of a community care facility.
At least one of the witnesses must make the additional declaration set out following the place where the witnesses sign.)

I declare under penalty of perjury that the person who signed or acknowledged this document is personally known to me to be the principal, that the principal signed or acknowledged this durable power of attorney in my presence, that the principal appears to be of sound mind and under no duress, fraud, or undue influence, that I am not the person appointed as attorney in fact by this document, and that I am not a health care provider, an employee of a health care provider, the operator of a community care facility, nor an employee of an operator of a community care facility.

Signature:.. Residence Address:...
Print Name:...
Date:...
Signature:... Residence Address:...
Print Name:...
Date:...

(AT LEAST ONE OF THE ABOVE WITNESSES MUST ALSO SIGN THE FOLLOWING DECLARATION.)

I further declare under penalty of perjury that I am not related to the principal by blood, marriage, or adoption, and, to the best of my knowledge, I am not entitled to any part of the estate of the principal upon the death of the principal under a will now existing or by operation of law.

Signature:....................................... Signature:..
Print Name:..................................... Print Name:..

STATE OF TENNESSEE

DURABLE POWER OF ATTORNEY FOR HEALTH CARE

WARNING TO PERSON EXECUTING THIS DOCUMENT

This is an important legal document. Before executing this document you should know these important facts. This document gives the person you designate as your agent (the attorney in fact) the power to make health care decisions for you. Your agent must act consistently with your desires as stated in this document.

Except as you otherwise specify in this document, this document gives your agent the power to consent to your doctor not giving treatment or stopping treatment necessary to keep you alive.

Notwithstanding this document, you have the right to make medical and other health care decisions for yourself so long as you can give informed consent with respect to the particular decision. In addition, no treatment may be given to you over your objection, and health care necessary to keep you alive may not be stopped or withheld if you object at the time.

This document gives your agent authority to consent, to refuse to consent, or to withdraw consent to any care, treatment, service, or procedure to maintain, diagnose or treat a physical or mental condition. This power is subject to any limitations that you include in this document. You may state in this document any types of treatment that you do not desire. In addition, a court can take away the power of your agent to make health care decisions for you if your agent: (1) authorizes anything that is illegal; or (2) acts contrary to your desires as stated in this document.

You have the right to revoke the authority of your agent by notifying your agent or your treating physician, hospital or other health care provider orally or in writing of the revocation.

Your agent has the right to examine your medical records and to consent to their disclosure unless you limit this right in this document.

Unless you otherwise specify in this document, this document gives your agent the power after you die to: (1) authorize an autopsy; (2) donate your body or parts thereof for transplant or therapeutic or educational or scientific purposes; and (3) direct the disposition of your remains.

If there is anything in this document that you do not understand, you should ask an attorney to explain it to you.

DURABLE POWER OF ATTORNEY FOR HEALTH CARE

(1) DESIGNATION OF HEALTH CARE AGENT. I, ...

....

(insert your name and address)

do hereby designate and appoint: ....

(insert name, address, and telephone number of one individual only as your agent to make health care decisions for you. None of the following may be designated as your agent: (1) your treating health care provider, (2) a nonrelative employee of your treating health care provider, (3) an operator of a health care institution, or (4) a nonrelative employee of an operator of a health care institution.) as my attorney in fact (agent) to make health care decisions for me as authorized in this document. (If the agent you designate is your spouse, he or she becomes ineligible to act as your agent if your marriage is dissolved or annulled, unless you expressly provide otherwise.) For the purposes of this document, "health care decision" means consent, refusal of consent, or withdrawal of consent to any care, treatment, service, or procedure to maintain, diagnose, or treat an individual's physical or mental condition.

(2) CREATION OF DURABLE POWER OF ATTORNEY FOR HEALTH CARE. By this document I intend to create a durable power of attorney for health care.

(3) GENERAL STATEMENT OF AUTHORITY GRANTED. Subject to any limitations in this document, I hereby grant to my agent full power and authority to make health care decisions for me to the same extent that I could make such decisions for myself if I had the capacity to do so. In exercising this authority, my agent shall make health care decisions that are consistent with my desires as stated in this document or otherwise made known to my agent, including, but not limited to, my desires concerning obtaining or refusing or withdrawing life-prolonging care, treatment, services, and procedures.

(If you want to limit the authority of your agent to make health care decisions for you, you can state the limitations in paragraph 4 ("Statement of Desires, Special Provisions, and Limitations") below. You can indicate your desires by including a statement of your desires in the same paragraph.)

(4) STATEMENT OF DESIRES, SPECIAL PROVISIONS, AND LIMITATIONS. (Your agent must make health care decisions that are consistent with your known desires. You can, but are not required to, state your desires in the space provided below. You should consider whether you want to include a statement of your desires concerning life-prolonging care, treatment, services, and procedures. You can also include a statement of your desires concerning other matters relating to your health care. You can also make your desires known to your agent by discussing your desires with your agent or by some other means. If there are any types of treatment that you do not want to be used, you should state them in the space below. If you want to limit in any other way the authority given your agent by this document, you should state the limits in the space below. If you do not state any limits, your agent will have broad powers to make health care decisions for you, except to the extent that there are limits provided by law.)

In exercising the authority under this durable power of attorney for health care, my agent shall act consistently with my desires as stated below and is subject to the special provisions and limitations stated below:

(a) Statement of desires concerning life-prolonging care, treatment, services, and procedures:

....

....

....

....

....

....

....

....

(b) Additional statement of desires, special provisions, and limitations regarding health care decisions:

....

....

....

....

....

....

....

....

(You may attach additional pages if you need more space to complete your statement. If you attach additional pages, you must date and sign EACH of the additional pages at the same time you date and sign this document.) If you wish to make a gift of any bodily organ you may do so pursuant to the Uniform Anatomical Gift Act.

5. INSPECTION AND DISCLOSURE OF INFORMATION RELATING TO MY PHYSICAL OR MENTAL HEALTH. Subject to any limitations in this document, my agent has the power and authority to do all of the following:

(a) Request, review, and receive any information, verbal or written, regarding my physical or mental health, including, but not limited to, medical and hospital records.

(b) Execute on my behalf any releases or other documents that may be required in order to obtain this information.

(c) Consent to the disclosure of this information.

(If you want to limit the authority of your agent to receive and disclose information relating to your health, you must state the limitations in paragraph 4(b) ["Additional Statement of Desires, Special Provisions, and Limitations"] above.)

6. SIGNING DOCUMENTS, WAIVERS, AND RELEASES. Where necessary to implement the health care decisions that my agent is authorized by this document to make, my agent has the power and authority to execute on my behalf all of the following:

(a) Documents titled or purporting to be a "Refusal to Permit Treatment" and "Leaving Hospital Against Medical Advice."

(b) Any necessary waiver or release from liability required by a hospital or physician.

7. AUTOPSY; ANATOMICAL GIFTS; DISPOSITION OF REMAINS. Subject to any limitations in this document, my agent has the power and authority to do all of the following:

(a) Authorize an autopsy pursuant to the Post Mortem Examination Act, compiled in title 38, chapter 7.

(b) Make a disposition of a part or parts of my body under the Uniform Anatomical Gift Act (compiled in title 68, chapter 30).

(c) Direct the disposition of my remains pursuant to title 68, chapter 4.

(If you want to limit the authority of your agent to consent to an autopsy, make an anatomical gift, or direct the disposition of your remains, you must state the limitations in paragraph 4(b) ["Additional Statement of Desires, Special Provisions, and Limitations"] above.)

8. DURATION.

I understand that this power of attorney exists indefinitely from the date I execute this document unless I establish a shorter time or revoke the power of attorney. If I an unable to make health care decisions for myself when this power of attorney expires, the authority I have granted my agent continues to exist until the time I become able to make health care decisions for myself.

(IF APPLICABLE) This power of attorney ends on the following date..................

9. PRIOR DESIGNATIONS REVOKED. I revoke any prior durable power of attorney for health care.

DATE AND SIGNATURE OF PRINCIPAL
(YOU MUST DATE AND SIGN THIS POWER OF ATTORNEY)

I sign my name to this Statutory Form Durable Power of Attorney for Health Care on ....(Date) at..............................(City),...................................(State).

....
(You sign here)

(THIS POWER OF ATTORNEY WILL NOT BE VALID FOR MAKING HEALTH CARE DECISIONS UNLESS IT IS EITHER (1) SIGNED BY AT LEAST TWO QUALIFIED WITNESSES WHO ARE PERSONALLY KNOWN TO YOU AND WHO ARE PRESENT WHEN YOU SIGN OR ACKNOWLEDGE YOUR SIGNATURE OR (2) ACKNOWLEDGED BEFORE A NOTARY PUBLIC.)

CERTIFICATE OF ACKNOWLEDGEMENT OF NOTARY PUBLIC
(You may use acknowledgement before a notary public instead of the statement of witnesses.)

State of Tennessee)
) ss.
County of....................)

On this ....day of ...., in the year ...., before me, ...(here insert name of notary public) personally appeared ....(here insert name of principal) personally known to me (or proved to me on the basis of satisfactory evidence) to be the person whose name is subscribed to this instrument, and acknowledged that he or she executed it. I declare under penalty of perjury that the person whose name is subscribed to this instrument appears to be of sound mind and under no duress, fraud, or undue influence.

NOTARY SEAL ....
(Signature of Notary Public)

STATEMENT OF WITNESSES

(You should carefully read and follow this witnessing procedure. This document will not be valid unless you comply with the witnessing procedure. If you elect to use witnesses instead of having this document notarized you must use two qualified adult witnesses. None of the following may be used as a witness: (1) a person you designate as the attorney-in-fact, (2) a health care provider, (3) an employee of a health care provider, (4) the operator of a health care institution, or (5) an employee of an operator of a health care institution. At least one (1) of the witnesses must make the additional declaration set out following the place where the witnesses sign.)

I declare under penalty of perjury under the laws of Tennessee that the person who signed or acknowledged this document is personally known to me to be the principal, that the principal signed or acknowledged this durable power of attorney in my presence, that the principal appears to be of sound mind and under no duress, fraud, or undue influence, that I am not the person appointed as attorney-in-fact by this document, and that I am not a health care provider, an employee of a health care provider, the operator of a health care institution, nor an employee of an operator of a health care institution.

Signature: .... Residence Address: ....
Print Name: ....
Date:...
Signature: .... Residence Address: ....
Print Name: ....
Date:...

(AT LEAST ONE OF THE ABOVE WITNESSES MUST ALSO SIGN THE FOLLOWING DECLARATION.)

I further declare under penalty of perjury under the laws of Tennessee that I am not related to the principal by blood, marriage, or adoption, and to the best of my knowledge I am not entitled to any part of the estate of the principal upon the death of the principal under a will now existing or by the preparation of law.

Signature:..
Print Name: .... Address: ....
Date:.......................................

COPIES: You should retain an executed copy of this document and give one to your attorney-in-fact. The power of attorney should be available so a copy may be given to your health care providers as well.

STATE OF TEXAS

INFORMATION CONCERNING THE DURABLE POWER OF ATTORNEY FOR HEALTH CARE

THIS IS AN IMPORTANT LEGAL DOCUMENT. BEFORE SIGNING THIS DOCUMENT, YOU SHOULD KNOW THESE IMPORTANT FACTS.

Except to the extent you state otherwise, this document gives the person you name as your agent the authority to make any and all health care decisions for you in accordance with your wishes, including your religious and moral beliefs, when you are no longer capable of making them yourself. Because "health care" means any treatment, service, or procedure to maintain, diagnose, or treat your physical or mental condition, your agent may consent, refuse to consent, or withdraw consent to medical treatment and may make decisions about withdrawing or withholding life-sustaining treatment. Your agent may not consent to voluntary in-patient mental health services, convulsive treatment, psychosurgery, or abortion. A physician must comply with your agent's instructions or allow you to be transferred to another physician.

Your agent's authority begins when your doctor certifies that you lack the capacity to make health care decisions.

Your agent is obligated to follow your instructions when making decisions on your behalf. Unless you state otherwise, your agent has the same authority to make decisions about your health care as you would have had.

It is important that you discuss this document with your physician or other health care provider before you sign it to make sure that you understand the nature and range of decisions that may be made on your behalf. If you do not have a physician, you should talk with someone else who is knowledgeable about these issues and can answer your questions. You do not need a lawyer's assistance to complete this document, but if there is anything in this document that you do not understand, you should ask a lawyer to explain it to you.

The person you appoint as agent should be someone you know and trust. The person must be 18 years of age or older or a person under 18 years of age who has had the disabilities of minority removed. If you appoint your health or residential care provider (e.g., your physician or an employee of a home health agency, hospital, nursing home, or residential care home, other than a relative), that person has to choose between acting as your agent or as your health or residential care provider; the law does not permit a person to do both at the same time.

You should inform the person you appoint that you want the person to be your health care agent. You should discuss this document with your agent and your physician and give each a signed copy. You should indicate on the document itself the people and institutions who have signed copies. Your agent is not liable for health care decisions made in good faith on your behalf.

Even after you have signed this document, you have the right to make health care decisions for yourself as long as you are able to do so and treatment cannot be given to you or stopped over your objection. You have the right to revoke the authority granted to your agent by informing your agent or your health or residential care provider orally or in writing, or by your execution of a subsequent durable power of attorney for health care. Unless you state otherwise, your appointment of a spouse dissolves on divorce.

This document may not be changed or modified. If you want to make changes in the document, you must make an entirely new one.

You may wish to designate an alternate agent in the event that your agent is unwilling, unable, or ineligible to act as your agent. Any alternate agent you designate has the same authority to make health care decisions for you.

THIS POWER OF ATTORNEY IS NOT VALID UNLESS IT IS SIGNED IN THE PRESENCE OF TWO OR MORE QUALIFIED WITNESSES. THE FOLLOWING PERSONS MAY NOT ACT AS WITNESSES:

(1) the person you have designated as your agent;

(2) your health or residential care provider or an employee of your health or residential care provider;
(3) your spouse;
(4) your lawful heirs or beneficiaries named in your will or a deed; or
(5) creditors or persons who have a claim against you.

DURABLE POWER OF ATTORNEY FOR HEALTH CARE

DESIGNATION OF HEALTH CARE AGENT.

I, ... (insert your name) appoint:
Name:...
Address:.. Phone ....
as my agent to make any and all health care decisions for me, except to the extent I state otherwise in this document. This durable power of attorney for health care takes effect if I become unable to make my own health care decisions and this fact is certified in writing by my physician.
LIMITATIONS ON THE DECISION MAKING AUTHORITY OF MY AGENT ARE AS FOLLOWS:
....
....
DESIGNATION OF ALTERNATE AGENT.
(You are not required to designate an alternate agent but you may do so. An alternate agent may make the same health care decisions as the designated agent if the designated agent is unable or unwilling to act as your agent. If the agent designated is your spouse, the designation is automatically revoked by law if your marriage is dissolved.)
If the person designated as my agent is unable or unwilling to make health care decisions for me, I designate the following persons to serve as my agent to make health care decisions for me as authorized by this document, who serve in the following order:
A. First Alternate Agent
Name:...
Address:...
Phone.....................
B. Second Alternate Agent
Name:...
Address:...
Phone......................
The original of this document is kept at ....
The following individuals or institutions have signed copies:
Name:...
Address:...
Name:...
Address:...
DURATION.
I understand that this power of attorney exists indefinitely from the date I execute this document unless I establish a shorter time or revoke the power of attorney. If I an unable to make health care decisions for myself when this power of attorney expires, the authority I have granted my agent continues to exist until the time I become able to make health care decisions for myself.
(IF APPLICABLE) This power of attorney ends on the following date.......................................
PRIOR DESIGNATIONS REVOKED.
I revoke any prior durable power of attorney for health care.

ACKNOWLEDGMENT OF DISCLOSURE STATEMENT.
I have been provided with a disclosure statement explaining the effect of this document. I have read and understand that information contained in the disclosure statement.

(YOU MUST DATE AND SIGN THIS POWER OF ATTORNEY)

I sign my name to this durable power of attorney for health care on.................. day of ....
19........... at .... (City and State)

....
(Signature)

....
(Print Name)

STATEMENT OF WITNESSES.

I declare under penalty of perjury that the principal has identified himself or herself to me, that the principal signed or acknowledged this durable power of attorney in my presence, that I believe the principal to be of sound mind, that the principal has affirmed that the principal is aware of the nature of the document and is signing it voluntarily and free from duress, that the principal requested that I serve as witness to the principal's execution of this document, that I am not the person appointed as agent by this document, and that I am not a provider of health or residential care, an employee of a provider of health or residential care, the operator of a community care facility, or an employee of an operator of a health care facility.
I declare that I am not related to the principal by blood, marriage, or adoption and that to the best of my knowledge I am not entitled to any part of the estate of the principal on the death of the principal under a will or by operation of law.
Witness Signature:...
Print Name:... Date.................................
Address:..
Witness Signature:...
Print Name:.. Date............................
Address:..

STATE OF UTAH

SPECIAL POWER OF ATTORNEY

I, ..., of ...., this .... day of ...., ..., being of sound mind, willfully and voluntarily appoint .... of .... as my agent and attorney-in-fact, without substitution, with lawful authority to execute a directive on my behalf under Section 75-2-1105, governing the care and treatment to be administered to or withheld from me at any time after I incur an injury, disease, or illness which renders me unable to give current directions to attending physicians and other providers of medical services.

I understand that "life-sustaining procedures" do not include the administration of medication or sustenance, or the performance of any medical procedure deemed necessary to provide comfort care, or to alleviate pain, unless my attorney-in-fact specifies these procedures be considered life-sustaining.

I have carefully selected my above-named agent with confidence in the belief that this person's familiarity with my desires, beliefs, and attitudes will result in directions to attending physicians and providers of medical services which would probably be the same as I would give if able to do so.

This power of attorney shall be and remain in effect from the time my attending physician certifies that I have incurred a physical or mental condition rendering me unable to give current directions to attending physicians and other providers of medical services as to my care and treatment.

....
Signature of Principal

STATE OF ....)
:ss
County of ....)

On the ....day of.., ..., personally appeared before me ...., who duly acknowledged to me that he has read and fully understands the foregoing power of attorney, executed the same of his own volition and for the purposes set forth, and that he was acting under no constraint or undue influence whatsoever.

....
Notary Public

My commission expires:
Residing at: ....
....

STATE OF VERMONT

DURABLE POWER OF ATTORNEY FOR HEALTH CARE

INFORMATION CONCERNING THE DURABLE POWER OF ATTORNEY FOR HEALTH CARE

THIS IS AN IMPORTANT LEGAL DOCUMENT. BEFORE SIGNING THIS DOCUMENT, YOU SHOULD KNOW THESE IMPORTANT FACTS:

Except to the extent you state otherwise, this document gives the person you name as your agent the authority to make any and all health care decisions for you when you are no longer capable of making them yourself. "Health care" means any treatment, service or procedure to maintain, diagnose or treat your physical or mental condition. Your agent therefore can have the power to make a broad range of health care decisions for you. Your agent may consent, refuse to consent, or withdraw consent to medical treatment and may make decisions about withdrawing or withholding life-sustaining treatment.

You may state in this document any treatment you do not desire or treatment you want to be sure to receive. Your agent's authority will begin when your doctor certifies that you lack the capacity to make health care decisions. You may attach additional pages if you need more space to complete your statement.

Your agent will be obligated to follow your instructions when making decisions on your behalf. Unless you state otherwise, your agent will have the same authority to make decisions about your health care as you would have had.

It is important that you discuss this document with your physician or other health care providers before you sign it to make sure that you understand the nature and range of decisions which may be made on your behalf. If you do not have a physician, you should talk with someone else who is knowledgeable about these issues and can answer your questions. You do not need a lawyer's assistance to complete this document, but if there is anything in this document that you do not understand, you should ask a lawyer to explain it to you.

The person you appoint as agent should be someone you know and trust and must be at least 18 years old. If you appoint your health or residential care provider (e.g., your physician, or an employee of a home health agency, hospital, nursing home, or residential care home, other than a relative) that person will have to choose between acting as your agent or as your health or residential care provider; the law does not permit a person to do both at the same time.

You should inform the person you appoint that you want him or her to be your health care agent. You should discuss this document with your agent and your physician and give each a signed copy. You should indicate on the document itself the people and institutions who will have signed copies. Your agent will not be liable for health care decisions made in good faith on your behalf.

Even after you have signed this document, you have the right to make health care decisions for yourself as long as you are able to do so, and treatment cannot be given to you or stopped over your objection. You have the right to revoke the authority granted to your agent by informing him or her or your health care provider orally or in writing.

This document may not be changed or modified. If you want to make changes in the document you must make an entirely new one.

You may wish to designate an alternate agent in the event that your agent is unwilling, unable or ineligible to act as your agent. Any alternate agent you designate will have the same authority to make health care decisions for you.

THIS POWER OF ATTORNEY WILL NOT BE VALID UNLESS IT IS SIGNED IN THE PRESENCE OF TWO (2) OR MORE QUALIFIED WITNESSES WHO MUST BOTH BE PRESENT WHEN YOU SIGN OR ACKNOWLEDGE YOUR SIGNATURE. THE FOLLOWING PERSONS MAY <u>NOT</u> ACT AS WITNESSES:

—the person you designated as your agent;
—your health or residential care provider or one of their employees;
—your spouse;
—your lawful heirs or beneficiaries named in your will or a deed;
—creditors or persons who have a claim against you.

DURABLE POWER OF ATTORNEY FOR HEALTH CARE FORM

I,..hereby appoint................................... of... as my agent to make any and all health care decisions for me, except to the extent I state otherwise in this document. This durable power of attorney for health care shall take effect in the event I become unable to make my own health care decisions.

(a) **STATEMENT OF DESIRES, SPECIAL PROVISIONS, AND LIMITATIONS REGARDING HEALTH CARE DECISIONS.**

Here you may include any specific desires or limitations you deem appropriate, such as when or what life-sustaining measures should be withheld; directions whether to continue or discontinue artificial nutrition and hydration; or instructions to refuse any specific types of treatment that are inconsistent with your religious beliefs or unacceptable to you for any other reason.

....

....

....

....

....

(attach additional pages as necessary)

(b) **THE SUBJECT OF LIFE-SUSTAINING TREATMENT IS OF PARTICULAR IMPORTANCE.**

For your convenience in dealing with that subject, some general statements concerning the withholding or removal of life-sustaining treatment are set forth below. IF YOU AGREE WITH ONE OF THESE STATEMENTS, YOU MAY INCLUDE THE STATEMENT IN THE BLANK SPACE ABOVE.

If I suffer a condition from which there is no reasonable prospect of regaining my ability to think and act for myself, I want only care directed to my comfort and dignity, and authorize my agent to decline all treatment (including artificial nutrition and hydration) the primary purpose of which is to prolong my life.

If I suffer a condition from which there is no reasonable prospect of regaining the ability to think and act for myself, I want care directed to my comfort and dignity and also want artificial nutrition and hydration if needed, but authorize my agent to decline all other treatment the primary purpose of which is to prolong my life.

I want my life sustained by any reasonable medical measures, regardless of my condition.

In the event the person I appoint above is unable, unwilling or unavailable to act as my health care agent, I hereby appoint .... of .... as alternate agent.

I hereby acknowledge that I have been provided with a disclosure statement explaining the effect of this document. I have read and understand the information contained in the disclosure statement.

The original of this document will be kept at .... and the following persons and institutions will have signed copies:

....

....

....

In witness whereof, I have hereunto signed my name this .... day of ...., 19 ....

....

Signature

I declare that the principal appears to be of sound mind and free from duress at the time the durable power of attorney for health care is signed and that the principal has affirmed that he or she is aware of the nature of the document and is signing it freely and voluntarily.

Witness: .... Address: ....

Witness: .... Address: ....

Statement of ombudsman, hospital representative or other authorized person (to be signed only if the principal is in or is being admitted to a hospital, nursing home or residential care home):

I declare that I have personally explained the nature and effect of this durable power of attorney to the principal and that the principal understands the same.

Date:.............................

Address:...

Name:...

STATE OF WEST VIRGINIA

MEDICAL POWER OF ATTORNEY

Dated: ...., 19........... I,...(insert your name and address), hereby appoint...
(insert the name, address, area code and telephone number of the person you wish to designate as your representative) as my representative to act on my behalf to give, withhold or withdraw informed consent to health care decisions in the event that I am not able to do so myself. If my representative is unable, unwilling or disqualified to serve, then I appoint ....
as my successor representative.

This appointment shall extend to (but not be limited to) decisions relating to medical treatment, surgical treatment, nursing care, medication, hospitalization, care and treatment in a nursing home or other facility, and home health care. The representative appointed by this document is specifically authorized to act on my behalf to consent to, refuse or withdraw any and all medical treatment or diagnostic procedures, if my representative determines that I, if able to do so, would consent to, refuse or withdraw such treatment or procedures. Such authority shall include, but not be limited to, the withholding or withdrawal of life-prolonging intervention when in the opinion of two physicians who have examined me, one of whom is my attending physician, such life-prolonging intervention offers no medical hope of benefit.

I appoint this representative because I believe this person understands my wishes and values and will act to carry into effect the health care decisions that I would make if I were able to do so, and because I also believe that this person will act in my best interests when my wishes are unknown. It is my intent that my family, my physician and all legal authorities be bound by the decisions that are made by the representative appointed by this document, and it is my intent that these decisions should not be the subject of review by any health care provider, or administrative or judicial agency.

It is my intent that this document be legally binding and effective. In the event that the law does not recognize this document as legally binding and effective, it is my intent that this document be taken as a formal statement of my desire concerning the method by which any health care decisions should be made on my behalf during any period when I am unable to make such decisions.

In exercising the authority under this medical power of attorney, my representative shall act consistently with my special directives or limitations as stated below.

SPECIAL DIRECTIVES OR LIMITATIONS ON THIS POWER: (If none, write "none.")

....

....

....

THIS MEDICAL POWER OF ATTORNEY SHALL BECOME EFFECTIVE ONLY UPON MY INCAPACITY TO GIVE, WITHHOLD OR WITHDRAW INFORMED CONSENT TO MY OWN MEDICAL CARE.

These directives shall supersede any directives made in any previously executed document concerning my health care.

X..............................
Signature of Principal

I did not sign the principal's signature above. I am at least eighteen years of age and am not related to the principal by blood or marriage. I am not entitled to any portion of the estate of the principal according to the laws of intestate succession of the state of the principal's domicile or to the best of my knowledge under any will of the principal or codicil thereto, or legally responsible for the costs of the principal's medical or other care. I am not the principal's attending physician, nor am I the representative or successor representative of the principal.

WITNESS: DATE:

....

WITNESS: DATE:

....

STATE OF ....,
COUNTY OF ...., to wit:
I, ..., a Notary Public of said County, do certify that..,
as principal, and .... and ...., as witnesses, whose names are signed to the writing above bearing date on the .... day of ...., 19 ...., have this day acknowledged the same before me.
Given under my hand this .... day of ...., 19..........
My commission expires: ....

....
Notary Public

Appendix D

Instructions and Form to Execute a Durable Power of Attorney for Health Care in States without Specific Legislation and a Model Form

(a) Print your name in the space provided at the bottom of page one (Name of Principal).
(b) Print the name, home address, and telephone number of the person you appoint as your health care agent.
(c) At the top of the second page, space is provided to designate two alternate health care agents in the event the person named on page one is not available or is unable to act as your agent.
(d) In the middle of the second page, space is available to indicate your specific wishes regarding medical treatment you want or do not want, as well as other special instructions, and any limitations you wish to place on the authority of your agent. As in the case of the Living Will, you can spell out exactly the types of treatments you specifically refuse and any you specifically request (see the title page of Appendix B for specific examples). You may give permission here for the donation of your organs, although the health care agent will automatically have the authority to make anatomical gifts from your body after your death *unless you specifically deny that right to your agent in this space.* If you need additional space to indicate your wishes, you may add additional pages. Be sure to date and sign each additional page.
(e) You are asked to check one of three boxes to show the level of life support you desire in the face of imminent death or in the event you are in a coma, including a persistent vegetative state.
(f) At the bottom of the second page, your signature is required, as well as the date and your address.
(g) On page three, you are given a witnessing procedure to follow as well as a notarization form. You must have two witnesses meeting the criteria indicated sign the form and provide their addresses. In addition, it is highly recommended that you have the form notarized as well.

DURABLE POWER OF ATTORNEY FOR HEALTH CARE

INFORMATION ABOUT THIS DOCUMENT

THIS IS AN IMPORTANT LEGAL DOCUMENT. BEFORE SIGNING THIS DOCUMENT, IT IS VITAL FOR YOU TO KNOW AND UNDERSTAND THESE FACTS:

THIS DOCUMENT GIVES THE PERSON YOU NAME AS YOUR AGENT (THE ATTORNEY-IN-FACT) THE POWER TO MAKE HEALTH-CARE DECISIONS FOR YOU IF YOU CANNOT MAKE THE DECISIONS FOR YOURSELF.

AFTER YOU HAVE SIGNED THE DOCUMENT, YOU HAVE THE RIGHT TO MAKE HEALTH-CARE DECISIONS FOR YOURSELF IF YOU ARE CAPABLE OF DOING SO. IN ADDITION, AFTER YOU HAVE SIGNED THIS DOCUMENT, NO TREATMENT MAY BE GIVEN TO YOU OVER YOUR OBJECTION AT THE TIME, AND HEALTH CARE NECESSARY TO KEEP YOU ALIVE MAY NOT BE STOPPED OR WITHHELD IF YOU OBJECT AT THE TIME.

THIS DOCUMENT GIVES YOUR AGENT AUTHORITY TO CONSENT, TO REFUSE TO CONSENT, OR TO WITHDRAW CONSENT TO ANY CARE, TREATMENT, SERVICE, OR PROCEDURE TO MAINTAIN, DIAGNOSE, OR TREAT A PHYSICAL OR MENTAL CONDITION. THIS POWER IS SUBJECT TO ANY STATEMENT OF YOUR DESIRES AND ANY LIMITATIONS THAT YOU INCLUDE IN THIS DOCUMENT.

YOU MAY STATE IN THIS DOCUMENT ANY TYPES OF TREATMENT THAT YOU DO NOT DESIRE AND ANY THAT YOU WANT TO MAKE SURE YOU RECEIVE.

A COURT CAN TAKE AWAY THE POWER OF YOUR AGENT TO MAKE HEALTH-CARE DECISIONS FOR YOU IF YOUR AGENT (1) AUTHORIZES ANYTHING THAT IS ILLEGAL, (2) ACTS CONTRARY TO YOUR KNOWN DESIRES, OR (3) WHERE YOUR DESIRES ARE NOT KNOWN, DOES ANYTHING THAT IS CLEARLY CONTRARY TO YOUR BEST INTERESTS. YOU ALSO HAVE THE RIGHT TO TAKE AWAY THE AUTHORITY OF YOUR AGENT, UNLESS YOU HAVE BEEN ADJUDICATED INCOMPETENT, BY NOTIFYING YOUR AGENT OR HEALTH-CARE PROVIDER EITHER ORALLY OR IN WRITING. SHOULD YOU REVOKE THE AUTHORITY OF YOUR AGENT, IT IS ADVISABLE TO REVOKE IN WRITING AND TO PLACE COPIES OF THE REVOCATION WHEREVER THIS DOCUMENT IS LOCATED.

YOUR AGENT HAS THE RIGHT TO EXAMINE YOUR MEDICAL RECORDS AND TO CONSENT TO THEIR DISCLOSURE UNLESS YOU LIMIT THIS RIGHT IN THIS DOCUMENT.

IF THERE IS ANYTHING IN THIS DOCUMENT THAT YOU DO NOT UNDERSTAND, YOU SHOULD ASK A SOCIAL WORKER, LAWYER, OR OTHER PERSON TO EXPLAIN IT TO YOU.

THIS DOCUMENT REVOKES ANY PRIOR DURABLE POWER OF ATTORNEY FOR HEALTH CARE.

YOU SHOULD KEEP A COPY OF THIS DOCUMENT AFTER YOU HAVE SIGNED IT. GIVE A COPY TO THE PERSON YOU NAME AS YOUR AGENT (AND ALTERNATE). GIVE A COPY TO YOUR REGULAR DOCTORS AND ANY HEALTH CARE FACILITY WHERE YOU HAVE BEEN A PATIENT AND WHERE YOU EXPECT TO BE A PATIENT AGAIN.

CREATION OF DURABLE POWER OF ATTORNEY FOR HEALTH CARE

I,..(Name of principal) hereby appoint:

....
name

....
telephone number

....
home address

....

as my agent to make health-care decisions for me if I become unable to make my own health-care decisions. This gives my agent the power to grant, refuse, or withdraw consent on my behalf for any health-care service, treatment or procedure. My agent also has the authority to talk to health-care personnel, get information and sign forms necessary to carry out these decisions.

If the person named as my agent is not available or is unable to act as my agent, I appoint the following person to serve in the order listed below:

1.

....	....
name	home address
....	....
telephone number	

2.

....	....
name	home address
....	....
telephone number	

With this document, I intend to create a Durable Power of Attorney for Health Care, which shall take effect if I become incapable of making my own health-care decisions as I direct below or as I make known to my agent in some other way.

(A) STATEMENT OF MY DESIRES REGARDING MEDICAL TREATMENT I WANT OR DO NOT WANT, OTHER SPECIAL INSTRUCTIONS, AND ANY LIMITATIONS ON THE AUTHORITY OF MY AGENT:..
....
....

In addition, I direct that my agent have the authority to make health-care decisions regarding the following: (Check one box)

❑ I do not want my life to be prolonged nor do I want life-sustaining or death-delaying treatment to be provided or continued if my agent believes the burdens of the treatment outweigh the expected benefits. I want my agent to consider the relief of suffering, the expense involved, and the quality as well as the possible extension of my life in making decisions concerning life-sustaining or death-delaying treatment.

❑ I want my life to be prolonged and I want life-sustaining or death-delaying treatment to be provided or continued unless I am in a coma, including a persistent vegetative state, which my attending physician believes to be irreversible, in accordance with reasonable medical standards at the time of reference. If and when I have suffered such an irreversible coma, I want life-sustaining or death-delaying treatment to be withheld or discontinued.

❑ I want my life to be prolonged to the greatest extent possible without regard to my condition, the chances I have for recovery, or the cost of the procedures.

BY MY SIGNATURE I INDICATE THAT I UNDERSTAND THE PURPOSE AND EFFECT OF THIS DOCUMENT.

I sign this form on .... (date) at: .... (address).

....

Signature

WITNESSES

I declare that the person who signed or acknowledged this document is personally known to me, that the person signed or acknowledged this Durable Power of Attorney for Health Care in my presence, and that I believe the person to be an adult, of sound mind, and under no duress, fraud, or undue influence. I am not the person appointed as the agent (the attorney-in-fact) by this document, nor am I the health-care provider of the principal or an employee of the health-care provider of the principal. Furthermore, I am not related to the principal by blood, marriage, or adoption, I am not entitled to any portion of the estate of the principal either by will or codicil, or according to the laws of intestate succession, and I am not directly financially responsible for the principal's medical care.

....	....
Witness	Address
....	....
Witness	Address

NOTARIZATION*

State of...............................)
) ss.
County of............................)

Subscribed and sworn to before me by.., Principal, and.................................. and ...., Witnesses, as the voluntary act and deed of the principal this ....day of ....,19......

My commission expires:

....

Notary Public

[*The majority of states with Durable Power of Attorney for Health Care Statutes at present require two witnesses to sign the document. Some states give the option of either witnesses or notarization. A few states require both. It is recommended that both witnesses and notarization be used.]

Bibliography

Anderson, Gene C., et al. "Living wills: do nurses and physicians have them?" *American Journal of Nursing* 86, no. 3 (March 1986): 271-275.

Angell, Marcia. "Prisoners of technology: the case of Nancy Cruzan." *New England Journal of Medicine* 322 (April 26, 1990): 1226-1228.

Annas, George J. "Do feeding tubes have more rights than patients?" *Hastings Center Report* 16, no. 1 (February 1986): 26-28.

Annas, George J. "Fashion and freedom: when artificial feeding should be withdrawn." *American Journal of Public Health* 75, no. 6 (June 1985): 685-688.

Annas, George J. "When suicide prevention becomes brutality: the case of Elizabeth Bouvia." *Hastings Center Report* 14, no. 2 (April 1984): 20-21+.

Beauchamp, Tom L. and Perlin, Seymour, eds. *Ethical Issues in Death and Dying*. Englewood Cliffs, N.J.: Prentice-Hall, 1978.

Berg, R.N. "Removing life support: a constitutional right." *Journal of the Medical Association of Georgia* 73, no. 12 (December 1984): 843-845.

Bermel, Joyce. "Living wills: when do they mean what they say they mean?" *Hastings Center Report* 13, no. 4 (August 1983): 2.

Burleigh, Michael. "Euthanasia and the Third Reich." *History Today* 40 (February 1990): 11-16.

Campbell, Peter. *Choices for the Journey: Durable Power of Attorney and Healthcare Decision Making for Religious*. St. Louis: Catholic Hospital Association, 1989.

Capron, Alexander M. "Right to refuse medical care." In *Encyclopedia of Bioethics*, edited by Warren T. Reich, pp. 1498-1507. New York: Free Press, 1978.

Colen, B.D. *The Essential Guide to a Living Will*. New York: Pharos Books, 1987.

Colen, B.D. *Karen Ann Quinlan: Dying in the Age of Eternal Life*. Plainview, N.Y.: Nash Publishing Corp, 1976.

Collins, Francis J. and Meyers, David W. "Using a durable power of attorney for the authorization of withdrawal of medical care." *Estate Planning*, no. 5 (September 1984): 282-287.

Cox, Stephen S. "Artificial feeding: laying to rest some common misconceptions." *Hastings Center Report* 14, no. 6 (December 1984): 48.

Culliton, Barbara J. "Helping the dying die: two Harvard hospitals go public with policies." *Science* 193, no. 4258 (September 17, 1976): 1105-1106.

Davidson, Kent W., et al. "Physicians' attitudes on advance directives." *Journal of the American Medical Association* 262, no. 17 (November 3, 1989): 2415-2419.

De Wachter, M.A.M. "Active euthanasia in the Netherlands." *Journal of the American Medical Association* 262 (December 15, 1989): 3316-3319.

Dempsey, Davis. "The right to die." In *The Way to Die: An Investigation of Death and Dying in America Today*, pp. 99-123. New York: Macmillan, 1975.

Derr, P.G. "Why foods and fluids can never be denied." *Hastings Center Report* 16, no. 1 (February 1986): 28-30.

"Dutch are quietly taking the lead in euthanasia." *New York Times*, October 31, 1986, 4:4.

Eichler, B.L. "Nursing home residents' right to refuse treatment." *Journal of the Medical Society of New Jersey* 82, no. 5 (May 1985): 359-361.

Fenigsen, Richard. "Euthanasia: how it works—the Dutch experience." *Current* (June 1989): 4-14.

Fleming, Gerald. *Hitler and the Final Solution*. Berkeley: University of California Press, 1984.

Fletcher, Joseph. "Elective death." In *Ethical Issues in Medicine: The Role of the Physician in Today's Society*, edited by E. Fuller Torrey. Boston: Little, Brown & Co., 1968.

Fletcher, Joseph. "The right to live and the right to die: a Protestant view of euthanasia." *Humanist* 34, no. 4 (July-August 1974): 12-15.

Fletcher, Joseph et al. "When should patients be allowed to die? Some questions of ethics." *Postgraduate Medicine* 43 no. 4 (April 1968): 197-200.

Friedman, Emily. "California hospitals design Natural Death Act procedures." *Hospitals* 51, no. 22 (November 16, 1977): 62-65.

Furlong, Francis P. "Conflicting Protestant views on euthanasia. *Linacre Quarterly* 18 (November 1951): 91-98.

Garbesi, Curt. "Questions and answers on the living will and durable power of attorney for health care." *Euthanasia Review* 1, no. 1 (Spring 1986): 57-67.

Goldman, Alan H. "Medical ethics: the goal of health and the rights of patients." In *The Moral Foundations of Professional Ethics*, pp. 156-229. Totowa, N.J.: Rowman and Littlefield, 1980.

Hackler, Chris. "Advance directives and the refusal of treatment." *Medicine and Law* 7, no. 5 (April 1988): 457-465.

Hackler, Chris, Moseley, Ray, and Vawter, Dorothy E. *Advance Directives in Medicine*. New York: Praeger, 1989. (Studies in Health and Human Values series; Vol. 2)

Healey, Joseph M. "Decisions at the end of life: the legacy of Karen Ann Quinlan." *Connecticut Medicine* 49, no. 8 (August 1985): 549.

Healey, Joseph M. "Withholding and withdrawing artificial feeding: the role of the living will." *Connecticut Medicine* 49, no. 11 (November 1985): 765.

Helm, Anne. "Final arrangements: what you should know about living wills." *Nursing* 15, no. 11 (November 1985): 39-43.

Hilhorst, Henri W. "Religion and euthanasia in the Netherlands: exploring a diffuse relationship." *Social Compass* 30, no. 4 (1983): 491-502.

Hubbard, R.D. "How to draw up your living will." *Colorado Medicine* 82, no. 11 (July 1, 1985): 186-187.

Humphrey, Derek. "Legislating for active voluntary euthanasia." *The Humanist* 48 (March-April 1988): 10-13.

"Implications of mercy; case in the Netherlands." *Time* 101 (March 5, 1973): 70.

Klutch, Murray. "Survey results after one year's experience with the Natural Death Act." *Western Journal of Medicine* 128, no. 4 (April 1978): 329-330.

Kung, Hans. "Dying with Christian dignity." *Commonweal* 111 (January 1984): 42-43.

Kutner, Luis. "Due process of euthanasia: the living will—a proposal." *Indiana Law Journal* 44, no. 4 (Summer 1969): 539-554.

Kutner, Luis. "Euthanasia: due process for death with dignity—the living will." *Indiana Law Review* 54, no. 2 (Winter 1979): 201-228.

Kutner, Luis. "The living will: coping with the historical event of death." *Baylor Law Review* 2, no. 1 (Winter 1975): 39-53.

Lankfer, Marilyn. "Living wills and durable powers authorizing medical treatment decisions." *Michigan Bar Journal*, no. 7 (July 1985): 684.

Larue, Gerald A. *Euthanasia and Religion: A Survey of the Attitudes of the World Religions to the Right-to-Die*. Los Angeles: Hemlock Society, 1985.

Lazaroff, A.E. and Orr, W.F. "Living wills and other advance directives: ethical issues in the care of the elderly." *Clinics in Geriatric Medicine* 2, no. 3 (August 1986): 521-534.

Lecso, P.A. "Euthanasia: a Buddhist perspective." *Journal of Religion and Health* 25, no. 1 (1986): 51-57.

Lefevere, Patricia. "Life, death: where law, medicine and religion intersect." *National Catholic Reporter* 24 (March 18, 1988): 9-11.

Lo, Bernard, Rouse, Fenelle and Dornbrand, Laurie. "Family decision making on trial; who decides for incompetent patients?" *The New England Journal of Medicine* 322 (April 26, 1990): 1228-1232.

Lombard, John J. et al. "Legal problems of the aged and infirm: the durable power of attorney: planned protective services and the living will." *Real Property, Probate and Trust Journal* 13, no. 1 (Spring 1978): 1-67.

Lubinsky, Marian S. "Constitutional law: right to refuse medical treatment: decisions to terminate life: prolonging treatment for incompetent patients." *Western New England Law Review* 2, no. 4 (Spring 1980): 759-774.

Lynn, Joanne. *By No Extraordinary Means: The Choice to Forgo Life-Sustaining Food and Water.* Bloomington, Ind.: Indiana University Press, 1986.

Lynn, Joanne. "Food and water can be withheld from dying patients: the very different situations of Claire Conroy and Karen Quinlan." *Death Education* 8, no. 4 (1984): 271-275.

McCarrick, Pat Milmoe. *Living Wills and Durable Powers of Attorney: Advance Directive Legislation and Issues.* Washington, D.C.: Georgetown University, Joseph and Rose Kennedy Institute of Ethics, Center for Bioethics, 1990.

McCrary, S. Van and Botkin, Jeffrey R. "Hospital policy on advance directives: do institutions ask patients about living wills?" *Journal of the American Medical Association* 262, no. 17 (November 3, 1989): 2411-2414.

Margolick, David. "Patient's lawsuit says saving life ruined it" (Edward H. Winter). *The New York Times* 139 (March 18, 1990): 1.

Martyn, Susan R. and Jacobs, Lynn B. "Legislating advance directives for the terminally ill: the living will and durable power of attorney." *Nebraska Law Review*, no. 4 (Fall 1984): 779-809.

Miller, Bruce L. "Autonomy and the refusal of lifesaving treatment." *Hastings Center Report* 11, no. 4 (August 1981): 22-28.

Mishkin, Barbara. "Part III. New approaches: advance directives." In *A Matter of Choice: Planning Ahead for Health Care Decisions,* pp. 19-35. Washington: American Association of Retired Persons, 1986.

Mitscherlick, Alexander and Mielke, Fred. *Doctors of Infamy: The Story of Nazi Medical Crimes.* New York: Henry Schuman, 1949.

Morison, Robert S. "Bioethics after two decades." *Hastings Center Report* 11, no. 2 (April 1981): 8-12.

Oden, Thomas C. "A cautious view of treatment termination." *Christian Century* 93, no. 2 (January 21, 1976): 40-43.

Orntlicher, David. "Physician participation in assisted suicide." *Journal of the American Medical Association* 262 (October 6, 1989): 1844-1845.

Overman, William and Stoudemire, Alan. "Guidelines for legal and financial counseling of Alzheimer's disease patients and their families." *American Journal of Psychiatry* 145, no. 12 (December 1988): 1495-1500.

Paris, John J. "When burdens of feeding outweigh benefits." *Hastings Center Report* 16, no. 1 (February 1986): 30-32.

Paris, John J. "Withholding or withdrawing nutrition and fluids: what are the real issues." *Health Progress* 66, no. 10 (December 1985): 22-25.

"Persistent vegetative state and the decision to withdraw or withhold life support." *Journal of the American Medical Association* 263 (January 19,1990): 26-30.

Peters, D.A. "Advance medical directives: the case for the durable power of attorney for health care." *Journal of Legal Medicine* 8, no. 3 (September 1987): 437-464.

President's Commission for the Study of Ethical Problems in Medicine and Biomedical and Behavioral Research. *Deciding to Forego Life-Sustaining Treatment: A Report on the Ethical, Medical and Legal Issues in Treatment Decisions.* Washington, D.C.: The Commission, 1983.

Quinlan, Joseph, Quinlan, Julia and Battelle, Phyllis. *Karen Ann: The Quinlans Tell Their Story.* Garden City, N.Y.: Doubleday, 1977.

Raber, Patricia E. "Ethical and legal problems of living wills." *Geriatrics* 35, no. 8 (August 1980): 27-28+.

Rachels, James, Beauchamp, Tom L. and Childress, James F. "Is killing the same as letting die?" In *Taking Sides: Clashing Views on Controversial Bio-Ethical Issues*, edited by Carol Levine, pp. 94-109. Guilford, Conn.: Duskin Pub. Group, 1984.

Raffin, T.A. "Value of the living will." *Chest* 90, no. 3 (September 1986): 444-446.

Ramsey, Paul. *Ethics at the Edges of Life: Medical and Legal Intersections.* New Haven: Yale University Press, 1978.

"Right to life, church-state cases before Court." *Christianity Today* 33 (October 6, 1989): 44-45.

Rubin, Hal. "Death with dignity in California: the story of the nation's first natural death act." *New Physician* 27, no. 5 (May 1978): 26-28.

Scully, Thomas and Scully, Celia. "The Living will, the durable power of attorney and naming a proxy: the pluses of thinking ahead." In *Playing God: The New World of Medical Choices*, pp. 92-123. New York: Simon and Schuster, 1987.

Self, Donnie J. "Moral culpability and the distinction between killing and letting die." In *The Life Sciences and Human Values: Proceedings of the Thirteenth Conference on Value Inquiry*, edited by James B. Wilbur, pp. 173-188. Geneseo, N.Y.: State University of New York College at Geneseo, 1979.

Sereny, Gitta. *Into That Darkness: From Mercy Killing to Mass Murder.* London: Deutsch, 1974.

Showalter, J. Stuart. "Withdrawing life-support treatment: a preferred medical-legal-ethical approach." *Legal Aspects of Medical Practice* 13, no. 7 (July 1985): 3.

Sprung, Charles L. "Changing attitudes and practices in forgoing life-sustaining treatments." *Journal of the American Medical Association* 263 (April 25, 1990): 2211-2215.

Squillace, Scott E. "Removal of a nutrient feeding tube and need for a living will." *Journal of Contemporary Health Law and Policy* 3 (Spring 1987): 253-280.

Staff, Marcia J. "Natural Death Act directives: their limitations and importance." *Barrister*, no. 2 (Spring 1984): 50-53.

Stenibrook, Robert L. and Lo, Bernard. "Decision making for incompetent patients by designated proxy: California's new law." *New England Journal of Medicine* 310, no. 24 (June 14, 1984): 1598-1601.

Towers, Bernard. "Irreversible coma and withdrawal of life support: is it murder if the IV line is disconnected?" *Journal of Medical Ethics* 8, no. 4 (December 1982): 203-205.

Vaux, Kenneth L. "The giving and taking of life: new power at life's thresholds." *Christian Century* 92, no. 14 (April 16, 1975): 384-387.

Vaux, Kenneth L. *Will to Live, Will to Die: Ethics and the Search for a Good Death.* Minneapolis: Augsburg Publishing House, 1978.

Wachter, R.M., et al. "Life-sustaining treatment for patients with AIDS." *Chest* 95, no. 3 (March 1989): 647-652.

Wanzer, Sidney H., Federman, Daniel O., Adelstein, James, et al. "The physician's responsibility toward hopelessly ill patients: a second look." *New England Journal of Medicine* 320 (March 30, 1989): 844-849.

Wennberg, Robert. "Euthanasia: a sympathetic appraisal." *Christian Scholar's Review* 6, no. 4 (April 7, 1977): 281-302.

White, Robert B. and Engelhardt, H. Tristram. "A demand to die: case studies in bioethics." *Hastings Center Report* 5, no. 3 (June 1975): 9-10.

"Why patients refuse treatment: a study of seven hospital wards." *Hastings Center Report* 12, no. 5 (October 1982): 3-4.

Williams, Phillip G. *Life from Death: The Organ and Tissue Donation and Transplantation Source Book, With Forms.* Oak Park, Ill.: The P. Gaines Co., 1989. (Contemporary Public Health Issues series; Vol. 2)

Winslade, William J. and Ross, Judith W. "The newly dead, the nearly dead, and the living dead." In *Choosing Life or Death: A Guide for Patients, Families, and Professionals*, pp. 52-84. New York: Free Press, 1986.

Index

A

C

D

L

M

T

U

V

W

Contemporary Public Health Issues
Volume 2

Life from Death: The Organ and Tissue Donation and Transplantation Source Book, With Forms

by Dr. Phillip Williams

Life from Death combines an overview of anatomical gifts and transplantation with an illuminating analysis of the legal "support system" underlying our program of voluntary donations in this country.

Topics covered in this volume include:

- The broad scope of current uses for anatomical gifts in transplants, restorative surgery, hormonal therapy, research, and teaching
- The emerging field of brain implants to treat Parkinson's and Huntington's (and potentially Alzheimer's) disease
- Severe organ shortages
- The key role of public and professional education in averting the growing crisis in available donations
- Organ donation and transplantation in the black community
- Children and anatomical gifts
- The stance of 22 of the most common religions in America, from Jehovah's Witnesses to Judaism, on organ donation and transplantation
- Hispanic outreach programs
- Contrasting approaches to organ donation in France and the United States
- Answers to commonly asked questions about organ donation

Life from Death **features:**

- Unabridged texts of key state and federal laws pertaining to donation and transplantation
  - ➢ Anatomical gift laws of all fifty states and the District of Columbia
  - ➢ The National Organ Transplant Act
  - ➢ The Uniform Anatomical Gift Act of 1987
  - ➢ The highly influential recommendations of the National Task Force on Organ Transplantation
- Copies of pertinent forms and instructions for adults and minors for making anatomical gifts
- Glossary of key terms
- Directory listing support services for both donors and transplant recipients, as well as organizations providing audio-visual aids, speakers, publications, and other educational materials, those active in public policy, and those seeking volunteers
- Annotated bibliography and comprehensive index

What others say about *Life from Death*

"An excellent sourcebook on a topic of great importance. Recommended for academic, legal, and public libraries."—*Library Journal*, March 1, 1989

"*Life from Death* is . . . thorough, up-to-date and well-organized. The P. Gaines Co. and Dr. Phillip G. Williams should be commended for painstakingly piecing together so many of the important facts and points-of-view related to organ and tissue donation."—Lee Gutkind, author of *Many Sleepless Nights: The World of Organ Transplantation* (New York: W.W. Norton, 1988)

"An excellent source and reference guide. . . a fine addition to the literature on this increasingly important medical frontier."—Frank Maier, author of "A Second Chance at Life," cover story of *Newsweek* (September 12, 1988 issue)

ISBN 0-936284-44-7 **$19.95, quality paperback, 8 1/2 x 11, bibliography, index, 252 pages**